Strawberry Panic

The Complete Novel Collection

WRITTEN BY
Sakurako Kumino

ILLUSTRATED BY
Takuminamuchi

Seven Seas

BOOK 1 | page 9   BOOK 2 | page 245   BOOK 3 | page 483

Strawberry Panic

written by
Sakurako Kimino

illustrated by
Takuminamuchi

STAFF CREDITS

novel 1 translation **Michelle Kobayashi**
novel 2 & 3 translation **Anastasia Moreno**
english adaptation **Christine Norris**
layout & design **Nicky Lim**
copy editor **Erica Friedman**
editor **Adam Arnold**

publisher **Jason DeAngelis**
Seven Seas Entertainment

STRAWBERRY PANIC: THE COMPLETE NOVEL COLLECTION
Content originally published as Strawberry Panic Novel 1-3.
© 2006 Sakurako Kimino / ASCII MEDIA WORKS
First published in 2006 by Media Works Inc., Tokyo, Japan
English translation rights arranged with ASCII MEDIA WORKS.

Visit us online at www..gomanga.com.

ISBN: 978-1-934876-99-2

Printed in Canada

First Printing: June 2011

10 9 8 7 6 5 4 3 2 1

Lovers Drawn to Each Other

The *Étoile* competition is held to find the best couple out of the three Astraea schools. We will introduce the favored lovely couples of this contest: Nagisa and Shizuma, and Hikari and Amane.

Hanazono Shizuma

St. Miator Girls' Academy
Sixth Year, Snow Class

Hanazono Shizuma

Eldest daughter of a prominent Japanese family. Those around her are enchanted by her beauty and flamboyance. Though she was the *Étoile* last year, she is paired with Nagisa this year to claim the crown for the second time.

St. Miator Girls' Academy
Fourth Year, Moon Class

Aoi Nagisa

A newly transferred Fourth Year Student to St. Miator Girls' Academy. She has been Shizuma's object of desire since her first day at school, and before she could even acclimate herself in this prestigious all-girl school, she was pulled into the *Étoile* Competition.

Aoi Nagisa

Precious Friends

St. Miator Girls' Academy - Fourth Year, Moon Class

Suzumi Tamao

Nagisa's classmate and roommate who has a crush on Nagisa.

St. Miator Girls' Academy - First Year, Flower Class

Tsukidate Chiyo

An underclassman who adores Nagisa. A well-mannered and modest young lady.

St. Spica Girls' Institute - Third Year, Class Un

Nanto Yaya

Hikari's classmate and roommate. Strongly desires Hikari.

St. Spica Girls' Institute - First Year, Class Deux

Okuwaka Tsubomi

Surefooted Student Council Secretary. Always full of energy.

St. Lulim Girls' School Second Year, Class B

Hyuga Kizuna

Innocent girl who loves sweets and Chikaru-sama.

St. Lulim Girls' School Second Year, Class B

Natsume Remon

Kizuna's classmate and member of Chikaru's Costume Club.

St. Lulim Girls' School First Year, Class C

Byakudan Kagome

Childish and always carries a teddy bear.

Konohana Hikari

St. Spica Girls' Institute Third Year, Class Un

Konohana Hikari

A quiet, timid girl, newly transferred to Spica. She and Amane, the campus star, are in love with each other.

St. Spica Girls' Institute Fifth Year, Class Trois

Otori Amane

The leader of the "Five Great Stars" of the school, and called the "Prince." She entered the *Étoile* Competition with Hikari to fulfill the expectations of the fellow students.

Otori Amane

St. Miator Girls' Academy's Student Council President

Rokujo Miyuki

Fifth Year, Flower Class. Daughter of an old, well-established family. A strategist, known as the "Princess of Rokujo-in." Rumored to have the ability to control evil spirits.

Rokujo Miyuki

The Beautiful Campus Leaders

Here we will introduce the student council presidents who bring together all three schools. They are highly respected and admired model students gifted with both intelligence and beauty. Each beautiful campus leader strives to have their chosen couple claim the *Étoile* crown for their school!

St. Spica Girls' Institute's Student Council President

Tomori Shion

Fifth Year Spica student known as the "Snow Queen." Very intelligent, but unlike her nickname, can become quite heated at times.

Tomori Shion

St. Spica Girls' Institute - Fifth Year, Class Trois

Kusanagi Makoto

Violinist who studied abroad in Russia after graduating Spica Elementary. Came back to Japan to return glory to Spica. Hates the Amane-Hikari couple.

Kusanagi Makoto

St. Lulim Girls' School's Student Council President

Minamoto Chikaru

St. Lulim Girls' School Fifth Year, Class A. Has a graceful demeanor, but is a definite go-getter. Known as the "Shadow Empress"..!

Minamoto Chikaru

Astraea Hall (Strawberry Dorms)

The dorm where Nagisa, Shizuma, and others live. Three buildings, one for each school, are arranged in a triangle.

Diagram of Astraea Hill

Here we introduce the facilities and other locations where the blessed young ladies enjoy their campus life. On Astraea Hill, there are the three all-girl schools, a dormitory, a garden, and a convent, which are isolated from the world.

Maiden Park

The park is surrounded by the three schools, with a church and a large lake in the center.

St. Lulim Girls' School

A free, relaxed school with many interesting clubs. The building has a homey air to it and sits closest to the Strawberry Dorms.

St. Miator Girls' Academy

The oldest school, with its British architecture, has the strictest educational standards.

St. Spica Girls' Institute

This school emphasizes the development of women who will advance in society. Well-built facilities with horseback riding grounds and an indoor pool.

SEVEN SEAS' COMMITMENT TO TRANSLATION AUTHENTICITY

Japanese Name Order

To ensure maximum authenticity in Seven Seas' translation of *Strawberry Panic*, all character names have been kept in their original Japanese name order with family name first and given name second. For copyright reasons, creator names appear in standard English name order.

Honorifics

In addition to preserving the original Japanese name order, Seven Seas is committed to ensuring that honorifics—polite speech that indicates a person's status or relationship towards another individual—are retained within this book. Politeness is an integral facet of Japanese culture and we believe that maintaining honorifics in our translations helps bring out the same character nuances as seen in the original work.

The following are some of the more common honorifics you may come across while reading this and other books:

-san – The most common of all honorifics, it is an all-purpose suffix that can be used in any situation where politeness is expected. Generally seen as the equivalent to Mr., Miss, Ms., Mrs., etc.

-sama – This suffix is one level higher than "-san" and is used to confer great respect upon an individual.

-kun – This suffix is commonly used at the end of boys' names to express either familiarity or endearment. It can also be used when addressing someone younger than oneself or of a lower status.

-chan – Another common honorific. This suffix is mainly used to express endearment towards girls, but can also be used when referring to little boys or even pets. Couples are also known to use the term between one another to convey a sense of cuteness and intimacy.

Sempai – This title is used towards one's senior or "superior" in a particular group or organization. "Sempai" is most often used in a school setting, where underclassmen refer to upperclassmen as "sempai," though it is also commonly said by employees when addressing fellow employees who hold seniority in the workplace.

Kouhai – This is the exact opposite of "sempai," and is used to refer to underclassmen in school, junior employees at the workplace, etc.

Sensei – Literally meaning "one who has come before," this title is used for teachers, doctors, or masters of any profession or art.

Oniisan – This title literally means "big brother." First and foremost, it is used by younger siblings towards older male siblings. It can be used by itself or attached to a person's name as a suffix (-niisan). It is often used by a younger person toward an older person unrelated by blood, in this case as a sign of respect. Other forms include the informal "oniichan" and the more respectful "oniisama."

Oneesan – This title is the opposite of "Oniisan" and means "big sister." Other forms include the informal "oneechan" and the more respectful "oneesama."

French Guide

Aînée: Older sister
Cadette: Younger sister
Étoile: Star
Examen sur l'Astraea: Exam about Astraea
Galette: A type of crêpe, a pancake-like pastry
Garçon: Waiter
Le Dernier Miracle: The final miracle
L'Épreuve d'amour: The test of love
L'Ouverture brillante: The brilliant overture (beginning)
Petite couronne: Small crown
Trois Lumières: Three lights

Strawberry Panic!

Girls' School in Full Bloom

Miator
Girls' School

May today be another good day.

Of the three girls' schools built on the hill, St. Miator Girls' Academy, with its lovely, old-fashioned one-piece uniform, is the school with the longest legacy. It has strict educational standards and is attended by many girls from distinguished families. On any given morning, students can be seen going to school with their friends.

ST. SPICA GIRLS' INSTITUTE

Let's have a party in the courtyard this weekend.

Many of the girls who attend St. Spica Girls' Institute are independent and active in society. Even students relaxing on the school's café terrace have an air of cheerful activity. The white miniskirt uniform is stylish and popular in the surrounding neighborhoods.

*Heh heh heh.
Are you
studying
hard?*

ST. LULIM GIRLS' SCHOOL

The girls who go to St. Lulim Girls' School always seem to be having fun, even when studying together in the classroom. The school's motto is "Nurturing modern wives and wise mothers." Maybe because of the school's independent and relaxed atmosphere, they seem to have a laid-back attitude when it comes to studying.

CHAPTER 1

A Goddess Finds Delightful Prey
in the Cherry-Colored Mist

Flutter flutter...

All around them, cherry blossoms scattered to the ground. In the middle of a cherry-colored mist, a larger figure and a smaller figure stood close together atop a hill, surrounded by thick, old cherry trees. Standing atop the gently rolling hill of bright green, the two figures looked like they were floating in a thin, cherry-colored cloud.

"The time has finally come to say goodbye, hasn't it?"

"Oneesama, I...still..."

Fwooo. A gentle breeze blew. It scattered the cherry blossoms again.

Flutter flutter...

"I still want to stay with you, Oneesama."

The larger figure leaned toward the smaller figure in admonishment. She gently pressed her finger to the other's lips.

"You shouldn't say things like that."

The smaller figure—the younger girl—wiped at her tears with a handkerchief. "Y-you're right... I'm sorry..." She'd been crying so much the handkerchief was already soaked, but she didn't care. In a daze, she rubbed her eyes with it.

The larger figure reached out her hand and softly, gently, halted the other girl's hand.

Twitch. The smaller girl's shoulders shook horribly.

"You shouldn't rub your eyes so much," the older girl said. "You're just as much of a crybaby as ever, aren't you? Your eyes will get puffy." She lovingly, gently traced the girl's eyelids with her finger.

The young girl shook so violently, she almost seemed to convulse.

Fwooo. A cherry-colored cloud enveloped them again. A halo-like aura surrounded them—mostly white, but with a single, faint drop of peach.

The older girl gazed at the younger. The school uniform suited her well, which made it seem even more like the time for her to transform into a grown woman had arrived. She felt an intense longing. *Ah, I can't take it any more.* She opened both arms wide and went to embrace the smaller figure, but suddenly she stopped herself. *I shouldn't. If I did...there would be regrets. I shouldn't hold her any more. It's time for us to say goodbye.*

She forced her arms under control, and instead of around the girl, gently placed them on her shoulders.

"Listen, my darling little daisy. The two of us have been

so happy until now, right? You were my darling angel. Really. Please understand, okay? I adore you so much, it's really hard for ME to be apart, too. Goodbye."

At that last, the girl's face snapped up. Her stream of tears stopped without a sound, her face as sad as it could be. Her oneesama, who was so beautiful, so sublime, she almost seemed to melt into the cherry-colored cloud that floated in the blue sky, slowly and silently shook her head.

Then her oneesama gave a casual smile. "You know the kind of person I am, right?"

"Y-yes..." The girl knew, but still...it was only to be expected. A new flood of tears streamed down her cheeks.

"Come on, don't cry like that any more." Once again, the older girl gently wiped them away with her finger.

Nothing but sobbing came from the younger girl; she was choked by tears.

"What am I going to do? When I see you crying like that, it feels like it'll make me sad, too," said the girl's oneesama— seventeen-year-old Hanazono Shizuma—her hands resting gently on the girl's back. In her own way, she was mourning the fact she had to part with the innocent girl.

Ah, you are my treasure, as beautiful as a delicate daisy. I wish this moment could last forever and ever. The flow of time is cruel. In the end, it's come to this again: We have to part. I thought for sure you would be the one who could tie down my wandering heart.

As Shizuma looked at the high, clear blue sky, her thoughts drifted back in time.

I wonder how many times something like this has happened since I came to St. Miator.

St. Miator Girls' Academy was known all over the world as a first-class girls' school. It accommodated the kind of refined girls who seemed to have all but disappeared from ordinary society—well brought up, beautiful in appearance and very wise, yet with noble hearts. Shy and innocent, they had respect for their elders and pure hearts filled with love for God.

It's hopeless trying to tell me not to let my eyes wander.

Shizuma had attended this school since kindergarten, and since the day she'd entered middle school had attracted the attention of the entire school.

Even in a school like Miator, which was filled with girls from prominent families, being the eldest daughter of the head of such a large, well-established business conglomerate with so many ties to prominent political and economic circles was enough to get the other students' attention. On top of that, Shizuma was, with no exaggeration, a handsome, talented girl who excelled both academically and athletically.

She had long, shiny, gently waving hair and pale, almost transparent skin, like porcelain. She was tall, with long, slender legs.

Shizuma was on the track team, specializing in the high jump. During the sports festival, she competed in the relay. And in the national practice exam, she was always in the top one hundred. Her high-bridged nose and sharp chin gave her a look of intelligence, her large eyes, fringed by long eyelashes, always shone and she brimmed with confidence. Anyone who saw her thought she looked like a bisque doll.

Smart, beautiful, athletic and talented—ever since she was a little girl, people had told her she was like a rose blossom.

Upperclassmen showered her with invitations to tea and underclassmen shot her admiring glances. It happened so often she didn't even feel uncomfortable about it. Shizuma never turned down those invitations—no matter who did the asking, she always answered with a smile. It was all a part of her glorious school life. Even if the other girls' admiration grew and turned into love, Shizuma didn't think it particularly strange. She enjoyed being surrounded by a bunch of sweet, beautiful damsels, and she certainly didn't dislike playing at romance when she was invited somewhere.

Sometimes Shizuma would fall in love—a mysterious feeling that only appeared when she was with her damsels, during the little games she would play with them. That thick, sweet, gentle, peach-like aroma that only floated in the air between two girls; an emotion that went beyond simple affection or impatience and made them wish they could touch each other's soft white skin forever.

Once this emotion had been born in her heart, it shifted intensely, and she found herself driven to control her partner.

I'm not going to leave your side for an instant. I want to be connected to you forever. You're so precious to me I won't let you lay eyes on anyone but me.

Blessed with talent and usually able to control everything, it was the first time in Shizuma's life she felt emotions she couldn't control, like an unruly, galloping horse. At some point, Shizuma had abandoned herself to the sensation.

Once she became an upperclassman, Shizuma started to change her "favorite" frequently. She thought she might have become numb to the feeling altogether. No, she knew that wasn't it. At what point had it started to fall apart? No matter whom she was with or what she did, it always came down to the same thing.

Deep in her heart, there was a void she just couldn't fill.

It could be because of *her*... For a moment, small cracks formed in Shizuma's heart. Whenever memories of that autumn began to surface, Shizuma pushed them down and sealed them away.

She had a feeling that somewhere out there, there must be someone who could fill that void.

Shizuma was silent.

The girl noticed the quiet, and before she even realized it, lifted her head. There were no more tears in her eyes. In their place was a determined expression.

"I'm sorry, Shizuma-oneesama. I cried in front of you even though I know you hate it when people cry." Her cheeks were soaked with tears, but somehow she managed to smile.

"Shizuma-oneesama, to me you are like a beautiful dream.

Like what I feel when I look at these cherry blossoms." As she pointed toward the sky, a single fluttering cherry-blossom petal came to rest on the girl's fingertip. "I will be okay. Please, do not worry yourself. Just having the honor of being a companion to someone like you was a dream come true for me, Shizuma-oneesama. Thank you for letting me live my dream—I feel as if I could die happy right now."

The girl gently kissed the flower petal and smiled. "I've been so happy, this month that I've spent with you, Shizuma-oneesama. That's enough for me. I'm so happy—almost happier than someone like me has a right to be." Her voice shook toward the end of the little speech. *Fwooo*. The wind was cold against her tear-soaked cheeks.

"Thank you. You're such a good girl." Shizuma couldn't hold herself back. *One last time*. She took the girl's wet cheeks gently in her hands and gazed steadily at her face. The image of Shizuma's face reflected in the girl's damp, dark eyes grew larger and larger. Soon the only thing reflected was Shizuma's eyes. The other girl slowly closed hers.

The two figures floating in the cherry-colored cloud became one.

Rustle.

Before long, the rustling of Shizuma's skirt could be heard.

"Please, go before me, Oneesama."

Shizuma gazed at the girl's face worriedly. With her hands folded in front of her chest, the girl closed her eyes and accepted Shizuma's scrutiny.

"I would like to stay here a little longer and look at the cherry blossoms. I will use them to help me remember my dear Shizuma-oneesama." She slowly opened her eyes and gave a bright smile. "This is our final goodbye. But please do not worry, Shizuma-oneesama. Starting tomorrow, I will go back to being a regular underclassman. It's just, at the end, I wanted to—" A single tear fell from the girl's eyes. "My memories... the memories in my heart...even if I lose everything else, I will always carry them with me. You don't mind that, do you? I will treasure this for my entire life."

Feeling a slight twinge of pain in her chest, Shizuma smiled at her. "Yes, of course."

Then she turned her back on the girl and, without a single glance back, left her on the hill alone.

"My beloved, you will always be my one and only little daisy."

Swssshh. The breeze grew stronger and the snowstorm of cherry blossoms veiled Shizuma from the girl's sight as she walked away.

The sight of scattering cherry blossoms made everything there seem more beautiful.

They would only last but a week.

Sparkle sparkle.

Along the fence by the pale, dry path, clusters of white double bridal wreath[1] flowers blew about. The sunlight pierced through them, making them appear to shine.

"*Wooow*, what cute flowers!" As the girl shouted for joy, she reached out an impulsive hand to one of the young double bridal wreath bushes planted along the long fence.

The flowered branches, touched by the girl's delicate fingers, seemed to flutter happily as they scattered their small petals, which gathered on the ground by her feet.

"It's like a warm snow is falling."

Swssshhh. A small whirl of wind stirred.

Rustle rustle rustle...

The double bridal wreath branches, bent with the weight of countless small white flowers, swayed in the breeze.

A shining white petal snow fell on the ground all around. The girl had no idea the adorable flowers had an equally pleasant name, but it was a bright, beautiful sight.

The girl, Aoi Nagisa, who was already in a cheerful mood, walking to her new school, felt it was a very good omen. She had a feeling a lot of fun things waited for her. She'd heard the school was for really high-class girls, so she was a little nervous, but...

Yeah, I'm sure it'll be all right.

Gorgeous weather, a cheerful mood—that's what a new semester is all about.

Her brand-new school uniform, which she'd tried on for the first time this morning, was very cute, but also kind of mature. She'd thought it might not look good on her. Now those worries were a distant memory, because the uniform looked great on her.

Right?

That morning, when Nagisa had stood in front of the full-length mirror to see how she looked in her new uniform, the image that had looked back at her appeared to be a completely different person.

Her ponytail was tied more securely than usual; the brightly-colored bundle of hair that fanned out behind her was pulled up too tightly—probably because she'd put too much energy into tying it up.

The charcoal gray one-piece dress, made out of thin, high-quality wool, with an off-white petticoat that peeked from under the long button-down skirt, had a classic style. The delicate lace collar and the short tie in the school's color, dark green, gave it a formal look. Nagisa's growth had begun to spurt only about six months ago, but when she put on the uniform, she unexpectedly found she looked almost mature.

My face looks childish for a fifteen-year-old, and I can't do anything about that, but at least my usual cheerful smile is as perfect as ever today, if I do say so myself!

She tried smiling at herself in the mirror—and saw a smile that was still innocent and childlike. A smile that looked like it belonged to a child that knew only the taste of sugary-sweet candy and nothing of heart-wrenching love.

People are always telling me I look like a child, but... Umm, I wonder if it's because of these big, round, droopy eyes?!

Nagisa put a finger on the corner of each eye and tried lifting them up a little. *Whoa, that looks weird!*

She burst into laughter, but she had a feeling the uniform really looked better on her than she thought.

I guess it's true after all—when you enter high school, you grow up before you even realize it. Ha ha! Nagisa, aren't you being just a little cheeky?

Even though no one else was around, Nagisa smiled embarrassedly at the mirror.

Right. I feel like I can do anything today, Nagisa thought as she watched the wild dance of the double bridal wreath flowers shining in the sunlight. Her first time wearing the uniform, her first time going to this school—from now on, Nagisa would be going to a school for really high-class girls. She might not quite fit in there, but still...

These adorable flowers came out to greet me! It must mean the girls at school won't hate me. How should I put it...a gift from God?

The weather was gorgeous this morning, the sun shone down on her, the little white flowers were so beautiful and adorable—and she didn't know why, but for some reason, she was in an amazingly cheerful mood.

Nagisa didn't know much about God, but she had a feeling that such a wonderful day as this was a gift from God to cheer her on. It felt as if He were telling her, "Do your best! If you make a little mistake or slip up a little, I will help you. So don't worry about the little things; just do the very best you can."

Yeah, that must be it! Today's the day I start out. God must be cheering me on! I have a feeling good things are going to happen!

Gently stroking the delicate white lace collar, Nagisa flung herself into an energetic spin. Her long skirt puffed out like a parachute. Flustered, she pressed it down again.

Oh no! Someone will see my underwear! I don't have time to be playing around like this—I'll be in big trouble if I'm late! Today's the first day of school and it's important. I went through all the trouble of getting up early, but I was so nervous after checking my uniform I had to drink cup after cup of tea to calm down, and now I only have ten minutes left! I have to hurry.

When Nagisa had put on the uniform she'd so longed for, she had taken a step forward in her life. It was the uniform of the venerable St. Miator Girls' Academy, which every single girl desperately wanted to attend.

The petticoat fluttered and floated in time to Nagisa's bouncy steps. She looked at the hem of her skirt dancing in the air—until she'd stepped into this uniform, Nagisa had never worn such a long skirt before—and thought, *I guess I have to walk a little more lady-like from now on.*

That is how Nagisa started on her way to St. Miator Girls' Academy on the day that marked the beginning of her school life.

When Shizuma reached the bottom of the hill, she looked back toward the top.

Astraea Hill. A convent, established here a long time ago, had served as the mother institution for St. Miator Girls' Academy since the school was built.

Two sister schools, St. Spica Girls' Institute and St. Lulim Girls' School, had since been built in the adjacent area. The three Astraea Schools, each with its own unique characteristics, were widely known throughout society as elite girls' schools. Teeming with the lush green of springtime, the hill rose out of the ground as if it wanted to pierce the high, blue sky.

Shizuma gazed up the hill. *Will she be able to go home alone? I hope she's not crying any more, but... No, I'm sure she's not.*

She shook her head. The fact that her relationships never lasted more than a month, no matter what girl she went out with, was entirely her own fault. She simply didn't have the ability to worry about the girl who was probably crying over her. Even Shizuma couldn't say exactly what the root of the problem was. Though she loved each one of them...the passion never lasted long.

It would have been simple enough to keep the relationship going even though the passion had disappeared, but she didn't want to do that. She didn't want to betray the other girl's honest feelings. She didn't want to hurt her.

Shizuma always wanted to love her partner as much as her partner loved her.

As she thought about all of this, a sharp pain ran through her chest again. *I don't want to hurt her. I want to love my partner just as much as she loves me. But what about her?*

Somewhere in Shizuma's heart, the question burned.

Yes, what about her? What about the girl I treated like that and had to leave... Could it be I feel guilty? Or could it be...I'm getting too old for this?

Shizuma forced herself to laugh, trying to fool herself into thinking it was a ridiculous idea. Suddenly her skin felt a little cooler.

Is this what they mean by crazy weather in spring? The wind seems like it's gotten stronger.

The white violets that bloomed on Astraea Hill bent in the wind.

I have to hurry back to the Strawberry Dorms. With a slight shrug of her shoulders, Shizuma went around the hill and walked along a path that headed in the opposite direction.

Rustle... She walked defiantly into the wind, which occasionally gusted at her. On the other side of the hill was the unconventional dorm Shizuma lived in.

I hope no one finds out I've broken up with her, at least for a little while...

Normally Shizuma would go directly to the salon. Since it was the last day of spring break, it was sure to be filled with students enjoying tea and snacks. A huge crowd of Shizuma's fans, who paid careful attention to her every move, would be there.

So Shizuma's absence today most likely had not gone unnoticed.

Because the schools and dorms both had strict rules regarding relationships between upper- and underclassmen, and Shizuma was going to be in the highest grade beginning this spring, it was rare for an underclassman to get close to her. An appearance by Shizuma at the salon was one of the few opportunities the underclassmen had to see her. It was almost like getting to meet a star.

Even though they knew all Shizuma's recent relationships had lasted only a month, there was still no end to the number of girls who admired her and wanted to be by her side. This was because all the girls Shizuma had loved said it had made them happier than anything else. It made them cry tears of joy, and they all said it was a memory they would put away in the most important place in their hearts for the rest of their lives.

And Shizuma used her overwhelming presence to reign over the other girls. There were many who would have loved to throw themselves into Shizuma's embrace and be held by Shizuma's long arms. She was more dignified than any man, smart, forceful yet beautiful...and endlessly greedy, the kind of girl who tried to control her partner.

This was Shizuma, the girl they all longed for.

I hope the girl I just broke up with doesn't get hurt by any gossip going around the salon.

Shizuma's feelings turned a little dark. With a sigh, she looked at her feet; she had stopped without even realizing it.

A girl's voice called out ahead of her. "Excuse me! Is this the way to the Strawberry Dorms?"

When Shizuma looked up, she saw a girl wearing a St. Miator uniform, carrying a big Boston bag. Shizuma didn't recognize her.

"Who might you be?"

"I'm a fourth-year transfer student! I'm going to start living in the dormitory today."

Shizuma took another good look at her. *Heh heh. She has a cute ponytail. Well, well, it looks like we're getting another super-cheerful girl to add to the crowd.*

Lured by the girl's bright, sunny smile, Shizuma found herself grinning.

Ah, if I go back to the Strawberry Dorms with this girl, maybe it will distract them from starting any other rumors about me. Because once everyone gets this new bit of news, they'll just have to jump on it.

Shizuma was more than a little relieved. "I'd be happy to lead you there. Please, come with me."

Shizuma gracefully extended her beautiful white hand, as if leading a dance.

CHAPTER 2

The Shining Star of the Campus Makes a Decision in the Flaming Greenery

As the end of the day's classes drew near, a gloriously uninhibited atmosphere floated over the entire campus. In the Fourth Year Moon Class' homeroom, in the new school building, the final class was being held.

The nun, wearing a dark gray habit and a warm smile, looked over the classroom from the podium. "That is all. I pray for the safety of every one of you as you return home. Class is over. Take care, everyone. The organ, if you please."

A small organ sat close to the door of the classroom. Two students wearing St. Miator uniforms were seated in front of the instrument. According to the daily routine of St. Miator Girls' Academy, it was time for hymns. In both morning and afternoon homeroom the students sang hymns in thanks and praise to God.

In response to the nun's smile, the two students gave a small nod. They looked at each other, exchanged gentle smiles, and raised their hands above the keyboard. At that signal, the entire class rose quietly from their seats and the sound of a prelude began. The girls' beautiful, pure singing filled the room.

> In Heaven up above
> The stars of the sky
> Give off
> Their brilliant light.

Wow! Singing hymns is cool after all!

Nagisa loudly flipped though the pages of her hymnal. *But I don't know this song. I wonder what page it's on? There are so many hymns I just don't know what to do!*

Rustle rustle rustle. Nagisa frantically searched the pages of the book. Since she hadn't been at the school very long, she didn't know where to find this particular song they were singing in the thick hymn book.

Found it! Found it! This is it. I see, it's a song for the Virgin Mary.

Nagisa finally joined the others. She came in late and she didn't know the song, but she sang proudly, without holding anything back.

Oh no! The girl in the next seat cast a long glance at Nagisa. *Oh dear. What am I going to do with you, Nagisa-chan. You let yourself get all frantic again. You look so serious. How cute!*

Suzumi Tamao, fifteen years old. This was her first spring

in high school, but her fourth year at Miator. She was tall for her age, and Miator's classic uniform suited her well. Her head looked small, perhaps because she wore her long hair tied up, but it did expose the beautiful, gentle slope of her neck. Fascinating, elegant wisps of hair that escaped the tie caught the sunlight that came through the windows and shone, black with just a tinge of blue. She was a very beautiful girl, who looked much more composed and much more mature than her actual age.

Whenever Tamao saw Nagisa, she almost felt compelled to tease her. It was a sickness that had begun the day Nagisa had transferred to the school.

It's like they've let a sinful child in here. I finally begin to enjoy a peaceful school life, but now it's just like I'm... Well, like I'm a pervert!

A pervert—

As soon as that word popped into her head, Tamao froze for a moment, startled. *N-no, that's not it at all. That couldn't possibly be. What am I thinking?*

She shook her head a little. *Phew*... Mentally, she took a deep sigh. She had to think of something to lift her spirits... She put on a vague smile and shook her head in total resignation.

Tap tap tap. She gently tapped Nagisa's shoulder and whispered, "Hey, Nagisa-chan, listen to this! It looks like Shizuma-oneesama is outside."

"Whaaaat?" Nagisa turned frantically and looked out the classroom window, almost toppling her chair in the process.

Several nearby students looked at her, still singing.

Flustered, Nagisa ducked her head and cast a questioning

glance toward the nun at the podium before looking back toward the window. The only thing she could see outside was the top of a large double-flowered cherry tree in full bloom.

A single, heavy-looking flower fell with a *plop*. Now that Nagisa thought about it, they were on the second floor.

"Jeez! Don't do that to me, Tamao-chan!!" With her face bright red, Nagisa posed as if she were going to punch Tamao and playfully tapped her chest.

In her heart, Tamao was tickled she could be so close to Nagisa, but on her face was an exaggerated frown. *Aah, Nagisa-chan really IS cute!*

"Excuse me."

The classroom door quietly opened. A calm, penetrating voice caused the atmosphere in the classroom to suddenly change. Nagisa's classmates, who would barely move even if someone made a huge sound, all turned at once.

Standing in the doorway was a tremendously beautiful woman—so stunning, it was as if she reflected the beauty of the flowers that fluttered outside.

"Shi-Shizuma-sempai—" Nagisa called out.

Remembering then what Shizuma had told her, she corrected herself. "Shizuma-oneesama!"

It had happened one week ago, on Nagisa's memorable first day at school.

When Nagisa saw Shizuma's delicate white hand stretched

out toward her in the midst of a shower of cherry blossoms, she didn't know what to do with it. Dumbfounded, she froze stiff.

Huh? Why does she have her hand out like that? C-could it be she wants to hold hands?! Uh, sh-she said "come with me," so she's probably going to show me the way, but why hold hands? I could understand if I was in elementary school or something, but, umm, I'm in my first year of high school, so... I know people tell me I look young, but I don't look like an elementary school kid, do I?! I can't just stand here like this forever, umm, umm...

When the panicked Nagisa stole a timid glance at Shizuma, she saw the other still standing there, not moving. She looked like she was kind and gentle, yet strong, with a noble smile that made Nagisa want to get closer to her.

As if she couldn't care less about Nagisa being shocked speechless, Shizuma simply stood there beautifully in the blowing wind, her outstretched arm not moving.

She just kindly kept it stretched toward Nagisa, her long hair swirling beautifully around her.

Nagisa looked at Shizuma's hand, patiently waiting for her, and...

Clench. Nagisa took it with both hands and squeezed with all her might.

Abruptly.

Suddenly.

Rudely.

Squeeeeeze. Nagisa's cheeks were bright red with nervousness. Even through the tight grip, the softness of Nagisa's palm was instantly apparent to Shizuma.

Shizuma was shocked at both her rudeness and the strong warmth of her hands.

I've never had anyone squeeze my hand with such genuine strength. My cute little flowers always take my hand so softly and timidly, like they're touching something that might break.

On the other hand, feeling the slenderness and coolness of Shizuma's hand, Nagisa was hit with a sudden panic. *Oh NO, I can't believe it. What did I do that for? Why did I just squeeze her hand like that? I thought how weird it was to hold someone's hand, then I thought how stupid I looked just standing there, THEN I thought how pretty she was, THEN I thought, "She doesn't want to hold my hand, does she?" and then I thought, "I wonder why she's still standing absolutely still?" and then, and then, I just couldn't take it any more—*

—Aah, what'll I do? I must have scared her!

—Aah, I wonder what happened? I feel like my body's gotten so warm.

The two of them lifted their gazes from their clenched hands to each other's faces.

Ahh...

A sort of electricity ran through their bodies.

"It's Shizuma-oneesama!"

"It's Shizuma-oneesama…"

"I wonder what in the world would bring her to a fourth-year classroom?"

In the midst of the whispering of golden voices, Shizuma slowly bowed to the nun and gave her a gorgeous smile as she spoke.

"I apologize for interrupting your homeroom, Sister. I have come to get the student who is in charge of the holy water today."

Sighs of admiration rose from the class. The girls looked like they were about to faint.

"Aaah… What a perfect, beautiful bow she made."

"I could watch her all day."

"I actually got to see Shizuma-oneesama. This is the luckiest day of my life!"

"Oh, why thank you," the nun said politely. "You are Hanazono-san, correct? Your duties must be hard today." With a cheerful grin, she turned the pages of the attendance book. "The student in charge of the holy water today is—oh my, it's our transfer student, Aoi-san!"

Nagisa and Tamao stopped their playful punches in mid-air.

Whaaaa…? M-ME?! Nagisa was so shocked she almost stopped breathing.

All eyes in the classroom were on Nagisa.

Oh, great. I feel like they're staring daggers at me…

"Well then, please come here, Aoi-san." With an air of calm, Shizuma walked slowly toward Nagisa. She stopped and reached out her hand to Nagisa and gave her a powerful look that said plainly, "Please take my hand."

"Go on, hurry."

When Nagisa timidly brushed her fingertips, Shizuma immediately clenched her hand and pulled the girl toward her.

Nagisa lost her balance and fell right into Shizuma's chest. A tiny scream rose from the back of the classroom. Wrapped in Shizuma's arms, Nagisa remembered. That day. Shizuma's large, strong-willed, almond-shaped eyes. Nagisa's round, childlike, innocent ones reflected in Shizuma's.

It was the same a week ago. Enveloped in a cherry-colored mist, the eyes of the two girls met. Neither of them saw their surroundings. Their eyes were wide open, but they gazed only at each other, as if they were trying to take in every last bit of each other's faces. They gazed at each other soundlessly, as if everything were suddenly in slow motion—and they simply gazed at each other.

The words Shizuma said next echoed in Nagisa's ears.

"From this day forward, you are my younger sister. Call me Shizuma-oneesama. If you break your promise..." *Sting!* Shizuma nipped Nagisa's finger.

"I'll punish you."

Shizuma released Nagisa's finger from her mouth. It glistened with dampness.

The spring breeze brushed coolly across it.

Nagisa felt like she could still feel that coolness on her finger, even now. Just as Nagisa was about to get lost in the memory...

"I will lead you." Shizuma's cool voice echoed through the classroom. For just a moment, she gave Nagisa a strong embrace. With a satisfied smile on her face, she led the blushing Nagisa out of the classroom with an arm around her shoulder.

Clatter. The closing of the heavy door echoed through the room. A second later, the classroom was thrown into commotion.

Oh, Shizuma-oneesama... Sting. Seeing Nagisa taken away right in front of her, Tamao was so frustrated she ground her teeth.

Around the same time...

"I wonder what Nagisa-oneesama is doing right about now." The words were only a faint mutter on the girl's lips. The girl was Tsukidate Chiyo, twelve years old. She was in the First Year Flower Class' homeroom at St. Miator. Her pitch-black hair was cut in a shoulder-length bob. The innocent, impressionable girl was also genuinely upper-class. She had gone to the same kindergarten as Shizuma, and was now attending Miator.

With homeroom over, the class had begun cleaning up.

Chiyo paused in her sweeping and looked outside the window at the double-flowered cherry tree, remembering. Remembering the day she'd met Nagisa. The day she had decided Nagisa was her oneesama…

It had been about a week ago—the day the Strawberry Dorms had opened for the year. Even now, she could see it clearly. The cherry blossoms had been fluttering that day, too. But it hadn't been a double-flowered cherry tree, which she found beautiful but somehow cheap-looking. No, it had been a Yoshino cherry tree, light pink and as delicate as a thin, ephemeral cloud.

Shizuma-oneesama had been there, beautiful and gentle, like a cherry-blossom spirit. Chiyo was captivated by the memory. Before she even noticed, she started shuffling her feet. She was fidgety for some reason.

Tomorrow is Easter… I don't really know why, but I get the feeling something wonderful is going to happen.

A voice coming from the hallway interrupted Chiyo's thoughts. "Chiyo-maru! It's time for the library committee meeting!"

"Okay! I'll be right there!"

"Wow! Look, it's Shizuma-oneesama!"

"How do you do, Shizuma-sama?"

"Shizuma-oneesama, you look as beautiful as ever."

The comments came from all around her. Cheers echoed around the red-carpeted hallway. A ring of blushing girls, their heads bowed reverently, opened up in front of her like a ripple.

"It's all right, it's all right, please don't go to so much trouble, my cute little daisies."

Shizuma was entirely unmoved by the girls' cheers and reverence. She simply kept walking and waving her hand with a grin on her face, looking like a queen, giving her subjects a royal smile. The cheering grew, like a bubble ready to burst on the water's surface.

Watching Shizuma act so much like a queen, Nagisa couldn't help blushing. *Shizuma-oneesama might be even more amazing than I thought.*

Shizuma strode majestically down the hallway with a huge smile, as she always did. But she noticed that Nagisa, walking next to her, hung her head. She dipped her own head and peeked into Nagisa's face.

"Oh dear. Whatever is the matter, Nagisa-chan?" Shizuma's long hair billowed and waved and the fragrance of flowers blossomed around her.

"It's nothing."

The smile Shizuma gave Nagisa was so beautiful it almost made her catch her breath. She looked even more like a majestic goddess than before. Flustered, Nagisa shook her head. Nagisa started to get the feeling someone like her shouldn't be next to someone like Shizuma. She was completely unsure of herself.

Shizuma enjoyed the expression on Nagisa's face. She tried hard to suppress her naturally flirtatious expression. "Oh Nagisa-chan, don't sulk!" She placed a hand under Nagisa's chin and forced her head up so she could gaze into her eyes.

There was more than ten centimeters' difference in their

heights. Shizuma had to bend down to peek into Nagisa's face. As Shizuma watched, Nagisa's big round eyes started clouding with tears.

What beautiful, adorable eyes.

Quiver quiver.

Devoted, adorable, just like a little puppy.

Quiver quiver.

Aah, I can't take it any more.

Shizuma's face moved closer to Nagisa's, as if pulled in by some force.

Smooch. Shizuma planted a kiss on Nagisa's forehead.

Screams rose from the crowd of girls that surrounded them.

"Aauggghh!!"

"Shizuma-sama! Shizuma-oneesama! She...!!"

Shoot, now I've done it! Shizuma mentally scolded herself. *I forgot we were out in public, right in the hallway of Miator.* She pulled Nagisa's wrist—"Let's go, Nagisa!"—and took off as fast as she could.

"Y-you're going too fast!"

The screams and angry roars of the girls faded away almost instantly.

Huff huff huff...

Shizuma stopped just as they reached the exit. Beyond the open door was a broad, lush green lawn leading to the back gate.

Nagisa finally caught her breath. *Wow, Shizuma-oneesama must be very good at sports, although I'm not so slow myself... I can't believe she can run so fast in such a long skirt, and she's*

not even breathing hard at all, Nagisa thought.

"Good, I think we fooled them about the kiss," Shizuma murmured in a low voice as she checked to see if there were any people by the back gate.

"Huh? What did we fool them about?"

"Uh, um, uh, it's okay, it's okay. I mean, look, we managed to baffle my adorable little flowers, right?" Shizuma waved her hand frantically right in front of Nagisa's eyes.

"Oh, yes, I guess you're right. That's good! But what a shock! I never knew you were so fast!"

Shizuma looked at Nagisa's beaming smile and chuckled to herself. *Heh heh heh... My, my, you really are innocent and sweet after all, aren't you, Nagisa-chan? You're the one who was fooled, my adorable little puppy.*

Shizuma slowly put her hand to her hip and spoke more seriously. "By the way, Nagisa-chan, did you know tomorrow is Easter? It's the most important day of the year for Catholics. So we're going to the church to bring some holy water to the classrooms."

"Oh, so that's what they meant about being in charge of the holy water! Do you mean the church in Maiden Park?"

"Right. So we're going to have a little date in the garden. Doesn't that sound nice?" Shizuma took Nagisa's arm and leisurely led her out the door.

St. Miator Girls' Academy: it was a girls' school with a long and distinguished history, built at the end of the Meiji era.

The old convent, sitting at the peak of the wide, hilly area that was originally called Astraea Hill, was the school's mother institution. When the school was first founded, only girls from families that were financially blessed could receive a higher education. Even among those, Miator gathered only young ladies from the most elite families.

That single school gave the girls a consistent education from kindergarten all the way through high school. The progressive education and rigorous discipline, imparted by Catholic nuns on the convent's vast grounds—in an environment completely forbidden to boys—made the school incredibly popular among nobles and certain rich families, who saw the need for higher education for their girls but faced limited choices.

This popularity, of course, raised the school's status, which grew even faster as the number of newly rich families grew. Sending a daughter to St. Miator Girls' Academy was seen as proof of success. The striking popularity brought in far more applicants than the school could handle with the space and number of staff they had. So St. Spica Girls' Institute and St. Lulim Girls' School were built as sister schools in order to take in the overflow.

Miator continued to focus on rigorous discipline and strict rules and an ideal, conservative, high-class education, and also boasted of the fact that over fifty percent of its girls became engaged while in school. In comparison, Spica was liberal and promoted the image of independent girls advancing in society. Lulim's goal was the happiness of its girls, and it sought to nurture modern wives and wise mothers. Each school had its own unique atmosphere, and the varied curricula attracted a variety of applicants. The three schools of Astraea Hill remained the most popular schools in the area.

Entering the campus from the base of the hill, Miator was in the center, Spica was to the left, and Lulim was to the right. Each had its own campus, gymnasium and courtyard, and each had its own entrance as well, so although they were sister schools, they were fundamentally separate and functioned independently.

The schools did share the use of several buildings and facilities, however. One building included a large auditorium where joint events were held, a large theater and other facilities that all three schools used. There was also the convent, the mother institution of the schools, and the church associated with the convent. The schools also shared a vast garden, called Maiden Park, which stretched behind the school buildings. In the middle of the garden was a small lake, and nearby, at the apex of the hill, was the large landmark church.

There was one other facility that the schools shared. It was a triangle-shaped building quietly tucked away in the farthest corner of the campus. Its nickname was the Strawberry Dorms.

The Strawberry Dorms were the dormitories for students attending Astraea's three schools. Some of the large numbers of students who attended these famous schools came from far away. The dormitory had been built for those students for whom it would be too far to commute daily.

It also served another purpose, pursued by only a small number of schools these days, even among schools with a long legacy such as Miator: the isolation and discipline of the students.

Even though many young ladies from strict families— many from the oldest, most noble families—could potentially have commuted to their schools for the purpose of getting an education, they were still boarded in the Strawberry Dorms. There, they learned the ability to take control of their everyday lives. At the same time, these rare beauties were protected from the outside world.

It was a reminder of a time long past, when attending a girls' school was part of training in the domestic arts in preparation for becoming a wife. The young ladies who boarded in the Strawberry Dorms went to school by walking a path through Maiden Park, and when classes were over, they walked back through the park again, back to the Strawberry Dorms. There was absolutely no chance for them to have contact with the outside world.

The girls lived entirely within the school, a pure world within the walls that was reserved only for young ladies. A world of classes, sports, friendship and love, as well as mental and emotional bonds and passionate physical aches.

All of it existing only between girls.

"Wow, it sure is a long walk just to the church, isn't it?" Nagisa swung her arms cheerfully as she walked on the shimmering lawn.

Shizuma's face softened as she looked at her. "That's right. The Miator campus is big, but Maiden Park is huge. Wait, is this your first time going to the church, Nagisa? I thought there was a Mass there during opening ceremonies."

"Oh, that day I had some transfer paperwork to fill out at the convent, and then a nun took me from the convent right to the church, so it's my first time going to the church from the school."

Nagisa turned to look at Shizuma, her face shining like a plump, fresh, white peach, ripened in the brilliant spring sunshine. She looked so soft and gentle… It was all Shizuma could do to keep herself from reaching out and touching her.

"Oh, I see. So then the first time you came here, Nagisa, you went through the real main gate, right?"

"Huh? The real main gate?" Afraid that maybe she'd messed something up again without even realizing it, Nagisa jerked to a stop.

When Shizuma saw the frightened expression on Nagisa's face, something welled up in her heart. Shizuma reached out to her. "You must not know, then. It was before Miator was built. Back then, the only thing on the hill was the convent and the church. If you look from the St. Miator's gate, you can see all of Astraea Hill. Look, can you see the large gate that leads to Maiden Park?"

"Oh!"

Shizuma's hand moved suddenly and brushed Nagisa's uniform at her chest. Her dark green tie swayed gently.

"That's the true main gate for the campus and all the

buildings on the hill. A proper and holy gate, reigning over these grounds where only pure maidens live."

Nagisa was tense for a moment, but Shizuma's hand swept far and high, gesturing toward the part of the hill farthest away from where they stood, just visible under the clear blue sky.

With a slight blush, Nagisa looked where Shizuma pointed. She couldn't see much, but if she strained her eyes, in the shadow of a huge tree, very far away, she saw something that looked like the corner of a giant bronze-colored gate. She looked at it and imagined what the giant main gate to this hill, where her time-honored school stood, must be like. A chill ran down her spine.

She couldn't help but think how beautiful Shizuma looked, pointing across the sky, and was a little moved.

Shizuma took the opportunity to swing around behind Nagisa.

"That's why the path from the gate to the church is called the old approach," Shizuma explained as she eyed Nagisa, who was fascinated by the gate.

"No one uses the old approach now—except during the coronation of the *Étoile*, when it's covered by countless beautiful flowers. It's magical. Astraea has quite a lot of events…"

Carefully, so she wouldn't brush against Nagisa, Shizuma spread her arms wide. "Hey, Nagisa. Do you know about the biggest and the best—the grandest event in Astraea? It's the *Étoile* Competition, where the students select the couple who will represent the three schools. That is the holy place, where only the *Étoile* and her *cadette* are allowed to go."

Nagisa's mind was still on the gate at the bottom of the hill.

Shizuma examined her innocent profile, her cheeks blushing slightly as if she weren't even aware of Shizuma's wicked movements.

"So you could say," Nagisa said slowly, "that Maiden Park is the heart of Astraea, and Miator, Spica, and Lulim are its back yard."

Shizuma had the sudden urge to eat Nagisa up. She closed the circle of her arms around her. "Do you have any interest in the *Étoile*, Nagisa? If you make it through all the trials, you will become part of the greatest couple in all three schools, blessed in the presence of God himself. There are a lot of girls who would love to come here and try to become the *Étoile*."

Squeeze. I've got you!

Shizuma was just about to say it when...

"Oooooh!" Nagisa screamed and ran two or three steps, as if she didn't even notice Shizuma's arms circling her. She flailed her arms frantically. "Ooh! Oh! Oh! Ooh! There's a CASTLE!"

When she looked back at Shizuma, Nagisa's mouth was wide open. *It looks perfect for stuffing a big onigiri in,* Shizuma thought.

Shizuma was dumbfounded for a second, but when she looked at the building Nagisa pointed to, she smiled meaningfully. "Ahh... Heh heh. The Secret Garden."

Scraaape.

The low sound of a chair scraping the floor disturbed

the pleasant silence of the large open space of the main hall of the library. A student wearing a white uniform pushed her chair back and got up from the large reading table. Her short, double-breasted jacket had a wide collar and a high waist. Her matching skirt was a tight mini. It was the uniform of St. Spica Girls' Institute, with its "sailor" look.

In the silence, which was as taut as the head of a drum, the tall student was acutely aware of the attention of the other students sitting around her, focused on her every move. Eyes peered at her from behind books propped up unnaturally on the table. When she stared back, those eyes slipped behind the books again to hide. One set of hands grasping a thick cover shook, and a book clattered against the desk.

Even here too, huh? The girl let out a small mental sigh, grabbed the book she had been reading, and left her seat, heading toward the checkout desk. At the counter was a small Miator student with bobbed hair.

"Thank you. Could you put this back for me?" the St. Spica's girl asked.

"Sure. I'm sorry it's reference only and you couldn't take it out." The girl at the counter with a library committee armband on her arm, who appeared to be a first-year, looked like she was about to cry.

The tall student, Otori Amane, couldn't help but think, *I wish you wouldn't get so nervous over me.*

"It's all right. Just looking at it here was enough to see what I wanted."

"Really? That's wonderful." The girl shrugged her shoulders

apologetically. "All of the Astraea directories are so thick and heavy, especially this Miator directory because it has so many student pictures. That's why it can't be taken out."

"I see. I was surprised, because I didn't think very many people would even need to use this kind of book. I wondered if the restriction is meant to protect privacy."

"There is that, too, but…here, take a look at this." The library committee girl opened the large book to a picture that filled the entire page.

It was of a tall, beautiful, mature-looking girl, standing nobly with a crown on her head and a scepter in her hand, just like a queen. Nestled close beside her was a fragile-looking girl with very light brown hair, a small tiara on her head and a kind smile on her face. They were both wearing the uniform of St. Miator Girls' Academy.

The page looked very well-worn. The library committee girl didn't even have to flip through the book to find it; it had been so often looked at that it naturally opened up right to that picture.

Amane flinched. *That's the part I was just looking at.*

"It's a picture from last year's *Étoile* competition. The entire school was excited because they saw it as the birth of the greatest Miator couple in a long time. I heard that everyone in the school tried to copy this picture, and the crowd caused a huge mess."

The girl lowered her voice. "There were even some who tried to tear it out and steal it." Flustered by Amane's silence, the girl hastily put on a smile. *Oh no, now that I've said that, what if she thinks Miator is a school with loose morals?!* She quickly tried to change the subject. "Um, it has a lot of pictures of many other wonderful oneesama, too. So I'm sure the restriction was also made to keep the book from going missing."

"I suppose you're right."

Noticing that Amane was at a loss for words, the library committee girl's expression turned to one of worry. "Umm, are you really sure it's all right?"

"Oh…yeah, I'm sure it's all right. There was a picture I wanted to see, just like you said. I wanted to look at it somewhere peaceful and quiet—which the St. Spica's library is not," Amane added with a somewhat bitter smile. Her words were packed with feelings of self-derision as she remembered the noise in her own school's library.

"Oh, really?! A lot of students from Spica and Lulim have been using our library lately. I'm so glad to hear people from the other schools like it here… Umm, if you like, please don't hesitate to come again. I think this is a wonderful, calm place for reading books, too! Next time I'll show you the best place in the whole library!"

She beamed, a truly genial, radiant and utterly innocent smile. Amane was just a little stunned by it, and couldn't help smiling back. *If students from Spica and Lulim are coming here often, I think it just means that the fame of the Secret Garden is spreading, that's all. Well, no matter.*

Amane put on her own smile. "Ah ha ha. Thank you. You really love this library, don't you?"

"Yes. It's like, whenever I come here, I can feel myself relaxing. I start to feel more positive, like as long as I try my best even with the little things, I'll be happy."

Amane leaned over the counter toward the girl. Her face drew close to the girl's, as if she were going to peer into it. "What's your name?"

"Umm, my name is Tsukidate Chiyo. I really hope everyone is comfortable using this library."

Her smile gave away her shyness, but at the same time said she took pride in her duty, protecting this dignified library.

"Oh, that's a cute name. I'm Otori—"

As Amane started to give her name, the corners of Chiyo's mouth curved into a smile.

"I know."

"Huh?"

"You are Otori Amane-sama, from the Fifth Year Class *Trois* at St. Spica Girls' Institute…correct? You're famous, so I recognize you. I am honored to meet you," Chiyo said to Amane, her voice entirely unpretentious.

So she knows me? But when Amane looked at Chiyo, she felt a little relieved there were girls like her. *So, this kind of thing does happen even when I go to other schools—and it's probably only going to get worse.*

She figured she could bear it for just this one year. "I'll come back again. I hope next time we'll be able to doze off together, reading an even better book. Goodbye. Good luck with your library committee job."

She turned around and left the counter, waving a hand behind her.

Clatter clatter clatter.

Chairs clattered as several students, who must have been eavesdropping on the girls' conversation, raced toward the counter.

It wasn't a castle, it was a library.

Since Nagisa had never been inside, Shizuma said with a meaningful smile, she would take a little detour and show her the way. Amid the profusion of small white flowers stood a white stone wall and a building that looked from the outside like an old castle.

Wooden doors three stories high were visible in the front façade. Nagisa had only ever seen such elaborate doors once before, on a school trip to an art museum.

These doors were so heavy and massive the two girls could only open one side. Beyond the doors was a cavernous entrance hall, almost as big as a classroom, with a high ceiling supported by several giant pillars.

Click. When Nagisa stepped inside, her footsteps echoed off the stone floor, which had a large black and white checkerboard pattern. The cool air brushed her skin, and it was so quiet she wondered whether there was anybody there. Coming in here from bright Maiden Park was like stepping into a completely different world. Nagisa instinctively looked up at the tall, dome-shaped ceiling. When she saw its stained-glass windows, with their beautiful geometric patterns and lily motif, she couldn't help but gasp.

Nagisa's jaw dropped. Ever since she had entered Miator, she had constantly been struck by the feeling she was on some sort of trip.

Shizuma watched with amusement. *It looks like Nagisa's ended up someplace she never imagined.*

"What's the matter? Oh, Nagisa, your mouth is hanging open like a slob!" Shizuma said, smiling as she drew up beside the flabbergasted Nagisa.

"Ah! Oh no, I-I'm sorry."

"You don't have to apologize." Shizuma reached a hand to Nagisa's lips. "Goodness, Nagisa! You're drooling!"

Nagisa was flustered, but Shizuma invited her deeper inside the library with a big smile.

Click. Click. Click. Click. The floor faithfully made a spectacular sound with every single one of Nagisa's panicked steps.

"Please wait for me!"

Chasing after Shizuma, Nagisa entered the sacred ground beyond—the main hall. Unlike the entrance, the high-walled interior of the building had a floor with a delicate mosaic of dark, polished wood and stone. It was dimly lit and wrapped in silence.

A few lamp-like lights were situated high along the wall, which made Nagisa wonder how they changed the light bulbs. She was stunned by this seemingly empty space, but when she took a more careful look, deeper inside, she saw what seemed to be a checkout counter, all the way in the back, and the shapes of people here and there, lit by orange, flower-shaped lights.

Even though she couldn't see anyone clearly, she could hear a very faint rustling coming from a variety of places around her.

It's so quiet I thought maybe there wasn't anyone here. But still...even though it's so cool and quiet...I feel like there's an air of excitement. Like a candle flame burning without a sound.

Shizuma came up and whispered to her, "This is called the Secret Garden. It's quiet and dark, yet full of excitement— doesn't it have an atmosphere of secrecy? There's even a rumor THEY come out here."

"What 'comes out?'"

"Well...something you probably hate, Nagisa-chan."

"Something that I hate? What could that be?"

"Well...something that starts with 'g' and rhymes with 'toast.'"

"Toast... Oh, ghosts!!" Nagisa shouted without thinking.

"Shh! Don't shout like that! This is a library, you know." Shizuma hurriedly put a hand over Nagisa's mouth to quiet her, but looked like she was having a lot of fun doing it.

I can't believe there are ghosts in such a wonderful library. Nagisa was a little depressed. She really did hate ghosts.

"Hey, look," Shizuma whispered into her ear. "There are some wonderful, adorable little ghosts!"

At Shizuma's urging, Nagisa looked. Not far from where they stood were movable book racks over two meters tall. Just beyond them, through the cracks, she caught a glimpse of people moving.

"It's all right. They won't see us from here," Shizuma said

in a low voice. Nagisa peered between the book cases and listened to the conversation.

"But…"

"You said you were going to do this, didn't you?"

"Yeah…but…"

"Leave it to me. You don't have to think about anything."

"…I think I…"

"Shh. Don't say it. I know what you want even without you saying it."

From between the book racks the arm of someone dressed in a white uniform reached for something, then tried to hug it close. Long, perfectly straight hair rustled against the uniform. A sweet, spicy musk emanated from the hair and wafted between the book racks toward Nagisa.

"My beloved Hikari-chan," the girl with the long hair said. "It's all right." She pulled the other girl close and gently embraced her.

"I want you to understand my feelings…just a little…"

"Ah! Ya-Yaya-chan?!"

"Shh! Be quiet."

"Ah! Aaaaugh."

The first girl squeezed the second girl tighter and tighter, twisting her body and making her skirt slide up. The short, tight skirt was part of the Spica uniform. The girl's skirt slid up so high it revealed her underpants, and her butt cheeks, pure and white, peeked from underneath the hem. The other girl slid her hands along them.

"Ah—" the young girl's voice trembled.

The hand that had been stroking her butt cheeks disappeared even further up her skirt, causing a loud cry from the girl. "Aaah…"

At that most important point, Shizuma forced Nagisa's face toward herself. "Any more will be too much for you, Nagisa-chan…right?"

Nagisa almost wanted to see more, but had the feeling it was a good thing she hadn't. *What the heck is this? What the heck is this? What the heck is this?!*

In answer to Nagisa's unspoken question, Shizuma whispered an explanation. She explained the rumors about this place and how to use it. Although there didn't *seem* to be any people, all around, in the shadows of the bookshelves, couples enjoyed secret rendezvous.

"They are sacred, modest rendezvous between maidens," she said. "Being a library, it's quiet and only certain people come here, so there aren't many interruptions. They say that ever since before anyone can remember, it's been a popular rendezvous spot for girls who long to see each other. People started calling it 'The Secret Garden.' Although the meetings are called 'rendezvous,' that doesn't necessarily mean that anything particularly 'big' happens."

That's what Shizuma said, but Nagisa wasn't sure she believed her.

It seemed one way girls had of confirming each other's love was to hide in the shadows of the bookshelves together, open books in front of them, and pretend to look into each other's book so they could secretly touch cheek to cheek. After all, that's just about all young girls are capable of doing. But they couldn't try even such a modest thing without being nudged on by the dignified, secretive, beautiful atmosphere of the library.

"At least for normal girls," Shizuma said. "That's why when you come to the library, it's definitely worth seeing the innocent, excited faces of underclassmen who are invited here by upperclassmen. Once in a while, there are girls who get wonderfully intense, like the ones you just saw. Heh heh heh. At times like that, I feel almost like I've won something. When two people love each other...it's only natural to want to touch each other more and more, Nagisa-chan."

This is bad, Nagisa thought. *I-is that what a rendezvous is?! That's just... That's just... After that, did they...?*

Nagisa's heart began to pound. In response to her thoughts, her body began to heat up.

Shizuma didn't seem to notice Nagisa's discomfort. "Heh heh. It looks like Spica girls have started to use it lately, too. But if they're doing it there, they must still be beginners. There's a better spot..."

THEY were just beginners? Nagisa was so shocked her jaw dropped again. And then...

Huh?!

Without realizing it at first, Nagisa found herself being hugged by Shizuma.

Nagisa's heart pounded. A cold sweat ran down her back. She remembered the couple they had just seen. The pure white uniform crumpled by the tight embrace.

The skirt that had slid up.

The hand that had gone up with it.

It's just coincidence. It's just coincidence that we ended up like this, I'm sure of it—it's because I yelled before. She tried to stop me, and... Nagisa desperately tried to convince herself.

But when she thought about where she was and what she had seen—*Could there really be girls who do things like that here?*—she felt like running away.

"Shizuma-oneesama...umm, if that's how it is, we must be bothering them, so maybe it's time for us to leave..." She tried to squirm out of Shizuma's arms, but Shizuma seemed to have anticipated Nagisa's actions.

"Tsk tsk tsk..." Shizuma gently stroked the nape of Nagisa's neck and softly whispered into her ear. "Aww, don't do that, Nagisa. You're the one who said you wanted to come here, and you invited me, you know?"

Shizuma's breath brushed against her cheek.

Shudder shudder.

Shizuma's voice was very sexy. Her breath had the fragrance of roses.

Nagisa's entire mind was suddenly a blur of pink.

"This is why we came here—isn't it? I'm so happy, Nagisa... It's all right, leave it to me. I'll be VERY gentle with you..." Shizuma's hand slowly crept its way from Nagisa's neck toward her chest.

Whaat?! Is this, is this, could this be... No, it couldn't possibly be... I mean, we're both girls!

The ribbon tie at Nagisa's chest swayed.

Ah, aaaah, it really IS!

When Nagisa thought she sensed Shizuma's fingers on her chest, she couldn't take it any more. "I-I-I-I think I'm going to leave after all! I-I have to go to the toilet." She closed her eyes, thrust herself away from Shizuma, and ran from the hall.

Shizuma was dumbfounded. "What? That is the first time something like that ever happened to me. Why—"

Moments before, Shizuma had been able to tell that a pink-colored mist had shrouded Nagisa's mind while she was in Shizuma's arms.

This is going to work, Shizuma had thought. Normally, once Shizuma brought a girl that far, she would fall right into Shizuma's hands.

"I've never brought a girl that far and had her slip out of my arms before."

"I have to go to the toilet?" Hmph. She has no sense for mood.

"But no matter. I've taken even more interest in you now, Nagisa."

You, who are actually capable of rejecting me...

Shizuma smiled with obvious delight and quietly walked after Nagisa.

"Jeez, Shizuma-oneesama, Shizuma-oneesama, Shizuma-oneesama!!"

Nagisa walked quickly toward the entrance, her head down and eyes glued to the floor.

I'm so embarrassed! I don't know how to face Shizuma-oneesama. Even if it was due to circumstances, I still pushed her away. Aahh, I probably made Oneesama angry with me. Even though she was nice enough to offer to teach me how to handle the holy water... That's right, what if she didn't mean it that way at all, and I just completely misunderstood? When I felt her fingertips brush against my bare skin between the buttons of my uniform, I might have been imagining things. Yeah, that's right. This uniform is really tight, so it wouldn't open up that easily, I'm sure of it.

And yet she still kept walking quickly ahead, not even looking in front of her.

Bwam.

She bumped into someone. She quickly looked up. "Oh! I-I'm sorry!" Standing there was the first-year library committee member, Tsukidate Chiyo.

"Nagisa-oneesama!"

"Chiyo-chan!"

Thwump thwump. Chiyo's arms turned to jelly, letting the books she held fall onto the floor. She was only a lowly committee member, and she had only become a library committee member because she didn't have any other talents.

I like doing an honest job in this beautiful library, and I'm happy working here, but up until now, I never really got anything special out of being a library committee member. But ahh, this time I'm thrilled! I was able to see Nagisa-oneesama in the library!

Chiyo's heart felt like it would burst with joy. *I just met the shining white Prince of Spica, Otori Amane-sama, and now I get to see Nagisa-oneesama, too!*

Chiyo hurriedly tried to figure out what she had done to suddenly deserve this. "Nagisa-oneesama! Did you come looking for a book? I'm a library committee member! I'm so glad to see you! By all means, please allow me to help y—"

Her joy only lasted a moment.

Click click click click.

From behind Nagisa came the sound of someone running— certainly an unexpected noise in a library. Chiyo gasped, in unison with Nagisa, who turned to look behind her. A girl ran toward them, her long hair flowing behind her. It was none other than....

"Shi-Shizuma-oneesama?!" Chiyo doubted her own eyes.

Shizuma didn't even give Chiyo a second glance. "Nagisa-chan! So here you are!" She suddenly embraced Nagisa. "I've caught you! And this time I won't let you go!"

Nagisa simply stiffened helplessly.

Seeing the two of them like that gave Chiyo a huge shock. Instantly, hot tears started to well up in Chiyo's large, round, doll-like eyes.

Drip...drip drip drip.

As she watched the two of them, tears that shone like jewels fell one after the other.

What's wrong with me? Why am I crying again? If I let her see me like this, it'll scare Nagisa-oneesama. Stupid! Stupid! Stupid! Come on, Chiyo, you shouldn't cry! But, but, but, but...

Waaaah! Nagisa-oneesama is—she's already taken by Shizuma-oneesama!

Chiyo ran off without a word, crying.

Nagisa was so dumbfounded she couldn't move. *What in the world just happened?*

When Shizuma looked at Chiyo, getting farther and farther away, and at the state Nagisa was in, she felt just a little bit guilty. With an unusually awkward look on her face, Shizuma said, "Now that you've seen the library, why don't we go to the Lourdes Spring next? It's along the path to the church. It's a mysterious spring that can make miracles happen. Something might even happen between you and me."

Chiyo ran and ran, until she found herself standing in the hallway in front of Nagisa's classroom. Recently this had become Chiyo's regular spot for secretly peeking at Nagisa.

It was sacred ground…that brought back the memory of when she had first met Nagisa.

At the time, Chiyo had been crying, as usual. *Nagisa-oneesama probably thinks I'm a big crybaby,* she thought, her tear-soaked face shining.

Chiyo had been having problems back then, too…

A small white butterfly had fallen right in the middle of

the hallway. For a moment, Chiyo had thought, *Oh, there's a beautiful white butterfly,* but then she realized the butterfly wasn't moving at all and froze. Her legs stiffened and she couldn't move.

But I have to go to the faculty room, so I need to pass it no matter what...

Chiyo loved flowers, so she was a part of the gardening club, and one of her strong points was her knowledge of insects. She could touch beautiful butterflies and adorable tent caterpillars.

But even Chiyo was too scared to get close to a dead bug. Just a few moments ago, it had been happily fluttering around in the sky, but now it was dead and nothing but a cast-off skin. When Chiyo thought about that, she got really depressed, and felt like she was being dragged down by something scary—it was frightening.

"Poor thing. And what a place for it to happen."

The voice belonged to someone Chiyo had never seen at the school before. When the girl saw the butterfly, she walked up to it, gently picked it up, and placed it in her palm. She did it so lovingly, with the smile of a gentle goddess.

The girl gently blew a breath across her palm, and the butterfly's wings trembled along with the breath. To Chiyo, it looked like she gave the butterfly its last rites—one last moment of warmth.

She's saying goodbye to it. How kind.

This girl gave love to something Chiyo was too afraid of to even get close to. The girl released the butterfly out the hallway window, saying, "Be a good girl—go on home, now!"

Even though it was already dead. Though Chiyo thought the upperclassman seemed to be under the impression the butterfly was still alive.

But it might be better for it to return to the ground, instead of staying in the cold hallway, she thought as she watched the older girl.

And then...

There was a miracle.

Chiyo had thought the dead butterfly would naturally fall to the ground. But just when she thought it was going to hit the ground, it stopped in mid-air. The next moment, it started moving again, flapping its wings.

It's magic, Chiyo thought. Chiyo's goddess, who was kind even to an insect that was almost dead, said her name was Aoi Nagisa.

🍓

My dream was to share lunch in the garden with Nagisa-oneesama some day. I thought I would be happy just watching Oneesama from afar. But then I thought Nagisa-oneesama might see me when she leaves the classroom, so I've been hiding behind this pillar whenever I have the chance... But that dream's not going to come true now. If Shizuma-oneesama has taken a liking to Nagisa-oneesama—there's absolutely no chance for me.

Tears streamed from Chiyo's eyes again as she thought about it.

This must be punishment for thinking such a brazen thing. Because I wanted Oneesama to find me.

"Huh?" someone said as she passed. It was Tamao. She looked like she was about to go back to the dorms. "Chiyo-chan? What's wrong? Why are you crying?"

"Ta-Tamao-oneesama," Chiyo sobbed, and told Tamao everything.

When Tamao heard about the situation, she burned with jealousy. "Shizuma-oneesama hugged Nagisa-chan?! I absolutely, definitely cannot allow it!"

The image of Shizuma doing things to Nagisa in the library, and the image of Nagisa having things done to her by Shizuma in the library, ran through Tamao's mind. She had a vivid imagination.

No, I cannot allow such a thing! Having fun with Nagisa-chan is MY job!

The dismissal bell rang.

Diiing dooong...

Diiing dooong...

The girl heard the bell and turned around. "Huh? Oh no, it's time to go home already."

The sunlight coming in the fifth-floor window shone sharply through the glass. The light wrapped the floor in a red glow and shone all the way to the back of the long room.

"Well, then, is that all for everyone for today?"

St. Spica Girls' Institute, the second school, was built to the east of St. Miator Girls' Academy. It was the tallest building in the area. On the top floor was the Spica Student Council meeting room.

The room had a white steel frame, four glass walls and a frosted glass partition, making it look like the inside of a modern office building.

"Then it's decided. For this year's *Étoile* competition, we'll be going with *Trois Lumières*. The first competition, *L'Ouverture brillante*, will be held at the end of April. We will inform the candidates."

The girl, wearing the white Spica uniform and looking majestic, stood alone in front of one of the glass walls, which was colored a bright orange by the sun. Passing her eyes over the documents in front of her, she continued.

"We have a number of couples who have already handed in their applications—four from St. Miator Girls' Academy, five from St. Spica Girls' Institute and three from St. Lulim Girls' School. Taking into account any last-minute applications, I think the total number is most likely going to be around fifteen couples. We will eliminate approximately half in the initial competition, and we will eliminate half of the remaining couples in the second competition, *L'Épreuve d'amour*. As is customary, the final competition, *Le Dernier Miracle*, will be held by the school attended by the couple who takes first place in the second competition. The coronation of the *Étoile* is planned immediately after the third competition. However, we need time to prepare, and I think it might cause problems for the school whose couple took first place in *L'Épreuve d'amour*, so…" *Phew*… She had said all of that in one breath.

Tomori Shion, President of Spica's Student Council, was a delicate girl, slim, who looked good in the white uniform. She let out a soundless sigh. Her long chestnut hair was left loose, with only the top part tied up. Her gracefully exposed forehead gave her an air of intelligence. Her small, tipped-up nose and sharp chin gave her an ever-so-slight aura of sternness. She gave such a serious impression that the only thing missing was a set of silver-rimmed glasses.

She was a tough beauty with a sharp mind.

I can relax a little now we've gotten this far. The only thing left to do now is leave things up to the flow of the river and take my time preparing. I've done everything I can for now.

Shion gathered the papers together and tapped them against the desk to stack them neatly.

"As all of you are aware…" She looked at everyone around her, checking every single person's expression. Sitting around the large meeting table in Spica's Student Council room were three representatives from each school—the Student Council President, the Vice President, and the Secretary—as well as other Student Council staff.

Shion gathered her strength once more, straightened up, and continued. "We at St. Spica Girls' Institute will be making preparations beforehand…"

"Wait just a moment, please, if you would?"

A girl, sitting across and to the left at the large triangular table, raised her hand.

"Is there some sort of problem, Lulim Student Council President?" Shion asked, knitting her eyebrows ever so slightly. *I wonder what it is? We're almost finished.*

"What do you mean, Spica will be handling the preparations this year?" she asked in a rather gentle manner, completely different from the sharp voice she'd used a moment earlier. She tilted her head sweetly to the side. She wore the St. Lulim Girls' School uniform, with its warm pink checkerboard pattern.

She was the Lulim Student Council President, Minamoto Chikaru, from Fifth Year Class A. Her long, luxurious hair flowed behind her and, in ladylike fashion, she wore a fine braid and ribbon beside each ear. Even though she seemed tall, she gave off a delicate impression. Underneath her black bangs, her large, kind eyes gave her a wise expression. When she tilted her head, her hair swayed airily, as if joining her in asking, "Why would you say that?"

Shion was stunned. "What is this about? Why are you bringing this up now…?" She suddenly shut her mouth. In the face of such a direct question, she couldn't say a thing, because bringing something like this up in the joint Student Council was not Shion's usual way of doing things.

The fact that Spica will win this year's Étoile competition is set in stone!

Or at least that's what she thought. Even if it was obvious that everyone in the room thought so too…she absolutely could not say something in such bad taste.

Shion's previous utterance had apparently not been phrased

diplomatically enough. She heard a smothered laugh coming from somewhere beside her.

"Heh heh heh heh…"

Another girl jumped to Shion's defense. "Oh, come now, President Chikaru. Everyone already knows why, even without saying. But of course! It is because our Prince of Spica is this year's *Étoile*! You know that, and yet you go and ask that question? President Chikaru, you really are a meanie, aren't you? Shion is working so hard, and you're teasing her. Do you think Shion is that cute? I'm a little jealous."

Shion panicked. "Hey, Mo-Momomi! I mean, Kiyashiki-san, what are you saying?! If you say something like that…"

The girl sitting next to Shion, Kiyashiki Momomi from Fifth Year Class *Un* and Vice President of St. Spica Girls' Institute's Student Council, saw the state Shion was in. She hid her mouth behind her fan and continued, "Oh, come on, Shion, don't be so surprised. You want to say, 'If you say that, it will all be over,' right? Heh heh heh. It's all right, everyone here already knows it. And everyone knows President Chikaru is so kind, even if she does love teasing you. Come on, cheer up!"

The girl's face was framed by loose curls of hair, and she had large, doll-like eyes, showy eyelashes, a long, slender, high nose, and a large mouth. She gave a smile so flowery it seemed to envelop the entire area in the aroma of perfume.

It appeared Momomi was friends with the Lulim Student Council President. In spite of Shion's shocked state, the conversation continued.

"Oh, I love you just as much as Shion-chan, you know,

Momomi-chan?" Chikaru said. "You're the only girl in all of Spica who looks good in those curls."

"Wooow! President Chikaru, that makes me so happy! Then next time let me be in charge of doing the rosary, okay?"

Momomi turned to Shion and said, "If you let something like this get you so flustered, you'll be a disgrace to your nickname, Snow Queen. You're supposed to be the greatest prodigy since Spica was founded."

She waved her fan, trying to get Shion to look forward.

Shion's mouth had been hanging open. When she heard the name "Snow Queen," she came back to herself. "Hmph. I couldn't care less about that nickname!"

Well, whatever. There's no use in trying to hide it NOW. Seriously. Everyone already knows it, right? This year, SHE is finally going to enter the Étoile competition. I mean, ever since she entered Spica, her first year of middle school, it's been said that if the Prince of Spica ever entered the competition, she would definitely win. She's tremendously popular but very shy, so up until now she's always declined to participate. But now that she's in her fifth year, it's her last chance. "Before I become a sixth-year student and am too busy with entrance exams to enter the competition, I just can't refuse any more." I'm sure that's what she's thinking. Fortunately, there aren't many significant rivals right now. She will become the greatest Étoile these schools have ever seen. And I will become the most famous Student Council President of all time, and make it a total "Spica Year" to enjoy to my heart's content!

Shion renewed the determination in her heart and composed

herself. "I am terribly sorry, Lulim Student Council President. It seems I spoke too soon. I heard that Otori-san was planning to enter this year, and I just… I have a slight habit of worrying about things that are still too far in the future."

"Yes, we already know that, of course, Spica Student Council President," her enemy muttered meaningfully with a sugary smile. Her voice was so soft Shion could barely hear her. "But I think it might be better if you did not let your guard down."

"Let my guard down?"

It was a remark no one could ignore.

Light from the setting sun shone through the window. For a moment, Shion entered battle mode. "Do you have some new information?" She took a step forward and shot Chikaru a sharp look. "Does Lulim have a strong candidate? Is that what you are suggesting, President Chikaru?"

Tension overwhelmed the entire room.

"Oooh, scary!" Momomi muttered. She opened her fan and seemed to be talking to the panda on it when she said, "She really IS the Snow Queen, isn't she?"

Chikaru didn't budge an inch. She gave Shion a wink. "Oh, come now, I'm hurt, Spica Student Council President. We've known each other since we were children, Shion-chan, so I wouldn't do something like that to you, now would I? I'm not THAT much of a bully. But, then again…do we really know each other that well? However…I've heard St. Miator has a new transfer student in the Fourth Year."

Across from Chikaru, sitting to Shion's right, a Miator

student council member twitched.

Shion was not to be intimidated. "I haven't heard anything about an upperclassman transfer student at Miator."

Tension rushed through the three representatives from Spica.

And worry flitted across the faces of those from Miator.

Chikaru slowly continued, "Just a little while ago, I heard a rumor… They say the previous *Étoile* has a strong interest in that transfer student."

Tomori Shion knocked her chair over with a loud noise. She glared at another girl seated at the table. "The previous *Étoile*?"

The object of Shion's stare, Miator's Student Council President, Rokujo Miyuki from Fifth Year Flower Class, let out a huge breath.

They're not here. They're not here. They're STILL not here. For goodness sake!

Tamao was about to unconsciously snap the tip of the tree branch in front of her when she came back to herself with a start. The shadows of the trees, which spread out as if to hide Tamao, were becoming thicker.

Before Tamao even noticed it, little Chiyo stood next to her, frightened and looking at her questioningly.

"Oh! Oh, I'm sorry," Tamao said. "I didn't mean to… Did I scare you?"

Chiyo shook her head, trying to say "No, not at all" without actually saying a single word.

Seeing Chiyo's cute face calmed Tamao a little bit. "Shizuma-oneesama and Nagisa-chan sure are late, aren't they?"

"Yes. At this rate, they might miss the dorm curfew." Chiyo looked at the large watch she wore, which didn't look quite right on her small arm.

Tamao continued looking through the trees. "Shizuma-oneesama did say they were going to Lourdes, right?"

"Yes. But I was kind of far away by then, so maybe I just THOUGHT I heard her say that..." Chiyo said, her voice trailing off.

"Knowing Shizuma-oneesama, it certainly seems possible. First the Secret Garden, then the miraculous spring—I'm sure she's plotting something bad again."

Chiyo was so scared she let out a soundless scream and stepped back.

Rustle. The sound of the evening breeze passed through the grass.

"News reaches you quickly, as always, President Chikaru," Miyuki said in a surly voice. Wearing Miator's classic charcoal uniform, she sat calmly with her eyes closed. Her luxurious black hair was bobbed, cut absolutely straight just below her chin, and glistened like it was wet. The sharp edge of it covered almost a third of her small face. Almost an expression of her personality, the blade-like edge swayed over her fine features.

"So you say you're only a semi-retired Student Council President, still doing it because there were no other candidates. How modest. You, Chikaru, have served as Student Council President for an unprecedented two consecutive terms, starting in your fourth year. It seems I can't call you 'The Holy Mother of Lulim, who has nothing to do with ambition,' after all. I'm impressed you heard the news long before Spica, when they are so desperate to take the title of *Étoile*. I suppose I should have expected—"

"Hold it, was that a sarcastic remark toward Spica?!" Shion's cheeks burned.

Miyuki, however, stayed in her seat and didn't meet anyone's gaze. She continued to speak, perfectly calm.

"—I suppose I should have expected nothing less from the person they call 'The Shadow Empress of Astraea.'"

Her eyes gleamed with a strong will as her clear leadership ability began to express itself.

Chikaru answered in a cold voice. "Thank you for the compliment. But I wonder if the nickname Shadow Empress isn't more appropriate for YOU? Aren't you the 'Princess of Rokujo-in,' a schemer with a reputation of being able to control vengeful demons? I know perfectly well that just because Shizuma-sama is a sixth-year student now, and just because Spica has Otori Amane, Miator isn't necessarily going to give up on taking the title of *Étoile* so easily."

Momomi started talking to the panda again. "Whoa, scary. I didn't know President Chikaru could be so shrewd. Scary..."

Meanwhile, Shion finally regained her composure. "So, is that how it is?"

Chikaru smiled gently at Shion. "Yes, so you finally understand, Shion-chan? I'm so glad. Amane-chan is truly wonderful, and I also think she would fit the role of *Étoile* perfectly. It's no wonder you are so fired up about the possibility of Spica winning the *Étoile* title this year. But—"

"I-I am not fired up!"

"But you were, weren't you?" Momomi said to the panda, in order to avoid the glare from beside her. "Didn't you look outside the dormitory window and shout to the night sky, 'To be Student Council President the same year the star, Prince Amane, is here! This must be my destiny. I was guided by the star of Spica!'"

Chikaru continued, ignoring Momomi, "Miator will never allow that, you know."

Gulp. When Chikaru said that, Shion caught her breath.

"It isn't personal, you know. That's just how Miator is. No matter how calm it may seem on the surface, if it's not always top on the list, if it's not always number one, it won't stop until it is. The fact that over two-thirds of all the *Étoiles* have come from Miator isn't simply coincidence, or simply because of Miator's long history. Like what is happening now. Even if there is a girl that everyone agrees should become the *Étoile*, if she's not a student at Miator, Miator is too proud to accept it, and anyone who makes light of Miator might find a painful trap waiting for them—"

"Ahahaha!" Miyuki suddenly burst out in throaty laughter.

"Oh, come now, President Chikaru, no need to say such things. I just have a bad temper, that's all. Please do not talk about Miator's dark side. It's just that I...I just don't want to worship an *Étoile* from another school while I am Student Council President. I think many of the other Miator students feel the same way."

With that, everyone picked up the documents and scissors strewn on the table and slowly prepared to go home, completely ignoring the dumbfounded Shion.

Miyuki began to speak candidly. "It is exactly as you said— we had half given up on this year's *Étoile* competition. After all, Prince Amane is a fifth-year student this year. Just for this year. If we could somehow fight the fact that Chikaru's been President for two consecutive years, we might have a fighting chance, but..."

"But?" Shion shot her a harsh look.

"But you know..." Chuckling to herself, Miyuki took a long hard look at Shion's face.

Making use of her famous family name, Miyuki's nickname was The Princess of Rokujo Institute. Her appearance was perfectly Japanese. Her glossy, straight black hair was fastidiously cut, and made her pale skin seem even paler. Combined with the delicate bridge of her nose, her kind eyes and her small, rosebud lips, she had the elegance and dignity of a princess.

"It's exactly as President Chikaru said." She cast her eyes down in embarrassment.

"Like Chikaru said?"

Shion remembered. *Chikaru said an upperclassman transferred into Miator this spring, which is unusual. And for some reason the previous Étoile has taken an interest in her—but so? Why bring up the previous Étoile now?*

"It looks like you remember. That's right...it seems that Hanazono Shizuma-sama, the previous *Étoile*, the oneesama that every student in Miator admires and adores—has shown a significant interest in a new fourth-year student who just transferred into the school. I only just heard it recently myself, but...I heard that when they embraced, the scene was so bright the people around them had to cover their eyes. So I predict there is a greater than ninety percent chance that Shizuma-sama will say..." Miyuki put on a fake smile, like one might see on a receptionist. "'I want to try becoming the *Étoile* with her.'"

"But Shizuma-sama's a sixth-year, getting ready for entrance exams. Not only that, but she's been the *Étoile* once already."

"That doesn't matter to her. To her, being the *Étoile* was just one more required school experience. Even if she didn't particularly want to become *Étoile*, it would've been even stranger for her NOT to, that's all. She might not seem like she has any particular attachment to the title, but if she can turn it into an excuse for love, it's a completely different story. According to my information, it's unusual for Miator to accept a transfer student who spent her middle-school years in a different school..." Miyuki's eyes narrowed. "Yeah...I suppose you could say she's the excessively cheerful, needy type? I'm a little surprised Shizuma-sama would set her heart on her, but it's obvious that she doesn't understand the logic of Miator, and she's giving Shizuma-sama trouble."

Before she even realized it, Momomi was pulled into Miyuki's story. She had an excited smile on her face as she listened. "She's giving Shizuma-sama trouble? Wow, she must be something else, then." Shion thought she picked a strange point to be impressed about.

Miyuki went on, "Of course, it's only a matter of time before she comes in front of our Student Council. It's just, the only problem is…"

Momomi looked entranced. "The problem is…?"

"That girl is a brand-new fourth-year student who doesn't know Miator's customs, who can't comprehend beautiful sisterly love. And yet Shizuma-sama seems TERRIBLY excited about having her as her partner."

"Wow…terribly…" Shion muttered, dodging the topic. "Won't they just end up breaking up? When she's chasing after slippery prey, Shizuma-sama—well, she uses up an incredible amount of energy. There's nothing she cannot achieve, but it takes a lot of energy."

Miyuki stood. She had an unexpectedly short, slender build. "When Shizuma-sama decides she wants to do something, no battle is too tough for her, not even the *Étoile* competition. Yes, I am already well aware of what the Spica Student Council intends to do this year. But we will not let an opportunity such as this slip by. Please understand, we look forward to competing against you."

She made a slow, courteous bow. It was unusual, for

although she lowered her head, it looked almost like she tossed it back in retort.

Shion noticed Miyuki's behavior. "Rokujo-san, is that...is that a declaration of war?!"

Bwsh. Without thinking, she whipped her arm around and pointed, almost hitting Miyuki's eyes and nose. So close, and so strong...

Ah...shoot.

But it was too late. Tension rushed through everyone in the room.

Miyuki slowly smiled. "My, my." She gently grabbed Shion's arm to move it away.

"I could ask you the same thing, Tomori-san. What you just did is forbidden in Astraea. It is the sign of a challenge."

"Oh, I, I didn't mean to..." In a panic, Shion tried to pull her arm back, but Miyuki already had a tight grip on it, so she couldn't move.

Pointing at someone with the index finger was taboo for young ladies. Especially if it stopped right in front of that person's nose. In Astraea, it was said to be a signal of challenging someone to battle.

Miyuki slowly drew closer, threatening. "Up until now, I hadn't thought there was any particular need to challenge you... However, thanks to President Chikaru's untimely interference, there's no longer any need to hide it." Miyuki slowly brought Shion's hand to her lips and kissed it.

"An oncoming enemy should be fought with love. The Miator Student Council accepts your challenge with all of its

power. Please go gently on us. Now then, it is past time to leave school, so if you will excuse me."

She turned around and walked quickly out of the room without looking back.

The two Miator students who remained, the Vice President and the Secretary, rushed after her. Shion could only stand there, speechless, and watch them leave.

Miator's first dismissal time was at 4:30 P.M. The second dismissal time was after club activities were over, at 5:30. There was also a special dismissal time of 6:00 P.M., which was used only for events like the Culture Festival. The second and third times could change by fifteen minutes either way, depending on the amount of daylight, but the first dismissal time was the same for the entire year.

The regular students had to leave when they heard the dismissal bell, because those precious students, entrusted to the school by their families, had to return home before it got dark.

Once they left the school, there were two places the students went. Some went directly down the hill to the path that led to the closest station. Others went alongside the school buildings, passed in front of St. Lulim Girls' School, walked around the outer edge of Maiden Park and headed toward the back. To the Strawberry Dorms.

The building, which was close to the deepest part of Maiden Park, was plain-looking but solidly built from brick and tile.

With the lush green Maiden Park as its landscape, it had an indescribable atmosphere, like a secret hideout.

The Strawberry Dorms, which only successful applicants could enter, were used jointly by all three schools. The building itself was an unusual triangular shape, and each of the schools had their dorm in a different section. In the center was a courtyard. The Miator dorm had a small place of worship attached to it, which looked like a strawberry stem, so the students affectionately called the whole dormitory the Strawberry Dorms. Its proper name was Astraea Hall.

Movement from one school's dorm to another school's dorm was fundamentally forbidden, and the tips of the triangle were not connected. There were skywalks on the second-floor level that linked the three buildings together. Only those who had permission from the dorm manager or the nun who acted as dorm mother could pass through.

Miator's second dismissal time was about to pass. Walking back to the Strawberry Dorms took a little less than twenty minutes, so Shizuma and Nagisa had to come back along this path. Chiyo and Tamao had decided to leave school and wait along the path that went to the Strawberry Dorms.

It had been mostly Tamao's idea.

Chiyo was so excited she thought she would die. *I can't believe I'm waiting for my longed-for oneesama! I want to see Nagisa-oneesama, too, but Shizuma-oneesama is—how should I greet her? She probably thinks this is all a huge bother, because Shizuma-oneesama seems to really like Nagisa-oneesama. And when Nagisa-oneesama is with a wonderful person like Shizuma-oneesama, someone like me doesn't even compare! I just know it! I just know it! I'll only be a nuisance…*

Just as large tears were about to fall from Chiyo's eyes again, she heard the sound of talking from the other side of the wall of trees, which was so overgrown it looked like a hedge.

It was a nun, and it sounded like she was scolding someone.

"This isn't like you at all, Hanazono-san. Be more careful from now on. It's already time for you to be back at the dorm, so please go home now."

Tamao opened a space between the tree branches and peeked through. Shizuma and Nagisa were there, next to the side door of the church, which was closed. They stood in front of the nun with their heads bowed meekly.

The church was closed because students used to just stop there along the way to somewhere else. It looked like even though Shizuma and Nagisa were in charge of the holy water, they hadn't gotten it quickly enough, so the nun had to make special arrangements for them to get in.

The nun left and Shizuma started complaining. "Honestly, Sister Sakaue is so annoying, broody and strict. She's a bully. They call it holy water, but in the end it's just water, isn't it?" She swung the heavy crystal bottle used to hold the holy water.

Tamao couldn't help but laugh. "My, are you sure you should be saying something like that, Shizuma-oneesama?"

"Who's there?!"

Tamao poked her head through the hole she had made in the branches.

"Tamao-chan?!" Shizuma and Nagisa were stunned.

When Nagisa saw Tamao, she looked incredibly happy. Shizuma seemed just a little uncomfortable. Tamao was convinced. *There's nothing between those two yet.* In a voice soft enough they wouldn't hear, she whispered to Chiyo, "It looks like I still have a prayer!"

Chiyo raised her head with a jolt.

"You were on your way home, correct, Shizuma-oneesama?" Tamao said as she slowly made her way forward.

"Yes." Shizuma had been looking off to the side, staring into the distance. But now she turned her head and gazed at Tamao's face. For a moment, Shizuma regained the aura of the poised, quiet, strong queen.

Tamao felt overwhelmed, but she managed to say in a clipped voice, "The dismissal bell rang a long time ago. It's not like you to stay behind until this late."

Shizuma responded indifferently, "Yeah, well, we were in charge of the holy water today. We got a little side-tracked, and we're late." She was nonchalant, like she was flicking away a little cocklebur pod that had gotten on her uniform.

Just a little sidetracked?! Nagisa shuddered. *It felt like she was leading me on an all-out tour of Maiden Park. And we even got yelled at by the nun…*

Nagisa threw a questioning look at Shizuma, who ignored it and turned her eyes to the trees, which were almost glowing red in the sunset. "The sun's already set."

Until a moment ago, Shizuma had been having fun and enjoying herself, and seemed like a perfectly normal high-school girl, just like the other ones Nagisa knew. But the quick change in her attitude worried Nagisa. *Oh, Shizuma-oneesama...up until a moment ago...up until a moment ago you were having so much fun.*

Overwhelmed by Shizuma's transformation, Nagisa wondered if this was who Shizuma really was, and was amazed.

When I look at her like this, Shizuma-oneesama really is beautiful and wonderful, and I guess mature. Using the word feels a little strange, but she seems stately, I guess. I was a little shocked by how Shizuma-oneesama acted in the library, but... I'm sure it was because of the special atmosphere the library has. I'm sure I was mistaken.

Thoughts ran through Nagisa's mind as she looked at Shizuma in profile, gazing at the trees.

I got caught up in the strange atmosphere, and it made me feel like Shizuma-oneesama was se-seducing me.

All of a sudden, she was embarrassed. *I wonder what Shizuma-oneesama thought... Maybe everyone could tell exactly what I was thinking and they think I'm stupid. Yeah, I'm such an idiot. That I thought even for a moment someone like Shizuma-oneesama might be in love with me...*

The wind blew.

Nagisa shivered. *It's cold!*

Shizuma's hair blew in the cold early spring evening breeze.

Shizuma-oneesama... Stealing furtive glances at Shizuma's beautiful profile started to make Nagisa a little sad, but she still kept looking.

Tamao caught sight of Nagisa out of the corner of her eye and could tell what was going on. She still wasn't crushed.

"Oh, is that what it was? Tsukidate-san just told me she saw you and Nagisa-chan in the library—oh, please let me introduce you. Nagisa is a new student, just transferred into the same class as me. By coincidence, she's also in the seat next to mine, and we are sharing a room at the dorm! We have a wonderful connection—"

"Right, by coincidence." Shizuma's voice was so low when she spoke, only Nagisa could hear her.

Tamao continued, "Chiyo-chan told me what happened, and... well, considering the place, I asked her for some details..."

Chiyo's face went beet-red.

"I was worried that maybe my Nagisa-chan made some sort of careless mistake with you..."

"...MY Nagisa-chan?" Shizuma said in an unexpectedly sharp voice.

"Yes, MY Nagisa-chan." Tamao smiled so broadly her eyes closed. It was as if the humble attitude she'd had up until now were a lie.

"Is that so? Your Nagisa-chan made a careless mistake with me?"

"Yes, that's right. My precious friend Nagisa-chan isn't used to it here yet, so when I heard she was caught by a star like you, Shizuma-oneesama, I was worried perhaps she was totally embarra—I mean, she did something rude."

The longer Shizuma forced herself to keep her mouth closed, the more Tamao piled on the taunts.

"Just like I thought, she really did do something rude, didn't she? Shizuma-oneesama, please forgive her. She isn't used to life here at Miator yet. If she did do something rude, it is the fault of the entire Fourth Year Moon Class. No, it is my fault, because I haven't properly taught her the customs at Miator yet, even though we share the same room. Please punish me. Punish me for all of the calamities Nagisa-chan caused…"

Tamao suddenly became overdramatic. With a flourish, she got down on her knees and bowed her head, then clasped both of her hands as if she were praying.

Shizuma looked down on Tamao silently.

Chiyo froze.

Snap snap snap snap.

When Nagisa heard the noise, she felt like a fat, cold, giant icicle had descended between the two girls. Frantic, she stepped between them.

"O-oh, come now, Tamao-chan, not another one of those jokes! Please don't kneel like that." *Honestly. Why do the girls from Miator make such a big deal out of everything?* "Jeez, Tamao-chan, you're always joking around like that!"

With a wry smile, Nagisa reached her hand out to Tamao. "You don't have to say stuff like that! You're pretty and smart and fun, and you're SO nice to a transfer student like me. I'm so thankful for everything you've done," Nagisa mumbled, helping Tamao stand up.

Tamao very happily took a gentle hold of Nagisa's extended

hand and stood up firmly. Tamao's hand was cold.

I wonder if Tamao-chan was waiting here a long time? Nagisa thought. "Listen, I might not be strong enough to be your best friend, Tamao-chan, but of course you're already my best friend in Miator!"

"Na-Nagisa-chan..." Tamao drew away from the words that had slipped out of Nagisa's mouth. *Incredible. How honest and up-front she is.*

Tamao felt like she had been shot through the heart by the straightforward words she couldn't possibly have said. Living in the feminine environment of Miator, Tamao had seen more "best friends" and "lovers" than she could count, but the words always seemed so empty when said out loud.

It felt like as soon as she said them, something was lost. Like desperately trying to stop a lie once spoken.

We're number one best friends, right? Every time Tamao had heard those words, every time she had responded to them, she had felt a part of herself fade.

But Nagisa's words were different. She'd felt that way ever since they'd first met, and she had a feeling she was beginning to understand why she was so attracted to Nagisa.

Tamao had a habit of trying to manipulate a situation by tossing around superficial words. But the words that fell from Nagisa's mouth were always just words, nothing more, nothing less. They had substance.

Nagisa simply grasped things as they were.

You're so honest and straightforward, Tamao thought.

Almost impossibly so. I wonder if I'm so warped because of the kind of home I was raised in. She looked back on her past and started to feel a little lonely.

Number one best friends… Tamao felt it was a little different from what she'd wanted, but now that Nagisa had said it, Tamao thought maybe she wanted really to be "number one best friends" after all.

Before Chiyo realized, she muttered aloud, her eyes gleaming, "Nagisa-oneesama is really a nice person, isn't she? She's like a pure angel. I think everyone who meets her will fall in love with her!"

Chiyo could almost see adorable white butterflies fluttering around Nagisa.

Tamao hid her self-consciousness. "Well, that makes me happy, Nagisa-chan. I think I could live on nothing but those words for a whole week. You must be vitamins sent by God just for me! Ooh, I just want to eat you up! I guess this means I'm Nagisa-chan's number one, right?" She winked suggestively.

"Ah ha! Ah ha ha ha ha! You're saying weird things again, Tamao-chan! You're so funny! Isn't she, Shizuma-oneesama?"

When Nagisa turned to look at Shizuma, the sound of silence echoed back to her.

Huh?

Shizuma radiated an icy aura, as if her whole body were frozen. "You two seem to be enjoying yourselves."

Chiyo's body shook, startled. *Oh no, I went too far—I think.*

Tamao instantly stepped away from Nagisa and stood there stiffly, her mouth open.

Without even looking at Nagisa, Shizuma placed her hand gently on the younger girl's head and took a small step forward.

"Nagisa-chan, I'm glad you seem to have such a good classmate."

The wind blew, sending Shizuma's hair whirling, further hiding her expression. "It looks like you won't have any trouble finding someone to recommend you."

The wind rustled through the trees. Suddenly the cold of early spring pervaded the area.

"Someone to recommend me?" Nagisa repeated with a questioning look on her face.

"Yes. Someone to recommend you for entry. *L'Ouverture brillante* is going to be at the end of the month, you know." Shizuma's low voice echoed from within the increasing evening shadows.

Chiyo went pale. "*La... L'Ouverture brillante*? Do you mean—"

"I-I've just now decided." Shizuma abruptly straightened and spun around to face Nagisa.

"Shizuma-oneesama…"

Chiyo's and Tamao's voices overlapped. Chiyo was frozen and Tamao went bright red.

"I am going to enter the *Étoile* competition this year with Nagisa as my partner," Shizuma said. She walked back to Nagisa, determined, and looked dolefully into Nagisa's face. "I would have been happy just to spend some time with you; I really don't want to get you wrapped up in something like this."

She stroked Nagisa's head again and then gently placed her hand against Nagisa's cheek. "But…" She spread her fingers. "You're going to have to understand, okay?"

Her thumb and index finger squeezed closed. She pinched Nagisa's cheek.

"Didn't I tell you? If you break your promise…" Shizuma slowly leaned close to Nagisa's ear and whispered, "I'll punish you."

Aah, but…weren't you just talking about calling you "Shizuma-oneesama?"

Overwhelmed by the pain in her cheek—or by Shizuma-oneesama's intensity—Nagisa couldn't put her thoughts into words.

"I am Hanazono Shizuma from St. Miator Girls' Academy, Sixth Year, Snow Class. As someone who has lived on this campus a long time, and has worn the shining *Étoile* crown once already, I will never play second fiddle to anyone. Ever."

Shizuma slapped Tamao's hand off of the edge of Nagisa's skirt. "I've only just met you, and I didn't even think of this before—it looks like I was soft. There are plenty of traps waiting for good seeds that have just been planted. Even a good seed can be eaten by a bird if it falls on the edge of the path. If it falls among the rocks, it dries up. If it falls among thorns, it gets choked. But…"

She glared at Tamao with icy eyes.

Tamao felt something cold run down her spine. *I wonder… I wonder how long it's been since I've seen Shizuma-oneesama act like this.*

Shizuma was filled with a dignified elegance and an intensity that seemed like it would overpower Tamao. It was like she was wrapped in a silent flame. A cold, silvery, soundless flame.

"A seed that falls on good ground will produce thirty, sixty or even a hundred times what was sown, growing thickly laden with fruit in the good ground. I must let everyone know that this good seed[2] is mine, and…for this good seed, the good ground is me, Hanazono Shizuma."

Shizuma gazed steadily at Nagisa and gently extended her hand.

Ah! This gentle, noble hand that seems like it belongs to a goddess. Nagisa couldn't help wondering how happy she would be if she took that hand. It was like the entrance to a dazzling other world, like a gateway to a land of bliss, a world flowing with milk and honey—an inviting hand that no normal person could refuse.

Shizuma gave a gentle smile from the bottom of her heart, one that looked sympathetic. "Nagisa. You didn't know, so I will forgive you. But I'm going to tell you right now, so be sure to remember. I am a good oneesama to everyone who lives in Miator. But this is what it *really* means to call me 'oneesama.' I will not allow you, my beloved *cadette*, to fall into another's hands again. As a sign of our promise, let's take the title of

Étoile together. I, Hanazono Shizuma, promise you the crown of miracles."

Shizuma's face lowered—and drew close to Nagisa's lips.

Nagisa blanked out.

What is this all about? What in the world is going on here?! Staring dumbfounded at Shizuma, whose hair was shrouding Nagisa and blocking Tamao's view of her, Tamao couldn't believe what she was seeing.

Could Shizuma-oneesama possibly be serious...?

Tamao had come to Miator directly from the elementary school. For good or bad, she'd thought she knew almost everything about this oneesama who was two years her elder. Tamao, an outstanding beauty who was always number one or two in her class, had even set her eyes on Shizuma once, and there had been many times when the two of them had worked together at functions such as Masses.

Shizuma was the prettiest girl in the school, and talented. Not only that, she knew how to make good use of her beauty to enjoy her school life to the fullest. Tamao secretly felt a bond with her.

Compared to what Tamao knew of Shizuma, this didn't seem like her normal behavior. Chasing and chasing and running down her prey—driving the girl she sought to the very edge of a cliff and then finally getting her to jump into Shizuma's arms of her own volition. She had heard that was Shizuma's usual method, and that's how she had imagined it to be, not this twisting of someone's arm, forcing her.

Getting someone to do what you want of her own will was the epitome of a white lily's love.

This, however... It's because Nagisa-chan is so cute. Because she's so normal. Because I teased her a little—right in front of Shizuma's own eyes. I wonder if she's serious? She actually wants to become the Étoile together?

It didn't matter that Shizuma-oneesama was so popular she had easily won the title of *Étoile* last year. Her partner was a transfer student who had only come here this month. There was no way such a ridiculous idea would succeed. There were only three weeks left until the first competition of the *Étoile* series, *L'Ouverture brillante.*

Clap, clap, clap, clap, clap, clap.

The sound of dignified applause echoed from nearby.

"Wonderful—this is exactly what we expected from our Shizuma-oneesama!" With a rustle, someone appeared out of the shadows.

"Who's there?!" Shizuma asked.

While Tamao and Chiyo stared in astonishment, St. Miator's Student Council President, Rokujo Miyuki, appeared, looking her usual calm self.

"Miyuki-oneesama! What are you doing here?" Tamao yelled.

"Oh my, what a coincidence, isn't it? The joint Student Council meeting ran late today, so I was taking a shortcut..." Miyuki put a leisurely smile on her face. Tamao was going to say something else, but Miyuki didn't even look at her. She stared straight ahead, looking only at Shizuma.

"And I see I came at the perfect time, Shizuma-oneesama. If I am not mistaken about what I just heard, you are going to enter this year's *Étoile* competition with this transfer student, Aoi Nagisa from Fourth Year Moon Class—am I correct?"

Chiyo's mouth fell open. "Whaaat? Miyuki-oneesama, were you listening the whole time?!"

Miyuki didn't even look at the shocked Chiyo; she merely silenced her with a gesture of the hand. "Splendid! Truly splendid determination!"

She clapped her hands again. "As president of Miator's Student Council, nothing could make me happier. Actually, there was a bit of an incident at the joint Student Council meeting just held at Spica. You simply must hear about it, Shizuma-oneesama."

Miyuki told them what had happened at the meeting. How Spica was so confident in one of their candidates, Otori Amane. How they seemed to think they had already won the *Étoile* crown. How Miyuki and the other Miator students present at the meeting had been frustrated when they heard it.

And about how Spica's Tomori Shion had provoked them and given them the sign of challenge, as if she were saying "If you think you can win, then go ahead and try!"

"Lulim's Council President, Minamoto, seemed to be supporting Spica, too. Shizuma-sama, you must understand how we in Miator's Student Council felt when we heard that." Miyuki's voice became tearful.

"I know what you're trying to say," Shizuma said in a low voice, still holding Nagisa in her arms. For some reason, Nagisa hadn't uttered a word since Miyuki had showed up.

"Thank you very much," was all Miyuki said.

Shizuma let out a huge sigh, mixed with considerable sorrow. She lovingly looked at Nagisa in her arms.

Tamao was shocked at the look in her eyes. The usually confident and cheerful Shizuma couldn't say a thing—she seemed to be feeling both heart-wrenching sadness and kindness at the same time.

"Tamao, please take care of Nagisa-chan and Chiyo-chan," Shizuma said without shifting her gaze. With a thwump, she gave Nagisa's immobile body over to Tamao.

For the first time, Tamao realized the state Nagisa was in. *Oh no! What happened to you, Nagisa?!*

Shizuma gave Miyuki a look. "Let's go."

Miyuki bowed deeply and said in a small voice, "Well then, let's go through the formalities as quickly as possible. The entry sheets are in the Student Council office."

The two of them left, walking quickly.

Shizuma, her silvery hair fluttering behind her, disappeared into the dark shadows of the trees.

"Tamao-oneesama, I wonder what's going on with Shizuma-oneesama," Chiyo said nervously after a long silence.

"I'm sure Shizuma-oneesama is—" Tamao started to say, but stopped. "I don't know, either. But right now, I have our Nagisa-chan on my hands."

She looked at Nagisa's face. Her eyes were closed and she was breathing regularly.

Goodness, I wonder when she fell asleep! I've never seen a girl so stunned by Shizuma-oneesama's kiss!

A totally peaceful feeling came over Tamao. "It's impossible for us to understand what the upperclass oneesama are thinking. But that's okay, Chiyo-chan, because we're with Nagisa-chan. Let's go back to the Strawberry Dorms, all three of us. We're already late, so let's take our time and pick flowers along the way. It's all right, I'll think of an excuse to give the nuns. I'm sure there won't be any problem if we mention the Student Council President, Miyuki-oneesama. Besides, we actually were with her. Knowing her, I'm sure she'll match her story with ours."

"Right!" Chiyo looked at Tamao trustingly, then peeked at Nagisa's face. "Ah! Oh, Nagisa-oneesama... It looks like she's fallen completely asleep! And she looks happy!"

"You're right. She looks so innocent when she's sleeping, just like a little child," Tamao said with a laugh. She shook Nagisa awake. "Come on, wake up. Wake up, Nagisa-chan! It's time to go home! I'm sure there's delicious cake and tea waiting at the Strawberry Dorms! Wake up, my cute little Nagisa-chan! If you don't wake up, I'll tickle your stomach!"

The wind blew, swaying Nagisa's hair. Her eyelids twitched. From somewhere, a sweet flowery scent, like that of a tropical island, drifted over them.

Chatter chatter chatter chatter...
The halls of the Strawberry Dorms rippled with the noise of the pre-dinner bustle. Groups of girls laughed happily, telling

each other about what had happened that day and talking about their plans for that night before each went her own way.

In a hall deep in the Miator section of the Strawberry Dorms was a public corner with shared facilities, like the dining hall and salon. It was the farthest corner of the hall and had a stone floor with a gray mosaic pattern. There was also a large wooden door made of oak.

A girl, passing by, looked at it, puzzled. "Huh? The common bath is closed? It looks like there's light coming from inside. Did someone mention we couldn't get in the bath before dinner tonight?"

Swsssh.

A watery sound, like a wave, echoed from the other side of the thick white steam. Miator's large common bath was designed in the Roman style, with large, bright terra cotta tiles. Three large goddess statues, each holding a vase, stood around the bathtub, which was big enough for thirty people. Streams of water flowed from the vases. Water that spilled out of the tub calmly flowed over the floor.

"Phew, what a nice bath," whispered one girl, her long hair pulled up as she soaked in the tub.

"It sure is," replied another girl with short black hair and a slightly nervous look on her face. "Two people hardly ever get a chance to use this huge tub by themselves."

The serious voice belonged to Rokujo Miyuki.

The other girl laughed and turned around. "Oh my." She chuckled inwardly. "You don't have to be so sarcastic. What's wrong with doing a little mischief once in a while?"

That was Hanazono Shizuma—even through the steam, it was clear her face was as beautiful as the goddess sculptures around the tub.

Miyuki puffed out her cheeks and blew out a slow breath. "Thanks to a certain someone it seems I have quite a few *more* things to do now."

Plunk.

Shizuma drew closer to Miyuki. "I wanted to take it easy. Didn't we used to talk secretly like this a lot before?"

Zwsssh... Water overflowed.

"Yes—until a year ago."

"A year? Has it been that long? No, I mean, is that all that has passed? It feels like much, much longer. And at the same time feels like just the other day."

"Yes," was Miyuki's short reply. Shizuma sat in front of her, facing her.

"Oh, you think so too, Miyuki? Heh heh. You know, you are the only one I can talk with about back then, Miyuki."

"This is the first time you've talked about it, Shizuma-sama," Miyuki replied with a serious face.

And the first time you've smiled so brightly, she thought.

"Oh, it is?" Shizuma chuckled as if she didn't know what Miyuki was talking about.

Now that I think about it, I guess it has been a very long time since I've felt so carefree, so cheerful. I feel like something

*good is waiting for me. It makes me want to do something really
showy. It's a feeling of excitement I have about the future—
something I'd forgotten.*

"Since it was you, Miyuki, I was positive—I knew you
would sense my mood and catch on. And the way you pretended
to cry—even Tamao was fooled, don't you think? I'm impressed.
But I knew from the beginning there was no way you were going
to give up on the *Étoile* competition. Of course, I had absolutely
no desire to enter, but…" Shizuma moved right next to Miyuki.
She brought her face so close to Miyuki's their cheeks almost
touched. "It's all right. I'll go along with it. Just this once."

"Shizuma-sama! I didn't mean to—"

The moment she started to speak, Shizuma's supple fingers
dug into the bulge of Miyuki's soft breast.

"It's all right. Our interests happen to be the same this time."
Shizuma smirked, lowered her voice even more and said, "You
look lovely naked, Miyuki-chan."

Shizuma passed Miyuki, walked to the edge of the tub and
stood with a loud rush of water.

The steam lifted and Miyuki unconsciously averted her
eyes. The sight of Shizuma standing there openly, stark naked,
was too—

—sublime.

Miyuki tried to play it cool. "If you'd like, shall I rinse you
off?"

Shizuma turned only her head turned to look back. "No, I
couldn't ask you to do that."

Miyuki blushed, even though her eyes were still averted.

"Oh, are you getting hot flashes from staying in the bath too long? Your cheeks are bright red, Miyuki-chan," Shizuma said, almost as if she was talking to herself. She chuckled and left to rinse herself off.

Shizuma disappeared beyond the steam.

Aaah… That was scary. Shizuma-sama sure is intense when it's one-on-one. Having managed to somehow withstand Shizuma's pursuit, Miyuki stroked her breast. She suddenly sympathized, just a little, with the transfer student Shizuma had her eye on.

"Hey, hey! Tamao-chan!" Nagisa was a little excited. *Today was—how do I put this—a dazzling day.*

"Hey! Hey! Hey! Come on!" she called. It had been a week since Nagisa had started sharing a room with Tamao. Usually Tamao would answer right away, and she'd always be concerned about whatever it was Nagisa wanted to talk about—but now there was no answer.

"Hey! Hey! Is this how you use a facial mask?" Nagisa turned from the mirror.

"Ha! Heh heh heh heh heh heh."

Tamao, who had been sitting by her bed absent-mindedly combing her hair, burst into laughter. "Oh, what am I going to do with you, Nagisa-chan… Ha, heh heh heh heh."

"Huh? It's not right, is it? When I put it on, my eyes get plugged up and I can't see."

Nagisa sensed Tamao was coming closer.

"Silly, it's absurd to wear it like that. The parts for your eyes need to be open. There are eye holes sewn into it, you know? Look."

Tamao's cool hands flitted about over Nagisa's head, and...

Nagisa's vision became clear. "Oh, I can see. There *are* spots for the eyes...but even the eye parts were covered in beauty cream, so I thought this was how I was supposed to use it..."

The facial mask with beauty cream on it that Tamao had given her was cool and felt good.

"If you wear it like that, the cream will get in your eyes. Are you okay? Do they hurt?" Tamao took Nagisa's face in her hand and took a long look into her eyes. Nagisa's desk light reflected and sparkled in Tamao's large eyes.

"Yeah, I'm all right. Tamao-chan, your eyes are twinkling."

"Wh-what are you talking about?" Tamao looked off to the side embarrassedly, which was not like her at all.

"Oh, I'm sorry..." *I have a habit of saying exactly what I think, don't I.*

Nagisa felt a little guilty about it, but at the same time she was surprised by the silent, embarrassed Tamao.

For the past week, after eating dinner, they had been going to the salon together. Even when they were in their room, they would do something fun—play a little game, do crafts, eat delicious snacks. Tamao had arranged all of it to cheer Nagisa up. This was the first time Nagisa had seen her quiet like she was tonight.

"What's wrong? You seem kind of down, Tamao-chan."

"I seem down? Not at all! I'm cheerful as ever," Tamao replied with a big smile. She fussed with the hem of her white negligée and went back to her own bed.

Nagisa didn't believe it. *She really is acting strange.* Normally, Tamao would shout something like "I'm so happy you're worried about me, Nagisa-chan!" and give Nagisa an enthusiastic hug.

Oh no. What am I thinking? Since when did I start thinking about things like that? It-it's not like I'm E-EXPECTING it!! Swiping the naughty idea away with her hand, Nagisa stood up.

Tamao sighed.

"Come on, what's wrong?! You're acting strange today. If you want, you can talk to me about it."

"It's all right. If I told you, it wouldn't help anyway."

"Oh, not at all? Well, I've only just transferred here, but I think I've started to get used to Miator."

"Then…Shizuma must have taught you a lot in one day!"

"It-it's not like that…" Nagisa said with a blush. "It's thanks to you of course, Tamao-chan, because you've been so nice to me since my first day here. Oh, now that I think about it, Shizuma-sama—no, I mean Shizuma-oneesama—suddenly disappeared this evening. I wonder what happened. Do you know, Tamao-chan?"

"Oh, come on, Nagisa-chan—you don't remember?"

"Huh? What do you mean?"

"But…" Tamao's mouth opened and closed soundlessly for a while and then stopped. *She was even kissed, for goodness sake.*

"Well, whatever. I suppose it's more convenient that you forget."

"Huh? Why do you say that?"

"Don't worry about it. It's none of your concern. Shizuma-oneesama left because she had sudden business with the Student Council President."

"With the Student Council President?! Wow, Shizuma-oneesama really is an important person after all. She even goes to the Student Council… Wait—but, if she's the oneesama that all the schools admire the most, why isn't Shizuma-oneesama the Student Council President?"

"Oh, because Miator's Student Council President is usually a fifth-year student, who wouldn't be studying for entrance exams yet. And last year when Shizuma-oneesama was a fifth-year student, she was the *Étoile*."

"*Étoile*? Now that you mention it, I think Shizuma-oneesama said something about that once. Exactly what is an *Étoile* anyway? Is it some sort of job within the Student Council?"

"You don't know what the *Étoile* is? Well…it's a little difficult to explain."

Tamao's face clouded as she tried to think of the best way to explain it to Nagisa. "You could say the *Étoile* is the symbol of this school—no, not just this school. The symbol for all of Astraea. One is picked each year, from all of the students. She is the kind of person who is the object of everyone's admiration, the target of their love and affection and a model to the other students. It's different from the usual beauty contest, because it doesn't focus as much on looks as it does on being loved by all the students in all three schools. It's not just one person who is picked; it's always a couple. The couples are formed voluntarily, but usually it's an oneesama type, like Shizuma, paired with a smart little sister type. They are a symbol—a model of how to care for each other and love each other as sisters. In reality, there are some couples who really do love each other, and some who are couples in name only, formed just because they look like model students together."

Tamao got a distant look in her eyes. "The *Étoile* is decided by three competitions, one each month for three months, beginning in April when the new school year begins. There is a coronation before first-term Ending Ceremonies. After summer vacation, there are many things she must take part in, like giving the opening speech at important events like the Culture Festival. So if the process of choosing the *Étoile* has begun, you will probably see her too, Nagisa-chan. She does not have the authority to decide anything substantial, so you could say it is an honorary position, but…it is a meaningful, almost royal position."

"Hmm, I see. I think I understand now. It's such an incredible position that you even speak more solemnly when you talk about it."

"Oh no, I always speak like that when I discuss the upperclass oneesama. But…you might be right, in a way. The person wearing the sacred crown of the *Étoile* is…how do I put this? It's like she's endowed with an indescribable, noble light that seems to have a magic spell cast on it. No one who lives on this hill can help but love and respect her. Shizuma-oneesama is beautiful and full of confidence, and she is a wonderful person. However, when she was the *Étoile*, she truly shone. No one could help but be fascinated by her. Everyone wanted to get close to her. She was like a goddess."

Wow—in my eyes, she seems like a goddess right now. Nagisa tried with all her might to imagine Shizuma when she had been the *Étoile*. Next she tried adding Shizuma's partner standing beside her. But it was beyond the limits of her imagination.

When she glanced to the side, she noticed Tamao's eyes shone with ecstasy. For some reason, Nagisa felt like she understood Tamao's feelings.

"Hey Tamao-chan, don't you want to try to become the *Étoile*? I think you would win for sure. Yeah, I'd definitely cheer for you!"

Tamao sprang up in a panic. "N-no, not at all! Someone like me would only disgrace the title of *Étoile*. Besides, I'm still in my fourth year. And this year, there is a great prince who attends Spica. Everyone thinks there's no doubt this year's *Étoile* is going to be Prince Amane."

"A great prince?!"

"Yes. A prince so great even the girls at Miator think we might not have a chance this year."

"You say prince, but…it's a girl, right?" Nagisa asked.

"Heh… Oh, Nagisa-chan. You are still so innocent! Yes, of

course she is a female. But I think even you would understand the instant you saw her. No matter how you look at her, there is no doubt she is a prince."

"Hmmm… Oh, I see… I want to see her right now!"

"Oh, Nagisa-chan, you cheater! I'll tell Shizuma-oneesama on you!" Tamao raised her hand in jest. "Oh, that might become another big problem…"

Nagisa imagined it and was a little disheartened, but for some reason it also made her very excited.

"I think you'd better go to sleep," Tamao said.

Reluctantly Nagisa turned toward her bed. "W-wait, I still have the facial mask on."

"It's all right. I'll watch over you until you fall asleep, and when the time comes I'll take it off for you."

"But I should do it!"

"No, no, if I left it up to you, Nagisa-chan, you would do something weird again and wake me up!"

"I don't care what you say, I'll be fine! All that's left is to take it off."

"Quiet! If you complain, I'll get into the bed with you!"

"Urgh…okay," she said. Wondering why Tamao was being so threatening over something so small, Nagisa got into bed. *Well, whatever.* Too much had happened today, and Nagisa was a little panicked.

If tomorrow is like this too, oh, it makes my head hurt, but… I still feel kind of happy. God, does that make me strange?

Five minutes later…

"Hey, Nagisa-chan, it's so boring, watching you like this, so…can I sleep next to you after all?"

Tamao suddenly invaded Nagisa's bed.

"Whoa! Whoa whoa whoa whoa whoa! Tamao-chan, you're too close!"

The silk of Tamao's negligée rustled against Nagisa's cheek and she smelled the gentle scent of soap.

Yargh! Whatever! Anyway, may tomorrow be a good day as well!

Even though Tamao had forced her way into Nagisa's bed, when Nagisa looked at her, for some reason she felt kind toward her.

"Well then, fine. Let's sleep together tonight! It's warmer that way!"

"…Nagisa-chan."

The early spring day at Miator finally came to an end. To Nagisa, the *Étoile* was really nothing more than a star in space, shining in the distance.

CHAPTER 3

The White Prince of the Stars Falls in Love with a Violet on the Roadside

"It's the Prince!"

"The Prince!"

"The Prince has graced us with her presence!"

The girls' murmurs spread like ripples. They stood in front of the main gate of St. Spica Girls' Institute, which shone in the white morning sunlight. They were there to see the main event of the morning—the arrival of the Prince of the Stars.

The girls, all wearing uniforms of pure white, which they called "Spica White," stood in two lines in front of the main gate. With the same anticipation in each of their hearts, all of their cheeks pink, they fidgeted with excitement. The aisle between the two lines looked like a glorious path up to a stage.

Around the corner of the path stood a person in anguish.

Aah, my head is spinning—even though I should be used

to it by now. It happens every morning. Why must it be like this every time I go to school? I feel like I'm going through intense scrutiny—though I should be used to it by now. Do I have no choice but to walk up this path? Just like this, forever?'

Otori Amane sighed from the depths of her heart.

Diiing dooong.

The sound of old bells echoed distantly from the direction of Maiden Park. It was the first bell, signaling that it was 8:15.

Not again.

She took a reluctant step forward.

"It's almost time!"

"She will be here soon!"

Amane almost always arrived at the school gate just past 8:00. And if the Prince couldn't find the resolve to appear early, the girls who waited for her stayed planted in that spot, even until this late time. They did it every morning.

The young ladies waited anxiously, their hearts swelling in anticipation of the moment she would finally step into view.

Oh well, there's nothing I can do. I have to go, Amane told herself desperately.

"Good morning!" She forced out the greeting in a strong, dignified voice. At that moment, Amane's face turned into that of a prince. She was completely unaware of this, but she was so used to the role she had played for so many years, it was already a part of her. Her role as Prince of the Campus.

The girls who waited trembled with joy as they greeted their Prince.

"Good morning to you."

"How is your health this morning?"

"May God's divine protection be upon you today, Amane-sama."

As each girl gave the greeting she had spent all morning thinking about, she took the edge of her skirt in her fingers and curtsied. It was a Western form of reverence—pinching the edge of the already short skirt of Spica's uniform and forcing it to spread a little, drawing the right leg toward the back and bending it and lowering the body as if kneeling. Then slowly, elegantly, bowing the head.

If Spica's uniform were black instead of white, and if they were wearing white caps on their heads, the girls would look exactly like maids serving a prince.

As Amane passed, a wave of beautiful curtsies flowed down the lines of girls, like a wave among spectators at a sporting event. The only sound was the rustling of clothes.

It was an elegant sight, without a single thing out of place. The very person for whom all this spectacle was put forth, who could be expected to lord it over those who showered her with affection, actually kept her eyes directly ahead as she walked, because she didn't want to see any of it.

Around the same time Amane reached the end of the lines, one girl from the very end walked gracefully to the center.

"Aaaaaaaa-Amane-sama!" The girl was so nervous, she had difficulty speaking.

Amane looked firmly into the other girl's eyes. "Yes?" Amane was strong as she prepared herself and stepped forward.

Now that it's come to this, I don't have a choice. Just like always, they'll release me after this.

"Uuuuuuuumm, umm, umm…" The young lady was so nervous she felt like she had to go to the bathroom. But she squeezed her thighs tight and endured it.

"What?" Amane asked with a good-natured tilt of her head. Her voice was slightly husky, low and mellow. Her bangs hung over her forehead and her eyes shone faintly in their shadow.

But her gentleness had the exact opposite effect from what she'd wanted.

"Uh, umm…" The young lady looked like she was just about to faint.

I guess I have no choice. Nothing's going to happen if we stay here like this.

In a calm voice, Amane asked her, "Did you have something to give to me?"

"Y-y-y-y-y-y-yes!" In one of the young lady's hands was a small package tied with a golden ribbon. She was holding it so tightly the paper it was wrapped in was completely wrinkled.

This happened every morning, and it had come out of something Amane herself had said. Before this spectacle had come to be, underclassmen would visit Amane's room one by one every morning. Blushing nervously, in small voices, they would tell her why they had come to visit. Not only would they not be able to get up the courage to give her the present they'd brought, but they would clutch it so tightly they'd leave wrinkles in the wrapping paper.

Because of these attacks, which had waited for her every time she'd opened her door to go to school, every time she'd turned a corner in the hallways, Amane was always late.

So she had made a request. The proclamation was called the "Adonis decree" among Amane fans. From that point on, waiting for Amane-sama was permitted only in the morning when she arrived at school, as a group at the front gate.

And only one person was permitted to give her a gift.

The truth was, Amane didn't want a single present. She didn't want them to wait for her arrival, either. But if she told them that she would be rebuked by the current Spica Student Council President, Tomori Shion.

"If you say that, a lot of girls will try to get a jump on everyone else, and you'll be bothered even more, you know? Forbidding your fans from doing ANYTHING isn't a good plan. I think it will be better to plan an escape route. Pressure cookers always need a proper release valve."

Amane had been impressed. It was just like the enterprising Student Council President to think of something like that. Shion was known in some circles as the Snow Queen. From Amane's point of view, the girl was energetic, a person of action. But she placed impossible demands on Amane and made Amane do exactly what she most didn't want to do—and do it over and over again.

Shion is a lot prettier and more adorable than me.

Amane thought about the Student Council President's long brown hair and her incomparable forehead above her beautiful face.

Why me?

To Amane, it was almost inconceivable that the underclassmen would be drawn to her androgynous looks. Her tallness, her short haircut, her gallant expression and her masculine way of speaking—she couldn't understand how people could be attracted to those things.

It was just chance she happened to be tall. Her hair was short because it was more convenient for riding her horse. She was always alone because dealing with the other girls was a pain. She was embarrassed every time they exclaimed she was "wonderful!" Instead of talking to other girls, she enjoyed talking to her beloved horse.

To Amane, this was just the ordinary truth.

I don't have a fan mentality, but if I were them, I would've become the fan of a much cuter girl.

The image of a certain girl came to Amane's mind. *She's… not like that at all.* Amane's thought denied her previous one. *Now that I think about it, if I look back to before the "decree," when I was still getting a mountain of presents every day, this is definitely much better—I just hope today's gift doesn't have sweet cookies in it again.*

As she accepted the package, Amane was a little absent-minded. Her hand lightly brushed the other girl's hand.

"Ah! Aaaaaaaah!"

The young lady fainted with a spectacular flopping sound.

"Amazing..." murmured Konohana Hikari, from St. Spica Girls' Institute's Third Year Class *Un*. Her shiny hair, which was twisted into curls that fell to her slender shoulders, gleamed in the morning light. Even her delicate features, which usually held a forlorn expression, were filled with an unusual radiance this morning.

She held her overly large bag protectively to her thin upper body. Today was Hikari's true school debut. She was still just a little embarrassed about wearing a miniskirt, but she was getting used to it. She still walked a little pigeon-toed, which was probably a habit.

Six months had passed since she had transferred to the school. She'd heard rumors about the lines that greeted Amane-sama in the morning. This was the first time she had actually seen it, because until today Hikari had been coming in earlier than the other students in order to go to special early-morning lectures given especially for transfer students.

I...I never knew she was incredible enough to deserve THIS.

She stood in a corner of the entrance to the school building, her eyes glued to the spectacle in front of her, and her heart trembled ever so slightly. Romantic feelings for this beautiful, extraordinary person, and the feeling she was out of place at that moment...

I wonder if meeting her alone back then was just a convenient dream.

"They're Amane-sama wannabes," said a mellow voice next to her.

Hikari turned around. "Oh! Yaya-chan!"

Nanto Yaya, who was in her class, stood there proudly and tossed her perfectly straight, supple hair. The uniform's miniskirt suited her well; it seemed to accentuate her glamorous physique. Her slightly tilted eyes and parted lips were alluring. From the first time Hikari had seen Yaya, she couldn't believe the girl could possibly be in the same year as her. And this morning, as always, Yaya looked like a sultry woman.

"Heh heh heh. Good morning, Hikari-chan. You look as cute as ever today!"

"Th-thanks..." Hikari looked down, her cheeks red, remembering what had happened in the library. *It was so embarrassing when she tried to see if my panties were provocative enough!*

Yaya looked at Hikari with a satisfied expression and said, "Hikari-chan, your special lectures are finally over, right? I'm so happy! From now on, let's walk to school together! It doesn't take much time to go from the Strawberry Dorms to school, but I want to be with you every little bit I can. Besides, I can't go with Amane-oneesama. So it's all right with you, right? Heh heh heh heh heh heh."

Completely ignoring Hikari's reaction, Yaya took Hikari's arm as if it were perfectly natural and smiled.

"Yeah," Hikari answered in a slightly gloomy voice. Her

eyes were rooted on Amane, who still held the student who had screamed and fainted. She was yelling for someone to take the poor girl to the nurse's office.

"Are you really that worried about those Amane-sama wannabes?" Yaya asked in a disappointed voice.

"N-not at all! But what do you mean, 'Amane-sama wannabes?'" Hikari obviously hesitated to ask, but apparently just couldn't help herself.

Hikari's anxious expression made Yaya shiver a little bit. *You're cute even when you're anxious, Hikari-chan. I had the same thought back in the library too, but you just make me want to tease you.*

"It's like…Amane-sama's fan club, I suppose," Yaya said bluntly. "She used to have something like official bodyguards, but as Amane-oneesama got older, the number of her fans grew and they couldn't handle it. The organization was disbanded and split into too many groups to count. At the request of Amane-oneesama herself, her fans are only allowed to have an audience with her in the morning at the school gate."

As she said this, Yaya raised the hand holding her bag and pointed to Amane, who was leaning over the girl in her arms and looking into her face to see whether she were okay.

"Oh no, it looks like they're kissing!"

Huh? When Hikari turned around to look, she could definitely see what Yaya was talking about. From Hikari's angle, though, their two faces were still definitely separated. What she did see was that the girl's face was bright red and she looked like she was so overwhelmed with joy she felt she could fly.

Hikari averted her eyes, her heart quivering. *Twinge twinge.*

My chest kind of hurts.

"So now people who call themselves Amane-oneesama fans are generally called Amane-sama wannabes," Yaya continued indifferently. "Of course, they don't have a membership certificate or anything, but there seem to be a lot of people who wear a white lace ribbon choker as a symbol that they 'serve the Prince.' I guess you could say their image is a little maid-like?"

She suddenly turned to face Hikari. "What are you going to do? Do you want to try wearing a white choker like the wannabes, Hikari-chan? It looks like you can make it as elaborate as you want. I think it would look good on you, Hikari-chan. It has a slave feel to it. I'm sure it would be wonderful!"

Yaya brought her face close to Hikari's. It seemed like she'd read Hikari's mind completely.

The look in Yaya's eyes was bright. Hikari instinctively turned away.

"N-not at all... Besides, I'm still just a new transfer student. I don't even know Amane-sama very well."

"Oh, that doesn't matter at all! Most of the girls lined up over there probably haven't ever spoken a single word to Amane-oneesama, you know? Compared to them, Amane-oneesama loves you so much, Hikari-chan. Aah, I just don't know what to do! Which one should I be jealous of? The beautiful Amane-oneesama, or Hikari-chan, who's loved by the beautiful Amane-oneesama?"

Yaya writhed like she was in agony, just to poke fun at Hikari.

"N-not at all! Me, loved by her? You're exaggerating!" But at that moment, Hikari remembered just a little bit about that night. She felt airy and happy. That night, she had felt like she was floating on a rose-colored cloud.

It was an episode that had completely changed Hikari's idea of what her life would be like at St. Spica, so much so that it had made Hikari feel as if they had probably been destined to meet.

The Strawberry Dorms were a facility that served as a dormitory for the three schools: St. Miator Girls' Academy, St. Spica Girls' Institute and St. Lulim Girls' School. It was located across from St. Spica, almost directly behind Astraea Hill, in a corner of the eastern edge of Maiden Park.

The Strawberry Dorms were built to look as if a rectangular building had been cut to form an equilateral triangle shape. The center was a courtyard. The three buildings were separated according to school: a Miator dorm, a Spica dorm and a Lulim dorm. Each was independent, the dorms only connected by three skywalks that passed over the courtyard, which it gave the girls a slight thrill to cross. Their nickname was the Bell Walkways.

In the Strawberry Dorms, going between the different

schools' dorms was forbidden. In order to go to the dorm of a different school, a student needed to get permission from the dorm mother. That was why the Bell Walkways started at the second level, close to the dorm mothers' rooms, which jutted out above the front entranceways located in the center of each of the dorms like lookout points.

The stairs that led to the walkways were built to be hidden, and the entrance to each walkway, which abruptly appeared in the stairwell wall, seemed as strange as one of Escher's optical-illusion pictures and gave them an atmosphere of forbiddenness.

When a student crossed one of the Bell Walkways, she rang a large bell by the entranceway and gave her name.

"St. Spica Girls' Institute, Third Year, Class *Un*, Konohana Hikari, passing through."

A student was supposed to perform this ritual in order to clear people from the walkway. No one knew exactly what purpose it served or when it started, but it was a strict rule of the strange Bell Walkways.

Hikari had been crying. Looking back on it now, she had probably been homesick. Several days had passed since Hikari had come to St. Spica Girls' Institute and started living in the Strawberry Dorms.

She was the only new student who had transferred into Spica that year.

In the Spica dorm, new transfer students stayed in a one-person room for the first two weeks.

The nun who had showed Hikari around was nice, and the dorm mother was kind too. The fifth-year student who was the dorm leader had seemed very wise, and Hikari felt like she wanted to get closer to her. She had treated Hikari so politely it was hard to believe she was an upperclassman.

She had said, "If there's anything you don't understand, you can ask me."

The room was of a style that gave it an air of having a long history, but it also had a very beautiful art deco floor lamp. It was just the kind of atmosphere Hikari liked.

Of course, it was lonely being in a room all by herself, even though she had been totally fine being alone in her own room back home. In fact, she had loved being alone in that room, drinking tea and looking at her collections of beautiful illustrations.

But here…

She grabbed her favorite book from the bookshelf. Gustave Moreau. Usually, as soon as she opened the book she would be sucked right into it, captivated by the pictures. But she wasn't moved at all today.

While her mind was someplace else, a single tear fell.

Drip.

Hikari just couldn't stay still, so she left the room. Before she even realized it, Hikari stood in front of the entrance to the bell walkway. She had no reason to go to one of the other dorms, of course, but when she stood there she could see the front entrance of the Spica dorm.

The door to the outside world.

People are always coming and going from that entrance, and if the dorm mother or one of the nuns found out, I'm sure they'd worry.

When she stepped onto the Bell Walkway, she was surprised there wasn't anyone there, but it seemed like no one would notice her. There was a thick, dark peach-colored carpet on the floor of the walkway. The lie of the carpet's long fibers was beautiful, and there wasn't a trace of anyone's having walked there.

It looks like this walkway isn't used very much.

Hiding in the shadow of the wall, Hikari stared at the front entranceway.

I know standing here like this isn't going to help anything, but still... If I go out that front door, I can go home. It's not like I hate this place, but... Everyone here is wonderful, but...

Hikari felt she couldn't blend in. It was probably because of her simple, shy personality. There were a lot of refined and sophisticated students at Spica, and they were all so dignified. Hikari felt she would be bothering them if she talked to them. She gazed at the glass entranceway below with its steel ivy growing over it and let her thoughts wander. The light from the entranceway, reflecting off the glass in front of her, began to blur.

Even though she didn't think she was that sad.

Even though there was no reason she could think of.

Drip.

Another tear fell.

Ring ring ring.

The sound of a handbell came from the entrance directly below her. In a panic, Hikari stepped back to hide against the wall.

Next came a voice. It was slightly low, mellow and dignified.

"St. Spica Girls' Institute, Fifth Year, Class *Trois*, Otori Amane, coming in!"

Hikari's heart jumped. *Oh no, she's coming this way...!*

She hurriedly looked for a better place to hide. *What do I do? There's no place to hide. It's just a walkway.*

Tmp tmp tmp. She heard the sound of someone climbing the narrow stairs to the walkway. From where Hikari was, she couldn't see the person.

Quick, quick, I have to hide somewhere!

At the end of the walkway was another school's dorm. There was no place she could go. She was trapped like a rat.

The sound of footsteps stopped.

Aaugh, what do I do... I'm going to get yelled at!

Hikari ducked her head and covered her ears. She heard someone murmur in a husky voice. "An angel...?"

Amane was on her way to Lulim's dorm. She had been called by St. Lulim's Student Council President, Minamoto Chikaru.

I don't have a very good feeling about it, either—it's probably about THAT. This year's Étoile competition. Chikaru wants to try and convince me to enter this year, I just know it. What a pain.

Even though Amane was half resigned to it, she still felt dejected over it. Chikaru was a friend; they used to go horseback riding a lot together. But she had a meddlesome personality and she worried about Amane even though she was from another school. This time Amane thought she was going too far and she should mind her own business.

The Étoile title, a beloved cadette—*I don't need either of those.*

Just as that thought went through her head—

Ktnk.

—There was a loud sound.

She sensed someone moving in the Bell Walkway. *Who is it?* She felt something wrong and raised her head.

Standing there was…

An angel.

She crouched directly under a warm arc of light in the walkway, her waist-length golden hair shining, casting a halo-like ring of light above her head. Her small, pale face shone like a dream shrouded in delicate silk gauze. Her short build was adorable and her slender shoulders trembled innocently. She looked exactly like a messenger from God who had been found by a savage person on earth and been struck with surprise.

She knew they weren't really there, but Amane was certain she saw them: large, white, shining wings behind her back, spreading out above her. Peach lotus-flower petals of light fluttered down, overflowing from the heavens, church bells rang and the sound of angels' singing echoed.

An angel had descended in front of Amane.

When Hikari timidly opened her eyes—

Oh no, I squeezed my eyes shut without even realizing. I always do that. When I get scared, I end up like a turtle shut inside its shell.

The image that struck Hikari's eyes at that moment was...

The...Prince?

Amane had certainly earned her nickname. Most Spica students who saw Amane for the first time got the impression of royalty, even without knowing her or her nickname beforehand.

Before Hikari's eyes was a prince wearing a skirt.

It wasn't details like her height or her hairstyle. It was her demeanor, her very existence that told Hikari a prince had arrived. There was also the funny story that said Amane was under the "curse of the prince."

The two of them silently drew close to each other, like magnets coming together.

Hikari was dumbstruck. Up until a moment ago, her heart had been full of fear because she was in the Bell Walkway without permission, but that was completely forgotten. She was fascinated by the person who had appeared before her.

Amane thought, *This is the first time I've seen such an adorable girl. She's just like an angel. It's more than her being cute... For some reason I don't understand, I feel myself strongly attracted to her. Both my body and my heart. I can't take my eyes off her.*

She couldn't stand still; she began to fidget. Otori Amane,

seventeen years old, experienced a sensation she had never felt before in her life. She might have been the White Prince of the Stars who was loved by everyone, but—though she didn't yet realize it—this was *her* first love.

"Are you lost?" Amane asked.

With that one question, Hikari suddenly relaxed and felt like she wanted to laugh.

Ah! Oh yeah, now that I think about it, this is a relief.

"Yes, I'm sorry… I just moved in…" The thread of tension was cut and she was able to talk smoothly.

"I see. I heard there was one transfer student this year. I guess it's you, then?"

For some reason, the fact that Amane knew about Hikari delighted her. "Yes."

"What year are you in?"

"Third."

"What class?"

"Class *Un*."

"What is your name?"

"Oh…Konohana Hikari."

"Hikari, huh? That's a wonderful name. It fits you well."

"Th-thank you very much."

Their conversation faltered. Suddenly Amane said, "If you're a transfer student, you're still in a one-person room, right?"

"Yes, that's right."

"Come with me."

"What?"

"I will show you the way." Amane reached her hand out to Hikari.

Hikari was startled for a moment, but, for some reason, she took Amane's hand without even a hint of shyness. Gently, elegantly, like Cinderella being invited to dance by the prince.

The two looked into each other's eyes. Hikari felt like her body was floating, like she was in a beautiful dream. Still they gazed at each other—they couldn't take their eyes off each other.

In a corner of this aging walkway, they had the sensation of being surrounded by a glimmering red bubble, floating away from the world together, just the two of them. They felt like they could go anywhere, holding hands, soar to limitless heights.

When Hikari saw Amane's dark, burning eyes staring at her, her body got hot and her heart pounded. Everything in the world around Amane and Hikari seemed to shine. Hikari felt her cheeks soften, and it made her happy.

With Amane holding her hand, she walked the path to her room. Along the way, Amane talked unfalteringly about the school, still holding Hikari's hand the whole time.

Back then, Hikari hadn't realized how incredible that was.

CHAPTER 4

The Cock Crows Three Times,
an Omen of Battle

Late afternoon, St. Lulim Girls' School. Most of the students were in the bright courtyard, playing and enjoying the glorious spring sunshine, when a poster was put up on the Astraea bulletin board in the center of the yard.

"Oh, a new poster. I wonder what that could be?"

"What? Did something change?"

In this carefree moment of relaxation after lunch, girls in light pink uniforms who had been walking with their friends in groups of twos or threes went to the board, seeking something unusual to talk about.

"Oh my!"

"Ooh, now that I think about it…"

"It's that season again."

<u>NOTICE</u>

THE COMPETITION FOR CHOOSING
THE NEXT *ÉTOILE*
WILL COMMENCE NEXT WEEK!

Étoile • Aînée
Étoile • Cadette
1 Person Each

The method of competition will be *Trois Lumières*.

The final selection and coronation
are planned for **July**.

From this point on, events related to the *Étoile* Competition
will have priority over all other events and activities in all
schools, so that the listed students may contend in this
contest, in which lies the pride of all students in all three
schools on Astraea.

– FIRST ROUND –
L'Ouverture Brillante
Month of the Virgin Mary
Held in the two days before the advent of St. Ranael

TWO DAYS PRIOR:
***Cadette* Competition:** Undecided*
Location: Chapel Hall or Maiden Park
**We are currently in the process of choosing the
event. It will be posted the day of the competition.*

DAY PRIOR:
***Aînée* Competition:** The Fortress of Promises
Location: St. Spica Girls' Institute,
Riding Grounds

**—*Étoile* Competition
Executive Committee**

The notice was followed by a list of the seventeen couples
who wished to participate in the competition. Included in the
names were St. Spica Girls' Institute's Otori Amane of Fifth
Year Class *Trois* and Kenjo Kaname of Fourth Year Class *Deux*.
At the end of the list, the last to apply, were St. Miator Girls'
Academy's Hanazono Shizuma, Sixth Year, Snow Class, and
Aoi Nagisa, Fourth Year, Moon Class.

"What? The notice for the *Étoile* competition! Oh, this is
that 'Star of the Campus' contest Remon-chan was just telling
me about, right?" said a short girl reading the bulletin board,

her conspicuously short, pleated pink skirt fluttering. Her short hair, pulled up in two ponytails, swayed, and a saïlor collar lay on her small back. "Let's see. St. Lulim Girls' School has…one, two, three… Huh? Only three couples!"

The girl next to her, with her hair in buns, gave a wry smile as she automatically pushed up her glasses, which had slipped down.

"'Star of the Campus' contest, huh? Well, you could call it that *too*, I guess." She scanned the bulletin board with a very curious look on her face. "*Étoile* means 'star' in French, and the *Étoile* competition is the event that decides who is the most wonderful couple in Lulim, Miator and Spica, so calling it the 'Star of the Campus' contest would be right, but…the *Étoile*, who wins the competition that runs for three months—it starts in April when the new school year begins—is a HUGELY prestigious position! The *Étoile* always appears as the main guest at all of Astraea's events, like the Culture Festival and the Sports Festival and Christmas. And the school that the year's *Étoile* attends gets excited no matter what the event."

"Hmm… It's really that significant?" asked Hyuga Kizuna from Second Year Class B with admiration in her voice. She had just recently entered the school, so didn't know much about it yet.

The serious girl with glasses and her hair in buns was Natsume Remon, also from St. Lulim Girls' School Second Year Class B. She was a very common-sense type of person, but a little timid. She turned her eyes from the bulletin board, struck a triumphant pose and answered knowingly.

"That's right! There are going to be three competitions to officially decide the *Étoile*. Each time, the couples in the lowest positions are taken out, until one couple is chosen during the last competition in July. In the meantime, there's a fierce battle between schools, and the feeling of competition is just incredible! Even girls who say they're not interested get caught up in all the excitement. Of course, everyone hopes her school wins. Oh, but there's a rumor…since Prince Amane from St. Spica Girls' Institute is entering this year, the winner has pretty much already been decided. It looks like Lulim has already given up; there aren't many entries." She leaned in close to check the bulletin board. "They're saying it's not going to be very exciting this year, but… Whoa! There really aren't very many.

"Yeah, it sure does look like Lulim's giving up," said Kizuna. "It's too bad. But you know, what you just told me is incredible! Spica has a Prince?! Wow, I really want to see! Is he blond? I wonder what country he comes from. I've never seen a real prince before, so I just have to…"

Just as she was about to finish her sentence…

Slap.

Someone hit her lightly on the head from behind.

"Silly, I can't believe you said that. 'Prince' is just her nickname, of course. No, I guess it's closer to a term of respect than a nickname. Just like we call our adorable second-year student Kizuna the 'Peach-Colored Sleeping Beauty.'"

"Ah, Chikaru-oneesama!" Kizuna turned to Student Council President Minamoto Chikaru, standing behind her.

Chikaru smiled at the two of them with her strikingly kind eyes. The scent of flowers drifted from her flowing black hair with its trademark braids. The Student Council President's sudden entrance made Remon so nervous she unconsciously blushed and rubbed her inner thigh. Kizuna, however, was completely unconcerned and left herself wide open.

"Ah! Oh yeah! I guess you're right. I mean, why would there be a real prince here? Oh, so then Spica has a prince, even though it's a girl! Incredible! I think I really want to see her!"

Remon timidly responded to Kizuna's words in a modest voice. "Yeah, she's handsome and gallant and valiant, just like a real prince! But she's really popular, so it's not like underclassmen from a different school, like us, have a chance to get close to her. She's even beyond the reach of the Spica girls."

Chikaru laughed, like she was making fun of Remon's dreamy tone. "My, you like Amane-chan too, Remon? This is certainly unexpected."

"Oh, n-no! N-n-n-not at all!! It's just, umm, I saw her up close, at the opening ceremony, and I thought, 'Wow, she has a strong aura about her.'"

Remon's face turned bright red, her eyes immediately clouding up.

How adorable! She looks just like a little red tomato.

With that thought, Chikaru really started to enjoy herself. "Well, if you like Amane-chan that much, Remon-chan, then please cheer for her too, okay? Everyone is saying that Spica is certain to win this year's *Étoile* competition, but it looks like the winds might have changed last week. Actually, I also think Amane-chan should be the *Étoile* once, for her own sake, so—"

"What? The winds have changed? Did something happen? Did a strong rival candidate come from somewhere? Does this mean you will be entering, Chikaru-oneesama?!" Remon yelled. Then she was stunned speechless, her mouth hanging open.

Kizuna was completely flabbergasted. She froze with her head tilted to one side and a stunned look on her face. Her two ponytails tilted as well, one up and one down.

Chikaru gave a bitter smile.

Dear me, to think Shion-chan said that same thing to me, and now Remon-chan too—I'm so naughty. I need to be a little more careful.

She embraced Kizuna lovingly from behind. "Heh heh heh, I would be happy if that were true, but I'm sorry. Instead of wearing the lovely robes of the *Étoile* myself, I would love to place those robes on the girl I like," she said with a wink.

"I see," Remon said. "Hey, why don't all of us go to the club building together? I'm sure Kizuna-chan hasn't chosen which club she wants to join, right? Many of the girls that go to Lulim have hobbies, so there are a lot of clubs. There are plenty I could recommend." She nodded her head proudly.

Chikaru looked at Remon with a bright smile; she also seemed to be suppressing a laugh. "Good idea. The art department Remon-chan is involved in is pretty large, and they have a lot of activities too, so if you have a recommendation, then please share it. But since you're at Lulim—what about joining the club I formed, the Costume Club?"

Remon had been smiling up until then, but when Chikaru impishly made a little peace sign in front of her lips, her brow wrinkled.

"Bring Kizuna-chan into the Costume Club? W-was that what you planned from the beginning, Chikaru-oneesama?"

"Huh? What do you do in Costume Club?" Kizuna asked innocently.

"It's a club where we have fun transforming together. You can become a cat, an angel—actually, you might look cute as a little bear cub or something. Anyway, it's really, really fun!"

"Wow—that's like magic!"

"Yes, that's right! I will put my spell on you. It's even more fun than the *Étoile* competition! Hey, come on, let's do something fun together!"

When Chikaru reached out her hand, Kizuna happily took it and innocently followed her. Chikaru smiled at her kindly, like the Virgin Mary. Remon saw the expression on Chikaru's face and felt a twinge of worry.

However, she didn't have the courage to be left behind.

"Wait for me!"

In a mad rush, she noisily chased after them.

"Unforgivable! Unforgivable! Unforgivable! I absolutely hate, hate, hate, hate this!"

A din spread through the hallway at lunchtime. Amane

marched quickly down the passage, a demonic look on her face.

"Oh, it's Amane-sama!"

"So you are going to enter this year's *Étoile* competition after all, right?"

"Now we will win for sure!"

"I am so thankful to God for sending Prince Amane to us."

Not a single one of those whispered voices reached Amane's ears. She stormed down the hall with a suppressed anger that made the girls' hair stand on end. She headed for…

Baaaam!

With a loud noise, she opened the giant double doors.

"Hey, Shion! Would you explain exactly what is going on here?" Amane rose to her full height and held out a crumpled piece of paper—the *Étoile* competition notice, which looked like it had been torn from the bulletin board.

The object of her glare was Tomori Shion, who tapped the documents in her hand on the desk to align them neatly and softly cleared her throat. Her long chestnut hair fluttered.

The usually calm Amane had stormed in, yelling. Shock and fear spread through the Secretary, Treasurer and the other Student Council staff in the immediate area. They were in the St. Spica Girls' Institute Student Council office.

Shion controlled the commotion in the room with a gesture of her hand. "Oh my, I see you made your arrival early today, Prince Amane—or should I call you the future *Étoile*?" she asked with a chuckle. Despite her calm tone, she looked a little worried.

"The future *Étoile*..." *Cht*... Amane made a sound in the back of her throat and gritted her teeth. Then she clenched her fists as if holding something back and continued in an even lower voice.

"Yes, I did consent to entering the *Étoile* competition. Momomi came and asked; she knew I didn't want to, but she begged me to do it. She asked me to do a favor for the White Star of Spica. Momomi pleaded with me, and she was serious, which isn't usual for her."

Amane lifted her head to the sky and closed her eyes. That unguarded expression made her seem even more determined; sighs of admiration went up from the Student Council staff who were watching her.

"People told me to accept the fact that I should enter. I thought it might be unavoidable this year. Even I like Spica *that* much. When people told me I had to enter so Spica could win, I didn't really think it was true, but—when even the usually goofy Momomi asked me so seriously, I thought, 'Well, okay, I don't have much of a choice. I'll endure it for one year.'"

"Yes, I heard the same thing from Momomi. We humbly accepted Prince Amane's cooperation, and we were just now formulating a plan to make the greatest possible use of it," Shion replied coldly, in response to Amane's intensity. She hoped Amane would lose that dense aura of hers that looked like white particles of light she just couldn't turn away from.

Amane almost shouted in response, "Then WHY! Why, of all people, does my partner have to be that...that—"

Amane's hands shook. She couldn't continue speaking.

Kchak.

A small sound came from the Student Council reference room, in the back of the office.

The door opened. A student appeared, spouting exaggerated lines with exaggerated gestures, as if she were an actor playing Hamlet on stage. "Are you really unhappy, entering with me? What...what sadness. What misfortune! I see that my feelings still do not reach you, Amane-sama."

The student was a little smaller than Amane, but still tall, with short hair. The darkish shade of her skin, her long limbs and slim body, and her thin lips, high-bridged nose and well-defined features made her look even more androgynous than Amane. Moreover, she had an aura of fearlessness that made her appear masculine.

"Kaname! What are you doing here?" Amane shouted.

"You should know that without my telling you, of course— because *your* feelings, my beloved, are always clear to *me*," said Hamlet, glaring at Amane. "At least, I wish that were true, but..." She glanced at Shion. "The Student Council President called me here. She said to come during lunch break."

Shion put her head in her hands. "I asked you *not* to come in, no matter what, did I not? I said for you to initiate our secret plan for the *Étoile* competition instead of Amane, because she hates petty tricks—"

"But while I was waiting, I heard my Amane-sama's voice, and she sounded really fired up. I thought, 'Ooh, my precious Prince Amane is having a crisis, I can't just stand here silently,'" the exaggerated dark Hamlet—Kenjo Kaname from St. Spica

Girls' Institute's Fourth Year Class *Deux*—said, with theatrical gestures.

"That's why…" Amane took a deep breath and yelled again. "That's why I said I didn't want to enter this thing!! Of all people, why is my partner Kaname?! I refuse! I absolutely refuse!! I withdraw!! If Kaname is going to be my partner, I am absolutely not going to enter the *Étoile* competition!!"

"Ahh, what a rejection. The only one who can thrust me, one of the Five Stars of Spica, into the depths of despair like this is you, my Prince," Kaname remarked to Amane, who was breathing heavily.

Contrary to her words, Kaname looked completely impassive as she slowly drew closer to Amane.

When Amane tried to shoo her away with her hands, Kaname drew a single red rose seemingly out of nowhere and offered it to Amane.

"Please give up; this is our fate. It's all right. It only hurts in the beginning… Please leave everything to me. If it's for your sake, then I, Kaname, will use every technique I possess to give you the greatest happiness. I make this promise to you: I will give you such pleasure, you will feel as if you were in heaven itself."

Amane let out a single word. "Idiot!"

The Student Council room went dead silent.

Shion finally opened her mouth. "Ahem. Umm… Uh, well, I can more or less understand why Prince Amane doesn't want to do it."

"If you understand, then WHY?!" Amane asked, flabbergasted.

"Princes never get to choose their partners."

"I thought as long as I entered, my duty would be fulfilled. And the one who came to talk to me was Momomi, so I thought she was going to be my partner."

"Yes, of course we considered that. Kiyashiki Momomi is one of the Five Stars of Spica, so she is fully qualified. However, considering that our primary responsibility is to capture the *Étoile* title this year without fail, for the sake of our school, we in the Student Council thought this would be the best choice."

"How is it the best, even for your purposes?! I thought my *cadette* would be feminine and cute, like Momomi. But with Kaname as my partner, it's like having two boys as a couple!"

"Yes, exactly." Shion nodded deeply.

"Two boys—" Amane repeated weakly. She was bewildered.

"Having a masculine couple is pretty popular these days, Prince. Were you not aware of this?"

Amane was speechless. Shion smiled broadly at her and continued.

"Prince Amane participating in the *Étoile* competition was joyous news for all the students at Spica. However, I couldn't possibly imagine that Prince Amane, who hates these kinds of events and has always refused to take part in the *Étoile* competition, would suddenly be so ready and willing to compete, simply because."

With a look at Amane, who had hung her head in disgust, Shion stood and reached her hand out to Kaname.

"The *Étoile* competition is a serious and surprisingly tough fight, with the honor of all three schools at stake. Even with

Prince Amane's merits, there is still a small possibility that something could happen to hurt our chances, even if your partner were to be Princess Momomi, who is one of the greatest of the Five Stars. So, as insurance against that…"

Shion pressed on Kaname's shoulder. "We decided to place Kenjo Kaname as your partner. Her unshakable, optimistic self-confidence, her fighting spirit and her strength in competition will be a plus in this battle. She will make the fight a lot easier for you, Prince. She herself is a core fan. And we do not want to see Prince Amane, who is adored by the entire school, fall to a girl. That is the wish of the entire school. We cannot allow it to come to nothing."

Amane became even more bewildered. *They don't want me to fall to a girl? But…I'm a girl too, aren't I?*

Kaname sneered. "Aah, my Prince Amane. This is fate! Come, please take my hand!" She held out her hand. It was wild and angular for a girl's, yet still beautiful.

Amane felt a lump in the back of her throat. *I guess I don't have a choice. I have to endure it. To me, becoming the Étoile is nothing but a pain. But just this year, for Spica…*

And here she had planned to go to Miator's library to do some preliminary research—which was totally out of character for her—to prepare herself…

"Come now, why do you hesitate? Let us engrave our names in history as the Star of Astraea, a binary star, the greatest *Étoile* of all time!"

Kaname took Amane's hand. *I…I will become the* Étoile, *as the Star of Spica. With Kaname…?*

Something inside Amane exploded. "No! Not in a thousand years!" She slapped Kaname's hand away, and a sharp sound rang out, as if Amane were parrying in a fencing match.

"Amane-sama." Kaname was dumbfounded by Amane, who hardly ever showed any emotion and absolutely never did anything violent.

"Do you hate the thought of entering with me that much? If you're sad when you appear with me in the *Étoile* competition, no one will take us seriously as a couple. Yet if you still refuse…" Kaname said without thinking.

Maybe looking at Kaname, who trembled during her lament, calmed Amane down a little bit; her voice was clear and quiet when she said, "No, that's not it. It's not that I hate you, Kaname."

She gave a slightly bitter smile. "Even I didn't know the reason clearly until now."

It feels like a dense fog, covering the ocean, has lifted…
Amane faced Shion.

I wonder what happened… Kaname thought. The look on Amane's face at that moment… Even Kaname, the former captain of the now-defunct bodyguard troop and self-acknowledged long-time Amane-watcher, had never seen that expression before.

Amane continued, her voice soft, "As long as I enter the *Étoile* competition seriously, and we win, then that's good enough, right, Shion?"

"Y-yes…" Shion was also overwhelmed.

"I will choose my partner. I have a partner in mind whom I have complete confidence in, and who I think can win."

"Of course I don't mind," Shion said. "But you did not have a special partner yet, Prince Amane, so we just looked at the qualifications of the girls in the school and picked a suitable partner—and of course it had to be one of the Five Stars…"

"A special partner—I have one."

"…And of those, Momomi is too feminine, so if you say you don't want Kaname, either—wait, what did you just say?"

"I said, I have a special partner. Well, actually, it's not that we've made any promises to each other yet or anything. I'm the one who wants the relationship, but still…"

"Whaaaaaat?!" Shion shouted in surprise, and the entire room joined her.

"Amane-sama has a partner, and not only that, it's a one-sided relationship?!" Kaname looked like she was about to faint.

"W-we didn't know that. Of course, if you have a partner like that, we will investigate immediately. Now then, what is your partner's name?" Shion asked sharply as she signaled with her hand for one of the Student Council staff to hand her the student directory. She couldn't control her curiosity—or the adrenaline rush that came with the sudden change in the situation.

"Hikari," Amane said bluntly, and then blushed. Even she knew her face was red, so she spun around to hide her embarrassment. "Konohana Hikari. I'm pretty sure she said she was in Third Year Class *Un*." With that, Amane rushed out of the Student Council room.

Hikari pointed to the bulletin board with a trembling finger. "Yaya-chan… Umm, I think this is it…" Even here in the Third Year hallway, the notice of the *Étoile* competition caused a stir. The gossip flew: "Which couples are major contenders?" and "Which couples are Amane and Kaname's biggest enemies?"

"I guess there's nothing we can do. Since Amane-oneesama is in her fifth year, everyone wants her to win the title of *Étoile*," Yaya said. "No matter how much she doesn't like to stand out, I had a feeling she was going to be in the *Étoile* competition this year. It's just that, no matter how you look at it, Amane-sama doesn't have a special partner. Everyone was talking about who might have been her partner… There were a lot of girls dreaming about it. I always thought Momomi-oneesama would be her partner, though. For it to be Kaname-sama—the Student Council made a bold move." She had an unusually impressed, meek look on her face.

Seeing Yaya's behavior renewed Hikari's impression that Amane was the school's number one star, and it made her a little sad. Looking at the bulletin board made her feel small and pitiful, like a tiny grain of sand washed up on the beach. She hunched her shoulders timidly.

Next to her, Yaya also looked at the bulletin board. Without noticing the tears that had welled up in Hikari's eyes, she gave a satisfied smile and gently hugged Hikari's shoulders.

"Hey, Hikari-chan, did you know? The *cadette* is the younger sister, and the *aînée* is the elder sister. Of course

Amane-oneesama is the *aînée*, so… Hey, on the day of the *aînée* competition, let's go and cheer for her! If Amane-oneesama's favorite person, Hikari-chan, comes, I'm sure she'll get fired up and win!"

I don't want to just cheer for her, I want to stand next to Amane as her cadette, *if I could.*

The thought was vain, but she couldn't help imagining it. And, of course, she couldn't actually say it out loud. It took everything she had for Hikari to reply in a frail voice, "Yeah…"

Yaya finally suspected something was wrong and was trying to take a peek at Hikari's face, when…

"Hikari-oneesama!"

She heard running footsteps and someone yelling in a loud voice from far away. "I recognize that voice… ahh, she's running so fast!"

In the direction Yaya looked, squinting, a small girl was running toward them. She was going much faster than was proper according to Spica's strict rules. Her hair flew every which way and she was out of breath.

"Jeez, Tsubomi, don't run!" Yaya scolded. "Even if you are on the Student Council staff, if you run like that, you'll get yelled at by one of the nuns, you know? I thought you'd had enough of doing early morning duties."

As the girl got closer, Hikari remembered. *Tsubomi-chan!*

Hikari knew Tsubomi from the early-morning lectures she'd had to take in the first two weeks she was at the school. Tsubomi had been a small first-year student, and even though she had just recently entered the school, she was on the Student Council staff, which had surprised Hikari. It seemed that when Tsubomi had heard that an oneesama she had been friends with since kindergarten was going to be Student Council President this year, she'd decided, even before entering the school, that she was going to join the Student Council.

The day Hikari had first met Tsubomi, the younger girl had been helping the nun prepare for the lecture. She happened to meet Hikari's eyes and walked up to her with a smile.

"Excuse me! Umm...I haven't seen you at Spica before. Are you a transfer student?"

Hikari was surprised that a girl who seemed younger than her would suddenly come up and talk to her, but attracted by the girl's cheerful, adorable smile, Hikari answered with a smile of her own.

"Yes, I'm Konohana Hikari. I just entered Third Year Class *Un*. Nice to meet you!"

When Hikari said that, the girl seemed so happy she could jump for joy. "Ah! I knew it! You're the transfer student who moved into the Strawberry Dorms, right? Wow, I heard rumors about you in the Spica dorm. Yaya-oneesama said she was going to be sharing a room with a transfer student this semester... Wow, I'm so happy! I got to meet the oneesama everyone's talking about on the very first day!"

Completely ignoring how dumbfounded Hikari was, the girl

jumped and clapped her hands. When she suddenly noticed the wide-eyed look on Hikari's face, she grabbed both of Hikari's hands tightly and started jumping again.

"I never imagined you would be so pretty! I'm Okuwaka Tsubomi, from First Year Class *Deux*! I hope we can be friends!"

She's a really friendly girl, isn't she? thought Hikari.

"Oh, thank goodness, you're here!" Tsubomi panted, interrupting Yaya's scolding. The first thing Yaya asked was why she was in such a panic.

"*Huff huff*... Um, we've got a big problem! Hikari-oneesama!!" Tsubomi said, her long, glistening pink hair bouncing behind her as she recovered from her run. Under the thick headband she always wore to hold back her excessive hair, her large, slightly droopy eyes drooped even further. With an unspeakably pitiful, tearful expression, she looked at Hikari.

"Hikari-oneesama, a-aaaaare you...really..." She swallowed. "Are you really...going to enter the *Étoile* competition with Amane-sama?"

The moment she finished, Tsubomi dropped to her knees.

And commotion erupted in the crowd around them.

"What exactly are you trying to do?"

But even when she was called out and blamed, Shizuma

didn't say a single word in reply.

They were just outside the courtyard, in a lonely place that almost no one ever passed through, probably because it was behind the faculty room. It was nicknamed the Garden Grave.

Shizuma turned her back on the two girls who had confronted her. There was a small stone monument which was almost buried in a thicket of wild roses that scattered a sweet, refreshing scent. The monument itself was a square stone slab, half buried in the ground, with a stone cross on top. It only reached knee height. Shizuma gently touched it with her hand and thought about what she should say.

"I don't have any...particular purpose." The words that fell from her mouth were even more emotionless than she'd thought they would be.

The words only enraged the girls even more. One, Togi Hitomi, stared straight at Shizuma's back. She took a step forward and raged, flames of anger shining in her eyes. Her short haircut, which was unusual for Miator students, exposed the nape of her neck, which was slightly red from anger. Her body was supple, like a slender, quick antelope, and it was obvious she was furious.

"It's not like you to enter the *Étoile* competition with a...a transfer student who just entered Miator, Shizuma-sama! You were bestowed with the *Étoile* title so spectacularly with Mizuho last year, and you were both so happy your names would go down in Miator history, and yet... Were your words of thanks for supporting you all just a lie?! Even we, your admirers who served you, thought it was a perfect year, and after it was over we felt like a weight had been lifted from our shoulders. This is a stain on your reign, Shizuma-sama!"

"A stain? Now, Hitomi-chan, that's going too far." A little worried she might be seeing the flame of hatred, Kano Mizuho, who had been standing off to the side, shielded her eyes and chided the other girl in a small voice. "I'm sure Shizuma-sama has some sort of plan."

Mizuho's kind voice calmed everyone a little bit. She gave a gentle, tranquil smile as her soft, slightly quirky hair billowed in the spring breeze. However, when Mizuho used her hand to try to keep her hair down, it looked to Hitomi like she was fidgeting to sooth herself, which made Hitomi even angrier.

"Come on, Mizuho, are you really okay with this?! Shizuma-sama is so worthy, of course she'd become the *Étoile* as soon as she even tried, but as her *cadette* you worked so, so hard to get the title, didn't you?! You said, 'It's incredible that I'm Shizuma-oneesama's partner!' and did things like study Astraea history all night and practice dancing whenever you had a break, all so you wouldn't embarrass Shizuma-sama. I know exactly how much effort you put into it. Are you willing to let some silly transfer student ruin that?"

With every word she spoke, more anger welled up inside Hitomi. "No one actually said it, but everyone worked hard together and fought the best they could, didn't they? No matter how sad it was, they did it for poor Kaori—"

"Hitomi! Don't mention that!" Mizuho screamed when she heard that name.

Twitch. Hitomi froze for a moment—but quickly regained herself and said bitterly, "No one will say it, so I said it. Because this is too much, Shizuma-sama! It's just too much!"

Her voice grew progressively weaker, and it sounded like she was about to cry. She thought, *Why is Shizuma so quiet?*

I knew it. So this is why Hitomi called me here. Shizuma's eyes fell on the stone monument again. The ancient stone relic, called the Garden Grave because the students saw it as being like Christ's sacred grave, was buried in a profusion of roses. With one hand touching it, Shizuma let her mind drift back— not even trying to offer any resistance to Hitomi's outburst.

I'm sure she's resting peacefully right now, buried under the lavender flowers she loved so much. Remembering made Shizuma's chest ache, but kindness filled her heart—much more than she had even imagined she had in her. Up until now, Shizuma had tried not to think about it.

It might be time for me to face it—yes, it is. This might be a good opportunity.

Shizuma looked over her shoulder and gave a sweet smile.

The two girls always thought of Shizuma in whatever they did. They were Togi Hitomi and Kano Mizuho, both in their sixth year, like Shizuma. Hitomi could be a little difficult at times, but Mizuho was always kind. The two were childhood friends, and they made a good team. Ever since elementary school, they had tried to get involved with Shizuma in one thing or another. Before they'd realized it, the two of them were like Shizuma's closest relatives.

Shizuma herself thought that having such good childhood friends had probably had an influence on her personality. There were times when other people treated them like just another pair of Shizuma's admirers. Yet Shizuma was fully aware that if she had a comfortable school life despite having a lot of fans, that was largely due to these two.

But they even called her Shizuma-sama, even though they were in the same year.

They really are serious, aren't they? So soft-hearted, my precious, adorable ones.

Shizuma always looked out for number one and was always fickle, but...

I really do love these two. Just like I loved HER. Now that I think about it, it was these two who brought her to meet me the first time, wasn't it? They said, "We know this adorable girl who really admires you, and on top of that, it looks like she would suit you."

Sakuragi Kaori.

I've changed since I met Nagisa, haven't I... Heh heh heh.

Despite herself, a laugh escaped her lips.

"What are you laughing about, Shizuma-sama?!" Hitomi yelled furiously.

"Now, now, Hitomi. Please don't get so mad," Shizuma said, smiling as if the entire previous discussion hadn't even happened. Hitomi was dumbfounded.

This was the first time she had ever argued with Shizuma like this. Shizuma was strong-willed, so when Hitomi had decided to speak her mind, she had been fully prepared for however much Shizuma might yell at her or hate her—or push her away or tease her. She knew full well she might never be able to talk to Shizuma again after this.

Shizuma continued, "It's not that I don't understand how you feel, Hitomi—my year as *Étoile* ended, and…that was such a tough time. There were so many events, and I couldn't even ask any cute girls out to have some fun. If I hadn't had the support of you and Mizuho, I really might not have been able to handle it. Thank you; I'm truly grateful. Especially to you, Hitomi."

She reached out and gently stroked Hitomi's hair.

Augh! It was so gentle it tickled and Hitomi cringed.

Now that I think about it, we've been friends for a long time, but I think this is the first time I've touched her like that, Shizuma thought.

Hitomi was astonished by the gesture.

"Mizuho was able to be center-stage as my *cadette*, but you were content to work behind the scenes—and I think it may have been much more difficult for you than for her."

When Shizuma drew close, she seemed to give off a fragrance more intense than the wild roses that bloomed around their feet.

"But, you know, now that I've finished my time as *Étoile*,

and I'm free…I've been thinking about my last year here at Miator. I've already fulfilled my duty, so I can do what I want; I can enjoy every day however I please, with all of the adorable girls here at Miator."

Shizuma laughed and looked at the sky. Even in this deserted, lonely place, the blue sky stretched above them, and white clouds floated lightly overhead.

"Even I didn't expect this. I never expected to feel like this. Heh heh heh… It's strange, isn't it? Even I don't understand how it turned out this way. I've only just met her, so I don't really know what kind of girl she is, either. I don't know about her home, her family—nothing. She just suddenly showed up in front of me, on the road to Astraea Hall, and I took an interest in her. Ever since then, I've felt myself constantly thinking about her. So you see, that day, when I saw her and Tamao playing around, for some reason I just couldn't stand it. I ended up having as much patience as a little child."

Hitomi became even more bewildered.

"Please understand, okay? I just want to try, that's all. It's not that I want to deny the *Étoile* title I won with you. And it's certainly not that I've…forgotten Kaori, either. But…"

Shizuma smiled, an unusually diffident look on her face, and she spoke in an unsure voice.

"It feels like if I take my eyes off her, she's going to fly away somewhere. Then I got the idea that if I become the *Étoile* with her, I'll be able to be with her forever."

Why would she think that? It's not like there's any girl who would leave Shizuma-sama, Hitomi thought, although she couldn't actually say it.

Shizuma turned her back on the girls, as if she were embarrassed. "This isn't for Miator or anything like that, I'm just being selfish—so I don't expect the two of you to help me. I want you to…let me be, just for a little bit. If you ever actually met her, I'm positive you would understand, too," she said, and she left them there.

"I think that was the first time I've ever seen you with such a soft look on your face, Shizuma-sama," Mizuho muttered in a troubled voice.

Diiing dooong…

Around the same time, in the classroom for St. Miator Girls' Academy's Fourth Year Moon Class, after-school cleaning was about to begin.

"Sigh…"

"Sigh…"

The sound of the young ladies' sighs echoed through the classroom, although there were only two there: Nagisa, holding a mop with a weary look on her face, and Tamao, next to her, pushing a bucket full of water.

"Sigh… This classroom sure seems big with just the two of us in it."

"I'm sorry, Tamao-chan. It's my fault we ended up cleaning by ourselves," Nagisa said innocently, not even realizing Tamao had the easier job.

Tamao grinned. "Oh, that's all right, don't worry about it. I'm really happy just being alone together with you, Nagisa-chan."

"…Right. Thanks."

Tamao was a bit surprised Nagisa didn't respond more to what was just one of her usual little jokes. *Oh dear, is she really that shocked?*

The *Étoile* competition notice had been posted in the fourth-year students' hallway at Miator in the middle of fifth-period class.

Tamao heard shouts coming from students who had just finished Classics and gone into the hallway. She didn't pay any particular attention to it, though; she just kept messing around with Nagisa, who was in the next seat.

Then a first-year student charged into the room. "Listen! Listen! Listen! Listen!"

The girl, Iohata Momiji, made a beeline for Tamao's seat. Momiji was famous for being the biggest gossip-monger in Moon Class. Both her naturally wavy dark hair and her famous luxurious eyebrows flew up as she yelled.

"What's wrong? Did something happen?" Tamao slowly turned around—but Momiji wasn't even looking at her.

Huh?

Her gaze went right through Tamao and…

"What in the world is going on here?! How could Aoi-san possibly be in the *Étoile* competition? She just transferred here!"

Momiji's frightening stare wasn't directed at Tamao, but rather at Nagisa.

"Huh? The *Étoile* competition?" Tamao said, confused.

"Don't give me that!"Momiji beat her fists on the desk as if she couldn't take it any more.

"Not only that! Not only is her partner that transfer student of all people, but this is Shizuma-sama we're talking about! Exactly what in the world is going on here?"

Ah, I guess the notice for the Étoile competition was posted. So Shizuma-oneesama really did decide to enter the Étoile competition with Nagisa-chan after all. Tamao suddenly realized something. *And she did it without saying a thing about it to Nagisa-chan, too… Heh heh heh, that's just like Oneesama.*

"The kissing-Shizuma-oneesama-in-the-hallway incident has even been hushed up. But this is the perfect opportunity. Since we're here, shouldn't we have Aoi-san explain about that?"

Momiji's voice echoed across the classroom; there was the sound of chairs scraping the floor and the crowd pressed in on Nagisa.

"Well, when I'm with Nagisa-chan, it's never boring and I always have fun."

"Oh, not at all…"

With a bucket in her hand, Tamao tried as hard as she possibly could to comfort Nagisa, who was hanging her head. "Look, it was the same that day Shizuma-oneesama and you got the holy water. And besides, I got to see something interesting—"

"Yeah."

Oh dear, she is depressed after all. Tamao tried to lighten things up a little. "Besides, if I had never met you, I'm sure I never would've seen a storm of jealousy that came from an entire class, or been made to do all the cleaning with just one other person."

"Oh…I'm sorry… Well, but even that was because you couldn't stand to see me all flustered trying to do it on my own, so you came and helped me, Tamao-chan."

It wasn't so much that I couldn't stand watching; it was more because I just couldn't let the chance be alone together with Nagisa-chan slip by.

Tamao stuck her tongue out in her mind, but pushed the bucket with a gentle, angelic smile. "Come on, let's work hard and get this over with fast. I'm sure those girls from class are regretting what they said right about now! If we clean up quick together, I just know they'll start to respect you more."

"Th-thanks, Tamao-chan. You really don't have to be so considerate of me…"

"Oh, no, it's all right. Don't worry about it. I'm sure it was God who put us in the same class together."

If we don't hurry up, I'm sure a bunch of Shizuma fans will get in the way and try to suck up to Nagisa-chan by pretending to help her.

The fact that Nagisa didn't see her hidden intentions was Tamao's joy.

"Yeah, I'm really glad I could be in the same class as you,

Tamao-chan. So, the *Étoile* competition, huh? I still don't know much about it at all, but…if I really do have to enter it, I wish it could have been with you, Tamao-chan. Then I'm sure I wouldn't feel so anxious," Nagisa said in a tearful voice.

Tamao thought, *Oh, how adorable she is,* and had trouble fighting back the urge to hug her. She looked off to the side to hide her embarrassment. "I really do wonder what Shizuma-oneesama's intentions are. I can't believe she forced innocent you into the *Étoile* competition—an intense battle of pride between all the schools. It's a festering pile of trickery—and on top of that, she did it without even asking you!"

In contrast with her statement, Tamao was thinking, *If Nagisa-chan enters the Étoile competition, more people are going to find out how cute she is and try to go after her!*

Twitch twitch twitch.

Nagisa huddled herself up as much as she possibly could. *Is the Étoile competition really that incredible?* She thought back on how everyone had acted when they'd stopped by earlier—and the blood-curdling looks on their faces.

They all asked, "Why are YOU entering the Étoile competition, and with Shizuma-sama, too!" And they all looked so serious. Uuugh…I'm scared.

"You know, Tamao-chan, I told everyone this, and it was the truth. I didn't do anything, you know? I never applied, of course. I never even knew there was something called the *Étoile* competition until just a little while ago. And besides, I was never even asked if I wanted to enter with Shizuma-oneesama."

Even as she was speaking, Nagisa realized the truth of the words. *That's right—I never DID say anything about entering the Étoile competition.*

"That's right! Hey, Tamao-chan, I wonder if this is some sort of mistake? That's it! Hey, hey, hey, hey, that's it! That has to be it! I never did anything, and no matter how incredible a person Shizuma-oneesama is, it's ridiculous to enter it so suddenly, when I didn't even know about it!"

Tamao looked at Nagisa with pity, and Nagisa sensed something from Tamao that made her stop talking. Tears welled in her eyes.

Tamao hugged Nagisa's shoulders to comfort her. "I think it's a pity, too. It's like...you're being made into a sacrifice, you know? But...since this is Shizuma-oneesama we're talking about, there's nothing we can do. There aren't many people in Miator— or in all of Astraea for that matter—who can go against her.

"No, don't cry—it's all right. If you're that unsure of yourself, you won't get past the first round. To tell you the truth... The first *cadette* competition is the *Examen sur l'Astraea*, a quiz on your knowledge about Astraea Hill. It's a preliminary test to see if the *cadette* has enough knowledge about all three schools to represent them, and to eliminate the weakest contenders. So it's okay. Since you've just transferred in, there's no way you can win. Which makes me wonder what in the world Shizuma-oneesama was thinking."

Nagisa reacted by jumping into Tamao's arms. "R-really?! Is that true, Tamao-chan?"

Oh my, her mood certainly changes quickly! Tamao thought.

Nagisa gazed at Tamao, tears of relief glistening in her troubled eyes.

She's just like a cute, loyal pet dog that's just been forgiven by its master. Tamao was so mesmerized she dropped her guard—and involuntarily said what she really thought.

"Yes, because there are seventeen couples in the first competition. Everyone who entered is popular, and has been enrolled in this school since kindergarten—but I still think at least half of them will be eliminated in the first contest. I think, since you're a transfer student, it will most likely be a hundred percent impossible for you to make it through, so probably... I don't think Shizuma-oneesama seriously thinks she can win the *Étoile* competition. I think she's just using it as a way to be with you, or doing it for fun. She's the kind of person who believes life is all about doing flashy things. She probably has feelings for you, and she wants to show everyone. It's like she wants to say, 'Look at my adorable little Nagisa-chan!'"

"I see, so she's not serious." Nagisa was starting to think of it as just a short ordeal she would have to deal with. After what Tamao said about Shizuma's expectations, Nagisa was overjoyed.

Aahh, I'm so relieved. Thank goodness! If Miator lost because of me, or I caused problems for Shizuma-oneesama, I don't know what I would do! If I'm an embarrassment to myself, I can't help it, but I don't want to cause other people problems.

Nagisa didn't quite realize other people were actually causing problems for her. But even as she thought about how relieved she was, she started to feel just a little bit lonely.

I see. So she's not...serious. I guess that makes sense. There's no way I could become a representative for the school. I'm so relieved! It did have me worried. Being blamed by everyone—being forced to report every single word Shizuma-oneesama said—if it's something so incredible everyone reacts the way they have been, just thinking about it makes me scared. My heart races, I break out in a cold sweat.

Just a little bit, in the deepest reaches of my heart, I'm actually kind of excited—now I can see Shizuma-oneesama again. A sixth-year student and a fourth-year student. The Queen of the School getting together with me, the transfer student who seems like she only got into this school because of some sort of mistake—that's impossible. Or at least it should've been. Now that I think about it, it makes me kind of sad. My nose is tingly.

Tamao sensed Nagisa was downcast and tried to look at her face.

Nagisa turned away. *I don't want anyone to see my face like this.*

When Tamao realized what Nagisa was thinking, she put her hand on Nagisa's chin to force her to face her.

Clatter clatter clatter clatter... There was a loud noise, then the door to the classroom opened.

"This is horrible! This is horrible! Nagisa-oneesama! If you don't hurry up, Shizuma-oneesama's fans are going to—oh! Tamao-oneesama is here, too!"

The one who had burst in was a small first-year student with bobbed hair, Tsukidate Chiyo.

"What's wrong? Why are you in such a panic?" Tamao asked calmly and maturely as she whipped her hands away from Nagisa.

"Oh! M-my apologies! I was in a hurry, and I just…"

"It's not like you to just barge into a room without asking if you can come in, Chiyo-chan. Like I always say, when you're visiting another classroom, you have to stand outside, give your name and ask if you can come in first."

It wasn't like Tamao to lecture. Even she didn't know whether she was giving one now because of the flustered state Nagisa was in or because she was embarrassed Chiyo had seen her with her hand gently on Nagisa's face.

"Y-yes, my apologies, but…" Chiyo was bright red, and she was constantly looking over her shoulder.

Is someone coming? Tamao was worried for a moment, but she continued on. "I also told you that if nobody answered, you shouldn't go inside. If you let manners like that slide just because this is a girls' school, it's all downhill from there…"

"R-right!" As Chiyo cowered from Tamao's unusual scolding, she kept stealing glances toward the door.

"What in the world happened? What are you so jittery for?" Just as the words left Tamao's mouth—

Tromp tromp. It sounded like a huge crowd of students was making their way down the hall.

"Ah! Ah! What'll I do?" Chiyo sounded like she was about to cry.

"What happened?" Nagisa and Tamao asked in surprise.

Clatter clatter clatter clatter—pssshak!

The classroom door opened again with a flourish. A crowd of girls wearing "Shizuma-Oneesama Is My Life" headbands surged into the room.

"This is Aoi Nagisa's classroom, right?"

"What do you think you're doing, entering the *Étoile* competition with our Shizuma-oneesama!"

"We are so going to tear into you for this one!!"

"Aaugh, Nagisa-oneesama, run!" The words turned into a little scream in Chiyo's mouth.

CHAPTER 5

Beautiful Sisters Fighting a Phantom
Tell the Truth Before the Sea God

Intermission: Nagisa-chan's Miator Diary

I've just gotten called out again, during lunch break today.

Fourth Year, Moon Class, Aoi Nagisa-sama.

There are a few things I would like to ask you regarding the Étoile competition.

Today during lunch break, come to the roof of John Hall.

We will discuss the particulars then.

President of the Association for Conveying the Love of Lady Shizuma and Kaori

Fifth Year, Flower Class, Yamashina Sen

Eek… This is a letter of challenge!

Waah. I'm scared!

Tamao-chan, who's sitting next to me, is pointing and chuckling, though. 'Goodness, Nagisa-chan, you got called out again? The same thing happened yesterday too, didn't it? Wow, you're really popular, aren't you! You're so popular with the upperclass oneesama—I'm jealous!'

Uugh—she doesn't have to tease me like that. It's only been a month since I came to Miator, and I feel like I'm between heaven and hell.

By hell, of course, I mean being called out by scary oneesama.

It seems weird to say this, but ever since the *Étoile* competition announcement, it feels like I've suddenly become the center of attention of the entire school. Just walking down the hallway, I can hear people whispering about me.

'Hey, look. It's that girl Aoi Nagisa!'

'She doesn't look like anything special at all.'

They whisper stuff like that as if they don't even care if I hear it. I feel so small.

—They're right, though. I'm really not anything special. I want to scream at them that it's all some sort of mistake, but I can't do that, either. But I can understand how everyone feels.

When I transferred in, and I happened to meet Shizuma-oneesama in Maiden Park...I didn't know she was such a special person. I just thought Miator had some really pretty girls in it.

That's right. Now that I think about it, there's no way

there'd be many people like her. I still remember the beautiful hand of the goddess, reaching out to me. I felt like if I took her hand, I could float all the way to heaven. I had no idea she was the number óne goddess in Miator. And when other girls saw her paying attention to me, a really normal girl who had just transferred to Miator...

It wasn't funny.

I guess the only thing I can do right now is do my best to endure being called out—just like I did yesterday, and the day before that, and the day before that—every day this week.

Tamao-chan says I'm being soft. But I feel like I can't calm down, even when I'm alone.

Shizuma-oneesama is falling in love with me, and it's kind of like, it just...doesn't seem real. It feels like I'm having some sort of self-serving dream.

And when I get called out by scary oneesama, I suddenly realize it isn't a dream.

Tamao-chan offers to go with me every time, and I'm grateful for that, but I turn her down. There's absolutely nothing I can do except bear with it and try with my whole heart to explain it to them—and hope they understand.

Doesn't that sound like I'm hopeless?

Ahh, the door is opening. It's another upperclassman—

"Excuse me. I am Ebisawa Koharu from Fifth Year Snow Class. Where is Aoi Nagisa-san, the girl who is entering the *Étoile* competition with Shizuma-oneesama?"

Waah, I'm scared...

Somebody help me—!!

Patter patter patter patter patter patter...

The distinct sound of flat shoes against the floor echoed through the pitch-black hallways of the Strawberry Dorms.

10:45 P.M. The blurry light of a flashlight moved dimly past the room.

"Room 218...no problems," Sister Catherine muttered with a smile.

Yawn...

This isn't good. If I'm not careful, I'm going to fall asleep. I guess I'll end my night watch here and go back to my room to get some rest.

She had been reading *The Legend of St. Francis*, a thick book, every night of late, so she was a little sleep-deprived.

It was a quiet spring night. When she glanced through the window, she saw a big, round, yellow moon shining in the sky.

"Try your best not to make a sound, all right?"

"Yeah!"

Tiptoe, tiptoe, tiptoe... Nagisa repeated it in her head, like a spell. She nervously left her own room, her body shivering in the pleasantly cool air, and followed Tamao.

Wearing a gown over her pajamas, holding her shoes in her hands, breathing as softly as she could, Nagisa looked down the silent hall and sighed in relief.

Thank goodness—somehow we've managed to get this far without being caught. Only a little farther to the courtyard, she thought, then suddenly started to worry again.

Doesn't it kind of seem—a little too quiet? It's really tonight?

"Hey, Tamao-chan, is there really a midnight party tonight?"

"Shh!"

"Ah, sorry, sorry." Nagisa lowered her voice even more. "But it's so quiet… It's like there's no one here—or, actually, like everyone's sleeping, but—"

"You're going to be shocked when we get to the courtyard. Oh, hey, try listening very closely." Tamao put a finger to her mouth to silence Nagisa.

Nagisa listened with a serious look on her face. A faint din reached her ears from across the silence. "Oh!"

"Did you hear it?"

"Yeah! But the Strawberry Dorms have someone patrolling at night, right? This is the first time I've ever been invited to a midnight pajama party, but won't we get yelled at if we get caught?"

"You don't have to worry about that, Nagisa-chan. We've got everything arranged."

"Oh, okay. I just transferred a month ago, so that's not something for me to worry about, huh?"

"Oh, come on, don't be like that. Your naïveté is the best thing about you. Besides, you might not have noticed, but we let the nun on patrol pass by us just a few minutes ago, you know?

Sister Catherine's on duty tonight. She's a heavy sleeper and she's nice. We'll be fine from here on out!"

"Oh, I see! Then I'll relax. I'm such a klutz, I've been afraid I'm going to mess up and make a loud noise."

As soon as the words fell from her mouth, Nagisa's shoes fell out of her hand.

Ktnk bthd clop!

"Ssshh!"

Nagisa cringed.

"You are seriously clumsy, Nagisa-chan. Come on, let's get out of here fast. I'm sure the party's in high gear by now. I don't think your coming will cause many ripples. But just in case, you'd better not get too far from me, okay? Don't go by Shizuma-oneesama! Tonight is a really important celebration, the eve of the *Étoile* competition. It's the most important social gathering for the Strawberry Dorms. If you cause some sort of trouble tonight…the oneesama are going to do a lot more than just call you out, you know?" Tamao said with a wink.

She picked up the shoes Nagisa had dropped and looked around to see whether the coast was still clear. Then she took Nagisa's hand as if she were a lost kindergartner, squeezed it tight and walked on.

The sound of elegant music—a three-beat song, maybe a waltz—came softly from somewhere. Someone had snuck a CD player into the party.

The courtyard of the Strawberry Dorms spread out in front of Nagisa. In the center were several large tables, decorated with white crosses and piled high with cakes and sweets. Lit by countless candles, there were dishes of various colors and even warm teapots. It was like an outdoor party. Around the tables were groups of girls talking and playing games, wearing different colored pajamas and negligées, enjoying the party.

"Wow, I never knew you did stuff like this in the courtyard at night."

In an effort to hide, Nagisa sat on the stairs in the shadow of a fountain. She was about to mutter something about high-class girls' schools like this being in a completely different league when someone spoke to her.

"What's wrong? Why are you sitting in a corner all by yourself?"

"Oh, Tamao-chan said she would go get something to drink, so I'm waiting for her. She said that since all that excitement about me entering the *Étoile* competition hasn't died down yet, it would be best if I didn't go near the tables in the center... Ha ha ha ha."

Nagisa had thought it was someone from her class, but when she turned around, her jaw dropped.

"Umm, umm, umm..."

"My, was there really that much excitement? It must have been horrible for you, Nagisa-chan. And now you can't even enjoy the party, you poor thing."

In her mind, Nagisa yelled, "I-I-I-I wasn't the one who started it all!"

Standing in front of her was Shizuma. She wore a velvet gown of deep crimson over a glossy off-white negligée. She gave Nagisa a flowery smile as if to ask "Would you mind if I sit here?"—and sat next to her.

She kindly offered Nagisa a glass filled with a clear liquid that sparkled with golden light. Tiny bubbles burbled through it.

"How pretty."

Shizuma laughed as if she could tell exactly what Nagisa was thinking and took a sip.

"It's all right, it's not alcohol."

Now that Nagisa looked again, she saw that Shizuma also held a glass. *She went through all the trouble of bringing it to me...* Nagisa blushed a little when she realized what that meant.

I wonder if she was looking for me. When the thought crossed Nagisa's mind, she got a strange buzzing feeling in her chest. *I wonder if it's okay to think Shizuma-oneesama is a little—just a little—interested in me after all.*

Nagisa blushed, and to hide her embarrassment, she gulped down some of the golden drink. The bubbles tickled her mouth as they burst.

Along with the buzz of the crowd, which was getting even more excited as the night wore on, Nagisa still heard the faint sound of the waltz.

I wonder what time it is.

Shizuma, though she had intentionally come looking for Nagisa, for some reason kept quiet. Eventually a comfortable silence settled between them.

Her beautiful profile as she gazed quietly at the party, the distant buzz of the crowd…

Nagisa just sort of…wanted to hear it from Shizuma. The words flew out of her mouth, straightforwardly, without any embarrassment.

"Shizuma-sama, why did you decide to enter the *Étoile* competition with me?"

Shizuma responded in a soft voice, "So, you really don't want to do it after all, Nagisa-chan? You really don't want to be in the *Étoile* competition with me?"

She hadn't answered Nagisa's question, but asked a question of her own. For the first time, Nagisa honestly, seriously faced what was in her heart.

"Well…at first… At first I thought it was ridiculous. I never would've even dreamed of entering on my own. And that's still what I think. For a transfer student like me to enter is absurd. Ever since the announcement, I've been called out by so many of the older students—and they all told me the same thing. If I entered, I would only drag you down. I have absolutely no idea what I should do. I don't even look right sitting next to you." Even as she spoke, Nagisa wilted at the sound of her own words.

"Oh, I'm sorry about that," Shizuma said. "I just did it on the spur of the moment. I didn't think there would be such a big reaction."

"Oh, you just did it on the spur of the moment? That makes sense, sure. That's what I told everyone. This is just Shizuma-oneesama's whim, she just did it off the top of her head, there's no way she's actually serious about making me her partner."

As she spoke, Nagisa's voice got smaller and smaller.

Up until then, Shizuma's tone of voice had been unusually kind, but now she raised her voice as if she were angry. "That's right, I just did it off the top of my head—but I am serious!"

Shizuma-oneesama...

Shizuma's face was so serious it was almost scary. Without even looking at Nagisa, she began to talk in a faltering, completely un-Shizuma-like voice. But she was so forthright about everything, Nagisa felt like she could feel Shizuma's very being as she made her unexpected confession.

"To tell you the truth, ever since then...people have been saying things to me, too. 'What in the world are you thinking?!' they say. There are some who think it's selfish of me to try and take the title when I've already won it once. And there are some who think it's absolutely impossible for me to win with a transfer student, just like you said, Nagisa. I've even been asked if I intend to defile the sacred crown of the *Étoile*."

Nagisa couldn't believe what she was hearing—there were actually people who would say things like that to a noble Queen of the School?

"Of course, I don't care what they think. No matter what other people say, I will do what I want. Even if it's something that began as a whim, now it's what I want most in the world. It doesn't matter how it started. I will get what I want. I will do what I want. There are times when even I think I'm impulsive. But that impulse always drives me. That is the way I live my life. There's not a single thing I regret. But..."

She suddenly stopped moving. "I don't want to…cause you problems, Nagisa-chan. And I don't…" She turned toward Nagisa. "I don't want you to hate me, either." She had a pained look on her face. "So please tell me the truth. If you really don't want to do it, I will drop out of the *Étoile* competition."

Nagisa looked at the expression on Shizuma's face—and was absolutely stunned.

"Oh, no! I would never hate you, Shizuma-oneesama!" She shook her head. "I don't think there's anyone in this entire world who could feel like that!! I… If there's anything I can do to help you, and I mean anything, I'll do it! If you want to enter the *Étoile* competition or whatever, then I'll enter it! Umm, actually, I'm really happy! It's really intimidating to me, but if I can be by your side, Shizuma-oneesama, it makes me happy. Because I love you, Shizuma-oneesama," she said earnestly.

Nagisa gasped. *That sounded like I was confessing my feelings to her!* She hastily put a hand over her mouth.

"Thank you. You're such a sweet girl," Shizuma said, lowering her eyes. "Are you…disappointed now?" She plopped her hand on top of Nagisa's head and smiled with a touch of self-derision.

"N-not at all! Shizuma-oneesama, you're… Shizuma-oneesama, you're absolutely gorgeous and stunning, like a goddess. Not only that, you care so much about everyone, even someone like me. You're really such a nice person."

Nagisa wanted to cheer up the downhearted Shizuma, but she was frustrated that those were the only words she could say.

"Thank you. But I knew you would say something like

that, Nagisa-chan. I don't know exactly why. I'm completely different when I'm with you. I didn't realize it before, but I feel like this is the real me," Shizuma said, drawing closer to Nagisa. "Hey, would you mind, just a little?"

Nagisa had absolutely no idea what she was talking about, but Shizuma didn't even wait for her to answer. She just suddenly rested her head on Nagisa's knee.

"Shi-Shizuma-oneesama—"

"Sshh, be quiet..."

Shizuma's face, looking unusually vulnerable, her eyes closed in rapture, was directly below Nagisa's face.

Nagisa could feel the weight of Shizuma's head, and her warmth, on her thighs. She couldn't move. Through the thin cloth of her pajamas, she felt Shizuma's warm breath on the hollow of her stomach. She prayed Shizuma wouldn't be able to hear her heart pounding.

A sweaty, damp feeling pervaded the depths of Nagisa's body.

Some time passed with the two of them in silence.

"Shizuma-oneesama, are you asleep?" Nagisa murmured timidly.

"Just a little more—let me stay like this just a little more, please. This is the greatest..." Shizuma's eyelids were still lowered. "This is the greatest feeling I've ever had."

"Here's to Spica's victory in the *Étoile* competition! Cheers!" Tomori Shion gave the toast.

Loud shouts rang out from the ring of Spica students surrounding her.

"Cheers!"

"Here's hoping Amane-sama is crowned *Étoile*! Cheers!"

In the center of the ring stood Amane, looking incredibly uncomfortable. She downed her drink in one gulp and whispered into Shion's ear, "Can I…leave now?"

"I understand how you feel, Prince Amane, but this is the long-awaited eve of the *Étoile* competition… So please stay, just a little longer," Shion replied with a smile, her face not showing a hint of the screaming going on inside her.

Amane went silent, a bitter look on her face. Somehow she managed to stay.

Shion bit her lip in frustration. *For heaven's sake! She has so much star potential. Her attitude is so disappointing. If she wasn't so shy, people would get even more fired up about her.*

But Amane usually didn't even come at all, because she said she wasn't interested in this kind of midnight party—this kind of open-yet-secret fun and games. So the fact that she had even showed up to the party probably made everyone admit Shion's methods had some merit.

Now if Shion could just get Amane to stay until the circle of admirers broke up to enjoy the rest of the party, she would have fulfilled her mission.

Just as the thought crossed Shion's mind…

"But still, are you really so sure we're going to win the *Étoile* competition?" Kenjo Kaname suddenly asked loudly. She grinned maliciously and gulped down her red drink.

Momomi, next to her, tried to interrupt. "Honestly, Kaname!"

Kaname didn't even slow down. "Now that Prince Amane is finally entering the competition, everyone seems to be getting caught up in the excitement, but I'm...worried...whether we can really win like this. Hanazono Shizuma-sama from Miator has decided to enter for an unprecedented second term. They say Miator Student Council President Rokujo Miyuki, sharp girl that she is, is putting together some serious strategies. But we at Spica are relying on Amane-sama, whose *cadette* is just a regular third-year student."

"But that was..." Shion rushed forward. "That was because Prince Amane insisted on her. With Amane-sama as the *aînée*, it doesn't matter who the *cadette* is, Spica's victory is certain. All of you acknowledged that already, didn't you?"

"That's right! What in the world is wrong with you? You're acting strange, Kaname!" Momomi went to take Kaname's glass. Kaname snatched it back, and blood-red liquid splashed all over the tile of the courtyard.

Kaname's rant continued. "Shut up! Do you really think I'll actually allow something like...like this? I've been waiting for this since elementary school, yet...my Prince chose that...that obscure third-year transfer student over ME!"

A single student moved out of the ring.

"I-I didn't mean it!" The small girl's eyes were full of tears and her slender shoulders shook horribly. She didn't say another word before—*tmp tmp tmp tmp*—she ran off.

"Wait, Hikari!" Without a moment's hesitation, Amane chased after her. She didn't even glance at the people around her; it was like Hikari was the only thing she saw.

"Kaname-sama, you made her cry!" the long haired girl next to her, Nanto Yaya, said teasingly.

"I didn't realize she was there!" Kaname spit out, trying to hide the little regret she had.

"Hikari-chan is small and adorable, so she must not have stood out enough for you to see her," Yaya said in a sing-song voice. Yaya and Kaname appeared to have known each other for a long time.

After Hikari and Amane left, Kaname lost all of her energy. However, in spite of the conversation between Yaya and Kaname, the can of worms had been opened. The rest of the Spica students reacted predictably, voicing their opinions on Amane's actions.

"What is going on with Amane-sama? The way she just acted, it looked like she was actually serious about that girl!"

"Amane-sama is adored by all the students at Spica. We can't let that transfer student monopolize her!"

Just as someone said they should go after Amane and find out what the situation was, Shion clapped her hands and frantically made an announcement.

"This ends the toast for our celebration! Everyone please enjoy the party! However..." The Student Council President tried to live up to her nickname of Snow Queen by putting on the coldest smile she possibly could. "Regarding Prince Amane's actions, from now until the end of the *Étoile* competition, the Spica Student Council forbids any interference by the Spica student body!"

It was a spur-of-the-moment decision. Everyone fell silent.

"Our dominance of the *Étoile* competition has been the dearest wish of all Spica students for many years. Now that Prince Amane has finally made the decision to enter, please be aware that if anyone interferes in Amane's personal affairs, or displeases her, the Spica Student Council will use all the power at its disposal to pursue punitive measures."

Somewhere in the distance, there was the sound of a waltz coming to its climax.

Amane eventually caught up to Hikari in the dark back yard of the Spica dorm. "I'm sorry…I'm sorry, I'm sorry, Hikari!" she said, hugging the girl, who was in a daze. "I didn't mean to hurt you, Hikari..It's just, if I absolutely have to enter the *Étoile* competition…you're the only one I can think of as my partner."

Hikari silently trembled in Amane's arms.

"I'm sorry, I didn't think it would be like this—that this would happen to you. It's all my fault, Hikari." Pain ripped through Amane's body and she held Hikari even tighter. Her cheek, which had been exposed to the wind, brushed Hikari coldly.

The shock brought Hikari back to her senses. Her heart began to beat fast.

I'm being held tight by Amane-sama. Up until now, I thought I shouldn't be Amane-sama's partner…

I think it was a mistake for me to come to this school. I

wish I hadn't...met Amane-sama, either... If I hadn't, I never would've felt this hurt.

Thoughts like those had swirled through Hikari's mind as she was running.

But she had been caught by Amane, who had held her without even being told if she could or not. And she was apologizing to Hikari over and over again, almost pleading with her in a fit of passion.

Hikari couldn't think any more. She finally spoke in a fragile voice. "...It's all right... I'm all right now."

Hikari squirmed and lifted her head, and right in front of her was Amane's face.

"Hikari—" Amane looked like she was about to cry.

Hikari wanted to cry, too. But something stopped her.

I shouldn't... I shouldn't make Amane-sama cry because of me.

Hikari forced herself to smile. "I was weak. I'm sorry. I-I might not be able to be any help, but if you say so, Amane-sama..." She smiled, but her eyes were full of tears. "I'll try as hard as I possibly can! I want to help you, Amane-sama, even if it's just a little bit."

"Hikari!" Amane didn't know what else to say. She just held Hikari tight. Even after something like this, she just couldn't bear to let Hikari go.

She simply thought, *I must protect her.*

"Chikaru-oneesama, these sweets are so good, aren't they?!"

At the site of the midnight party, Minamoto Chikaru, the St. Lulim Student Council President, who loved dressing up, and the cheerful-as-always second-year student Hyuga Kizuna tasted the sweets Chikaru recommended.

"Oh, really? That's great. These *galettes* are made at the convent in Nagano. The Astraea Hill order has a facility there. They're special pastries, not usually sold. Only people from Astraea can eat them. I guess you could say they have a homemade taste because our own nuns made them," Chikaru responded, smiling as she prepared a fresh pot of tea.

"Oh, I didn't know that. They're so good. I wish they were sold regularly so I could eat them whenever I want."

"These *galettes* are almost always delivered for events and celebrations at Lulim, so you'll be able to eat them again soon. For the time being... Oh yeah, when the *Étoile* competition's *L'Ouverture brillante* is over, there's the first *Petite couronne* presentation ceremony, so I wonder if they will be there...?"

"*Petite galette*?!"

"Heh heh heh heh... *Petite couronne*. It means 'little crown' in French. The *Étoile* competition is designed to have three competitions, after which only one couple is left. But the couple that places first in each of the other two competitions receive small crowns. The couple that places first in the last competition becomes the *Étoile*, so the *Étoile* must get at least one crown, but in the first and second competitions, several of the top couples can pass on to the next stage even if they didn't place first and win the crown for that competition, so the couple that eventually becomes the *Étoile* might not necessarily have gotten a crown in one of the first two competitions.

"If a couple places first in all three competitions, they get to place three crowns on the large scepter the *Étoile* carries, and they are highly honored—I'm really looking forward to seeing if Amane-chan can accomplish it this year," Chikaru added, glancing at the group of Spica students in the distance.

"Oh Chikaru-oneesama, you're talking about the Prince again! I know! You love the Prince too, don't you? Oh, I just had a great idea! Why don't Chikaru-oneesama and Prince Amane—"

With the *galette* still stuffed in her mouth, Kizuna hopped up. She was about to say "enter the *Étoile* competition together..."

Cough cough cough cough!

She started choking.

"Oh no! Here, drink some tea." Chikaru picked up Kizuna's cup and held it out to her.

Kizuna drank the tea, her face bright red.

As she looked fondly at Kizuna, Chikaru thought, *What suits me isn't a prince, it's a princess... No, it might be an adorable girl like you.*

The next day, and the morning of the first *cadette* contest of the first of the *Étoile* competitions, *L'Ouverture brillante*, had finally come.

The hallways of St. Spica Girls' Institute were abuzz with conversation.

"Hey, did you hear?"

"Yeah, I did!"

"Is it true today's *cadette* competition isn't *L'Examen sur l'Astraea*?"

"It looks like it! They said for just this year, they're going to go with the Mouth of Truth."

"Why?! They should first have to test the *cadettes* to make sure they have the minimal amount of basic knowledge about Astraea—they do that every year, don't they?"

"Well…see, this year there are transfer students…"

"Ooh, them! Oh yeah, Miator's Shizuma-sama's and our Amane-sama's partners—both new students who just transferred in this spring. They would definitely be at a disadvantage in *L'Examen sur l'Astraea*… I can't say this out loud, but that's—"

"—Yeah, I think so, too."

"What, I haven't even said anything yet!"

"But I could tell what you were going to say! 'Favoritism,' right?"

"Yeah."

"You're right. I want Amane-sama to get the *Étoile* title, and it's for Spica, so I don't like mentioning it, but—"

"—It seems like favoritism, doesn't it."

"Yeah."

"I wonder if the other contestants are mad. Most of the members of the executive committee are from Spica this year, right? Spica could be criticized for going too far, but—"

"—I agree."

Diiing dooong diiing dooong diiing dooong...

The special bell announcing the beginning of the *cadette* competition rang at 1:00 in the afternoon. Today, all afternoon classes were cancelled at all three schools on Astraea Hill.

Although it was part of the glorious *Étoile* competition, *L'Ouverture brillante* was nothing more than the first of three competitions. Not only that, the *cadette* competition was just the warm-up.

In any other year, some students not actually involved in the competition would simply go home, but of course there would still be a lot of students who would stay to watch. But this year, with the dream standoff between Amane and Shizuma becoming reality, all of the schools were filled with excitement.

And it wasn't going to be the typical, plain *Examen sur l'Astraea*, the paper test on knowledge of Astraea Hill, either. This year, it was going to be the more dramatic Mouth of Truth.

The Mouth of Truth.

The nickname came from the famous Mouth of Truth[3] in Rome. The Astraea version, part of the relief carved into the wall close to the entrance of Maiden Park, bore the images of angels and saints instead of the face of the fearsome sea god Neptune.

No one knew when and why it had been made; it was simply

part of history, along with Astraea Hill.

A single large shining star—a pentagram—was carved deeply into the center of it. Young ladies who passed by jokingly called it the Mouth of Truth. This had continued for a long time, and at some point it had started to be used in an oath ritual between friends and lovers.

There were many different legends about it. One said that if two people placed their hands in the star-shaped hole together and made their oath, and one of them lied, that one would have her hand cut off, or be hit by a meteor and die. Another said that if two people made an oath there, they would be blessed by a holy archangel.

Of course, most of the young ladies used their judgment when they heard those legends. But there were some who really believed them. There were even some who insisted it could be used like a lie detector. And some went so far as to say it made everyone face the truth in her heart, and that anyone who faltered, even a little, in front of the Mouth of Truth was not trustworthy.

And yet those same young ladies grew into fine women.

Today, students gradually gathered in front of the gate to Maiden Park.

A white ribbon had been placed across the Mouth of Truth, as if to seal it off.

Tmp tmp tmp tmp tmp...

Nagisa ran down the empty hallways of Miator, blushing so badly it seemed as if steam would come out of the top of her head any moment.

I have to hurry, I have to hurry, I have to hurry—I'm going to be late for the cadette *competition! But before the* cadette *competition, I absolutely must...*

I absolutely must go to the library!

As she hurtled down the hall, Nagisa remembered the spell Tamao had placed on her with a smile as she left their room this morning.

"It's all right, I'm sure the first competition will be easy for you. Of course, I don't really want to accept your coupling with Shizuma-oneesama, but...I'm a Miator student too. I want you to do your best for Miator."

With those words, Tamao tossed a handful of rose petals and rose water over Nagisa just before she made her usual mad dash from the room.

"It's just a little spell we use here in the Miator dorm. There, now everything will be fine. The scent of the roses will always calm you. Good luck, Nagisa-chan. When you get nervous, you get giddy, so I'm just a little worried..."

Tamao remembered when Shizuma had kissed Nagisa, and she chuckled.

Nagisa laughed nervously, smiling in an effort to show

she would try her best. The truth was that she felt like she was under unspeakable pressure, and she had left the room with her shoulders slumped.

It occurred to Nagisa that if Tamao had been her usual self, she would've said it was a given Nagisa would lose, and that the ruckus would thankfully end today. Even though Tamao was normally quite cynical, saying things like Miator was a school for high-class girls who didn't know a thing about the real world, she had another side as well, one that wasn't so depressing.

"Right, even if you are a transfer student, you can still enter to represent Miator. If it gets ugly, well, that's the way it goes."

Sigh.

Nagisa's sigh faded away, as if absorbed by the quiet hallway of the Strawberry Dorms.

Then, at the very end of morning classes, which had begun so gloomily, the letter had come from someone behind Tamao.

"This is from someone behind me," Tamao said as she handed it to Nagisa. Miator green paper folded in the shape of a small star—a pentagram.

Nagisa looked behind her, but no one gave any kind of signal identifying them as the letter-writer. She didn't sense any kind of ill intent from the folded paper, which had "To Nagisa-chan" written on it.

Nagisa—who had gotten called out every day for days— opened the letter without any trepidation, read it, and...was shocked.

Aoi Nagisa-sama,

Before the first cadette contest begins, there is something I would really like to show you.

Without you seeing this beforehand, it will be impossible for Miator to win. Even though you are a new transfer student, I have been deeply moved by your heroic efforts. The way you went forward undaunted, heeding none of the great deal of wise advice given to you by upperclassmen! Ahh, the only word for it is heartbreaking.

We would like to assist you from the shadows, so that you may survive today's cadette competition and make your debut in Astraea stardom.

Please, you must, must meet me before the cadette competition.

I will be waiting at the library. At the noble green Miator star. There you will learn the truth behind this year's Étoile competition and Shizuma-sama.

I pray Shizuma-oneesama and the honor of Miator's victory will be protected forever.

From one of your fans.

Wise advice? Heartbreaking? There are a lot of parts I don't really understand, but... Ahh! This means the person's cheering for me, right?

Of course the people in her class were nice to her, but ever since the confusion with Shizuma had started, Nagisa had been the frequent recipient of both open and concealed jealousy and spite from the students who attended Miator. This was the first time someone she didn't even know had reached out to her and shown her warmth.

Yeah! There are people who support me, like this, too! The note was really polite and a little mysterious, so there were parts that were hard to really understand, but still... Anyway, I'm really happy! I'll do my best!

When lunch was over, she barely evaded Tamao, who urged her to hurry to the site of the contest.

"Sorry, I forgot something, so I'm going to go back for it, okay?"

Nagisa left the classroom alone.

Murmur murmur...

People gathered and the air filled with enthusiasm.

Bcht!

The microphone was switched on and Shion's voice echoed around the crowd.

"Thank you all for coming. It is now time to begin the *cadette* contest of this year's first *Étoile* competition, *L'Ouverture brillante*. All candidates please gather here."

The noise of the crowd that had gathered in front of the gate to Maiden Park grew louder for a moment. Within the throng were Shizuma and Chiyo, talking about Nagisa.

"That Nagisa-chan, I haven't seen her yet. I wonder what in the world happened?" Shizuma said.

"She's late, isn't she... I'm worried. Nagisa-oneesama

might even be lost somewhere," Chiyo said, standing beside Shizuma. Since the day Nagisa had been in charge of the holy water, Chiyo and Nagisa had become friends.

"Yeah, I should have gone to meet her after all. Nagisa is so clumsy, you know? She's the type who would make a huge mistake right at the most important time!" declared Shizuma.

Chiyo thought it was so funny to see Shizuma in this state, she couldn't help laughing.

"Ahh, I wonder if entering the *Étoile* competition with her was a mistake after all?"

Chiyo responded to Shizuma's little joke with a nod. "But it is because of Nagisa-oneesama that you entered the *Étoile* competition for the second time, right? To tell you the truth, I saw it in a photograph—Shizuma-oneesama wearing the *Étoile* crown last year. It was so sublime, it almost brought me to tears—it was truly splendid. Even though they say a moment like that comes only once in a lifetime, to think you are going to try again... You must truly love Nagisa-oneesama."

When she realized what she had said, she gasped. "Oh, umm, I-I didn't mean it like that. I'm sorry, Shizuma-oneesama..." Chiyo looked like she was about to cry.

Shizuma stood quietly, then finally said, "No, it's all right, don't worry about it. That was the truth of who I was then."

Even though that's what she said, Shizuma's face still stiffened subtly.

Togi Hitomi, one of Shizuma's followers, hid in the shadows, watching the *Étoile* competition that was about to begin.

Huff huff huff...

I finally made it.

Standing in front of the large library doors, Nagisa caught her breath. She'd been to this giant building—this Secret Garden—only once before, when Shizuma-oneesama had brought her. She was a little scared to go in by herself, because she was afraid she'd see something like she did last time. But there wasn't time to think about that.

"All right, here I go!" She psyched herself up and placed her hands on one of the doors.

Creeeeak... There was a heavy, dull sound as the door opened.

The now-familiar black and white checkerboard floor lay before her.

Chk chk chk...

Nagisa walked forward timidly, her footsteps echoing through the building. Once her eyes adjusted to the dim light inside, she saw several people in the hall. She didn't feel the air of excitement she had before, though. The place had the atmosphere of...a quiet, deserted library.

"I guess there aren't many people here today," Nagisa muttered.

"Because the *cadette* competition is today; everyone went to watch it," someone answered, right beside her.

Waugh!

Startled, she looked in the direction of the voice and found she stood next to the checkout counter. Sitting behind it was library committee member and previous *Étoile cadette* Kano Mizuho. With a grin, she explained her presence in the library to this underclassman she had never seen before.

"Hello. If you are here for something specific, please ask. Since today is my day to be on duty for the library committee, here I am, unable to watch the *cadette* competition. I want to help everyone as much as I possibly can."

Oh yeah, I have to hurry. There's someone here who's cheering me on! I have to be useful to Miator, even if it is just a little. Then I'm sure everyone will understand me, I just know it!

This upperclassman member of the library committee, who complained she couldn't see the *Étoile* competition but looked like she didn't care anyway, seemed nice, Nagisa thought.

"Um, I'm waiting for someone! I got a letter saying that someone had something she really wanted to show me before the *cadette* competition. Umm, I ended up being a little late, but do you know if anyone came here looking for Aoi Nagisa from Fourth Year Moon Class?"

"Aoi Nagisa from Fourth Year Moon Class?! Then you're—" Mizuho stopped mid-sentence, her mouth wide. "But why are you here?! By now the *cadette* competition has begun," she said frantically.

"It's all right! No, I mean, that's not the point—there's something I absolutely have to see before the *cadette* competition! Because the way things are now, I have absolutely no confidence I can win, so…umm, so once I see what I came to see, I'll run as fast as I can, so it'll be all right. I'm sure I'll make it in ti—"

Something leaped into Nagisa's vision. A green pentagram. The Miator star, the exact green color of the necktie of Miator's uniform. The words of the letter came back to Nagisa.

"I will be waiting at the library. At the noble green Miator star."

This star was on the cover of a thick book, sitting on the counter where Mizuho sat, with special large print and shiny foil leaf. It was placed between the white star of Spica and the red star of Lulim.

The book was the Astraea directory.

"Excuse me, is that—"

"Yes, they're the Astraea Directories. They contain the history of each of the three schools—"

Carried away by an urgent impulse, Nagisa grabbed the book, completely ignoring the rest of Mizuho's attempt to explain. Between the pages of the book was a green slip.

The words "To Nagisa" were written on it in small cursive letters.

What's this?

When she opened up to the page where the slip was, she saw a large picture that took up the entire page. The picture was of Shizuma-oneesama, wearing the *Étoile* crown and smiling so elegantly, so beautifully, it was almost scary. Next to her was a pretty girl wearing a small tiara.

"Ooh, is this—" Nagisa's thought faded away; she was speechless.

Mizuho peeked at the page Nagisa had opened to and smiled wryly. "Oh, that. That's right. Shizuma-sama asked me to be her partner, so I didn't really have a choice—you know. It was an awe-inspiring thing, though."

Mizuho noticed Nagisa's expression and hurriedly continued, "But it's not what you're thinking! You don't have to worry about it. I... I've known Shizuma-sama for a long time, since elementary school...so we get along, but I'm not the kind of person who can be her partner. Come on, relax. She is out of my reach. There just wasn't an appropriate partner for her back then, either."

Mizuho let her eyes water. "I happened to be by her side by chance...so it's nothing you need to worry about. Besides, this is something everyone who was at Miator last year knows," she said, and smiled weakly.

Deep down, Mizuho sympathized with the underclassman. No, you might even say she was...cheering for her. And for the one she loved—the goddess she adored.

The sunlight pouring through the skylight reflected beautifully off Mizuho's soft chestnut hair. Nagisa was drawn in by her kind aura, and she knew, instinctively, that this girl really did love Shizuma-oneesama.

She's much more important and beautiful than I am. If Shizuma-oneesama is out of reach for HER, then someone like

ME and Shizuma-oneesama must be like a turtle and the moon, a mole and a goddess, a stone and the galaxy!

As she was thinking, she caught sight of some very small writing—the text that went with the picture.

"Okay, next couple, come forward, please."

At the entrance to Maiden Park, Spica's Student Council President, Tomori Shion, presided over the *cadette* competition, which was progressing smoothly.

The two candidates called forward by Shion stood in front of the star-shaped hole in the center of the angel relief.

Shion placed transparent white veils on their heads. Then the two knelt, joined hands and put their hands in the hole.

"Go further in…"

Following Shion's instructions, the two of them put their hands in so deep they couldn't be seen from the outside. Then the questioning began.

"I ask the *aînée* candidate, Yonogi Maya of St. Miator Girls' Academy, Fifth Year, Moon Class. Do you swear to protect and help the *cadette* candidate next to you, no matter what?"

It seemed that, as a general rule, the correct answer to the question was "yes."

"Yes, I swear," the *aînée* candidate answered.

"Then please give a sign of that oath," Shion continued.

The Miator *aînée* candidate took her hand out of the hole, stood up, summoned the *cadette* candidate close to her and whispered something in her ear. The *cadette* candidate's face went bright red.

Then she lifted the *cadette* candidate in her arms.

Murmurs of approval ran through the crowd.

"So cool…"

"Protect me, too…"

Tumultuous applause rose and many flowers were tossed into the wicker basket that had been placed in front of the spectators. Vascs of flowers were placed around the site, and when the spectators thought a couple was good, they threw some of them.

"Next, I ask the *cadette* candidate, Takeda Estelle of St. Spica Girls' Institute, Fifth Year, Class *Un*. Do you swear to protect and help the *aînée* candidate next to you…?"

At the most, there would be five questions. If the basket was not filled with flowers by the end, that couple had to drop out. Almost all of the "star" candidates would remain, but generally, about a third of the entries would be eliminated at this point in the competition.

The ranking of the couples who remained would be determined in the *aînée* contest the next day. The couple who placed first would receive the first small crown, the first *Petite Couronne*.

Usually, the Mouth of Truth was used as the second competition. It was essentially a popularity poll.

Tamao appeared among the ring of spectators surrounding the *cadette* competition without a single worry on her mind.

"Oh! I found Chiyo-chan!"

"Ah! Tamao-oneesama!"

For an instant, Chiyo looked so relieved she might cry. However, when she realized Tamao was alone, she looked even worse.

"Nagisa-oneesama is… Nagisa-oneesama is missing!" *Drip*. Chiyo couldn't hold it back; a tear fell.

Tamao was shocked. "Whaaat? Oh no! But just a few minutes ago, she said she forgot something, and we separated—she said it was all right, she would be coming soon. Ahh, and here I was so happy because she was more excited than I thought she'd be, like she had some secret plan or something, so I thought she'd finally gotten fired up about the competition…"

No matter how scary things get, she's not the kind of girl who would run away.

Tamao remembered Nagisa's smile, which had never faltered as she had bravely endured being called out by so many upperclassmen over the past few days.

"I wonder if something's happened?" Tamao's face suddenly became serious, which made Chiyo even more uneasy.

"What should we do? It's going to be Nagisa-oneesama's and Shizuma-oneesama's turn soon. Once Shizuma-oneesama gets called, it's all over," Chiyo said, trembling.

"What number couple are they on now?"

"They're almost halfway, number seven. Nagisa-oneesama and Shizuma-oneesama are number ten, so…"

"We don't have a choice; the only thing we can do is try

and get them pushed back in the order. I'll go and try to work it out. Chiyo-chan, after I do that, let's go look for Nagisa-chan together. All right?"

"S-sure!"

Looking at Tamao's strong profile, Chiyo was able to relax a little, and her heart gently warmed. *Tamao-oneesama is so reliable.*

Nagisa still stood in the library, looking at the page of the Astraea Directory. The text that accompanied the picture of last year's *Étoile* coronation was written in small letters.

The Étoile aînée Hanazono Shizuma-san, from St. Miator Girls' Academy, Fifth Year, Snow Class, and her cadette, Kano Mizuho-san, also from the Fifth Year Snow Class. At the coronation, Hanazono Shizuma-san looked to the sky and confessed, "This Étoile title is dedicated to our irreplaceable friendship and to my adorable little sister, the late Sakuragi Kaori, who truly should have been standing with me as my cadette. I give all of my love to you..." The speech brought every Miator student to tears and the day went down in Étoile history.

Nagisa felt like she had been shot through the heart.
The words of the letter came back to her:

"There you will learn the truth behind this year's *Étoile* competition, and Shizuma-sama. I pray Shizuma-oneesama and the honor of Miator's victory will be protected forever."

What in the world is going on...?!
At that moment, the library's clock rang.
Gong gong gong gong...
The hands of the clock pointed to 2:00.

"I ask the *aînée* candidate, Otori Amane of St. Spica Girls' Institute, Fifth Year, Class *Trois*. Do you swear to protect and help the *cadette* candidate next to you, no matter what?"

Instead of the noise that had come from the crowd during the previous couples' questioning, the spectators watched this couple with bated breath. Despite the dramatic shift, Shion had asked the first question calmly.

In front of the entrance to Maiden Park, kneeling at the middle of the Mouth of Truth, Amane said, "Yes, I swear," and looked at Hikari. Hikari knelt beside her, trembling. She didn't even try to look at Amane, just faced forward with her eyes closed.

Amane felt sorry for her. *She must be nervous.* In the next moment, she thought, *Ahh, how adorable she looks!* Other feelings like that bubbled inside her, and Amane laughed to herself.

Shion said, "Then please give a sign of that oath."

Amane wasn't the kind of person to think up some kind of sophisticated performance at a time like this, so, just like the previous couples, she helped Hikari to her feet and said, "I swear to protect her, like this."

She embraced Hikari proudly, as though she were a princess.

The sight of Amane standing with her face to the sky—simply embracing Hikari to her chest, gently, without any kind of trick, her tall height and gallant face magnificent—was refreshing.

Amane's indescribably bright, relaxed smile, unusual for her to show in a public setting, overflowed with her sense of euphoria. The happy, loving couple's golden aura—which was apparent even to the people who watched—shone brightly in the spring sunlight.

Shouts that weren't quite cheers and weren't quite angry roars rose from the spectators at a terrific volume several times higher than for any couple before.

"Aaugh!"

"Stop, I can't take any more!"

"But it's too incredible!"

"Prince Amane!"

"Hold me, too!"

"I don't want to see that!"

The Amane fans didn't want to see any more, but they tossed many flowers, which flew around and into the basket. At first, Shion smiled wryly at the response. "That was...to be expected, I suppose... Heh heh."

She asked the spectators for silence. "Everyone, I understand how you feel, but please quiet down. Now for the next question."

One group of Amane fans, who had been suppressing their desire to toss their flowers of praise in order to watch Amane's proud moment just a little bit longer, leaned forward in anticipation.

Shion, feeling as if she were tossing food to carp in a pond, smiled broadly and asked the next question.

"Now then, I ask the *aînée* candidate, Otori Amane. Do you swear to love the *cadette* candidate next to you always, and offer her your unchanging love, even if either one of you should take a husband, for as long as you both shall live?"

Otherworldly screams rose from the crowd.

"Aaaugh!"

Nanto Yaya stood in a corner, grinding her teeth. *Honestly! I can't believe that Shion-oneesama, pulling a trick like that. It's no fair changing the questions during Amane-oneesama's turn.*

"If Shion-oneesama keeps doing stuff like that, Hikari-chan's going to fall even more in love with Amane-oneesama! And if innocent little Hikari-chan does fall in love with that awkward Amane-oneesama, they're just going to get hurt! No one understands that!" she muttered.

From behind her came the sound of laugher.

"I feel exactly the same way. The star of the campus and a transfer student—yeah, right. This isn't a novel. It's obvious they're going to get hurt. But it seems this particular 'illness' is more severe in your couple, doesn't it?"

When Yaya turned around, Tamao was standing there grinning, with an expression on her face that showed her pity for her fellow sufferer.

"Oh, I didn't mean…" Tamao started.

"It's just for now. Once the initial fever goes down…even Hikari-chan understands. If she stays with Amane-oneesama, she's going to be hurt, more likely than not. She's going to be hurt and suffer. I want to be there for her when that happens," Yaya said.

"You have a lot of patience, unlike me. I'm jealous," Tamao said, and pointed to the front of the crowd. "If you let your guard down this time…you might not be able to recover, you know?"

High-pitched, lovely voices and an even bigger commotion raced across the site. When Yaya frantically spun around, there was Hikari, slumped in Amane's arms. She had been about to receive a kiss on the forehead from Amane, to seal their oath, when she had fainted.

"Aaugh! Stop, I can't take any more!!"

With shouts that were closer to screams, the students scattered countless flowers into the sky.

"Ah! Nagisa-oneesama! Thank goodness! I've been looking for you. Where have you—" Chiyo couldn't finish the sentence. She was struck dumb by the strange, unusual feeling she got from Nagisa.

Chiyo had been watching the intense scene between Amane and Hikari from between her fingers, her heart pounding. She had been surprised when Nagisa had suddenly appeared, and had run frantically to meet her.

Nagisa apologized, embarrassed, with a stiff expression on her face. She didn't even look at Chiyo. "Did I make it on time?"

"Just barely! Tamao-oneesama negotiated with them and got them to change you to the last couple! Shizuma-oneesama is getting ready, down front. She said she knew you would come..."

Nagisa thanked Chiyo in a small voice and headed toward the administrators. She looked incredibly lonely as she walked away.

"Excuse me, Oneesama," Chiyo called from behind.

"What?"

When Nagisa looked over her shoulder, Chiyo didn't know what to say.

"Good...luck."

Nagisa gave a weak smile. "Thanks."

In front of the relief, a sharp voice called her. "Over here, Nagisa." Someone pulled on her arm.

Nagisa was surprised, but Shizuma didn't care, or even give Nagisa a chance to speak. She just quickly fixed Nagisa's hair, put the veil on her head and gave her a complete once-over, a stern expression on her face.

"That should do it," Shizuma said, and relaxed. "I was

worried, you know? What happened, did your stomach get upset? Did you suddenly have to go to the toilet?" She poked Nagisa's cheek.

Before Nagisa could say anything...

"Come on, it's our turn. It's all right, you don't have to do anything, Nagisa. If you just follow me, it'll be fine," Shizuma said, misunderstanding Nagisa's stiff expression.

They stepped forward, toward the Mouth of Truth.

"Now then, I ask the *aînée* candidate, Hanazono Shizuma of St. Miator Girls' Academy, Sixth Year, Snow Class. Do you swear to protect and help the *cadette* candidate next to you, no matter what?"

The first question was the same as the other couples'. However, Shizuma, who loved theatrics, didn't take Nagisa into her arms like the other *aînées*. She surprised Nagisa, kneeling to make her oath.

Nagisa accepted it with a dumbfounded, aimless gaze. Both loud cheers and boos rose from the crowd, and of course countless flowers flew through the air, but it wasn't enough to fill the basket in front of them.

And then, the second question. Shion cleared her throat. Just like she had with Amane, she said, "Now then, I ask the *aînée* candidate, Hanazono Shizuma."

Here her voice wavered, and her breath stopped. She was hesitant after all. It was cruel, what she was doing. She had felt like a demon when she chose the question. Now she asked herself whether she should really do this to Shizuma.

However, Shion's hesitation had made the spectators even more expectant. Passions flared as they waited for the next bit of excitement. Shion's goal was to drop a bomb that would blast across the entire site in one swoop, and also, as a natural consequence, lead Spica to victory, but—

When she looked at the sight of Nagisa, her expression rigid—probably out of nervousness—and Shizuma kneeling beside her with a charming smile, Shion unconsciously lifted her face to the sky and closed her eyes.

Shizuma-sama, please forgive me for being so sinful.

"Do you wish to be bound to the *cadette* candidate next to you as your one and only partner, both in this life and the next?"

"Waaaaaah!"

That cruel question, which asked Shizuma to declare that she wanted to become one and only lovers with Nagisa, who would be together even after they were reborn, caused a thunderous storm of shouts and applause from those gathered at the site.

Somewhere along the way, Nagisa became confused about what was going on. The only thing she heard was something about being one and only partners, even in the next world.

Shizuma's hand, which held hers deep inside the hole of the Mouth of Truth, shook badly. The picture of Shizuma as the *Étoile* jumped into Nagisa's mind. Her incredible beauty, her strong will and her dignified smile, like a queen's—and the text: "To my adorable little sister, the late Sakuragi Kaori… I give all of my love to you…"

Ahh, now I understand. No matter how thickheaded I am,

even I can understand this. Shizuma-oneesama had someone once who was much, much better matched to her than me. Someone much more appropriate. She had a real, steady partner...

But I didn't want to know about it. Everybody probably thought I was weird, being so sure of myself...and some people are angry at me, too. That's it. That has to be it. Someone like me with Shizuma-oneesama? Now that I think about it, the idea was strange from the start.

Nagisa's mind went completely blank and she froze.

Shizuma stood. Still holding Nagisa's hand tight, she pulled her to her feet. Shizuma faced the crowd, almost as if she were challenging them, raised Nagisa's hand high and shouted, almost in a roar.

"I do—I swear it. I take Aoi Nagisa as my one and only partner for the rest of eternity."

Even before Shizuma finished speaking, the loudest swirl of screams, roars and shouts that day rose from the crowd.

"Oh, please don't say any more!" the young ladies screamed.

The sky was dyed crimson with flowers, thrown about like a defeated fighter's towel.

"Nagisa, you were so great today! I'll forget all about the toilet thing. Let's do our best again tomorrow, in the *aînée* competition, okay?"

Once the *cadette* competition had ended, Shizuma said those parting words, joined some girls who seemed to be her followers and quickly disappeared from Nagisa's sight.

Without telling Nagisa a single thing about the truth.

Left behind, Nagisa lost all her steam. She almost thought the whole thing might have been just her imagination. She watched, dumbfounded, as the spectators left, and then spotted Chiyo standing alone. She ran over to her.

"Chiyo-chan!"

"Nagisa-oneesama! That was so…so splendid!" Tears welled up in Chiyo's eyes.

Now that I think about it, Nagisa thought, remembering, *Chiyo is a member of the library committee.*

Chiyo had been sitting at the counter on the day Nagisa had been in the library with Shizuma.

"Um, Chiyo-chan. Could I…ask you something?"

As if she had anticipated this, Chiyo silently nodded. Then Chiyo told her. She didn't know everything that had happened, because she hadn't been at the school yet back then, but…

What she did know was this sad story.

Chiyo and her friends had been upperclassmen in the elementary school—the age when little girls experience the joy of moving to the middle school they've always longed to attend, the feeling of wanting to grow up and the desire to get even just a little bit taller. These little girls felt they would be getting a glimpse into the world of adults—the world of the oneesama they admired.

It seemed like no matter how many times Chiyo and her friends had talked about it, it had always produced sighs.

Shizuma had still been a fourth-year student then, and the center of the Astraea universe. Everyone was expecting Shizuma to become the *Étoile* the following year, and she had a partner accepted by everyone.

Sakuragi Kaori of Third Year Snow Class.

They had said she was just as incredible a beauty as Shizuma, but that she was delicate, giving the impression she was made of glass so fragile she would break if you touched her.

She had worshipped Shizuma completely. Many girls had even said she wouldn't be able to live without Shizuma. She totally relied on the oneesama, but from an outsider's point of view, her position had been an enviable one.

"It's just that..." Chiyo said timidly to Nagisa, "Kaori-sama's devotion to Shizuma-oneesama was obvious to everyone. As for Shizuma-oneesama... Well, ever since she was very young she's been popular, so she wasn't like that with Kaori at first. But there was an incident... Kaori became sick and collapsed. It was tragic."

It seemed that within a month after she'd become friends with Shizuma, Kaori had discovered she was stricken with an incurable illness. Filled with despair, Kaori had tried to withdraw from the relationship.

"I don't know if it's true or not, but that's the rumor," Chiyo said apologetically. "It made Shizuma flaming mad, and from that point on, Shizuma was constantly by Kaori's side. If she saw flowers, she would give them to Kaori. She would always be looking for delicious food or pretty things for Kaori. A sick room was set up inside the Strawberry Dorms as a special exception. Because Kaori wanted to stay at school until the end. As much as possible, anyway. And she wanted to be with Shizuma."

She had started showing signs of her illness in the fall. And in the middle of winter, with the cold wind blowing, she had left the school.

In the spring, news of her death had arrived…

"That's what I heard," Chiyo said with a sorrowful look on her face. "Everyone said that when Shizuma-oneesama entered the *Étoile* competition that spring, she had truly become an adult. That is all I know. But I'm sure Tamao-oneesama knows more about it than me." Chiyo smiled demurely.

Lured by her infectious smile, Nagisa was able to smile herself, just a little bit. It was the kind of story that made her cold to the very core of her body, but…

"Yeah. I have a feeling Tamao-chan would be too worried about hurting me to tell me the truth. Thank you so much… Chiyo-chan. I forced you into a position you didn't want to be in. I'm sorry."

Seeing Nagisa's weak smile, Chiyo had doubts about whether this had been the right thing to do.

That night, in the large Roman-style bath of the Strawberry Dorms…

"Oh no, what's wrong, Nagisa-chan? What are you moping for? You don't look very happy…"

Sploosh sploosh sploosh—Tamao sent some of the bath water flying. "At times like this…" She jumped into the large tub with a big *sploooosh*.

"Aaugh!"

"Stop it!"

"Jeez, Tamao!"

The shouts came from all over and echoed around the mist-filled room lined with brightly colored terra cotta tiles.

"Come on, it's okay to swim like this, right? You can't do it in your bath at home, now can you? I guess this is one of the good things about the Strawberry Dorms."

But no matter how happy and playful Tamao was, Nagisa just couldn't get into the same spirit. She fumbled with the soaking wet sponge in her hand, but didn't wash or rinse herself off, just sat there absentminded and sighed.

"Yeah, thanks. But I don't think I will today; I'm kind of tired," Nagisa said with an exhausted look. Nagisa put on her best smile, but it came out stiff. *After all, Tamao-chan is going through all the trouble to cheer me up!*

"A lot happened today that I wasn't used to, so I'm sure I'm just tired from being so nervous. Ah ha ha ha!"

"Oh Nagisa, what am I going to do with you…" Tamao's heart twinged. Even she couldn't do anything. "Yeah, I understand. Then today, as a special service, I'll wash your entire body!"

She stood up to her full height.

"Whaaat? You don't have to do that!"

"Don't be shy. It's all right."

"Aaugh! That tickles!! Stop it, Tamao-chan! Ah! Not there! Aaaaaaaahh!"

Across the mist, bubbles flew into the air.

In another part of the Strawberry Dorms, another girl stood worrying.

"I wonder if it's okay this way?"

Standing on the balcony alone, gazing at the moon, which had passed through the full moon of the pre-competition party and was now entering its last quarter, was Otori Amane, age seventeen, who lived in the Spica section of the Strawberry Dorms.

Spring love... Amane had been hit hard by this powerful sickness. The look on Hikari's face when Amane had kissed her on the forehead, and when she had fainted from the strain... Amane still couldn't get it out of her head.

Whether she liked it or not, the conflicting emotions of terror at making her faint and rapture at the sight of Hikari's face when her eyes were closed had controlled Amane's body—and now she writhed in agony.

"Aah! This is almost like—" *It's like I'm the same as Yaya.*

She remembered her kouhai, who was well-known for being a "genuine lesbian," who hated men and was only interested in girls.

I wonder if I'm strange, Amane pondered.

CHAPTER 6

A Rainbow Shines in the Valley of Tears That Have Dried

The weather on Astraea Hill the next day was gorgeously sunny, almost like an early summer preview. It was the morning of the second half of the premiere contest, the morning of the *aînée* competition.

"Wooow…look at the crowd!"

Spica Student Council Secretary Okuwaka Tsubomi, a first-year student with long, shiny, peach-colored hair, was making preliminary arrangements. When she entered the horse-riding grounds, she was startled at how many people were there.

Even though the competition was being held early in the morning, before classes started, there were a lot of girls there who wanted to see the race.

Yes, the first *aînée* competition was a horse race.

What else could be expected from a famous school for high-class girls? The *aînée* candidates must know how to ride a horse or else they were completely unfit to represent the schools.

In a corner of the horse-riding grounds, which lay to the west of St. Spica Girls' Institute, the *aînée* candidates were lined up, each riding her favorite horse.

The horses, all of them large thoroughbreds with shiny coats, all pampered and obviously highly valuable, neighed loudly.

One white horse stood out from the many chestnut-colored ones. In the saddle of this horse, named Starbright, was Otori Amane. Wearing white riding pants, a white jacket and a royal blue tie, Amane looked exactly like a Prince.

Next to her was a jet-black horse with a white star on its forehead—*L'éclair noir*. Riding him was Hanazono Shizuma, wearing a riding jacket that matched her steed's coat. Her silvery hair was tied up, which was unusual, but it looked attractive against the black of the horse.

Sighs flowed from the spectators as they watched the Prince and the Queen. Suddenly a light fanfare sounded, signaling that everything was ready. Then the early-morning events developed quickly.

The horses, warming up in one corner, had been waiting for the signal, and leapt into the riding area as soon as they were given the okay.

They were ready to go.

The noble young ladies—all of them elite and capable enough to be more than a match for any ordinary male—turned their horses toward the "Tower of Captivity" set up in the center of the riding area.

Just like the scaffold used during Festivals, the Tower was a simple tall framework with four pillars and a platform with a light roof. The platform was high, higher even than the roof of the nearby stable. In one part of the base, there was a slope even a horse could climb, but that was only one meter high, and the only way to get any higher was to use a set of narrow stairs.

The *cadette* candidates climbed to the platform, each dressed in a unique costume. There was a Snow White wearing a red ribbon, a Cinderella with glass slippers and even a long-haired Rapunzel. They were the "captured" princesses.

The costumes had been chosen and designed not only for style but for ease of movement. None of them were grandiose, but each had been made with the help of the couple's supporters, and they were all the kind of costume that would tickle a girl's fancy.

Every young girl who saw them sighed and thought, *I wish I could wear a costume like that and be saved by the oneesama I adore so much.*

The way the competition would go was that the captured *cadettes* would stand on the platform, held at a height that could only be reached on horseback. There they would wait, expectant, for their gallant princes—their *aînées*—to come and rescue them.

In yesterday's *cadette* competition, twelve of the seventeen couples who had entered had been able to get their baskets filled with flowers by the end of the five questions. In order to reduce the original number by half, only the top nine after this *aînée* competition would be allowed to go to the next competition.

The second fanfare blared: the starting signal. The gallant horses dashed from the riding grounds all at once and galloped toward Maiden Park, where a special course had been set up.

The *aînée* candidates would leave the riding grounds, ride down the narrow horse trail that wound its way through lush Maiden Park, and return to the riding grounds and the Tower.

This course, used only on special occasions, was quite long—one full lap around the vast Maiden Park—so the start was more elegant than frantic.

The spectators stood in the small area set aside for them, which encircled the riding area, and enjoyed ogling the elegant *aînée* candidates on their horses to their hearts' content. Among the spectators was a student with an opera glass in one hand, looking as if she belonged at Ascot.

The Tower of Captivity was rather small. The platform where the young ladies stood had a guardrail with a single white ribbon wound around it, but it was flimsy and swayed in the wind. Not the kind of thing they could grab onto in an emergency.

The twelve *cadette* candidates pushed and shoved each other in the center of the platform and waited for their *aînées* to rescue them. While they waited, a restless atmosphere hung over the crowded *cadettes*.

"There's not enough room!"

"It must be because there are two last-minute entries here who don't belong."

They didn't exactly make a big scene, but it did make some wonder where the crowded princesses got their ideas from.

"The transfer students stood out; that helped them."

"They used force to get the format of the first competition changed."

"They have no idea how many years we've been trying to be chosen as *cadettes*."

"They're seriously annoying!"

Ahh…they're talking about me, aren't they? It sounds like there are some people who are really angry after all… Still not able to think quite clearly, still shocked by yesterday's events, Nagisa listened to the girls from a corner of the platform, not knowing what to do.

Tamao and Chiyo had asked their classmates to help them make Nagisa's costume. It was an angel outfit with lots of real white feathers. Tamao had said that everyone's a sucker for a pretty costume, and had put everything she had into making Nagisa's.

Shizuma's black riding clothes had been designed to look demonlike. Tamao's idea was that the couple would bring the theme of Forbidden Love to life.

Although Nagisa was grateful for Tamao's help, she was somewhat sad as she absent-mindedly gazed over the area.

It's not like I'm going to win anyway. And it's not like Shizuma-oneesama was serious when she invited me. She just did it for fun. I don't care about anything any more. I just want this aînée *competition to be over with soon,* Nagisa thought.

The other *cadette* candidates kept up their chatter.

"Her partner is Amane-sama, so it's a given that no matter what happens, she'll make it to the final competition."

"Kenjo Kaname-sama, one of the Five Great Stars, was really supposed to be Amane-sama's partner."

"A lot of people really wanted to see those two paired together, you know?"

"And yet look who ended up her partner!"

"Yeah!"

When she heard the talking, Nagisa looked to her side—and noticed a Spica student who looked like she wanted to run away. Hikari, wearing an ephemeral mermaid-princess costume, stared at her feet, trembling.

Oh, I see... It's her, huh? I feel sorry for her. No one expected Shizuma-oneesama to enter when I was made her partner—so I'm sure this poor girl is getting treated a lot more harshly than me.

Nagisa had heard a little about the situation in Spica from Tamao. Forgetting her own situation, she completely sympathized with Hikari. Despite the tension of the race, Nagisa's thoughts turned to the poor girl beside her.

That's right... Even I've heard about Spica's Prince. That's what all that fuss was about yesterday... Yeah, if she's not careful, people might be even more jealous of her than me. Poor thing... If I get kicked or stepped on, I'm strong, I can handle it, but this girl's different. She seems pretty weak-spirited. She looks like she would burst into tears if she got shoved or fell. I'm the kind of person who can smile even when stuff like that happens!

Thinking about it got her charged up and she scratched her nose.

Ah ha! I got a little embarrassed, just saying it to myself!

With those thoughts in mind, Nagisa turned to Hikari. She was about to ask whether she was all right and tell her not to worry so much when…

"Waaah!" Cheers rose from the spectator area.

The gates to the riding grounds opened wide.

The horse at the head of the pack, kicking up an impressive amount of dust, was…

White. Starbright, ridden by Amane! Close behind her was a glistening jet-black horse, *L'éclair noir*, with silver-haired Shizuma on his back.

Just as most people had expected, it had come down to a one-on-one battle between Amane, Spica's ace of the horse-riding club, and Shizuma, who came from a powerful ranch-owning family.

Loud cries rose from the spectators.

"Yay! Amane-sama, keep going!!"

"Shizuma-sama! Please pass that white horse!"

Now comes the real battle, was what they were all thinking.

The *cadettes* in the Tower of Captivity crowded along the edge of the platform, each leaning over to try and see what place her beloved *aînée* was in.

"Augh!"

A small scream reached Nagisa's ears.

Nagisa looked for the source of the scream and saw Hikari right next to her, just about to slip off of the edge of the platform.

She also caught a glimpse of a single arm reaching out through a gap in the crowd.

The edge of the platform was as crowded as a packed train, so Nagisa couldn't tell who it was, but whoever that arm belonged to pushed Hikari. She was going to fall from the top of the Tower of Captivity.

The scene seemed to unfold in slow motion before Nagisa's eyes as she had a sudden thought. This girl was loved very much by the oneesama she loved—Amane-oneesama. She was envied by the other girls, so much that one of them would do something like this to her. Yet she was also loved enough by other girls to be on this platform in the first place. If Hikari failed here, Nagisa had no idea what kinds of things they would say to her...

"You got in the way of Spica's chance to win!" or "You're just a burden to Amane-sama."

Compared to that... They've accused me of using "strong-arm tactics" and said I only entered "on the spur of the moment." But it was Shizuma's idea in the first place. I don't seriously think I could become the Étoile. And Shizuma-oneesama has already been the Étoile once. And she has really precious memories of a girl who was more beautiful and wonderful than me, and...

Then everything seemed to happen in an instant. Nagisa didn't know what to think any more. Before she even realized it, she had started to move. She launched herself into the panicked crowd...and saved Hikari.

But she started to fall instead. Nagisa wasn't concerned about it in the least. She suddenly felt like she wanted to fall.

I wonder how much easier it would be for me if I fell from this stage. If I had never met Shizuma-oneesama, I never would have suffered so much.

Such despair might have been what threw Nagisa off balance.

"Aaaugh!"

When they saw Nagisa about to fall, all the *cadettes* panicked. In a split second, Nagisa had launched herself at Hikari and pushed her toward the center of the Tower, but her momentum had destroyed her balance. She had knocked over the flimsy guardrail and was slipping right off the edge of the platform.

It was obvious that if she fell from that height, even if she wasn't critically injured, she certainly wouldn't come away unhurt. More importantly, Nagisa dangled over a route traveled by horses, and the horses were just about to arrive. If she fell... in the worst-case scenario, she would be trampled before she could escape.

Despite the panic around her, Nagisa managed to hold on to the platform with the tips of her fingers. She smiled weakly at Hikari and said, "Don't worry, it's okay... I'm fine. Unlike the other princesses, I'm strong, so I'll be fine even if I fall from here. Even if I get disqualified for this, I'm sure Shizuma-oneesama won't be angry."

"Oh, no, you mustn't. If you do, then you'll... Your oneesama will be sad, I just know it!" Hikari cried.

As she looked at Hikari, Nagisa remembered how Shizuma's face had stiffened at the second question of yesterday's Mouth of Truth. And how she had turned away from Nagisa and left with her followers.

And then there was that picture she had seen at the library. The words beside the image: "I give all of my love to you."

"No, that would never happen," Nagisa said feebly. "Right about now, I'm sure Shizuma-oneesama is regretting entering the *Étoile* competition with me." That was all Nagisa said. She felt weak, like she had a fever.

Just as she was about to intentionally let go of the platform, a gust of wind arrived at the Tower of Captivity.

"Ahh, she's not going to make it!" and "She's falling!" rose from the nervous spectators.

From the slope at the base, a horse like a white wind jumped into the air. The mounted Prince reached her hand up to the white princess. Seizing Hikari's arm, she snatched her off the platform.

Not noticing the situation, Amane just kept going. But from within Amane's arms, Hikari tried desperately to reach Nagisa, tears in her eyes. She yelled, "Help her, please help her! Please help that girl from Miator! She's going to fall instead of me."

When Amane heard Hikari's screams she looked back and noticed Nagisa about to fall from the edge of the platform. Nagisa was tired, barely hanging onto the edge with one hand.

Amane no longer cared whether she were first to the goal; without a moment's hesitation, she pulled the reins and turned the horse around. She cantered up the slope again, but at the moment she was about to grab Nagisa from underneath, she heard a sharp yell.

"Idiot! Stop it right now, Amane! Are you trying to take something that belongs to someone else?!"

Trrmp trrmp trrmp trrrmp... The galloping got closer.

"Get your hands off her!!"

A black figure leapt into the air, and before Amane could even turn to look, Nagisa's body was floating.

A sigh rose from the crowd. "Ahhhhh..."

"Stupid girl... You really are stupid, my angel." Held in Shizuma's arms, the only thing Nagisa heard was Shizuma's soft murmur—such a soft voice no one else could hear it. The scent of Shizuma's body, which was sweaty from riding, enveloped Nagisa.

Before she even knew what was going on, Nagisa had found herself on a horse, saved. The only things she could see were the vast blue sky and a face looking into hers. Half-blinded by the backlighting, Nagisa couldn't see Shizuma's face, beautifully fringed by her long, silvery hair.

But she did see a single, shiny teardrop.

No, it might be just sweat...

The release from all the tension was sudden and Nagisa felt overwhelmed. Shizuma squeezed Nagisa tight, and suddenly corrected her body position. The momentum she had needed to save Nagisa had carried her in front of Amane, who had been

leading, before she even realized it. She turned around and yelled again.

"You let your guard down, Amane! Now Miator has the win!! My strategy has paid off!"

"Hmph… That's just like you, Shizuma-sama." Amane was stunned by how admirable it was for Shizuma to decide to cover for the disgrace committed by a Spica student.

Hikari was the one who was falling first. If Shizuma-sama had said that, people would suspect jealousy from the other Spica students. That Miator cadette *saved her—she saved my Hikari. On top of that, Shizuma-sama shifted the blame to herself, to make it seem like this was planned from the beginning.*

After a moment, the corners of Amane's mouth curled into a smile—and she told Hikari to hold on tight, stood in her stirrups and used both her whip and spurs.

I understand, Shizuma-sama. Now that it comes to this, I will fight seriously too. From now on, I will protect Hikari with my own hands!

The neighing of her horse echoed across the sky. The two of them took one final lap around the grounds in a dead heat. Everyone there held their breath and strained their eyes to see the outcome.

Which one would win?

Amane?

Shizuma?

Spica?

Miator?

Which one would grasp victory?

CHAPTER 7

The Crown of the Most Beloved Blesses
the Two with its Holy Light

$\mathbf{A}$ gentle breeze blew across the garden in Maiden Park. Enveloped by the quiet spring sunlight, Shizuma sat next to Nagisa. "Thanks for your hard work. It was a really fun *Étoile* competition, wasn't it?" Shizuma said.

"Yes. We had just a little bit of trouble, but still…" Nagisa remembered how she had almost fallen off the platform and grinned wryly.

Shizuma looked lovingly at Nagisa. "I'm truly thankful. Thanks to you, I was able to have that much fun again."

"Not at all—it wasn't me. You're such a wonderful person, wonderful things always happen around you. You have such a spectacular school life, yet you chose someone like me… someone like me…"

I can't let myself get drawn in by Shizuma's relaxed attitude. I can't let myself become arrogant. Nagisa hung her head. She smiled, biting her lips the whole time.

"I'm sure I misunderstood a little. I didn't know anything. I had just transferred in, so I didn't know anything. I didn't even know how popular you were at this school. Or that someone like me doesn't even deserve to be next to you."

Or that you used to have someone who you loved, and that you made such a perfect couple with her no one could help but admire you...

That was what Nagisa wanted to say more than anything, but she couldn't say it, and it echoed in her heart.

With a sad expression, Shizuma said, "I don't know how much you know or what people have told you. I don't want to know, either. I have a feeling it's better if I don't. But I do want to say this."

She took Nagisa's chin in her hand and made her look into her eyes.

Ahh, she really is an undeniably beautiful goddess, Nagisa thought as she gazed into Shizuma's eyes.

"When it comes to my personal affairs, please believe only what I tell you. I am Hanazono Shizuma. I do not lie."

Nagisa nodded.

"I have memories of days that were like a dream, fun and beautiful, and memories of days that were so painful and sad they tore me apart inside. And together they make up all the wonderful memories that live inside me. Of course, there are some I would rather not remember ever again."

Days that were as fun and beautiful as a dream, and days that were so sad they tore her apart inside—something about those words pricked Nagisa's heart a little.

"Even so, I don't want to deny those memories. I don't want to erase them. Because no matter how bitter they are, they make up a part of the life I've lived. They've made me who I am now—Hanazono Shizuma."

Shizuma looked off into the clear blue sky, her gaze unwavering. Her profile gave off a deep, profound silence.

Nagisa was filled with new feelings toward Shizuma—a little different from the sadness she'd felt since learning about the existence of the girl named Sakuragi Kaori.

Painful memories she doesn't want to ever remember again... I see, Shizuma-oneesama lost someone very...very precious to her.

Nagisa suddenly realized something. *Maybe I've been thinking only about myself all this time. I'm positive Shizuma-oneesama loved Kaori a lot more than she does me. Why would she pick someone like me to take her place? I'm sure she just wants to have fun with me, and I can never replace the one she lost.*

Nagisa felt sorry for herself.

I wonder what it feels like to lose someone you love. No matter how much you miss her, you'll never be able to see her again. No matter how much you want to hear her voice, you'll never be able to talk to her. No matter how much you want to touch her, you'll never feel her warmth. All that's left are memories that grow hazier and further away as days go by.

Nagisa hadn't lost anyone that important to her yet, but... just imagining it made her body tremble.

Shizuma lives with memories like that—and such painful feelings—inside her.

Shizuma-oneesama…Shizuma-oneesama…waaaaah! I feel so sorry for Shizuma-oneesama!

Nagisa wanted to cry.

Looking at the sky, Shizuma spoke.

"What I love is…right now, this very moment, the one I want to have with all my body and soul is you and only you. The person I've been up until now never had such a feeling before."

The person she's been up until now… Which means…

A faint sense of expectation arose deep in Nagisa's heart, but she worked desperately to suppress it.

"I don't want to compare people… I don't want to compare the person I was in the past with the person I am now. But there's something I want to tell you. No matter what other people have said."

Shizuma brought her face close to Nagisa's. "I love you. Even right now, even being together like this right now, I'm afraid that you're going to jump out of my arms and leave. You're the only one who can make me feel so vulnerable."

Nagisa had a feeling she already knew what was coming next, but…

"May I? Nagisa?"

For some reason, today she was able to relax.

If it can make Shizuma-oneesama happy, even just a little, then…I'll do it. I can only do a little bit. If that's what Shizuma-oneesama wants, then no matter how much of a mismatch I am, even if people laugh at me, I will stay by Shizuma-oneesama's side. Until the day when Shizuma-oneesama can truly shake off those painful memories...

On top of the bright, lush hill, the two figures became one. Flower petals fluttered on the spring breeze.

Shizuma lay on the slope of the green hill and gazed at Nagisa's profile as she slept. In the distance, from across the hill, she heard cheers and fanfare.

She murmured softly, "It couldn't be helped this time, because you weren't used to it. But the bond between us is stronger now, so we absolutely must clear the second competition. You'd better prepare yourself."

As she grinned, a yawn came out of nowhere. The brilliant spring sunlight shone down, warming Shizuma's body.

"But, well, this is enough for today." *Because I got what I really wanted.*

Shizuma turned on her side, stretched her hand toward the bright sky, and closed her eyes. She felt like she could enter Nagisa's dreams.

EPILOGUE

The Coronation

The main gate to Maiden Park was open wide. A shower of flower petals danced and fluttered from the gate and through the sky. The spring sky, which was once again clear and blue.

A hymn, sung by a chorus of young ladies, echoed across the clear blue sky.

> Sacred
> Skylark in the sky,
> Sacred
> White lily in the field.
> The Lord's glory fills heaven and earth.
> It rains down upon us.
> Hosanna
> In the highest!

The couple, finished with the ceremony, appeared in front of the church in the middle of the young ladies. Accompanied by thunderous applause and cheers, enough flower petals to bury heaven were scattered through the sky.

"Congratulations."

"Congratulations!"

"Congratulations, holder of the *Petite couronne!*"

In the midst of the congratulations stood a Prince, wearing a jeweled white crown small enough to fit in the palm of her hand, holding hands with a princess who wore a pendant with identical jewels.

The couple gazed into each other's eyes, blushing. And just for today, no one said anything mean or spiteful to them.

The prince was cheerful; the princess looked shy. Together, they shook hands with some of the audience, then gently placed their cheeks together and gave their best smiles.

They were smiles from the heart, and everyone who saw them broke into a broad smile of her own.

Afterward, a grand party was given by the Spica Student Council. Tea and sweets were passed around.

Thus ended the first contest of the *Étoile* competition, *L'Ouverture brillante.*

Strawberry Panic!

Girls' School in Full Bloom

Summer has arrived, and the three Astraea schools have begun their swim classes in P.E. The students all wear their respective school swimsuits. Only Shizuma-sama is different—she wears her personal, virgin-white swimsuit rather elegantly.

We look forward to the pool!

After a little break, we'll practice our shots!

Girls from all three schools play basketball in the gym. They're taking a break, relaxing. The Lulim pair in the back, Kizuna and Remon, must have too much energy… They're enjoying themselves as they wrestle for the ball.

The girls who go to St. Lulim Girls' School always seem to be having fun, even when studying together in the classroom. The school's motto is "Nurturing modern wives and wise mothers." Maybe because of the school's independent and relaxed atmosphere, they seem to have a laid-back attitude when it comes to studying.

PROLOGUE

With the Goddess Absent, Tender Tears Fall from the Little Nymphet

*P*itter patter pitter patter…

Rain drizzled on the lush green forest of Maiden Park. It was the second week of June, a bit early for the rainy season.

Three famous all-girl schools sat atop the hill. Rain poured from the dark gray skies and soaked the whole area, acting as a precursor to the upcoming long monsoon.

Nagisa looked out from under the umbrella and sighed.

"Haaaah…"

She covered her mouth, surprised at the loudness of her sigh. In St. Miator Girls' Academy, it was taboo to sigh. She didn't know whether this rule was simply good manners to prevent others from feeling uncomfortable or a superstition to avoid bad luck, but she kept making little mistakes like these at this prestigious all-girl school. Fortunately, her classmates were well-mannered and didn't treat her coldly, but…

Nagisa tilted her head and thought, *Oh no, I did it again!*

From under her umbrella, all she could see was the thick, green forest that surrounded her. She was alone on the wet path.

Yeah…

She wouldn't chase me all this way…

She's not allowed to be with someone unimportant like me anyway…

Nagisa detested her cowardice.

"Haaaah…" she sighed again.

She had become self-deprecating ever since she'd started attending this school. Before that, Nagisa had never cared about nor paid attention to what others thought of her. She had used to scratch her head and laugh, and her friends had envied her simplicity…she was simply immature.

But Nagisa had changed quite a bit since she'd transferred to this school.

She reflected on things now, on her existence. And thought about what she could do for others.

This was merely a step toward maturity.

Nagisa tried to be optimistic.

Well, this is the first time I've been the center of attention at school, so…I should grow up a little… Tsk tsk, the star on campus is so influential, whomever the star likes, even if it's an ordinary transfer student like me…gets so much attention…

Nagisa wryly smiled, but deep inside…her heart tightened at the thought of the large shadow that had begun to fill it. The feelings swelled so much, she couldn't stare into her own heart.

She couldn't admit her true feelings to the one who had taught Nagisa to feel so melancholy…the one who had entered her heart and controlled her life.

That special person.

Ever since she'd met the goddess…

Nagisa used to spend her days peacefully, but ever since that fateful encounter, she had been attacked by violent waves of emotion that repeatedly rocked her feelings up to the heavens in happiness and at the same time dragged her to the bottomless pit of anxiety, over and over. And day after day.

Though it wasn't a conscious wish, somewhere in her heart she longed for something to happen.

Maybe I'll bump into her around the next corner…

Maybe, in the middle of a boring class, she'll burst through the door and ask, "May I speak to Nagisa-san?"

Nagisa's heart throbbed at the joyful anticipation.

But on the other hand…while the excitement of seeing the goddess surged through her like a tsunami, it was coupled with immense anxiety, freezing the pit of her stomach. Feelings of both joy and agony could overcome her at any given moment…

Ever since she had met Hanazono Shizuma, a large, mysterious shadow had begun to dwell in Nagisa's heart.

It was her heart's very first growing pains.

Another form of anxiety began to grow now.

"Will I never see her again…?" she started to lament, but stopped herself. *No, no way. This is only temporary. It's only for two weeks.*

And…it's been one, two, three…

Nagisa counted on her fingers the number of days she had been separated from Hanazono Shizuma, the number-one star on campus.

"See, it's been four days already," she tried to say cheerfully, but it was in vain.

Sigh... Oh, it's only been four days, and I'm already this miserable... It's like there's something large missing from my life...

She was depressed. *What's wrong with me, anyway?*

I haven't done so well today... At the science lab, everyone told me I looked so sad...

Even during breakfast with Tamao-chan, I didn't have much of an appetite. Tamao-chan looked at me with pity, like I was an abandoned kitty or something.

She even patted my head and said I was a good girl, trying to comfort me...

Oh, how did I get myself into this in the first place?
Come to think of it...

CHAPTER 1

The Hazel Comet Strengthens the Attraction of the Full Blue Tide

*A*ve…

   Ave…

   Verum Corpus…

Young, fine voices came from a distance.

   This song…I think I heard it in class before. It wasn't an English song, but in a language from a strange country…a hymn.

   Where is it coming from?

   Hyuga Kizuna, St. Lulim Girls' School Second Year Student, B Class, looked at the trees that surrounded her.

   A puff of breath left her small mouth. *Where am I…?*

   She looked at the circle of sky above, closed in by the surrounding trees.

   The clouds drifted along rapidly in the blue sky that continued infinitely upward.

"Wow, great weather!" Kizuna reached into the sky, almost throwing the paper bag she carried.

The scent of the green wood filled the air, and her double ponytails swung around as her little body skipped.

She was in the deep recesses of Maiden Park, which was behind her school, St. Lulim.

Not many people visited the deep, secluded areas of the forest. In fact, this was Kizuna's first time venturing this far.

Kizuna had entered the forest alone...because Chikaru, the Student Council President, had invited her to come. Her classmate, Natsume Remon, had also been invited, but Kizuna had had to stay back for clean-up duty after school, so...Kizuna had had to come later, on her own. She had tried to follow the directions on the map that she'd been given, but the more she walked, the more she got herself lost deeper in the forest.

She had walked for at least thirty minutes, but...

"Oh gosh...I'm lost."

Kizuna wasn't good at reading maps, so she glanced at the small one in her hand one last time before tucking it back into the paper bag.

"Instead of relying on a map...it's better to rely on your senses, right?"

Kizuna rubbed her tiny nose with her forefinger and closed her eyes. She concentrated on the singing voices...and sniffed around.

Vere passum, immolatum

in cruce pro homine…

As she closed her eyes, she heard the lovely, secretive song of a strange tongue, flowing like a magical spell…

Kizuna was drawn to the sweet, honey-like resonance.

Is it this way…?

She walked toward the soft voice, which seemed to invite her.

The singing voices came closer…

Suddenly, a bright light shone on Kizuna's closed eyes.

Ah…

Kizuna, surprised at the brightness, cautiously opened her eyes. In front of her was not a thick forest, but a small meadow, softly illuminated by the early summer sun.

There were people in the middle of the clearing. She squinted to see them better…

The person who sat in the center was a white goddess. A slender, graceful, and beautiful goddess. Her lush black hair fell in waves—she wore a white Greek chiton and a semi-transparent rainbow-colored scarf around her shoulders, with a rattan basket placed on her knees.

The goddess raised the basket high into the sky, and an angel descended.

An angel in a tunic, with golden locks of hair and large white wings on her back, pranced lightly toward the goddess and…gently placed flowers into the basket.

The goddess tenderly stroked the angel's head…

The angel's mouth slightly opened.

Cujus latus
perforatum…

A free, innocent voice sang, softly lingering.

It was that hymn.

Drawn to the song, Kizuna entered the clearing. *Puff*…her foot sank into the thick grass with a strange softness.

Another small angel appeared in front of her.

This angel, with her hair tied in two buns, seemed a little more energetic, and she approached the goddess with a single flower in her hand, ready for offering…

But that angel stopped in her tracks. She noticed Kizuna and greeted her.

"Oh, Kizuna-chan. Great, so you've finished clean-up duty! I was worried about you since it was getting a little late. Were you able to find this place without getting lost?"

The friendly angel with glasses and hair buns was none other than Natsume Remon, Kizuna's classmate. She handed a flower to Kizuna.

"Ah! Remon-chan!" Kizuna, surprised, carefully inspected the scene. The beautiful goddess smiling at her was actually St. Lulim's Student Council President, Minamoto Chikaru.

Her long, lush black hair rippled about her, and the large red ribbons, which tied off the braids that draped beside each ear, looked hazy and illusionary under the bright sunlight, like red butterflies…

President Chikaru warmly welcomed Kizuna with a gentle gaze befitting her nickname, the "Holy Mother" of St. Lulim.

"Welcome, Kizuna-chan," Chikaru said softly. "Any later, and I would have become really worried. I'm so relieved. Come join us as we pick more flowers."

There was a thick book beside the basket on Chikaru's lap. The aged yellow page that read "Faceless Devil" flipped over as the leather cover closed.

The angel next to her, singing innocently, was Byakudan Kagome, a St. Lulim first-year student, who smiled happily.

Seeing that cheerful smile pleased Kizuna. She skipped toward the center of the field, because she couldn't wait to join them.

"Here, change into this outfit, my cute little angel," Chikaru suggested gently. She took the paper bag Kizuna was holding, opened it, and pulled out an angel's outfit for Kizuna.

"The Costume Club will dress as angels today. Let's gather lots of flowers to decorate our rooms at the Strawberry Dorms."

Kizuna replied, "Yes, Angel Kizuna will do her best!"

As Kizuna received her angel wings, she grinned and wondered if Chikaru-oneesama had baked a *financier*[4] as a reward for gathering the flowers.

Kizuna's smile was so sweet and delightful, and it made Chikaru blissful. *I want their school, St. Lulim, to shine more brightly.*

For a moment, a secret wish that she had recently begun to think about—and truly desired—resurfaced.

There were three prestigious all-girl schools on Astraea

Hill, and every year they held an *Étoile* competition to choose the best students to represent the three schools. One week had passed since the end of the first round. While Spica and Miator had entered strong couple candidates and had fought fiercely in the *Étoile* competition, the apparently unmotivated students at Lulim had made it seem as if they were unaffected by this event, letting yet another peaceful school day pass by.

Of the three schools, Lulim was the youngest and had a laid-back atmosphere, uninterested in sending out a couple that would win the *Étoile* crown for the glory of their school.

In fact, most of the students there just wanted to have a pleasant girls' school life in which to enjoy their various interest clubs.

Even today, Chikaru had invited three of her favorite underclassmen to take part in an activity at the edge of Maiden Park, otherwise known as the "Rear House" of Lulim.

My girls are so adorable... I want them to...

Chikaru, while as content as she could be, still felt an underlying ambition from the past that she had thought was too much to ask for.

An ambition she had secretly fantasized about.

Seeing the smiles of her endearing younger sisters, though...

Well, maybe for my girls' sake, I should...put that plan into action...I suppose.

For Kagome-chan, Kizuna-chan, and Remon-chan... Because I now have the three of you, my new stars, finally...it is probably time to execute a plan I've had on the backburner for such a long time.

A dream I thought would never be fulfilled…until now.

Yes…

Everyone has probably long forgotten, but just like the dark green brilliance of Miator's emerald star, and the silver intensity of Spica's white star…the red, burning passion of Lulim's crimson star also shines…

Everyone must be reminded of this…

Chikaru placed a hand on her heart and closed her eyes.

To the beloved girl with beautiful, crystal-clear eyes, Kusanagi Makoto,

This year, during the month of May, the time for the fresh green leaves of spring has arrived. How have you been, Mako-chan? Things over here remain…chilly, I suppose. Though it has been a while since the new school term began, I am still alone… I still cannot bear the fact that I sincerely feel your absence.

Why did you choose to go to such a cold, distant country like Russia?

I am so…lonely.

Yet another beautiful and pleasant day has passed for the innocent girls living on Astraea Hill. Even though it has only been a few years since that incident, I sometimes ponder about the strangeness of it.

But…maybe it was for the best.

A beautiful memory like that shouldn't be shared by everyone, but rather by a few people, such as you and I, who truly knew her…and it should shine and be cherished in only our hearts.

While she attended school here...she was known as one of the Five Stars of Spica, whose spot was never to be filled again, an unprecedented glory that will stay with her for eternity.

Tsk...I recall your habit of making exaggerated declarations like that, Mako-chan. Maybe I picked up the habit from you?

But...

I have since removed myself from such rigid expressions, reputations, and pride, and transferred to the peaceful Lulim, where I have settled down as the Student Council President, but...

You know what? Mako-chan...if you'd only come back...

I sometimes wonder...what Spica would have become. The reason being...as the windy month of May approaches, Astraea's most popular topic is the Étoile competition, of course. Had you been here, my strong-willed Mako-chan, you'd probably disregard this as an awful tradition of the all-girl schools, I'm sure—tsk—but in this year's Étoile competition, a new star has appeared.

A new star that would bring a wonderful, new wind to Astraea Hill.

In fact, it isn't just one—there are two stars!

News from Maiden Park crossed the ocean and traveled to the cold, northern country.

Fierce, gusty winds. A continent frozen over almost all year round.

A mosaic of stars shone above the cold Russian winds...

Crumple, crumple, crumple...

Kusanagi Makoto crushed the elegant letter from Chikaru with all her might.

She gripped it as hard as she could, not caring that she wouldn't be able to read the mangled paper ever again…

"I can't allow this to happen!!"

Her unbridled rage caused her fists to tremble. She felt the blood rising to her head.

She couldn't stand it anymore. She rushed to the window and swung the right and left window panels wide open, letting the freezing wind rush in and rustle her hair wildly.

The cold, continental winds of May chilled Makoto's cheeks. From the edge of the window, she glimpsed the thickly thronged Lenin Square in the distance.

Inside Makoto's humble apartment, where she had lived during her entire study abroad, she felt her old passion rekindled almost instantly. She closed her eyes and saw memories, flashing one after another in short clips.

The wonderful times she had spent with her dearly beloved, who was no longer there.

The tensed corners of Makoto's eyes gradually relaxed, but her face hardened like a cold porcelain doll's.

After years of surviving fierce competition and discrimination as a foreign student in Russia's St. Petersburg Music School, Makoto's smile had evolved to become just as horrific as the evil smiles of Alexander the Great and Ivan the Terrible. Her skin was a little lighter than a Caucasian's, and her pale but bright hazel hair was thin and straight, with razor-sharp ends falling over her light gray eyes.

She was small in stature but had well-proportioned limbs—it seemed as if she hadn't fully matured yet. But she had a womanly aura about her: cold and cruel, yet somewhat powerful.

Her eyes gleamed like a conquering emperor, lording over the world, and her thin peach-colored lips, which were delicate but seemed unyielding, finally moved.

"I…need to crush them."

She smirked. "I have to go back."

She clenched Chikaru's letter once more. Her grip almost tore the fragile stationery.

She glanced back at her room. It had been five years since Makoto had graduated from Spica Elementary School at the age of twelve and left to study abroad, so her room definitely reflected her tastes. Delicate antique furniture, black lace curtains, and a small chandelier purchased from the local flea market. Her closet was full of small, black tuxedos, and her cabinet contained several of her favorite violins.

Only those who have experienced life abroad, away from the luxuries of a wealthy home, could understand the starkness of these meager living conditions.

But even so…Makoto had chosen to live like this. She had made her decision after she had lost her beloved, back when she hadn't known any better, vowing to be true to her heart and to achieve her dreams for both herself and the person she had lost, ignoring her parents' objections to this path.

She gazed at the photo placed atop the bedside table.

Under the soft shade of bright young leaves, young Makoto

sat on a makeshift swing that hung from a large branch. Pushing her from behind was an older girl, who sort of resembled Makoto but seemed a little gentler. She was quite beautiful, with an endearing smile. The older, slender girl wore the stylish white uniform of Spica—an outfit Makoto had often dreamed she'd wear one day. She was the only gloriously brilliant, beautiful goddess, indomitable in this filthy world.

She shines upon me forever like Apollo, the sun god.

Makoto tried to repress the image—which seemed like a bubble, about to burst.

An image flashed through her mind.

Phaethon, who looked up to his father, Apollo, rode the chariot into the sky but fatally plunged to Earth. She saw herself looking to the sky and being burned, getting too close to the sun.

Eventually, Makoto recalled the content of Chikaru's letter.

Spica is rumored to have a strong chance of winning this year's Étoile competition, because Spica's supposed number-one seed, Otori Amane, the "Prince," is in the running...

Many students from the three schools have predicted the victory of Spica's biggest star in history...

If she succeeds in defeating Miator's strongest candidate, Hanazono Shizuma, who is running in the Étoile competition for an unprecedented second time...she will surely make her mark in Spica's history as the best Étoile ever...

The Spica students seem to place so much hope on her, as if they waited for the Messiah...

But in reality, this self-proclaimed "shy, bashful" star of Spica is rather unmotivated, and we cannot overlook the fact that she openly displays favoritism toward a particular third-year student...

The Five Stars are not allowed to be monopolized by any single person, but as the top star, Otori Amane has abused her status and popularity to openly show her affection for one specific girl, mentioned above...

On top of that, the girl receiving her affection is a new transfer student who just arrived this spring... an average girl with no outstanding traits whatsoever... Because of Amane's desire for a cheap thrill with this new girl, one of the rules of the Étoile competition, which are based on Astraea's long traditions, was "revised" to accommodate this selfish couple...

Amid the excitement surrounding the rule-bending antics and the upcoming second round of the Étoile competition, Spica students who have upheld the traditions of Spica have begun to have deep-rooted concerns...

If Spica isn't careful, the clever sixth-year student, Shizuma— with the help of the crafty Miator Student Council President, Rokujo Miyuki—might claim the crown for Miator instead...

The soft-spoken Chikaru sprinkled her letter with beautiful, eloquent expressions...but Makoto got the gist of the situation.

Though Chikaru mentioned "two new stars of Astraea," she only focused on Spica's star—Makoto didn't think that was a problem.

But in the letter, Chikaru had written about last year's *Étoile*, Hanazono Shizuma—Makoto had heard her name back in elementary school. A gifted student from a prominent, influential family, who seemed to be infatuated with a rare transfer student who had arrived this spring…and even though sixth-year students like her were supposed to remove themselves from school activities…she had insisted on entering the *Étoile* competition for the second year in a row…

Makoto didn't care much about the Miator student, because she was obsessed with the situation brewing in Spica.

"I can't believe this…"

How could such a thing occur at St. Spica, the place where her dearly beloved had shone?

At Spica…the valiant and well-ordered St. Spica that Makoto's dearly beloved had adored…

Makoto really had loved her. She had truly adored and admired the person who had been the reigning star of Spica.

That's why…

It's unforgivable. I can't let a fake star bring down the Spica she loved so dearly…before it gets any worse, I'll just have to…

Makoto pulled open the drawer to take out her passport, as she thought about the ending of Chikaru's letter.

The past several days…I don't know why, but for some reason I sense I'll be seeing you soon, Mako-chan. Even though I know it's not possible, since you still live in Russia.

Perhaps I was just dreaming. But it would give me pleasure if, perchance, you saw the same dream, Mako-chan…

I have enclosed a four-leaf clover, picked from Lulim's secret garden. I must tell you, it required a lot of effort to find it.

I hope the power of this legendary charm will somehow bring us together in our dreams.

I truly want to see your beautiful face once again…

Your childhood friend who shares the same adoration of her,
Chikaru…

Ding dong…

At St. Miator, the warning for the first dismissal bell rang.

"Oh no! It's time already…"

At the front of the classroom, Nagisa wiped the aging, cream-colored keys of the organ that stood next to the podium.

Nagisa's ponytail bounced energetically—it matched her bubbly personality—and her brand new, charcoal-gray school uniform, with its classic and elegant design, rustled noisily.

Four fifteen…only fifteen minutes before the first dismissal bell.

Because Nagisa was not involved in after-school activities, she had to leave school immediately after clean-up duty, or she might not make it back to the Strawberry Dorms in time for the first curfew.

"Listening to all the fun conversations…made me lose track of time," Nagisa remarked. She scratched her head with the hand that held a dirty rag, leaving a dust bunny caught in her hair.

"Goodness, Nagisa, don't do that…your head will be filthy."

Shizuma stood halfway inside the classroom doorway. She took a step closer and reached for Nagisa's hair.

When Shizuma's delicate hand brushed the nape of Nagisa's neck, she shuddered at the sudden, strange sensation, and her neck twitched.

Shizuma made to brush off Nagisa's hair, but because of Nagisa's ticklish reaction, her hand stayed on the neck and instinctively moved...

"Kyahahaha!"

This time, Nagisa squirmed and trapped Shizuma's hand under her chin.

Shizuma found herself amused at this unexpected turn of events...she hadn't meant to tickle Nagisa, but...she decided to wiggle her fingers, caught between Nagisa's chin and collar bone...

Tickle, tickle, tickle...

Nagisa responded to Shizuma's tickles with a "Gyahahaha, eeeek!" and laughed loudly.

She was extremely ticklish.

"Ah, no, please stop, Shizuma-oneesama... I'm very ticklish! I have been since childhood..."

Nagisa, reacting in such an honest and innocent manner, blushed as she giggled, which only urged Shizuma to tease some more...

Shizuma snickered as she continued to tickle Nagisa. "Goodness, Nagisa, I want to let go, but...I can't move my hand if you keep clamping down on it..."

"Kyaah, it tickles so much...oh no..."

By the time they stopped laughing, they noticed the stares.

Cold stares, from the other students on clean-up duty.

Jealous stares…

When Shizuma came to the fourth-year classroom to invite Nagisa to come to her home in Hokkaido, the other classmates were both nervous and elated to see the number-one star of the school, but at the same time they closely observed them…

Oh no, I did it again…

Nagisa shook her head and tried to remind herself. *I need to get used to this treatment when I'm with Shizuma-oneesama…*

About three weeks ago, after the first round of the *Étoile* competition had concluded in early May, Nagisa had made a decision…because during the first half of the first round, the *cadette* event, she had uncovered Shizuma's shocking past.

Shizuma used to have a "younger sister," whom she had truly loved. Her name had been Sakuragi Kaori—she had been a very beautiful girl—and she and Shizuma had been a perfect couple, accepted by everyone, but Shizuma had had to bid her a painful, eternal farewell.

Last year, Shizuma had claimed the *Étoile* crown just for her…

Nagisa felt that she didn't have the right to stand next to Shizuma and participate in the *Étoile* competition… During the second half of the first round, the *aînée* event, she had wanted to disappear. When the round, the first of three in the *Étoile* competition, was about to conclude, Nagisa had wanted to withdraw from the competition, but Shizuma somehow had convinced her to stay…and had swept her away.

She had cried and embraced Nagisa. And after the event ended, Nagisa had discovered Shizuma's true feelings. Once she understood Shizuma's loneliness…and her emotional scars…Nagisa, who didn't have much to offer, wanted to help Shizuma any way she could.

For Hanazono Shizuma, the proud star who had lost her most beloved.

Shizuma's most beloved younger sister in the past… It was agonizing to think about, so Nagisa vowed not to dwell on it.

She recalled what Tamao, her classmate and best friend, had said to her.

"*Shizuma only seems at peace when she's with you… Shizuma-sama might just be flirting with you, though, so you can't be so serious about it…*

"*After all, how often do you get the chance to partner with the school's number-one star—much less a person coming from one of Japan's most influential families? You should take this opportunity to have the experience of a lifetime and enjoy the Étoile competition for all it's worth.*"

Nagisa remembered Tamao-chan's calmness and lighthearted smile and felt relieved.

Okay, Tamao-chan…I'll go for it!

Nagisa reaffirmed her decision. After the *aînée* event, Nagisa hadn't had the heart to tell Tamao what Shizuma had revealed to her. She knew she shouldn't be the one to tell Tamao about Shizuma's deep sorrow and loneliness.

But Tamao had said something that rang a bell with Nagisa.

"*Shizuma-sama definitely likes your happy-go-lucky attitude.*"

Nagisa said to herself, *If there's one thing I'm confident of, it's being cheerful...right? Even at my previous school my classmates said my most outstanding trait was being cheerful...*

So I shouldn't be depressed like this any longer. I need to bring Shizuma-sama's spirits up...

Collecting herself, Nagisa hopped around and spun toward Shizuma.

"But Shizuma-oneesama! Your home has a ranch so big that horses can run around? Wow! But I didn't know your home was in Hokkaido, Shizuma-oneesama... With your family so far away, you must be quite lonely...ah, maybe the reason you like to have cute girls around you is to cover your loneliness or something."

Shizuma was taken aback by Nagisa's babbling. She just stared back. "Oh, Nagisa-chan, I have several ranches. The home in Hokkaido is just one of them..."

"No, don't hide your feelings! I just..." Nagisa choked on her words.

Worried, Shizuma tried to peer into Nagisa's face, but Nagisa blocked her with one hand.

"You came all by yourself from Hokkaido, so far away... you must have been really lonely. To tell you the truth, I was worried when I was told I was transferring to Miator. I didn't know if I could handle living in a dormitory...um, but Shizuma-oneesama pulled me into one thing after another, so I never had a chance to feel homesick... Ahahaha," Nagisa laughed in embarrassment.

Nagisa suddenly became serious and peered into Shizuma's face for a closer look.

"Shizuma-oneesama, you've attended Miator ever since kindergarten, right?"

Shizuma was unusually surprised and over-whelmed by Nagisa's intensity. "Y-Yes…that's correct." *What is my adorable little Nagisa up to now?*

Nagisa's large eyes grew even larger, and she stared at Shizuma. "Shizuma-oneesama, I feel so sorry for you…"

A small tear rolled out of Nagisa's eyes. She hastily rubbed it away.

"You've endured so much since kindergarten, being really far apart from your mother and living all alone in the Strawberry Dorms…"

The world of *A Little Princess* came to Nagisa's mind, and she imagined Shizuma as the character from the book.

Images of little Shizuma flashed one after another. Little Shizuma unable to sleep alone in her room, crying. Little Shizuma running toward the sunset because she missed her mother so much. Little Shizuma on the phone in tears as she talked with her mother…

"Nagisa…"

Shizuma was stunned by Nagisa's reaction, and was about to explain that her home in Hokkaido was just a vacation home, that her real home was only an hour away, and she visited her family at least once a month…but she couldn't.

What a kind-hearted girl…

Her heart felt so warm and fuzzy, and she slowly cradled Nagisa in her arms.

Most of the students here, including me, are used to this

lifestyle, so as a new transfer student, you're probably more homesick than we are, Nagisa.

"Nagisa..." Shizuma said, as she raised Nagisa's face. She looked into Nagisa's tear-filled eyes and thought, *Oh, I messed up. Instead of inviting her for horseback riding at my home in Hokkaido, I should have asked her to visit a castle in Ireland or something. That way, Nagisa would have become even more flustered and cried out, "Oh, Shizuma-oneesama, I feel so sorry you're so far away from your homeland," or something like that...*

Wicked thoughts crossed Shizuma's mind as she placed a finger under Nagisa's chin.

This maneuver was quite natural for Shizuma, who was experienced with girls... Her face approached Nagisa's...and she planted her lips on Nagisa's forehead.

"Err, I don't mean to rain on your party...but may I interrupt for just a moment?"

"Ah... Aaaaaaah!" Nagisa cried out.

Shizuma and Nagisa were blocking the doorway. Beside them stood a girl, her black hair bobbed, the bladelike ends slightly swaying... Rokujo Miyuki, the extremely intelligent Student Council President of Miator. She hugged a large, black attendance roster book and leather folder to her chest.

Nagisa hastily pulled away from Shizuma and used her hands to wave off the puff of peach-colored sigh that Shizuma had left behind in the air.

Then they realized...all the other students in the classroom had left.

Miyuki's comment was cold. "Whatever drove you to flirt with her, even though she is…" She gave a sideways glance at Nagisa. "Even though she is a rather plain transfer student, I believe you lack grace with such behavior, Shizuma-sama…"

Nagisa flapped her mouth, as if trying to apologize silently… *Oh no, I'm sorry for looking down…*

She noticed a different shadow arrive from behind her, and cautiously looked up to see…

"Ah, Tamao-chan…"

Tamao was a beautiful girl who was mature and calm for her age, with long, bluish-tinted hair tied up in a ballet bun, revealing her amazingly white and beautiful neck.

Tamao stood behind Miyuki and chuckled silently.

Shizuma caught Tamao's movement out of the corner of her eye and replied, "Oh, I don't believe so, because one of the great things about being with Nagisa-chan is the openness of our relationship."

Shizuma stood before Miyuki, fully poised, and smiled in a way that was different than when she was alone with Nagisa… an expression that was somewhat cold and conceited. She looked down at Miyuki.

Nagisa noticed Shizuma-oneesama's eyes had a tendency to tighten at the corners a bit when she was around people other than herself.

Miyuki didn't flinch. "Tsk…well, I suppose I can overlook this today, because soon you won't be able to share intimate moments with her quite as freely…so please enjoy it while you can…"

"What do you mean by that?" Shizuma snapped.

Miyuki was pleased to have evoked such a harsh reaction. She smiled and lowered her eyes. "I cannot say it here... But if all of you are available for a bit...will you please follow me?"

Nagisa just stood there, gaping, and Tamao, amused at the sight, muffled her laughter. Shizuma just frowned in discontent.

While the uncomfortable meeting between last year's *Étoile*, the Student Council President, and the two girls ensued...

"Okay, is the hat tipped at the right angle?"

"Yup. Put that pipe in your mouth, and you're all set!"

"Let Mr. Teddy Bear join us, too..."

Inside one of the rooms at St. Lulim's Club Building. The Student Council President—or more accurately, the Costume Club President—Minamoto Chikaru, was in the center, with Kizuna, Remon, and Kagome surrounding her, excited.

They were changing into their outfits.

Clothes were strewn about the club room. On the sewing table lay a beige, caped trench coat with a Burberry checked lining, a large, glossy pipe, and the distinctive deer-stalker cap... Today's transformation theme was "Famous Detective."

Kizuna assisted Kagome, fumbling with her blouse buttons. Byakudan Kagome, a first-year student, was the smallest of the four, with her hair in spiral curls like a French doll—a distinctive feature not commonly found among St. Lulim students. For some reason, she was really fond of Kizuna and tagged along… and naturally, she had become a member of the Costume Club. Kagome looked really great in silky blouses with large frills.

"Okay, once you tie this ribbon, you're all set!" Kizuna said, but Kagome tilted her head to the side and muttered, "I don't know how to…tie a ribbon."

"Oh, of course…*I figured so,*" Kizuna mumbled. She picked up a small ribbon from the table. "Shall I tie it on for you?"

Kagome responded with a smile, which in turn made Kizuna smile too.

Their exchange of smiles brightened the room like a warm spring day.

Next to the two girls… "I wonder…were there eyeglasses during the time of Sherlock Holmes?"

Remon, sweating slightly, wore the coat and cap and fiddled with her glasses. The stems of the glasses didn't seem to fit inside the deer-stalker cap.

Watching Remon, Kizuna exclaimed, "What, so Holmes is a *real* person?!"

Chikaru clapped her hands, "Okay, no more talking! Those who are ready to play out their roles, please line up here."

"Okay!" The three girls lined up.

"Well then, are you ready? My cute Kizuna 'Holmes,' Remon 'Watson,' and…my little Kagome 'Mrs. Hudson.' You girls have a secret mission to accomplish!"

Chikaru smiled gently. "Soon, a little prince will arrive in

Spica. She is sad and lonely, but nonetheless is a pure-hearted and very cute prince. The three of you will help the prince…"

Chikaru stopped in mid-sentence and gave a teasing wink.

Back in Spica…

"She's so snobby because Prince Amane likes her…"

"Shh…she can hear us, you know…"

The bitter criticisms could be heard from afar.

Konohana Hikari leaned on the window ledge and looked at the sky outside. When she heard the wisecracks, her back twitched a bit, but she didn't have the courage to turn and face the gossipers. Her facial expressions indicated her worsening insecurity, and she hunched her small, fragile shoulders even more.

She tried to ignore their comments as she looked to the sky. Her hair swirled about her shoulders, creating soft shadows on her white uniform.

Sigh… Hikari sighed in her heart.

White clouds slowly drifted across the vast blue sky above Astraea Hill. The green grass below billowed violently in the wind, almost to the point of snapping in half.

The air was damp. Maybe a storm was approaching…the rainy season would arrive soon.

The deep inner part of Hikari's nose suddenly became hot, and tears formed in her eyes. Teardrops rolled down her cheeks. She was ashamed of herself.

Before anyone noticed, Hikari wiped her tears with the back of her hand.

I can't...I can't cry over things like this...

She tensed her stomach.

I am allowed to be with Amane-sama. I can't cry over things like this...I need to be strong. I have to do my best for Amane-sama. Amane smiled and said, "I didn't want to enter the Étoile competition, but I can bear through it as long as I'm with you, Hikari..."

There's nothing special about me, but the least I can do is not be a burden for Amane-oneesama.

So, I can't cry over things like this...

The caustic remarks behind her back escalated.

"She doesn't realize how much trouble she's causing Amane-sama... Because of her, Spica is split between the Student Council followers, who have allowed Amane-sama's favoritism, and those who oppose the Student Council's decision...it's split the school in half! She's the reason behind the loss of Spica's unity..."

Ohh... Hikari couldn't hold back anymore. The tears trickled down uncontrollably.

Gadunk...

As Hikari began to cry...Nanto Yaya, who had watched Hikari the whole time, rose from her chair at the back of the room. Yaya's long, straight hair swayed, and underneath her sharp, jagged bangs, which hung down to the middle of her forehead, her eyes were full of determination.

"Hikari…" Yaya's tight uniform squeaked across her chest as she reached out to place her hand on Hikari's back.

Yaya had mixed feelings.

She was definitely fond of Hikari. Ever since she had first laid eyes on her, she had known that Hikari was her type. She was cute like an angel, innocent and naïve, and of course shy but honest. On top of that, Hikari liked anything and everything beautiful, like paintings, sculptures, even interior decorations… which revealed a bit of Hikari's self-absorbed nature. There were times when timid Hikari acted out in bursts of unpredictable and outrageous behavior.

She was perfect in every way.

Hikari was Yaya's favorite type, period. Yaya wished she could pamper Hikari.

But she didn't want to protect Hikari. Not like Amane, the silent prince.

In Yaya's mind, Hikari didn't need any protection, since she had the inner strength to shine on her own. In contrast to herself, who had no doubts about her way of life, and lived it the way she wanted to…Hikari had a brilliant radiance and was quite precious.

Yaya believed the way she felt toward Hikari was indeed friendship. But somehow it didn't seem like a friendship…it just didn't sit right with her.

Somewhere in her heart, Yaya wanted Hikari's body and soul all to herself.

She enjoyed holding Hikari's hand as they walked. But in reality Yaya yearned for something more intimate. She wasn't satisfied with the casual physical contact gained from holding hands.

She wanted something more from Hikari…a more basic and instinctive desire to have somebody as her own.

Yaya knew Hikari's body had many hidden attributes, and she wanted to feel every inch of her body, to touch her…and to explore each other's bodies.

Ohh, I just want to tear everything apart and melt away with Hikari.

Yaya's desire was to connect deeply with the other girl…

Maybe…I should've been born a man.

Yaya sneered at herself. *If I was a man, I'd force myself onto her…and take Hikari once and for all. But of course I wouldn't dare say that to Hikari…*

Even if I said it, I probably wouldn't act on it anyway.

Yaya mouth went bitter with those thoughts, and she called out to Hikari once again.

"Hikari, don't stand there alone. Come here…"

Suddenly…*rattle rattle rattle…*

The classroom door slid open, and Yaya's voice was drowned out by its sound.

The whole class fell into silence at the sight of the person at the door. Yaya's hand stopped in mid-air.

"Hikari!"

When one visited a different classroom, the school custom was to announce your name and state the purpose of your visit to the student closest to the door…but the person at the door didn't bother to follow that rule. She just barged in and called out to Hikari.

The voice of St. Spica's tall, short-haired prince, Otori Amane, pierced the classroom, stopping everyone in their tracks. The reaction of the students in the class was a mixture of excitement and surprise.

The heroine of the scene, Konohana Hikari, spun around as she dried her tears. "Amane-sama!"

Hikari scampered across the room to greet Amane. The two of them rushed out of the room together and disappeared down the hallway.

The door slid back weakly.

As soon as it closed, the class erupted.

"What was *that* all about…?"

…*Oh well.* Yaya sighed to herself. *Hikari takes all the heat, because Amane-oneesama is so boorish…*

Yaya couldn't do anything about it but sigh.

Though Amane claimed to have no interest in girls, she somehow felt so hopelessly attracted to Hikari. Yaya had a vague understanding of Amane's unexplainable feelings.

The couple acted like a boy and girl, attracted to each other, but didn't understand the true meaning of love.

Amane-oneesama is probably in constant suspense, watching frail little Hikari being so cute and tantalizing… She probably feels she must protect Hikari.

But Yaya didn't want to meddle in their affairs. She could have easily given advice—based on her own torrid affairs with girls—on how to avoid friction with other students.

The reason she refrained from giving advice was not because Amane was a superstar or an upperclassman. Whether

Yaya realized it or not, her feelings held worry and anticipation intermixed…

Hikari and Amane were leaning precariously over a dangerous ledge, and they would either walk toward a happy ending or end in a painful breakup. Yaya wanted them to travel the natural course of fate and didn't want to alter it with her advice.

Amidst the flurry of excitement still buzzing in the classroom, Yaya walked to the window where Hikari had stood moments ago. And just like Hikari, she looked to the sky.

Thin gray clouds steadily drifted across the sky like muddy streams.

Envisioning Hikari looking to the sky and having obsessive thoughts of Amane tortured Yaya's heart.

"Oh well, what can I do now…?" Yaya murmured, while a bird—a pure white dove—flew across the dewy sky.

The dove flew in a gentle curve to the west and disappeared toward St. Lulim's School.

Marks of dried tears remained on Hikari's cheeks. Amane was brimming with anger when she saw Hikari's predicament, and she vented her frustrations. "I'll explain to everyone that you entered the *Étoile* competition just for me, Hikari," she blurted as they walked down the hall.

"I-It's okay… If you did that, Amane-sama, then I would only cause…"

...Amane-sama to have more pain.

Hikari couldn't finish the sentence, because she was too afraid...

Unfortunately, Amane misread Hikari's silence. "Yeah...I understand. If I said that, then it would cause you even more trouble, right?"

Amane laughed...but she looked a bit sad. *I wish she'd depend on me more.*

"I'm sorry, Hikari. It's all my fault. I can't even help you at a time like this..."

Hikari saw Amane's troubled look and didn't know what to say next. "N-No... It's my fault, because I'm such a coward." She looked at Amane with eyes still moist from tears. "I've come to realize that maybe I don't fit in at...at this school. I haven't been able to keep up with Spica's customs...and I sometimes feel like I should just vanish or something... It's quite embarrassing, but I admit there are times when I've wanted to run away from it all...so I wouldn't have to go through all this grief..."

She recalled the painful incident in the classroom just a few minutes ago. What Hikari had actually meant to say was *"with Amane-sama"* instead of *"at this school."*

"But...if I did that..." Hikari's voice shook. "If I did that... then I'd never..."

She tried to hold back her tears again. She didn't want to be a crybaby in front of Amane. She bit her tiny lips as hard as she could, and looked off to the side to avoid showing her tear-filled eyes.

"I thought I'd never...see you again, so..."

Hearing Hikari's quivering little voice was so enthralling, Amane curled her arms around Hikari's shoulders.

Squeeze...the tight, form-fitting Spica uniform wrinkled at the shoulders.

At the same time, Hikari's heart was also squeezed tightly. "A-Amane-sama…"

Amane brought her lips close to Hikari's ear as she whispered in the sweetest, gentlest voice, "Hikari, please feel better."

Her hair brushed Hikari's ear. "And…please be with me forever."

A light, peach-colored mist dizzily formed above Hikari's head. Amane chuckled in pleasure as she continued, "You know, Hikari, what a strange coincidence. I had the same thoughts run through my mind a while back. I also thought that maybe I didn't fit in at this school at all…and I wanted to run away from here once and for all…"

Amane remembered when she had begun to be called the "Prince" of Spica.

She hadn't received much attention during elementary school. But once she'd made it into junior high, the students had begun to treat her like a star. The shy and bashful Amane had felt really uncomfortable with the sudden attention.

The presents and love letters Amane had received only added pain to her grief, since she had just wanted to be left alone. Longing for a peaceful school life, she had often thought of transferring to a different school.

Amane could laugh about it now…because it had happened so long ago.

Her face lightened as she chuckled and thought, *Oh, when did I get over those feelings anyway...? Did I overcome this depression...when I met Hikari?*

Hikari, unable to believe that Amane had had a similar depressing situation, stared back at her, though it was still a sidelong look. "You felt helpless too, Amane-sama?"

"Yes, I did. I wanted to run away so many times from this restrictive hill full of girls. So I was just like you, Hikari." Amane smiled. "Well, let's go..."

Amane led Hikari down the hall.

She was looking for a place outside to be alone with Hikari.

CHAPTER 2

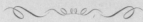

On Festival Night, the Omen of a Misfortune Avoids a Red Sign and Jumps

Despite the adverse conditions that surrounded Amane and Hikari, their love for each other deepened at Spica…and in the classroom on the top floor of the school, which overlooked the spacious Maiden Park, the students discussed the future of the couple.

The brilliant white star of Spica shone as bright young minds gathered in this room…known as the Student Council room.

"I told you so! If you had entered me in the *Étoile* competition, none of this would've happened!! But…instead that *little girl* is partnered with *my* Amane-sama…grr!"

Cough cough cough…

Kenjo Kaname got so excited, she violently choked on her own words.

Long limbs extended from Kaname's tan, fit figure. She looked rather masculine, and her brutish mannerisms and attitude, coupled with a lack of feminine qualities, only emphasized her macho demeanor.

"Oh please, Kaname, just chill out." Kiyashiki Momomi, who sat next to Kaname, offered her a cup of tea.

Coughing, Kaname dumped the tea down her throat in one gulp...

"Ack! W-W-What is this stuff...?"

"Oh, do you like it? I've been drinking *dokudami cha*[5] these days."

"*Dokudami*...?"

"It's good for health and beauty."

"How lame! I don't need a weird tea to improve my health or beauty! The only person in the world who doesn't think I'm beautiful is probably Amane-sama anyway...don't get me off track now!"

"Aww, I just wanted to soothe your throat because you yelled so much, Kaname-chan."

"Enough! Anyway, I think we got ourselves into this mess because the Student Council is so half-assed."

"Gee, you're such a party-pooper, Kaname." In response to Kaname's raised fists, Momomi gave back a very fake smile with her non-Japanese facial features and mumbled something to the panda on her folding fan.

"Kenjo-san, this matter has been settled already!" Spica's Student Council President, Tomori Shion, pounded the table as she stood, but her eyes seemed dark and gloomy from fatigue.

The other students who sat at the large triangular table fell silent. Shion's slim body seemed thinner than usual. Her long, chestnut hair framed her prominent cheeks, which lacked their normal, intellectual sharpness. Even her chiseled chin seemed recessed and pointier than usual.

The table still vibrated from the impact. White papers slid out of a black envelope, and a folder glided out of a clear plastic portfolio, scattering across the table.

Kaname viciously eyed the black envelope, and so did Shion, looking at it with cold, hollow eyes.

Kaname huffed and calmly sat back down. Though she seemed to have been put back in her place, she spoke again as her reflected silhouette filled the crystal glass wall behind her.

"Shion, you might be acting high and mighty because you're known as Spica's intellectual Snow Queen and Student Council President, but maybe you were careless about this one. I can't believe you didn't choose me, a sure-fire winner, but instead chose a pathetic newcomer—a third-year transfer student who only arrived at Spica last fall—to enter into the *Étoile* competition as Amane-sama's partner. And taking advantage of our weak entry, Miator unexpectedly entered last year's *Étoile* for this year's contest, to compete for a second time!

"Well, they've got their problems too, and at least Amane-sama managed to win the first round, just barely. But knowing how Shizuma-sama hates to lose, she'll strive to win the second round to regain her pride. Spica is split between the supporters and non-supporters of Amane-sama's partner. And Amane-sama probably isn't even aware of the concerns of the Spica students! Argh, I hate to say this, but Amane-sama has lost her senses, chasing after that transfer student!

"Humph. You know, the Miator Student Council President—the Princess of Rokujo-in—probably schemed this whole plot from the beginning!" Kaname scowled.

"Kaname-oneesama, your comments are a bit too harsh," Okuwaka Tsubomi, a first-year student and Student Council Secretary, remarked cautiously, mustering all her courage to do so.

"Well, I knew this would happen! I was against this from the start, but the Student Council President supported Amane-sama's stance and forced us to..."

Momomi cut in with a small voice. "But Kaname, you eventually agreed to the idea because you didn't want Amane-sama to hate you, right?"

"Wha—? N-No, you're wrong, Momomi! I agreed for the benefit of Spica!" Kaname was flabbergasted, her face red.

Tsubomi interjected again, "A-Anyway, Kaname-oneesama! Spica did win the first round, so please don't attack President Shion so harshly." Tsubomi wore a headband, which neatly gathered her long, peach-colored hair. She tilted her head and eyes toward Shion.

Shion, lost in her thoughts, stared intently at the scattered documents on the table. Kaname sensed Shion's dilemma and finally zipped her lips. Everyone else at the table re-examined the opened documents.

On the black envelope, the addressee's name was written in silver.

To All Spica Students

The contents of the letter explained at great length the

writers' dissatisfaction regarding the proceedings of the *Étoile* competition and concluded in an angry and almost threatening manner.

...Who is responsible for depriving Spica of the sure victory, which was supposed to be claimed with a flawless plan and Prince Amane's participation, but has instead resulted in such a mess?

We believe that all Spica students, including ourselves, have long awaited the day when Amane-sama would become a fifth-year student and enter the Étoile competition.

We cannot accept the fact that Amane-sama was forced to partner not with any of the Five Stars on campus, but rather an unknown, less-than-reputable girl...we can only imagine the tribulations of Amane-sama, having to deal with such a lame duck dragging her down, and Spica students will surely lament our star's dire predicament.

In fact, in order to give the new transfer student an advantage, a new rule, that worked against currently attending students, was forcefully established, causing the other schools to raise suspicions of foul play, and as a result we have utterly insulted St. Miator, our long-standing rival, by our lack of fairness.

The truth is, no matter what the obstacle may be, the invincible Amane-sama would have surely claimed victory. But because of poor, unnecessary decisions, resulting in an unfair advantage, Amane-sama's reputation has been marred...a truly unforgivable act.

The longstanding dream of regaining the Étoile crown brought all of the Spica students together, but these recent disturbances are great sins which have divided the unity of our students. The blunders of the

Spica Student Council are much too obvious.

Be prepared to receive God's judgment.

May the wrath of God punish all of you for the arrogant sins you have committed… for you are all in the twisted Tower of Babel, about to fall to its doom.

Pheew… Shion sighed. She smiled self-mockingly and reached for the file next to the letter. She was apathetic as she flipped the pink plastic cover of the report file open.

Sponsored by the Spica Student Council
Étoile Competition Round 2:
> Love Ordeal *(L'Épreuve d'amour)*

Event: Astraea Cup

The Astraea Cup—a small tennis tournament held between *Étoile* contestants.

This sport, which had originated in ancient Egypt and had later been known as the French nobles' sport, was often selected as a competition event because it required fairness and teamwork between partners.

The tennis tournament was the second-round *cadette* event. The rules went on for several pages and ended with the tournament chart.

It was a doubles tournament. The nine couples that had survived the first round were listed in the tournament brackets.

The last couple listed on the chart was not placed in any of the brackets.

Exempt—will proceed to the third round:
St. Spica Girls' Institute
Otori Amane, Fifth Year, Class Trois
Konohana Hikari, Third Year, Class Un

Tap tap tap...Shion's forefinger tapped on the couple's names.

"You know...this was the result of the drawing, fair and square..." Shion muttered.

Tsubomi stood up again in excitement. "Absolutely! I'm the one who made the drawing box and made sure there was no cheating involved when choosing the ticket! Besides, there were nine couples, so everyone knew one couple would be exempt from this round! When the ticket I chose last was Amane-sama, I was ecstatic to know that Amane-sama was not only beautiful and strong, but also had good fortune on her side..."

Momomi walked to the end of the room—where Tsubomi and the other underclassmen sat—and placed a hand on Tsubomi's shoulder...

"Yes...we know that, Tsubomi-chan. But unfortunately, they're not upset about that. The Spica Student Council is under suspicion for conducting the first round of the contest unfairly, and then Amane-sama's couple ends up being exempt from the second round, based on Spica's Student Council's selection method..."

"Basically, people think it's fishy the Spica Student Council did the drawing in secret, inside the room, rather than doing it out in the open. Do you get it, little girl?" Kaname interjected— deliberately cutting off Momomi. She pulled out a red rose and used it to indicate the black envelope.

"No matter how fair the selection was, if the result is this, then the skeptics will see everything as very black and very wrong. Especially with Amane-sama, who is seen as an impeccable prince on a white horse who can do no wrong. Suspicions swirl around her more than ever, so the blame easily flies towards scoundrels like us at the Student Council."

Kaname eloquently pronounced "scoundrels" with a thick, heavy French accent.

"That's why I should have been her partner…"

"No, the Student Council is not made up of scoundrels— no, no—you're the only scoundrel here, Kaname-oneesama!" Tsubomi retorted.

"Wh-What!?" Kaname roared.

"Pfft, how true…" Momomi chortled. "You lost this one, Kaname-chan." Smiling at Tsubomi, she eyed Kaname.

Please shut up already… Momomi thought. "So…Shion-chan." She turned back toward the head of the table, where the Student Council President sat.

Momomi faced Shion squarely and asked in an unusually calm but serious manner, "Well, President Tomori—since you are called our Snow Queen—I assume you've devised a plan to get Spica out of this crisis? Will you please…share your thoughts with us?"

The room went quiet…again.

Shion, who until then had been flipping through the files silently, smirked. No one could tell whether her smile indicated certain victory or was just another self-mocking gesture. She responded to Momomi's question with a chilly laugh.

"My thoughts…? I don't have any…and even if I did, I assume nobody would care to listen to them…"

She glanced at Kaname.

Kaname felt awkward. "I didn't mean it that way…"

But before the talkative Kaname could blabber on, Shion continued, "If…I have everyone's trust and confidence…I might have a way to get Spica out of this crisis. But…this will definitely go against our Student Council's policy to fully support Prince Amane—a total 180-degree turn."

She looked at the file she was holding and bit her lip—full of regret.

"If everyone here is interested, I will introduce the person who brought this plan to me…"

She spoke slowly, articulating every word, as if she hated the words coming out of her mouth.

And outside the room…

Tnk tnk tnk tnk…

The top floor of St. Spica's resembled an office building, full of white walls, glass, and steel—and the sound of graceful footsteps, echoing on the white marble floor.

The footsteps grew louder as they approached…

The silent Student Council room…

Creak…

One side of the large double doors opened.

"Oh my…everyone is here…"

Outside the open door, smiling…was St. Lulim's Student

Council President, Minamoto Chikaru.

"We were waiting for you, Lulim Student Council President…please, come in." Shion looked defeated as she offered the chair next to her…to Chikaru.

A warm puff of air.

Warm steam rose, carrying the strong aroma of the thick and smooth Assam tea.

"Today I prepared the Assam Tiger tea with lots of golden tips!"

Chiyo, wearing an apron full of frills, offered the tea to the assembled girls. She had been assigned to Tamao and Nagisa's room the previous week—as a room assistant. Room assistants were a tradition at the school: a first-year student would be assigned to a room of upperclassmen, where she was supposed to serve tea and assist with cleaning. Chiyo was always tagging along with the two girls, so Miyuki had caught her and strong-armed her into becoming the pair's room assistant.

"Would you like some milk?" Chiyo's cheeks flushed as she held the warm pot of milk, because she was delighted at this unusual gathering. There were five teacups on the round table.

"Just a little…" said Tamao.

"Yeah, I want lots of milk!" said Nagisa.

"I'll have some," said Miyuki.

"I…don't need any," Shizuma said.

Everyone stopped at that last piercing comment.

"Wh-What?" Hanazono Shizuma blurted, surprised as everyone looked at her. She received a barrage of protests.

"But…this is Assam tea?!"

"And because it's served as afternoon tea, you're supposed to have milk in it…"

"I cannot believe that you'd ignore our tea customs…"

But between the objections…

"Um, is it really…really…strange not to have milk in this tea…?" Nagisa inquired.

"Ahahaha… Oh, Nagisa…" Shizuma chuckled, feeling quite relieved and refreshed at last.

"Well, these girls are…how should I say this? Basically, they have very rigid, conservative mindsets. Assam tea must have milk in it, Earl Grey tea must be served as iced tea, and Darjeeling tea must be straight…it's a ridiculous rule, really."

"*Sigh*…so tea has all these rules… I didn't know, since we only ever had teabags at home…eheheh."

As Nagisa rubbed her head in embarrassment, Shizuma hugged her around the shoulders, looked at everyone, and stated proudly, "Goodness, Nagisa, you don't need to conform to these standards—there's nothing wrong with drinking straight Assam tea. We won't get punished for that, will we? You should be able to drink it any way you'd like. And live your life any way you'd like…"

Other students looked toward Shizuma as her voice became unexpectedly high-pitched.

Roughly a third of the lounge located in Miator's section of the Strawberry Dorms was occupied by students who had returned before the first dismissal bell and were enjoying conversations over afternoon tea.

A dark green—Miator green—carpet, with small star emblems scattered about, covered the floor. Small one-person and large three-person silver-gray couches were randomly placed throughout the room, and the warm afternoon sunlight softly illuminated the lounge, creating a relaxing atmosphere.

Behind the mantelpiece in the center was a large unused hearth, which was decorated with many enormous Chinese peonies almost at full bloom. The tables were adorned with seasonal flowers—small roses—which added to the serene ambiance for the students enjoying their afternoon tea.

"Shizuma-sama…" Miyuki requested quietly.

"I know…" Shizuma lowered her voice.

"You garner a lot of attention, especially since you won last year's *Étoile* competition, so you must be more careful…"

"I get it already!"

"No…I don't think you fully understand. Please…"

Miyuki flicked a sidelong glance at Nagisa, which stopped Shizuma.

Garnering too much attention is not good, for Nagisa's sake was what Miyuki must have been thinking, and Shizuma was forced to nod in agreement.

Chiyo sensed a bit of tension in the conversation, so she offered Shizuma another cup of tea. She was very attentive and good at reading between the lines. The tea she offered was a hot cup of Assam tea—served straight. It went well with the thick slice of banana cake she also offered.

Shizuma beamed as she thanked Chiyo.

Chiyo was stunned by Shizuma's refined, beautiful smile—and suddenly became nervous at Shizuma's overwhelming power. As she served tea to the other three—Miyuki, Nagisa, and Tamao—the china clanked slightly.

Phew...the warm tea made the girls relax.

"Well, may I begin?" Miyuki said, her voice calm. "I would like to explain something today. After seeing the results of the first round of the *Étoile* competition, I've thought of a few things..." Like a dealer in a casino about to challenge a professional gambler, she stared intently at the other girls as she spoke about the commotion at Spica.

Nagisa thought back over the events as they were being explained. She recalled meeting Hikari during the first-round *aînée* event, known as the Maiden Horse Race.

During the event, the other *cadette* candidates had been jealous of Hikari and had almost pushed her off the tower. Nagisa had assumed that the other candidates' jealousy had been born from their desire to win the *Étoile* competition—but she had been wrong.

It's so tough to go out with a very popular person...

She started to hunch her shoulders, but she stopped herself.

Oh gosh, what am I thinking...girls don't "go out" with each other! She'd thought she had become numb to this strange subject...and she scratched her nose in dismay.

But...I wonder...how is Hikari doing these days? I haven't seen her since that event... I hope she's doing well with her upperclassman, the handsome prince. Hikari was so eager and cute...and was a perfect match for the prince.

Nagisa smiled, lost in her thoughts.

"Um...there are more things to be worried about than other people's troubles, Aoi-san," Miyuki cut in coldly. "This directly involves you, of course..." She glared at Shizuma and Nagisa.

"Oh, what do you mean by that?" Shizuma mumbled, acting as if she were absorbed in busily eating her banana cake.

"Stop pretending that you don't know," Miyuki said. "While Otori Amane is Spica's most revered, number-one Prince... Shizuma-oneesama is St. Miator's Queen..."

She looked straight at Nagisa. "And you, the new transfer student? Though it may be one of the Queen's short-lived flirtations, you have been officially chosen as her partner. You are exactly like Spica's 'Snow White,' and the target of the jealousy of every Miator student—well, you're *supposed to be,* anyway."

Nagisa ducked her head in shame, and almost choked on the second slice of banana cake she had just gobbled.

Yes, I'm sorry for being with Shizuma-sama even though I'm not worthy... It's all my fault...

She suddenly realized something. *But huh? She said, "supposed to be"...?*

"Yes, supposed to be... You should have been the target of everyone's jealous outrage. But...do you remember? The fake letter that lured you to the library?"

Miyuki, her face cool, drank her tea.

The letter luring me to the library—I'll never forget that one! Nagisa gritted her teeth.

After the announcement of her entry in the *Étoile* competition, Nagisa had been called out by upperclassmen many times and picked on. So she had been relieved to read that letter, which had seemed to be a saving grace, but...

Telling Nagisa about Shizuma's past had actually been a plot to depress her and set her up for failure in the *Étoile* competition.

Though Nagisa had been shocked that someone was jealous enough to send an anonymous letter and was out to get her, she had definitely felt a greater shock when she'd found out about Shizuma's past.

Sakuragi Kaori—Shizuma's most beloved "younger sister." Kaori had passed away the spring Shizuma became a fifth-year student. Nagisa hadn't known about her until the letter incident.

Shizuma was cheerful, strong, and beautiful, and she constantly teased me, being the playful Shizuma, so I couldn't sense her painful past...

I was just so clueless...

Nagisa didn't notice Tamao, who was looking at her saddened face with concern.

Miyuki continued, "Of course, being a new transfer student, you can't possibly imagine the immense popularity of Shizuma-sama—so that letter was rather mild compared to the myriad of other horrendous things that *could* have happened to you. The truth is...the reason why you weren't harmed any more than you were...is because of Shizuma-sama's...virtuous presence, I suppose? Even from an objective perspective, Shizuma-sama's love for the one she favors is rather overbearing...and I believe no one would dare to go against her wishes. Besides…most of them were half in doubt. Even when they saw Shizuma-sama's name entered in the *Étoile* competition, they knew that she had won the *Étoile* crown last year already, so they didn't really believe that she would participate, especially since the students in her class are preparing for the college entrance exams—but Shizuma-sama actually participated. But because of Spica Student Council President Tomori's plot…"

Miyuki looked down, her eyes darkening.

"Plot…?" asked Chiyo. She sat on the edge of the table, nervously listening to the conversation at hand.

"Yes, a plot. That question—'Do you wish to be bound to the *cadette* candidate next to you as your one and only partner, both in this life and the next?'—was a total setup. I couldn't believe Shizuma-sama had to answer that in public. I'm sure it caused the Miator votes to split. Had I known about this insidious scheme, I would have objected. But that question wasn't in the list of questions attached to the *Étoile* competition schedule of events, which was given in advance to the Miator Student Council. President Tomori pulled a simple strategic maneuver to ensure that Spica would claim the *Étoile* crown. Considering President Tomori's faithfulness to Spica's creed of fairness, I was surprised by her sly maneuver…"

Miyuki turned deliberately to Shizuma. Shizuma sipped her tea, acting as if none of this affected her, and Miyuki continued.

"Unfortunately, the Spica Student Council President's scheme has had its effect—Shizuma-sama, the glorious *Étoile* of last year, had to announce to all of her fans in Miator. Shizuma-sama…"

Miyuki nodded at Nagisa, her expression grave.

Huh, me…?

Nagisa was confused—but Miyuki chuckled. "Shizuma-sama proclaimed that she loved this newbie *cadette*, Aoi Nagisa, out of the whole wide world…"

"L-L-Loooove…?" Nagisa shouted.

"Shhh, no, Nagisa-chan, not so loud…" Tamao, worried about the murmurs around them, grabbed Nagisa-chan, who almost fell out the chair.

"So…what are you trying to say?" Shizuma asked as she blew on the tea.

Miyuki faced Shizuma and looked at her intently—and the tone of her voice changed.

"At this point, whether your proclamation was true or not isn't the problem. Those who believed it will, and those who denied it won't…but…"

"But what…?" Shizuma didn't raise her face, and kept staring at her teacup.

"The problem is that Shizuma-sama—whether it was the truth or not—declared her love in front of the whole school. Shizuma-sama's declaration—true or not—may have caused those who voted for you in last year's *Étoile* competition to feel betrayed. Of course…love takes many forms and could change over time. Even I…"

Miyuki took a breath. She thought for a bit…then continued.

"Even I…believe that love, as beautiful and perfect as it

is, can change over time, or be lost. I think it is very natural that it should do so. Unlike the fantasies of many of the Miator students, there is no such thing as eternal love. In fact…the more perfect and beautiful it is…the more it could vanish in an instant, like a dream…"

She looked away. "But because you won last year's *Étoile*, Shizuma-sama, many people placed their hopes and dreams in you—and the beautiful girl who passed away. There are still many students in Miator who saw the dramatic fate, the limitless love, beauty, and adoration between the two of you. Knowing that, your declaration…might have caused many problems. Hanazono Shizuma now loves Aoi Nagisa out of the whole wide world, and even in the next life—so where does that leave poor Sakuragi Kaori…?"

K-tink…

The place froze.

Sakuragi Kaori…that name again…

Nagisa came to her senses. *If the things in the Astraea School Directory and what Chiyo-chan said are true, then Shizuma-sama…can't possibly love me more than Sakuragi Kaori…*

What Shizuma-sama said during the Mouth of Truth was just an act, to win the Étoile competition. No matter how clueless I am, that *was obvious…*

But I didn't care… I knew I can't even come close to…the beautiful girl who everyone feels belongs next to Shizuma-oneesama…

But…just for a bit…I wanted to understand their relationship…

It had been such a dramatic fate. A story of limitless love, beauty, and adoration.

In her heart, Nagisa heard Miyuki's words. Certain thoughts and feelings grew in Nagisa's mind.

Shizuma-oneesama told me to believe her. Though I just met her, I believe her...I believe this beautiful, beaming person. Looking at her powerful eyes, there's no way she'd lie or fake anything.

Shizuma-oneesama's feelings toward me can't be fake... Nagisa was sure she'd felt Shizuma's love.

But...

I'm curious about Shizuma-oneesama and her most beloved girl. What was Sakuragi Kaori like? And what were Shizuma-oneesama's feelings toward her? How did Shizuma-oneesama love and...care for her...and when did they have to say goodbye...?

"Um, about Sakuragi Kaori..."

Just as Nagisa mustered enough courage to ask her question, Shizuma's sharp and strong voice drowned her out.

"What sort of problem is supposed to affect *me?*"

As if she had been waiting for that question, Miyuki responded quickly.

"It is *definitely* a big problem. Let's disregard Aoi Nagisa's reputation for a moment—Miator students do not think highly of her, for sure, and to be blunt, regard her as garbage. An average transfer student with no significance whatsoever—oh, excuse me!" Miyuki coughed as she put Nagisa in her place.

Tamao laughed weakly.

Miyuki composed herself and went on. "To see this transfer

student receiving a large amount of attention from Shizuma-sama certainly doesn't please your fans at all. The fans accepted the special existence of Sakuragi Kaori, so they forgave Shizuma-sama's flirtatious behavior and admired from afar in a peaceful manner—caring for you. But even the Miator students who half-doubted your intentions heard your declaration and witnessed the dramatic dead-heat match of the *aînée* event, where you saved Nagisa-san as she fell from the tower…and they might be irritated. If we're not careful, a riot might occur."

Miyuki's tone was serious, but Shizuma laughed in her face.

"Tsk tsk… Riot? Oh great, I'd love to watch that happen… the peaceful Miator students causing a riot. It'll surely be a glamorous affair…"

"Oh, how true…" Tamao chuckled.

Miyuki's eyes tightened, and her face grew hard. "As the Student Council President…I don't want to see the Miator students lose their unity and squabble over this. I don't want to sit idly by if I can prevent what happened at Spica from happening here…and…"

She grinned fiercely. "I really hope we *do* win… *Étoile* two years in a row? A new historical record in Astraea. Wouldn't that be a wonderful glory for our legendary Queen, everyone?"

Nagisa's face went white at those words, while Tamao shrugged her shoulders in disbelief.

Chiyo gulped in surprise…and Shizuma, without saying a word, silently reached for her teacup.

Taking a deep breath, Miyuki said, "I have a plan." She scanned the faces of all four girls. "It will drive the Amane couple to certain defeat, raise Miator's odds of winning, and protect Aoi Nagisa-san from future petty, jealous antics, like the sinister letter."

The large gate of Maiden Park.

Maiden Park spread from east to west behind the three schools, and its main gate, which stood opposite the schools' front gates, protected the holy park of maidens—so it was usually closed. It would only open during special events.

Standing in front of it that day, full of deep emotions, was a girl. Propped next to her was a large, dark blue suitcase, and she seemed to have just arrived from airport, because the airline's luggage tag still hung from the side.

From Russia...

"The time has finally arrived..."

Standing erect, she used her hands to sweep her bangs from over her eyebrows...with eyes ready for battle, she stared at the symbol on the center of the gate.

Three small iron stars.

Against the large gate, the girl, who was small for her age, looked smaller than ever, yet she had an overpowering aura about her.

I will save Spica in your place...

As she made the promise in her heart, a drop of rain fell on the tip of her nose.

From the gray skies, *drip drip*—small droplets came down.

It had finally started to rain…

Black clouds approached the foothills.

I need to hurry…

Makoto grabbed the suitcase strap. Her scrawny legs made unusually large, confident strides.

She headed straight toward…Astraea's holy ground.

Past Maiden Park, to a place officially known as Astraea Hall—and nicknamed Strawberry Dorms.

But before she went there, she needed to meet someone.

Makoto changed direction…toward Spica's school building.

"…that's pretty much it." *Grin.*

Chikaru gleefully finished speaking.

When she had first entered, the Spica Student Council room had stirred in surprise, but they had simmered down as the explanation continued. Now—the air had gone cold, and no one dared break the silence, even with a cough.

The pressure inside the room grew. Outside the large glass wall, the skies turned from gray to almost black.

Tsubomi broke the tense air of silence. "But…"

As she nervously shifted her eyes around, her young voice shrilled a octave higher, making her sound even cuter. She had just graduated elementary school the previous year.

"Um, if that plan is carried out…and the former Spica Elementary School graduate came back…the first round of the *Étoile* competition is already over so…isn't it too late and rather impossible to have that oneesama enter the *Étoile* competition...?"

Her voice released the tension in the room.

"Yes...it's too late," Kaname grumbled. She looked pissed as usual—but also seemed to be afraid of something.

"Well...that's true," Shion agreed. "Even if she did return to school, the first round has concluded already, so it would be difficult for her even to compete in the second round. Had she returned during the first round, we might have been able to do something about it. Of course, considering Spica's current situation, even if we had forcefully pushed this new entry, the Student Council would surely have received another harsh wave of criticism—either way, I don't think we can enter her in the *Étoile* competition at this point. It might be possible next year..."

Bam!

The Student Council room door crashed open.

Nobody had noticed the person's presence—before now. Everyone turned to look. The outside air rushed into the stuffy room...

The double doors had been forcefully pushed open...

In the middle of the doorway stood a boy—no, a girl.

She had short, hazel hair that appeared almost luminous. Her frame was small, but her head was also small, so she was well-proportioned and had a beautiful profile.

Though she wasn't voluptuous, and in fact looked rather androgynous, she stood in a manner that relayed her conviction, and she folded her arms like a fresh, handsome, and powerful boy.

Her unbelievably small face was perfectly composed.

"Hello…good day, everyone… I'm back."

As she gestured with one arm, she seemed at the same time mysterious and alluring.

Everyone was taken by surprise at such perfect timing.

Everyone but Chikaru.

"Ahaha…oh, were you guys in the middle of a meeting? Or were you waiting on me, perchance…?" Makoto asked as she slipped into the room.

She looked at the papers in Tsubomi's hand. "Oh…you were talking about the *Étoile* competition, right? Great. I'm glad I made it in time."

Smiling at Tsubomi, she said softly, "Don't worry—I'm back, so everything will be all right."

Her smile was so beautiful—and captivating.

"Wh-Why do you say that?" *How do you know about this?* Tsubomi tried to ask, but Makoto had already shifted her gaze to Kaname.

She looked at the red rose placed in Kaname's breast pocket and remarked, "I'm pleased to receive such an adorable welcome."

She gave Kaname a proud and elegant smile. Kaname's knees went weak, and she almost melted to the floor, but she braced herself and looked away.

Makoto finally made her way to the furthest spot in the room—Student Council President Tomori Shion's seat, with the large glass wall behind her.

"It's been a while…Shion-kun, do you remember me? Even when I transferred to Russia, I always thought about

Spica—because I was proud to have been a Spica student. Do you understand? It has to be a place of pride, for eternity—I can't allow it to be anything else."

Makoto smiled again, like a totally pure and innocent angel.

She came close to Shion's face. A strong but dizzily sweet, musky aroma wafted in the air. She whispered into Shion's ear.

"Leave everything to me. You're foolish, Shion. Instead of relying on the unmotivated Prince Amane, you should have asked for my help in the first place. Or…did you hesitate to call me back from Russia, Shion? Aww…don't worry, just watch. I'll defend Spica's honor in your place. Oh gee, don't ruin your pretty face. You don't need to look so scared anymore. I'll take on your heavy burden…"

She smiled happily, like a pure, beautiful angel…

Or rather, like an evil, cunning devil…

Shion's face quivered in sudden astonishment.

The winds drifted away, leaving behind thick, dark clouds…

"I…I hate the commotion my beloved Spica is experiencing…and I can't stand to see the students fighting each other. The strong, white star of Spica, glowing in the beautiful sky… that was the star I came to adore. It was the image I held onto in faraway Russia. Spica, my favorite school, was the source of my pride."

Makoto's last sentence ended in a sad tone.

Her boy-like, pure sorrow moved everyone's heart.

We love Spica just like you do. For Spica's honor…we all share the desire to win the Étoile crown, for the school…

"So I want to do what I can for Spica. Of course, I went to Russia to chase my dream—to become a professional violinist. But Spica is more important than that... I finally realized I needed to keep the star of Spica shining brilliantly. So I left everything behind... I know that's dumb...but I knew I had to—so I came back."

...Yeah. The only thing my beloved left behind was the star of Spica and its honor...

Makoto couldn't hold her anguish inside. She looked away to hide her pained expression...but everyone misunderstood her behavior and felt bad.

Tsubomi was miserable. *We made even made a student studying abroad worry and feel troubled...*

"Though we appreciate your coming back...what *can* you do at this point...?" Momomi wondered.

Makoto suddenly chuckled. "Oh—well, actually..."

Her laughter sounded so innocent and fun—as if sunlight had broken through the dark clouds. It was like a pleasant moment after the quelling of the storm, and it spread warmly into everyone's hearts.

The beautiful, carefree angel continued, "Well...I have a wonderful idea. I'm pretty sure everyone will be surprised at it. But...Spica is really loved by God. I had a sudden revelation come to me, like an angel descending from Heaven..."

Giggling, Makoto resembled a mural of the young, playful angel Michael.

Her eyes turned cruel—for just a second. This was show time.

Makoto—the Emperor's—cold, cruel true form was revealed for only a moment before she spoke.

"I request that the *cadette* event of the second round of the *Étoile* competition be the Faceless Devil!"

The jovial atmosphere in the room turned into bewilderment.

Momomi left her mouth open, and Kaname's face turned blue.

Tsubomi and the other council members were flustered—really flustered—at the ominous phrase and refused to accept it.

Makoto was pleased at their shocked reactions and smiled innocently at Shion.

"This event will allow me to enter the competition at this stage. Right, Shion-kun? And…Spica students—especially Prince Amane fans—will surely enjoy this selection. What do you think?"

Shion's face crumpled as if she had eaten a bitter bug.

"Don't look like that," Makoto said sweetly. "I'm pretty sure that by the time I enter and the *Étoile* competition's second round is finished, you won't have to rely on Prince Amane anymore. But…she wasn't interested in participating in the *Étoile* competition in the first place, right? You know, we should allow the prince and princess to live happily ever after on their own. I'll be the star of Spica in their place. I left for Russia without realizing that Spica would turn out like this—I'm so sorry. But now that I'm back, there's nothing to worry about."

Makoto went to Shion's side and hugged her shoulder as if they were long-lost friends…

She looked directly into Shion's eyes, as if she were challenging her.

"I will be Spica's new *Étoile*. I want to revive the brilliance of the Five Great Stars…with my own hands."

Inside the Strawberry Dorms lounge…

"First, I would like to propose a change of events for round two."

Miyuki's bold comment caused Chiyo, Tamao, and Nagisa to gulp. Watching the puzzled looks of Nagisa and the others—except for Shizuma, who was indifferent as she sipped tea—Miyuki continued to explain in her cool, demure Student Council President manner.

"According to the announcement from this year's *Étoile* competition host, the Spica Student Council have chosen to have a tennis tournament for the second round—a very Spica-like choice, since they're known for their strong athletics program."

She smirked. "But this event follows the previous Maiden Horse Race…an arbitrarily chosen event that also gave Spica an obvious advantage. President Tomori is so simple-minded—well, she probably plotted to select as many sports events as possible to ensure Spica's victory. Of course, Shizuma-sama is very skilled in tennis…and at least Nagisa-san seems to be physically capable, so Miator still has a strong chance to win this round, but…"

Nagisa gulped during Miyuki's pause.

"Based on the reasons I stated previously…we cannot afford to miss this opportunity. As the St. Miator Student Council President, I propose a change of event—to give our school the highest advantage."

Tamao and Chiyo looked up and eagerly awaited Miyuki's next words.

"We propose that the second-round event be—the Faceless Devil."

Ukk… Tamao and Chiyo were horror-stricken.

"Instead of a boring tennis tournament, as the Student Council President I believe that this event is more appropriate for the long history and traditions of the *Étoile* competition. Does everyone agree with my opinion?"

Miyuki gently smiled at the group. Tamao and Chiyo ducked their heads in fear, and the clueless Nagisa shuddered at the sight.

Shizuma quietly sipped her tea.

"Well then, everyone. I need to fill out some paperwork so I can move into the dorm, so please excuse me. Uh, can someone show me the way?" Makoto scanned the room with her sparkling eyes.

One of the second-year students came running from the far end of the room, leaving behind her pile of work. "Yes, I'd be honored to, Makoto-sama!" She was overcome by Makoto's charm, her face flushed and eyes moistened.

Out of the corner of her eye, Makoto saw St. Lulim's Student Council President, Chikaru...

Makoto turned away. *Okay, I'm back...Chikaru.*

Your letter...is an overture for Spica's revolution!

After Makoto departed, the Student Council room was filled with an eerie silence and a series of colorful, beautiful smiles.

Like an expensive, foreign kaleidoscope...the faces changed expressions. Each was exquisite, quite captivating and mysteriously attractive...

Tsubomi was stunned...pale-faced Kaname bit her lips... and Momomi stared at Shion painfully.

Shion...glared at the meeting table.

Her original thought had been to rely on Spica's pride and the great star Prince Amane, even though she had a weakness in her personality, and to claim the *Étoile* crown, which Spica had not won for a long time.

She had known that she had to accomplish this feat—for the glory of Spica.

But her own hidden agenda—to create Astraea's first male-like couple of Amane and Kaname—had crumbled with the appearance of Konohana Hikari.

And Prince Amane, who claimed to be normal, who found girl-girl couples to be strange—had actually fallen in love with a girl.

Shion had believed victory was still attainable even with this unexpected turn of events.

In fact, she had hoped that the forthright Prince Amane

would become more masculine—and turn into a real prince—to protect her new love.

But that decision had taken a turn for the worse. While nobody disliked Amane, the school was being dominated by jealous outrage and resentment toward Hikari.

Now…a new star had appeared.

Would this star be a premonition of victory, or merely a trap leading to the downfall of Spica?

Shion didn't know. But for now…she had no choice.

Lifting her determined face, she said, "Well, I suppose we have no other option. Okay, everyone…"

She was interrupted.

Knock knock knock…

Someone softly knocked on the door.

Had Makoto come back? Tension ran through the room again.

But the person who quietly opened the door and entered was a Miator student, wearing their charcoal-gray uniform. She carried a tray with both hands.

"Excuse me. I am here to deliver a message from the Miator Student Council…"

The tall, slender Miator student bowed at the door. Keeping her face down, she slipped into the room and walked straight toward Shion.

She finally lifted her face and stared at the Student Council President.

Shion thought, *I've seen her before. She's one of Miator's Four Saints…*

But before Shion could remember her name, the girl spoke.

"Are you the Spica Student Council President?"

"Y-Yes…"

The Miator student never smiled. Her face was emotionless and mask-like as she offered the lacquered tray at chest height.

"I am here to deliver a message from the Miator Student Council President."

In the center of the tray was an envelope stamped with the Miator seal.

Shion carefully retrieved the envelope—and the messenger from Miator bowed her head and took a few steps back.

Shion nodded in confirmation. Without speaking another word, the messenger quietly retreated.

Shion was dumbfounded, but immediately opened the envelope.

She read the letter out loud.

Request to Change the Event for the Second Round of the Étoile Competition

Regarding the current situation, in which the Spica Student Council is under suspicion of foul play in the Étoile competition…

While I do not believe that any unlawful acts have occurred, our school believes in strict adherence to the traditions and preservation of the Étoile competition, and feels this grave situation should not be taken lightly.

In addition, regarding the announcement of the second-round event, it was written that Spica's strong candidate, the Otori Amane couple, has been exempted from this round and automatically proceeds to the next round…

As the St. Miator Student Council President, I truly believe the selection process was conducted in the fairest manner, but if the results of this selection were to be announced, it would only add oil to the fire that has already ignited at Spica—and could spread to Miator, bringing out the hidden resentment at our school...

"And so, this may be a bit presumptuous, but I request a change of events..."

For some reason, Shion stopped.

"What's wrong, Shion-chan?" Momomi asked, worried.

Shion continued in a quaking voice, "We request...for the event..."

"What?" Kaname and Tsubomi piped up.

"The Faceless...Devil..."

Shion's knees gave out, and she slumped back into her chair.

What an astronomical coincidence...

Chikaru took in the whole situation.

She sensed the arrival of a turbulent storm. She actually felt pleasure, waiting for the inevitable storm. There was a strange tingling down her spine.

Ohh...silly me... I actually...love this thrilling situation.

As she chuckled to herself, she thought of a particular Lulim student.

"What is the Faceless Devil anyway?" Nagisa inquired carefully.

"Well..." Miyuki answered...eventually. "The Faceless Devil is..."

The Faceless Devil was one of the *Étoile* competition events, much like the Mouth of Truth and the Maiden Horse Race.

But it was a very unusual event that had been chronicled but was rarely conducted.

It hadn't been conducted for a long while because…it was boring and actually quite cruel.

The *Étoile* couple, revered as the best "oneesama and her younger sister," had once been more pure and idyllic, an object of adoration among the girls.

Over time, though, as the fans had become more organized, and the popular students had begun to show unique qualities, the students had grown away from the original intent of finding the couple with the purest, strongest emotional ties, and the *Étoile* competition had evolved into a search for the popular star of the schools.

So recent *Étoile* competitions had involved more events that showcased the candidate's "showmanship," rather than the tests of true love, and the Faceless Devil had been used less and less.

Even Miyuki and Shion, who were pillars of their respective schools, had never seen this event being conducted. Only the concept had been passed on, as a legend.

…Why?
The rules of the Faceless Devil…

1. For two weeks, the aînée *and* cadette *will not be allowed to see or speak to each other.*

2. During these two weeks, they must endure and affirm their love toward each other.

3. Those couples who have succumbed to the temptations of the devil will be disqualified.

4. Those couples who have resisted the temptations of the devil will proceed to the next round.

The *aînée* and *cadette*—Shizuma and Nagisa—would go to school as usual, but for two weeks they must not see each other. They must endure a long-distance relationship for two weeks.

And during that time, the devil would tempt them.

A student from another school—in this case, probably a Spica student—would be selected to tempt the couple. That student would never announce that she was the devil, of course.

So this nameless, unidentifiable devil would come to them unannounced and without suspicion. With a sweet smile, the devil would tempt either Nagisa or Shizuma.

The devil would try to squeeze certain keywords out of the lonely, depressed target by any means possible.

For example, direct statements such as "I like you more than Shizuma-sama" or "Please take me away."

The devil would turn in a list of pre-selected keywords beforehand, and if the targeted individual uttered any of those keywords, the devil would win.

When the devil approached the target…and the target swayed…or seriously fell in love with the devil, then the target couple would be disqualified from the *Étoile* competition.

And the devil would be able to choose a partner and participate in the second event of the second round. Or the devil could choose *not* to participate in the *Étoile* competition.

This event had originally been used by weaker schools to reduce the number of strong candidates from their rivals—it was like a system of checks and balances. But except for the parties involved, the Faceless Devil wasn't particularly dramatic or entertaining. The two weeks would pass by quietly—and it was a very boring event for the spectators.

At the same time, the general consensus had been that it was a sinister event, designed to tempt the couples or break them up, and it didn't seem appropriate for the peaceful *Étoile* competition...

Thus, this dark, hair-raising *L'Épreuve d'amour* (Test of Love) event had been buried for a long time.

Shizuma chomped on yet another slice of banana cake. It was her third.

Miyuki remarked, "For now, our biggest threat is Spica's Prince Amane and her partner, Konohana Hikari. But this couple...consists of the shy, bashful, and un-prince-like lead character, and a partner who has newly transferred, and who also happens to be very timid and shy."

Hmm, that's true... Hikari didn't seem too strong, Nagisa thought. *She seemed really sweet, cute, and sensitive...*

"And it seems that they can't hold back their puppy-love affections for each other, even in public...basically, it's a *morganatic love*—like Cinderella. Of course, it also includes a whole crew of mean older sisters around them..."

Morganatic love—Nagisa winced at the dramatic choice of words. *That's such an outdated phrase.* But she couldn't laugh at it.

Miyuki tapped the table. "To be blunt, this couple will probably freak out at the thought of not seeing each other for just two weeks. We don't even need to send in a devil—if the event is changed to the Faceless Devil, this couple will be disqualified in no time."

Miyuki's evil grin and eyes were frightening. They made Nagisa gulp fearfully.

The Student Council President went on, "And next…oh yes, Aoi-san…I found out who wrote that letter to lure you into the library—are you interested in knowing who it was?"

Rattle rattle rattle… The table shook violently as it shifted.

It was Shizuma who stood up. "Who? Who was it?! Who troubled my dear Nagisa…!"

Shizuma's lips trembled, and her hair flared violently about her as she confronted Miyuki. She had turned red with anger, and Miyuki was overpowered, rendered speechless.

Oh, she's quite serious…

A brief pause.

"…Oh my, Shizuma-sama, please don't get so worked up, even if it is about your adorable little Nagisa-san!" Miyuki remarked sarcastically.

Shizuma came to—and blushed slightly. Bashfully, she fumbled to fix her hair. But she shot back, "But…the culprit did such a terrible thing to my Nagisa… I'm much too curious to find out…"

Shizuma-sama is blushing!!

Pfft...Chiyo and Tamao covered their mouths to keep from laughing out loud.

Miyuki looked at the group with deep emotion. *How long has it been since Shizuma-sama...showed such emotions? No, this may be the first time I've ever seen her get so flustered...*

She took a deep breath. *This is it. I need to convince all of them to agree with me.*

"Ahh, I thought so..." Miyuki put on her most pitiful expression.

"*What* did you think...?" the irritated Shizuma asked.

"Well...though the Faceless Devil would prove to be a disadvantage for the Prince Amane couple...it would be a disadvantage to Miator too—because we have the same weakness."

Miyuki further probed Shizuma's guilt. "Compared to Prince Amane, Shizuma-sama is rather invincible, of course. But with your reaction just now, Shizuma-sama, if something—no matter how small—happened to Aoi-san, it would worry you, possibly causing you to break the rules to go and see her. Considering that you previously said 'My words *are* Miator's rules'...ohh, even if my request to change to the Faceless Devil event goes through, it might be our Miator that crumbles to ruins..."

"I'm not...that foolhardy," Shizuma muttered.

"Then do you agree to this idea, Shizuma-sama?"

"Hey, hold it. I don't agree to this at all—I can't bear to be away from Nagisa for two weeks..."

"...Oh, of course not. I knew you wouldn't go for it. This is just an idea, but…" Miyuki gave the most delectable smile.

"Regarding the 'library culprit,' I believe it was one of Shizuma-sama's fans."

The words rolled off her tongue so easily.

The next moment, Shizuma froze. *Does Miyuki know something…?*

Miyuki continued, "The incident occurred behind Shizuma-sama's back, and was an effort to make Nagisa-san withdraw from the *cadette* event. Judging from the motive, they are the only suspects. It could possibly be someone really close to Shizuma-sama—which is all the more reason they don't want Shizuma-sama to know about it. But we can use this to our advantage."

She paused. Shizuma had finally fallen silent.

A lightbulb turned on in Tamao's head as she realized—*so that's why I was invited.*

"During the Faceless Devil event…the two of you will have to stay apart," Miyuki said. "That means the enemy—the library culprit—will know about the separation. She will surely take advantage of this chance. She will definitely try to lure Aoi Nagisa-san into another trap."

"Eeehh, oh nooo! If you know she'll do it, then why can't we just catch her…?" Nagisa whined, which caused Tamao to laugh.

"Oh gosh, Nagisa-chan, have you forgotten a very important person? Tsk tsk," she said, all smiles.

"Important person? Are you going to participate in something, Tamao-chan?" the bewildered Nagisa asked.

Miyuki responded cheerfully, "Oh, if you haven't gotten it by now, then this plan might actually work. During Shizuma-sama's absence, the library culprit will be…"

"…nabbed by…" Tamao took over with a broad grin, "…your very important and reliable friend, Suzumi Tamao-san!"

Chiyo smiled too. "Woow…that's splendid!"

"Well then, Suzumi-san—please stick close to Aoi-san for those two weeks. In addition to the library culprit, Spica might send in a devil or two…but you're sharp, Suzumi-san, so I'm confident of leaving you in charge. Yes, in fact…I keep saying you'd make a great Student Council President. Are you interested? I can bring you on as one of the executive committee assistants, so please consider a role in the Student Council…"

"My…oh goodness…I've declined several times already. I wouldn't be able to handle such a heavy burden. And…I don't like to take on too much responsibility. I just want to spend my days in peace, with a cute girl like Nagisa-chan…"

Tamao hugged Nagisa.

"Kyaaah!" Nagisa couldn't comprehend the conversation.

Ehh? Then that event—the Faceless Devil—will actually become the second-round event? That means…I won't be able to see Shizuma-sama for two weeks…

And…I want to know…Shizuma-sama's true feelings…

Satisfied that her idea had gone through, though in an unusual manner, Miyuki gleefully pointed at Nagisa.

"Hello, Aoi-san, snap out of it. I need you to do something during those two weeks. You're not good at dancing, are you?"

"Huh, dance?"

Nagisa was dumbfounded. How many times had she said "huh" today?

Miyuki answered, "Yes, dance. Social dance. The main event of the Faceless Devil is a dance. After two weeks of separation, the couple will dance, for the *aînée* event, in front of a large audience. It will be a test of compatibility between the two people who have been separated—the separation is only the first half of the test. Those couples who lost to the devil's temptation will be disqualified immediately, but those who endured will need to prove their close bond with their partner with a perfectly matching dance. It is the hardest part of the event. In Astraea, all the schools have dance classes, but I doubt your previous school had them, so you probably don't have much experience..."

"Eh, Nagisa-oneesama's old school didn't have any dance classes?" Chiyo asked, surprised.

"Oh...then we must do lots of dance practice!" Tamao's smile broadened at the thought of an additional task.

Miyuki looked on, content.

"Dance...? I've never danced in my life...!" Nagisa wailed.

Trrriiing...

A soft organ melody rang through the speakers in the lounge.

"Strawberry Dorm residents...it is almost time for the Social Exchange Dinner...we ask all residents to make preparations... We say again...Strawberry Dorm residents..."

"Ah!"

"Oh gosh, it's time!"

Chiyo and Tamao blurted in unison.

They noticed the lounge was almost empty.

Miyuki felt a bit guilty. "We were quite engrossed in our conversation…"

Nagisa turned around to see Shizuma, sitting alone.

She was lost in her thoughts.

CHAPTER 3

A Prophet Appears, Dividing the Obstructive Sea and Showering Manna

The Bell Walkways was a three-way aerial bridge that connected the buildings of the Strawberry Dorms. It was usually vacant year round. The bridge had three entrances, and it was the only passageway that connected the dorms. Though the dorms formed a strawberry shape when seen from above, from the inner garden below the bridge that joined them looked like a Y in the sky.

Except for official business, the use of this hall was restricted. Thus, the Bell Walkways were usually quiet, with a few students conducting school business shuffling across it occasionally.

But that night the Bell Walkways bustled with girls.

Girls lined up properly in single file, announced their names at the entrance, and entered the skywalk.

"St. Miator Girls' Academy, Fourth Year Moon Class, Suzumi Tamao, passing through!"

"St. Miator Girls' Academy, Fourth Year Moon Class, Aoi Nagisa, passing through!"

The excited girls' voices rang through the hall. Nagisa held a quiet conversation with Tamao as she walked across the Bell Walkways for the first time.

"Hey, Tamao-chan...this is...a really large gathering."

"Yes, it is...because it involves all dorm residents. Ah, that's right... Nagisa-chan, this is your first time, isn't it? Your first Social Dinner. We hold one every quarter."

"Yup! I've never seen another school's dining hall, so I'm really excited... And it must be luxurious, with a special menu and all, right? I really like that sort of stuff, like the rainbow fruit bowl with seven different kinds of fruit at kindergarten birthday parties, and the steak cutlet lunches they served on field day in elementary school, so that we could *teki ni katsu!*"[6]

"Fruit bowls and *teki ni katsu*, huh..."

Tamao looked at Nagisa with pity...but Nagisa's eyes sparkled innocently.

Tamao gazed at her with gentle eyes. "Yes, those can be quite fun, too. But today's menu might not be to your liking, Nagisa-chan..."

"Eh, Tamao-chan, you know the menu? Wow, what's on it? Spica is so extravagant, so maybe it's stew or steak... I can't wait..."

Nagisa drooled a bit.

Sister Fujii came out of the duty room at Miator's hall entrance and walked down the line of girls.

"Now, now, refrain from unnecessary chatter. Don't disgrace Miator!"

Nagisa and Tamao both straightened their postures.

"Yes, ma'am!"

Sister Fujii was Miator's strictest and scariest dorm mother. If you were caught by Sister Fujii, you'd go straight to the Repentance Room…and worse yet, miss out on the whole dinner.

Eeek—if that happened, that would ruin everything! Nagisa thought.

Nagisa and Tamao ducked their heads and tried not to stick out.

"St. Lulim Girls' School, Second Year Class B, Hyuga Kizuna, passing through!"

"St. Lulim Girls' School, Second Year Class B, Natsume Remon, passing through!"

From Miator to Spica.

From Spica to Lulim.

And from Lulim to Miator…

The line of girls continued to grow…

Knives and forks clanged softly in the dining hall.

Black iron and glass tables with carved legs lined the room, placed on top of the stunning royal blue stone floor.

The white walls had bold, geometric patterns. The oval

tables, each with room for twelve, were lined up in an organized fashion, with perfectly draped white table linens that had no wrinkles.

Several side tables were placed against the walls, decorated with vases full of white roses.

The low, soothing music of Schubert floated through the room.

This was Spica's main dining room.

Pheew...

Nagisa grew tired of eating and sighed as she looked down at her plate. In the center of the huge dish were duck confit, wild rice, and salad.

The two plates, stacked one on top of the other, were definitely too big for the portion of food, and Nagisa awkwardly fumbled with her utensils, wobbling the top plate.

It's so difficult to eat...aren't there any chopsticks?

She bit the end of her fork in frustration and blankly stared at the menu sheet, but Tamao laughed at her antics.

"Oh gosh, what's wrong, Nagisa? Does it taste bad?"

"N-No, that's not it... I'm having trouble eating it...because I didn't expect it to be so extravagant..." Nagisa rubbed at her head.

"Really? Well, they do serve special meals for Social Exchange Dinners so we can practice our table manners...oh wait, you prefer Japanese meals, don't you, Nagisa-chan? You're always saying you love tofu. It's all right. Even though they served French today, there are days when they serve Japanese food. They'll perform a tea ceremony and use tea ceremony dishes. And of course, you'll use chopsticks…"

Nagisa breathed a sigh of relief, because the smiling Tamao totally understood her frustrations.

The other people at Nagisa's table were two Miator upperclassmen, four Spica second-year students, and four Lulim fourth-year students.

The groupings at the Social Exchange Dinner were split by class and year—Miator's Snow, Moon, and Flower Classes… Spica's *Un*, *Deux*, and *Trois* Classes…and Lulim's Classes A, B, and C—to avoid seating the same students together every time.

This dinner wasn't the boisterous kind, but rather was a "social exchange" in which the students would have soft, pleasant conversations with their neighbors.

According to Tamao, the sisters observed students for proper table manners as they ate, so it wasn't much of a party. The only part that was exciting was the lively conversation held over dessert.

Despite the strictness of the event, Nagisa, the new transfer student, was fascinated to see the uniforms of the two other schools.

"Hey, is that student sitting at the back table…the Spica Student Council President?" Nagisa asked in a low voice.

"Yes, that's right. Tomori Shion, Spica's smartest student, known as the Snow Queen. Miator's Miyuki-oneesama seems reeeally smart too, but Shion-sama has a different coolness about her. Why, do you know her, Nagisa-chan? Do you…like her?" Tamao smiled.

"N-No way! That's not why I know her…" Nagisa stuttered. "I saw her at the *Étoile* competition…because she was the hostess of the program. So I sort of remember her face…"

Shion sat at the table furthest from Nagisa. She wasn't really engaged in any friendly conversations and ate silently.

"Oh, that's right. She was the one who asked the cruel question. There's no way you could forget her, huh…"

Tamao wiped her mouth with a napkin and turned to Nagisa.

"Speaking of the *Étoile* competition, that reminds me… Nagisa-chan?"

Tamao's sudden seriousness made Nagisa a little nervous. "Yes…?"

"Nagisa-chan, what did you think about Miyuki-oneesama's conversation earlier?"

"What did I think? What do you mean?" Nagisa didn't understand her question.

"I'm talking about the Faceless Devil, of course. Are you afraid of the devil approaching you…"

Nagisa laughed and waved off Tamao's question. *Jeez, I'm not scared of that…*

"Or are you worried about not seeing Shizuma-sama for two weeks…"

"Well…" Nagisa was at a loss for words. *Oh yeah, that's what happens, huh…*

It finally hit Nagisa.

"Yes, she probably…was prevented from saying the name."

"Prevented?"

"Yes. She could only hint that it was one of Shizuma-sama's fans, right? From the looks of it, the culprit is probably very close to Shizuma-oneesama…"

"Very close to Shizuma-oneesama…" Nagisa repeated her words like a dumb parrot.

She became…a bit scared. Her nervous body locked up… it caused her to clatter her fork and knife on the plates even more.

"Ah, s-sorry…"

As she said that… *Fling.*

Her duck meat flew under the table.

"Here, Hikari, have one more. It's delicious."

While Nagisa was flinging her duck confit out of unexplainable anxiety over her future with Shizuma-sama… Yaya, at another table, offered Hikari a piece of bread from the basket she was holding.

Ever since she came back to the Strawberry Dorms, Hikari has been quite cheerful, for some reason. She's so obvious. She's happy because she was able to walk back to the dorm with Amane-oneesama…

Yaya wasn't amused, though. She was suspicious of Hikari—smiling in a positive, almost confident manner, enjoying dinner.

Miyuki-sama said all sorts of things one after ano
I couldn't digest them all…but…

If President Rokujo's plan goes through, then I c
Shizuma-oneesama for a while…

Something…burst inside Nagisa's heart and dissolved

"N-No way…it's no big deal! It's only for two shor
so I'm not worried about it at all!" Nagisa replied, as ch
as she could.

"Besides, normally I would never have had a ch
meet a sixth-year student like Shizuma-sama anyway..
fact that we even *met* at all is so strange…and unimporta
me isn't worthy to see Shizuma-sama…"

Nagisa tried to talk down to herself.

Tamao replied slowly, "You don't believe that…do
She sighed in her heart. *Why do you say that about yo*
Nagisa-chan…?

"Oh well. If you can handle it, then it's okay—
stick really close to you for two whole weeks without
interrupted by Shizuma-oneesama!"

Tamao gave Nagisa a hug…but it caught Nagisa off g
and she almost spilled her glass of water.

Tamao continued, "But…was Miyuki-oneesama spe
the truth…about that?"

"Eh?" Nagisa didn't expect that remark, either.

"You know, about knowing the identity of the lit
culprit. Well, to be more accurate, she said, 'I have an idea
it is'…"

"Yeah, come to think of it…she didn't mention any nam

So…Yaya inadvertently…made a slip of the tongue…

"Oh, Hikari, you're so elated…just because Amane-oneesama came to see you. I'm a bit…jealous."

"Oh gosh, Yaya-chan…no… Amane-sama felt obligated to come see me because I was chosen to be her partner in the *Étoile* competition…so there's no reason for you to be jealous, Yaya-chan. I can't meet with her that often…because she's such a star…"

Yaya-chan is so funny… Hikari giggled and her cheeks reddened.

Hmph! What's up with that? She's so sure of herself… Yaya was frustrated. Hikari wasn't even aware of Yaya's feelings toward her.

"You say that, but I'm sure you'd prefer to have Amane-oneesama sitting next to you rather than me, right? Oh gee, it's too bad Amane-sama isn't in the same class as you."

Yaya pouted, acting jealous… *This is…weird*. She couldn't attack more aggressively…she felt something different inside and seemed somewhat vulnerable. Did Hikari sense Yaya's feelings at all?

"Don't say that, Yaya-chan. You're my special friend. If you weren't here…I wouldn't know how to survive Spica…"

Hikari's voice trembled at the end of the sentence.

Yaya understood Hikari's feelings. Hikari was having a hard time at Spica. She knew what Hikari was going through and wanted to provide support for her, but the one who could comfort her most was Amane-sama…so Yaya had mixed feelings about the whole thing. She knew she was confused, too…

"Oh…really?" Yaya asked sarcastically.

Hikari replied confidently, "Of course," and smiled like a pure white lotus flower.

Looking at Hikari's smile made Yaya's body tingle—she felt a lustful desire brewing inside her. When out of the blue…

"Oh, wonderful—you must be the little white princess of Spica. I finally found you…tsk. So, how was the dinner?"

A girl in a monochrome waiter's outfit approached them.

"Oh, Chikaru-sama!" Yaya exclaimed.

"Eh, Chikaru-sama…?"

Surprised, Hikari turned around to see the St. Lulim Student Council President, Minamoto Chikaru, wearing a white shirt and black necktie—a typical waiter's outfit.

Smiling, Chikaru said, "Good evening. So, did you have a pleasant dinner tonight?" The black ribbon on her chest bounced. "It's so nice to meet you. Congratulations on winning the *Petite couronne* in the first round of the *Étoile* competition. Our school was excited to see a new star appear in Spica, too."

She smiled and talked to Hikari as she swept away bread crumbs with her silver crumb scraper.

Hikari was so stunned her mouth stayed open. "Wh-Why is the Student Council President providing table service…?"

"Tsk…isn't this wonderful? St. Lulim's Costume Club members sometimes offer to provide table service at Social Exchange Dinners. Of course, we'll only do it if we're allowed to wear new outfits. So, how do I look in my *garçon* outfit? Ooohhh, would you like to wear this outfit too, Hikari-chan? I think you would look very cute in it. Unlike the rigid and veeery scary Spica and Miator, you can transfer to Lulim *anytime!* Tsk…if you'd like to, that is. But of course, your white prince on a horse—Amane-chan—wouldn't allow that, would she?"

"Ah, are you friends with Amane-sama?!"

"Yes, sort of, because I've been in Astraea for a long time… But I've heard about your tribulations…just because Amane-chan seems to adore you, you've been treated badly, right? Poor girl…"

Chikaru seemed overly concerned.

Hikari replied, "Well…but it's understandable, because…it's quite brash for a new transfer student like me to enter the *Étoile* competition. It can't be helped. But some students, like Yaya-chan and Tsubomi-chan…treat me very nicely…so I'm okay."

Hikari bravely smiled back, making Yaya feel somewhat unsettled.

"Oh, really? You're such a good girl, Hikari-chan. And so cute… I want you to join my Costume Club even more."

Yaya sensed something strange. *Something isn't right about Chikaru's jolly behavior. She's attentive and gentle as usual, but her excitement is quite odd. Maybe she's excited because she's in the middle of her Costume Club activities…or…*

Maybe she's up to something…

Chikaru raised her voice on purpose. "Oh, it's almost time for dessert! I need to go back and help out. There are eight different kinds of dessert, but I recommend the *groseilles*-and-*fromage* tart. I'll bring it to you later." She collected the plates from the table.

As she started to push the black service cart away…

"Oh yes…Hikari-chan? This is a secret but…I'll tell you

since you're such a good girl. Umm…" She whispered in Hikari's ear, "I believe another student will transfer to Spica. Soon you might be able to break free from the craziness surrounding the *Étoile* competition. If that happens, I hope you'll be with Amane-chan happily ever after. At first, I hoped Amane-chan would become the *Étoile*…but after seeing her and you together, I changed my mind. It was the first time I'd ever seen Amane-chan so happy and carefree. I am a secret supporter of both you and Amane-chan." Chikaru winked in such a charming, leave-it-to-me sort of way.

"Ohh, I must hurry back…" she cried as she trotted off, pushing the cart.

Hikari didn't know what to make of situation.

"Hey, Chikaru-sama, what did you say to her…?" The impatient Yaya caught at the departing Chikaru's shoulder.

Behind them, about three tables further along, near the wall…

"Hey, Tamao-chan…should I pick that up myself?" Nagisa asked bashfully.

"Oh, please…the *garçons* will take care of it. That's etiquette…" Tamao answered, and she dabbed at her mouth with the napkin.

"But that piece of meat sticks out like a sore thumb, and I feel bad for making them pick it up…"

"No, it's fine. By the way, the Lulim's Costume Club is helping out the *garçons*…"

"Eh, what's that?"

"Lulim's Student Council President, Minamoto Chikaru. Oh, you probably don't know her, Nagisa-chan. She usually stands at the front stage during the combined Mass…and she's a very sweet and gentle person, known as Lulim's Holy Mother. She's very smart, and rumored to be a strategist, much more than our Miator's Princess of Rokujo-in…"

"Oh, what rumor is that?"

Tamao started at the voice behind her. "Ch-Chikaru-sama…"

The surprised Nagisa turned around and saw Chikaru, smiling, standing beside her cart in her waiter's outfit.

"Ohh, that piece of meat, right? Pity, you dropped the largest piece…did you have enough to eat? I'll pick it up, so don't worry. It's all right, I'll do it discreetly so nobody will notice…"

Chikaru dropped a white handkerchief…and picked it up, along with the meat. In two seconds, the meat was gone.

"Th-Thank you so much!" Nagisa said.

"Oh gosh, it's part of my duties. The meat must have been tough. It's not your fault, Nagisa-chan. I will notify the kitchen staff and ensure this won't happen again."

Chikaru's nonchalant smile stupefied Nagisa.

She's such a nice Student Council President. So different from Miyuki-sama. But why is she dressed like that and serving us…?

"Oh, you're giving me strange looks too," Chikaru said. "Do I look bad in this outfit…?"

"N-No, absolutely not! You look great! And you're so nice and very helpful…" Nagisa said, flabbergasted.

"Oh, really? That makes me so happy. You're so nice, Nagisa-chan. All the transfer students this year are so sweet. Ohh…I want you to transfer to Lulim too, Nagisa-chan…"

Chikaru smiled innocently as she looked at Nagisa. "Ah, but if I said that, it might upset Shizuma-sama?" She stuck out her tongue.

"Oh, Chikaru-sama, you know Shizuma-sama?" Nagisa asked, her cheeks reddening as she beamed with pride, talking about her favorite oneesama.

Chikaru noticed Nagisa's cheerfulness and smiled back, thinking—*my, she looks so happy.*

"Yes, of course I know her. And about her dealings with you, Nagisa-chan. But what an enviable story…to have the gorgeous and proud Shizuma-sama…fall in love with you at first sight."

Chikaru clasped her hands in front of her chest and looked at the ceiling.

"Oh, how romantic…the Queen, who closed her heart after the loss of her beloved princess…met a sweet, honest angel that descended from the skies…and thawed the Queen's frozen heart…" Chikaru opened her arms as if to embrace Nagisa.

"Nagisa-chan is Shizuma-sama's rescuing angel. Come to think of it, Sakuragi Kaori was also very calm and lovely…and a frail, beautiful girl," Chikaru recounted sadly.

"The young lady returned to Heaven quite early, because her beautiful soul was loved by God…so they say. She was probably too pure and beautiful to remain on Earth. That's why she had to depart so soon…"

Nagisa felt a piercing stab in her heart.

"After she passed away, Shizuma-sama…lost her usual kindness. She had me worried. She played it off with her usual flirtatious behavior, but I somehow knew… Shizuma-sama was very lonely…"

"Chi-Chikaru-sama…" Tamao murmured.

"Oh, I'm sorry for talking about this…" Chikaru let go of Nagisa's arm, which she was still hugging. She peered into Nagisa's face.

"Nagisa-chan…the Miator students may say all sorts of things to you. But…Shizuma-sama is definitely cheerful when she is with you. Please stay with Shizuma-sama, no matter what. If things get worse, Shizuma-sama will probably withdraw from the *Étoile* competition, as a last resort. Please don't lose sight of what's important, regardless of what people around you say, okay?"

Her smile was like that of a goddess.

Shizuma's smile was dignified and almost overpowering, like a Greek goddess, but Chikaru's smile was warm and comforting, like a gentle spring breeze.

"…Yes…" Stunned, Nagisa almost choked on her answer and couldn't say another word.

Chikaru patted Nagisa's shoulder. "Good, Nagisa-chan… that's the *Étoile* candidate representing Astraea that I know. We are lucky to have so many wonderful transfer students arrive this year. I just met Hikari-chan a few minutes ago…you know, the new Spica transfer student?"

Nagisa finally began to focus on the conversation. "Oh, yes…I met her in the Maiden Horse Race…I was just wondering how she was doing."

"Oh, so you've already met her? She's adorable, too. She's cute, sweet, and quite sharp…and she seems strong-willed, to withstand the bullying by Amane-chan's fans." Chikaru chuckled.

Nagisa looked where Chikaru pointed—and saw Hikari-chan, sitting two tables away.

Hikari noticed them and waved back shyly.

"Come to think of it, you and Hikari-chan seem a lot alike. Nagisa-chan, if you ever get tired of Shizuma-sama…won't you transfer to Lulim? If you and Hikari-chan join me, then the Costume Club will be sooo fun…"

Tamao laughed at Chikaru's joke.

"Hmm—so, Kagome-chan, you never attended school until you entered Spica's junior high?"

Kagome gave a small shake of her head in response to Miyuki's question. "No."

They were in the St. Lulim Girls' School dining hall.

Bright maple wood floors and off-white plaster walls were easy on the eyes. A large fireplace stood at the far end of the room, but there was no fire in it during this warm season.

A domed ceiling made the room seem spacious, and in the center of the large hall was an oval table, roughly five meters wide, that held numerous pink roses in a vase and had a spotlight shining down on it.

The tables and chairs had bright, casual colors, and the central table's motif was pink—Lulim's school color.

It was time for dessert, and the atmosphere had become relaxed but lively.

This dining hall gathered students from Miator's Flower Class, Spica's *Trois* Class, and Lulim's Class C.

Many of the tables were close to the center. Sitting at the head chair of the center table next to the grand piano was the Miator Student Council President, Rokujo Miyuki.

Miyuki was curious about the tiny girl who sat across from her, clutching a small teddy bear. She talked to her and found out that she came from a very affluent family.

She was a first-year student, but she had just come back to Japan recently with her wealthy parents, and she had had a private tutor teach her at home until now.

Miyuki thought… *A child like her could…*

"You're very cute. If you transferred to Miator, there'd be many oneesama who'd love to take care of you as their younger sister. You'd be extremely popular," Miyuki said with a smile.

Kagome, feeling lonely, muttered, "But…Kizuna-oneesama isn't at Miator."

"Oh, you already have a favorite oneesama? Don't worry, we have many lovely oneesama too…"

As the Student Council President, Miyuki couldn't shake the habit of scouting everyone for her school.

A sudden restlessness swept the room, beginning at the entrance.

"What is it?" Miyuki slowly turned around.

A student, being led by one of the sisters, entered.

What's going on, at such a time as this? Is someone tardy? Or...

The student, who wore the white uniform of Spica, made a beeline to the center table where Miyuki sat.

Spotlights shining from the walls seemed to create shadows that first ran ahead, then bounced behind, as if chasing the walking student—which made her stand out even more.

Miyuki...squinted. *That face...*

Excitement filled the whole room. The sister stopped next to the grand piano, right under the main spotlight shining from above...and clapped her hands over her head.

"Everyone, be quiet... I would like to introduce a new transfer student who has moved into our dorm today..."

Before the sister could finish her introduction, the transfer student stepped in front of her. She introduced herself with a clear, smooth voice—which matched her sleek, white Spica uniform.

"Everyone...good day, I'm Kusanagi Makoto. I'm a fifth-year student in Class *Trois*... Nice to meet you."

Everyone was in awe of her energetic voice and beautiful profile. The small-framed girl was shorter than average but had long, skinny limbs. Her figure lacked womanly curves and looked androgynous—like a boy.

Yes… The spotlights revealed a skinny but poised uniformed figure that looked boyish—a really handsome boy.

The bangs of her short hair fell upon an unbelievably delicate face, with prominent nose and eyes and an expression of mingled elegance and self-composure. It caused the crowd to sigh in admiration.

She's so handsome…yet so cute… Miyuki thought. *Who in the world is she…?*

Makoto pulled a single large rose from the center table's vase, sniffed its wonderful scent, almost closing her eyes—and flung it aside.

Like a dart.

The rose-arrow flew straight for Miyuki, who was clutching the back of her chair as she turned to look behind her at Makoto.

What in the world…

Before she could finish her thought, the flower nicked Miyuki's cheek, continued its flight to the table beyond her… and landed on a dessert plate.

The light pink rose bloomed on a slice of devil's food cake.

The dessert sat in front of…

Otori Amane.

Hah!—Miyuki turned back around.

Amane's face crumpled. She slowly looked in the direction of the dart-thrower.

Makoto, poised for action, glared menacingly at Amane,

her body seeming to give off a purple aura. She finally broke the silence.

"Are you Prince Amane? Nice to meet you. I've returned to Astraea Hill, just to save you," she sneered. "Oh, how shall I say this? For the longest time, even before I attended Spica Elementary School, Spica was a shining star, a pure garden of maidens. But now I'm back, and I see Spica has turned into…a chaotic place, much like the cities of Sodom and Gomorrah, which received God's wrath. It's been tossed about over ridiculous romantic involvements, and all because of the cheap love affair of one foolish prince. On top of that, even the holy *Étoile* competition has been reduced to nothing more than a tool to capture her love…ohhh, I can't stand it anymore!"

Looking to the heavens, Makoto grabbed her head in exaggerated agony.

"That's why I challenge you, Prince Otori Amane…"

She pointed her forefinger at Amane. In Astraea, it was a gesture that was regarded as a challenge to a duel.

Amane didn't say a word, so Makoto snickered.

Chuckle… "Well, you certainly are a beautiful, pure, and wonderful prince, eh? But are you really Spica's number-one star? You really don't seem like much of one. But from now on…you are no longer Spica's number-one star!" she suddenly roared.

"The true leading star of Spica is, and will always be…" Makoto closed her eyes, enchanted. "The star whose position as one of the Five Great Stars has never been filled since she left…that star!"

Most of the upperclassmen…were slightly agitated.

The star that had left one of the positions of the Five Great Stars open…for eternity.

Several years ago, a legendary star had won the *Étoile* competition, but she had left the school while she wore the crown, for some unknown reason…

In order to leave a record of her glory in Spica's history, the Five Great Stars system always kept the top seat vacant…to remember the most powerful Star of all time…

Now that you mention it…Makoto looks like her, Amane thought.

"Are you related to her by any chance?" she inquired. She remembered seeing that page in Astraea's school directory. She had seen the picture on the day she had decided to enter the *Étoile* competition…even Amane had been convinced that the person in the picture was worthy of being an *Étoile* and being adored by all….

Makoto opened her razor-sharp eyes. "Maybe, who can tell? It doesn't matter anyway. You don't have the right to ask any questions about her. Especially because you are the one who has ruined the honor of beautiful Spica—something she left behind—over a ridiculous romantic affair!" With that retort, she lightly stalked between the tables.

"I love only her out of the whole world. That's why I want to protect Spica, the school she dearly loved and protected. That's all."

Amane watched, flabbergasted. *Is she trying to make sure everyone sees her face…?*

Makoto called to the entire room, "So, everyone—follow

me from now on! The silliness of this year's *Étoile* competition ends here. We, as residents of Astraea Hill, don't need peach-colored romance. She, the first star, said so herself. There is no such thing as choosing which girl you love. She said that everyone should be able to live in an all-girl world, with a larger mindset and more generosity, working together and looking to the future. So…this brief time of youth shouldn't be wasted on cheap romance, which is like a firecracker, an alluring, but temporary, burst. Nor should it be wasted on jealousy, which stems from an attraction as powerful as the gravity of the planet Venus, but which reduces humans to cruel beings. Your present beauty should be gathered with others to live a whole and peaceful life together, as one, just the way she hoped. Everyone here has a pure heart, beautiful as a pearl. So…you shouldn't use that positive energy for something petty, like jealousy or romance."

Makoto reached toward the domed ceiling, as if she were talking to the heavens.

"We need to live more freely… We must find…" Her face sparkled under the chandelier lights hanging from the ceiling. "The pure, beautiful, and precious treasure in all of us… That's why I will love all of you alike…"

Makoto spread her arms as she faced the crowd, like a radiant ancient Roman statue.

"I will give my love to everyone. So I ask for you to love me in return…"

Makoto's searing gaze pierced through all the students' hearts. The hall fell silent…then…several students sighed deeply… *Ooohh*…

She is…so beautiful and brimming with confidence…

We were looking for her to lead us…

The Spica students blushed. Even the Miator and Lulim students felt a bit jealous of Spica.

Snap…Makoto snapped her fingers, and two Spica students came out, holding a box about a foot square. They opened it.

They were already under Makoto's spell, so when she thanked them for bringing the box out to her, their faces turned beet red. From inside the box, Makoto pulled out a large number of sparkling blue items.

Kyaaah!—cries and screams intermixed as the students at the center table went wild first.

Makoto explained matter-of-factly, "As a token of our meeting…I brought a little gift. Please accept it. This symbolizes my feelings for everyone here. Starting today, all of you are my precious family. I've come alone to Spica…so I welcome anyone that loves me to please come to my room. I will always welcome you. I don't like ugly romance…but I love to give hugs and kisses to my precious family and sisters…"

She gave a wicked smile.

Eager to see Makoto, the students seated at the far tables kicked their chairs over as they stood.

"Aoi Nagisa…right? Thank you very much for helping me the other day!" Hikari bowed. She had stopped Nagisa as she was leaving the dining hall, headed back toward the Bell Walkways.

Nagisa waved her hands bashfully. "Oh, don't worry about it… Anyone would have done that."

"But it was my fault you almost fell from the tower instead of me… And the atmosphere at Miator and Spica became sour after that, so I wasn't able to say thanks… I'm so sorry."

Tears welled in Hikari's eyes. Nagisa gently placed her hand on Hikari's shoulder. "No, really…don't worry about it. You didn't do anything wrong, Hikari-chan…"

Hikari was relieved to hear Nagisa's reassuring words, and she felt her heart warm.

Nagisa continued, "But, umm, can I ask you something? You're also a transfer student, right, Hikari-chan?"

Hikari looked up. "Yes…"

Nagisa, observing a tiny teardrop in the corner of Hikari's eye, said, "Hikari-chan, how do you feel about being in the *Étoile* competition, even though you just transferred here?"

"How…?"

"Well, you know…did you feel like it was more than you could handle…or something that absolutely freaked you out…?" Nagisa struggled to explain her question.

Hikari finally understood what she was being asked. She smiled shyly as she answered, "I always feel everything is more than I can handle. But…"

"But…?"

"Amane-sama told me…even she wanted to run away, long ago. So, I should stay by her side…" Hikari blushed as she continued, "The only thing I *can* do is be by Amane-sama's side…"

Hikari's beaming smile was too bright for Nagisa.

That evening, the students who had eaten at the Lulim dining hall spread rumors like wildfire.

"Wow, is that a real sapphire?"

"Of course! Makoto-sama wouldn't give out any fake jewelry."

"But real sapphire pendants for everyone—even though we have many students from wealthy families in Astraea…this may be crude, but…I wonder how much it all cost?"

"Oh, forget the price… Makoto-sama doesn't care about money. I've finally realized she is the only one who truly loves Spica and Astraea with all her heart! That's why her overflowing love became a beautiful sapphire and…"

"Hey, why do you call her 'Makoto-sama'…?"

"Ah… Well, that's the only thing we *can* call her. I wish you'd been at the Lulim dining hall to see the whole thing, Yoshi-chan… She was really beautiful. Proud, poised, and strong…"

"But I swear you talked about Amane-sama like that yesterday…right…?"

"Oh…but it can't be helped. Amane-sama is also very lovely, handsome, and really beautiful when she's riding horses…she is like a real prince of Spica. But…"

"But?"

"But you know…Amane-sama…is… Well, Amane-sama used to say she wasn't interested in girls, but…didn't you see her at the *Étoile* competition, Yoshi-chan?"

"Yeah. I was pretty shocked, too…"

"Shocked is an understatement. Sad is more like it. The cool Amane-sama, who never batted an eye at anyone, so… frantic…for that girl…Konohana Hikari. The image I had of Amane-sama sort of crumbled at that moment…but…you know, Yoshi-chan…"

"What?"

"As a fan, I still wanted to see Amane-sama claim the *Étoile* crown… I was so intent on cheering for her. I was sad that Amane-sama liked that girl, but a true fan must wish for the happiness of Amane-sama. But…"

"But?"

"But…after the way Makoto-sama explained it… I don't know…how shall I put it? Compared to Makoto-sama, I wonder how Amane-sama feels about us. It somehow made me sad. Yes…we knew it all along. Amane-sama was shy from the get-go, and didn't like to show off, and blushed at the thought of having fans in the first place. Her bashfulness was one of her most endearing qualities. Amane-sama is the prince we look up to, but…she doesn't care about Spica as a whole…so I became a bit sad. I know it's not Amane-sama's fault, but…"

"I see…"

"Makoto-sama is very strong, noble, and confident…and absolutely awesome. I was instantly drawn to her, and I feel I can follow her. Makoto-sama will…take care of us…and Spica and Astráea…and lead us from the front."

"So basically…you're going after your desires, right?"

"Oh gosh! Yoshi-chan, that's not it… Well, if you see Makoto-sama, you'll see. She's really great! Almost as great as…Amane-sama. I didn't know much at first, but she claims to hold the traditions passed down to her from the legendary star that holds the unfilled position…"

"Hey, what are you talking about? Legendary star that holds the unfilled position…?"

"I didn't really understand that part, but…the upper-classmen obviously knew about her. Ah, but…that's beside the point. Makoto-sama was really beautiful, confident, and overflowing with brilliance! So Yoshi-chan, let's go see Makoto-sama tomorrow!"

After a few minutes…the room lights were turned off.

The dark Strawberry Dorms at midnight.

Nagisa couldn't sleep.

She kept tossing in her bed.

"After she passed away, Shizuma-sama…lost her usual kindness…but I somehow knew…Shizuma-sama was very lonely…"

Chikaru's words echoed in Nagisa's heart.

So she was…such a special girl. Sakuragi Kaori-san…

Tamao really tried to downplay it, claiming Chikaru-sama

tends to exaggerate things, so I shouldn't take her that seriously, but…everything Chikaru-sama said seemed so…true.

Everyone else hesitated to tell me about the truth behind Shizuma-oneesama's past. Chikaru-sama was quite different from Shizuma-oneesama, but to me she seems like a kind and gentle beauty.

To hear a person like that speak about the girl in such a way…

"Sakuragi Kaori was also very calm and lovely…and a frail, beautiful girl… She was probably too pure and beautiful to remain on Earth…"

Chikaru's words continued to pierce Nagisa's heart, but she tried to comfort herself.

The day the first round of the Étoile competition ended, after the coronation ceremony, Shizuma-oneesama asked me to believe in her.

Right now, Shizuma-oneesama wants to be with me. I believe Shizuma-oneesama, even now. She really cares about me, I really felt that. Sometimes I'm overwhelmingly happy, but—I've finally became accustomed to it.

But Shizuma-oneesama also said she didn't want to deny her past…the beautiful memories that were like a dream…and the painfully sad days that ripped her heart…

The girl Shizuma-oneesama had strong feelings and bonds with…Sakuragi Kaori.

I only know her name…and a few stories about her elementary school years from Chiyo-chan. A frail, beautiful girl who was perfect for Shizuma-oneesama—the first girl the flirtatious Shizuma-oneesama had a serious relationship with.

But she was stricken by a disease without a cure, and less than a year into their relationship she left the school—and eventually passed away.

When I first heard it, I was a naïve fifteen-year-old who didn't quite get it, because it seemed like a fairy tale. But now... I've heard the story from Shizuma-oneesama, Tamao-chan, and even from Chikaru-oneesama...

About Shizuma-oneesama's past.

And how Shizuma-oneesama feels about me.

Is Shizuma-oneesama comparing me and Kaori?

Instead of Chikaru's words of encouragement, the story of Sakuragi Kaori stayed in Nagisa's heart...and echoed.

What was Sakuragi Kaori like...?

And Hikari's confident smile at the Bell Walkways...it also pricked my heart.

CHAPTER 4

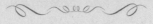

Vulnerable Girls Blossom Under the Conquering Shadow of a Young, Gallant Emperor

"There are more students here than usual."

Otori Amane, as always, stood at the front gate of St. Spica Girls' Institute, which shone in the white morning sunshine. She stared at the long line of girls waiting for her on the other side of the gate. There seemed to be almost twice the usual amount.

She felt dizzy. Despite the various rumors that were flying around, ever since the *Étoile* competition had begun the number of Amane-sama wannabees had increased by the day.

Amane refused all fanclub activities on campus, so the only chance her fans had to express their love was at this gate.

Last night...a mesmerizing Social Exchange Dinner, a peculiar transfer student jumping in to pick a fight with me... and now this humongous crowd this morning...

She shook her head, wondering how much worse things could get.

Did I do something wrong? Or am I extremely unlucky? Or possessed? She pondered her predicament, which was unusual for her.

She pressed on her temples. *My stomach feels queasy. I wonder why…maybe the pressure from competing in the Étoile competition is getting to me. Shion told me the next* cadette *event is a tennis tournament.*

I'm okay at tennis…but I wonder if Hikari can play? If she hasn't played too much, I'm pretty sure she'll get really nervous… I'll have to back her up as much as possible… But if Hikari gets into any danger, like what happened in the Maiden Horse Race, then I'll…

As Amane got lost in her thoughts…*Ding dong…*

The first warning bell rang from Maiden Park.

Oh no, not again. Amane always fidgeted in front of the gate until it was time.

I need to go.

Giving up, she tried to enter the gate between the rows of fans.

"Oh, excuse me."

A Spica student flitted past Amane like a breeze. Her short hair waved in the wind, and an aroma of authentic musk lingered in the air.

Amane, surprised by the sudden turn of events, heard loud screams break out…

"Kyaaaah, Makoto-sama has arrived!"

"Makoto-sama, we've been waiting for you…!"

"Our new star, Makoto-sama!"

"Kyaaah, Makoto-sama, please kiss us…!!"

Half of the students lined up at the gate were waiting for Makoto.

In one night, the news had spread throughout Spica. The students at the gate were Spica students who had become instant Makoto-sama fans and other students that those fans had dragged along to ogle Makoto-sama.

It was almost time for school.

Makoto had probably waited until the last minute to see how far the rumors had spread.

Her fans raged with excitement, and the Amane-sama wannabees, wearing their trademark black chokers, glared at them with envy.

Makoto raised her hand high and boldly walked the gauntlet of fans.

Her erect posture enhanced her graceful strides. It was a very alluring sight.

Even the Amane-sama wannabees, waiting for Amane's long-anticipated arrival, locked their eyes on Makoto's movements.

When Makoto entered the gate, she blew kisses at the crowd. High-pitched screams filled the air.

"Kyaaah, Makoto-sama, you're so wonderful!"

Amid the commotion, a student scampered toward Makoto. In her hand was a small, wrapped gift.

"Umm…here…" the girl said in a frail voice.

"This is a gift in return for the sapphire necklace I received from you last night—though it might not be much of a gift…but I…umm…"

The other students were agitated by the girl's selfish act, but Makoto quietly raised her hand and controlled the crowd.

"Thank you... I'm so glad. Not for the gift itself, but rather your proper feelings of wanting to give me a return gift. I'm deeply moved by the thought. Thank you, my sweet little star of Spica. I love you."

Makoto hugged the second-year student's shoulder, pulled her over, and kissed her cheek. The second-year student was a bit taller than Makoto, but Makoto's actions made her seem larger than life.

Kyaaaaaaah!

A mixture of screams and cheers rang through the air.

Makoto waved at each student and entered the school building.

"I love you, my little stars of Spica. I'd like to kiss all of you...but I'll just send you my feelings. I will accept everyone... so please don't hesitate to come to me."

The wannabees looked at Makoto with a bit of hatred. But they were still a little jealous.

"Awwww, only if Amane-sama would be like that, too..." a young first-year student lamented.

"Shh, stupid. Amane-sama's coolness and sensitive nature make her alluring..." a third-year student, following Makoto with her eyes, commented.

Amane saw the whole ordeal. *I'm amazed to see she isn't embarrassed to do all that...*

A person like her should be in the Étoile competition...not me...

The revolutionary fire slowly spread.

A Revolution.

The small Emperor, Makoto, had arrived, and the news created big waves in Astraea.

In the hall in front of Spica Second Year Class *Deux*...

"Hey, have you seen the Emperor, Kei-chan?"

"Yes, of course. She gave gifts out already."

"Ehh, really?! Oh...what luck. You should have taken me out there, too. So, how was it?"

"How...?"

"Well, there are rumors saying that the Emperor will receive all gifts and thank the gift-bearers with...a kiss..."

At the Lulim inner garden bench during break time...

"Hey, did you hear? Something exciting is happening in Spica!"

"Yes, I know. It all began at the Social Exchange Dinner, right?"

"Oh yeah, the girl who gave out sapphire necklaces to everyone. It's rumored she's aiming to enter the *Étoile* competition..."

"*Étoile*? That's impossible, since round one is over already.

Besides, Spica's Prince Amane won it anyway, so they don't need to try so hard anymore..."

"Well, the girl who passed out the sapphires keeps picking fights with Prince Amane. And they're in the same class. They say the air in the class is so tense..."

"Hyaaah, Toki-chan, you know so much. Ah, of course, you were such a Prince Amane fan, weren't you, Toki-chan?"

"Awww, if the Student Council President, Chikaru-oneesama, would just enter the *Étoile* competition, Lulim would be a little more excited... Don't you think it's a great idea? Lulim's Holy Mother, Chikaru-sama! Her Madonna smile would worry the Miator and Spica candidates, for sure..."

"No, it won't happen. She hates those kinds of things. Doing it would cut down on her time at the Costume Club, watching cute girls in outfits. And she doesn't like to call attention to herself anyway. She's definitely Lulim's number-one star, but...for some reason, I think...Lulim shouldn't get involved in such a mess...yeah..."

In Miator's Student Council room...

"President Rokujo...did you hear?" Marikoya Aiko asked as she lowered a heavy box full of documents from the shelf.

"Hear what?" Miyuki shifted her dust mask to answer.

"About Spica's new transfer student. According to the rumors, she's a really showy character. I was curious about her, but I haven't had a chance to see her yet. I believe you saw her in the Lulim dining hall during the Social Exchange Dinner?"

Aiko's stern, virtuous face was unusually filled with curiosity.

If Aiko, the most monotonous person, is curious about Makoto, then Astraea Hill must be overcome with the "Makoto-sama" windstorm... The thought worried Miyuki a little.

"Yes, I saw her. She came back from Russia, where she was studying music. She was powerful...and quite impressive."

"Impressive...?" Aiko said, bewildered.

"And let's see...she was very confident. She was quite small, though...really small. But she had so much presence I didn't notice it. And since she was small, she seemed pretty androgynous...kind of boyish, I suppose? She definitely has the looks to be really popular. Especially in Spica, since macho stars are their claim to fame."

Miyuki laughed at her own comments.

"She actually promised to rebuild the slightly ruined Astraea, bringing it back to its former glory...an egalitarian who loves everyone equally. She had the gall to hand out sapphire necklaces to everyone as a token of appreciation. I'm surprised Sister Fujii didn't stop her from bribing everyone in the room—such an indecent act, mind you. Maybe she overlooked it because Makoto had just come back from Russia or something."

Aiko placed her forefinger on Miyuki's lips to stop her. "I've heard quite enough, Miyuki-sama. A troublesome person has arrived, hasn't she?" she asked bluntly.

"Absolutely..." Miyuki inspected the old labels on the box. "This has become quite bothersome. But..."

Ah... Miyuki smiled at the box she had been looking for and pulled it out.

The old, faded letters on the cover were barely visible… "Astraea *Étoile* History… But currently…" *Cough cough cough*…Miyuki coughed on a cloud of dust.

"Are you all right, Miyuki-sama…?" Aiko—who was usually emotionless—was flustered as she hastened to Miyuki.

"Yes, I'm fine. We at Miator should lay low for a while, to see how things develop. Even if a new so-called hero has arrived, the fact of the matter is that she can't do much because she's new to the place. And the bane of her existence is Otori Amane. If we allow the Spica students to fight among themselves, Miator might have a better chance of winning the crown. As the saying goes, 'If you chase two rabbits, both will escape.' Let's just pray the Amane couple will be eliminated…"

With the change in the second-round event, the Amane-Hikari couple would surely be disqualified…and by using Tamao's wall of defense, the anti-Nagisa movement inside Miator could be eliminated, and the devil that Spica would probably send to tempt Nagisa—Kusanagi Makoto—could be deflected, thus preventing Makoto's entry into the *Étoile* competition.

Miyuki laughed quietly as she thought—*I can kill not two, but three birds with one stone.*

Aiko looked worried as she said, "If you say so, Miyuki-sama…" and smiled weakly.

As the chaos continued…

The notices for the *Étoile* competition's second round were posted.

<u>ANNOUNCEMENT</u>
This year's *Étoile* Competition
SECOND ROUND
Starting next week, the second round of the
Étoile Competition will be conducted.

– SECOND ROUND –
L'Épreuve d'amour (Tests of Love)
Birth Month of St. John the Baptist, for two weeks and a
day after the Day of St. Meriadoc

PRELIMINARY CADETTE EVENT
Faceless Devil
Location: Astraea Hill
Time: *Two weeks, starting from the Day of St. Meriadoc

MAIN AÎNÉE EVENT
Return from Temptation
Location: St. Miator Girls' Academy Koubu Hall

<u>PARTICIPANTS LIST</u>
(in ranking order from the first round)

ST. SPICA GIRLS' INSTITUTE
Fifth Year, Class Trois   Third Year, Class Un
Otori Amane   Konohana Hikari

ST. MIATOR GIRLS' ACADEMY

Sixth Year, Snow Class   Fourth Year, Moon Class
  Hanazono Shizuma   Aoi Nagisa

**********   **********

**********   **********

Total: Nine (9) Couples

REMARKS:

* Due to the unique characteristics of the *Cadette* Round, *Faceless Devil*, there will be nine anonymous participants, equaling the number of couples during this event.

* If an anonymous participant claims victory over a participating couple, that participant will be allowed to enter the competition, starting with the main event, *Return from Temptation*.

* Detailed rules will be provided on a separate document at a later date.

—Étoile Competition Executive Committee

While the announcement was being posted on bulletin boards, Tomori Shion sat alone in the Student Council room, drinking tea.

A very strong and bitter green tea, which matched how she felt.

She thought about Makoto. Why had she suddenly returned, and why now?

Shion remembered when she had been in the same class as Makoto, in elementary school. Compared to the brainy Shion, who had received a lot of attention even back then, Makoto hadn't stood out much.

Makoto had a very pretty face, but she looked really childish then... I think I was in her third-grade class...I remember having a conversation with this non-charismatic girl.

Considering that's all I can remember about her, we probably weren't that close.

She said she really loved her older sister. They were far apart in age, but they got along very well, and she looked up to and respected her.

Her sister used to go to Spica—and, she said bashfully, that she wanted to attend Spica just to be like her sister.

Around that time, she began to play the violin.

Shion stood at the large glass wall and gazed out. From there she could only see the wide sky and the thick green forest of Maiden Park.

What is Makoto doing right now?

Shion was dubious about Makoto's claims of wanting to save Spica from its downfall and to revive sisterly love in Astraea.

And why is she so bent on taking down Prince Amane? Why did this girl, intent on becoming a violin player and studying abroad since junior high, suddenly give it up...and come back here at such a strange time?

How in the world did she know about Spica's current situation?

A flock of white doves skimmed over Maiden Park's forest in one straight, beautiful line…

Shion recalled the day Makoto had come to Spica.

That day…were the doves flying like this, too?

As the birds flew toward St. Lulim Girls' School,

—I wonder if Lulim has a "White Dove Lovers" club?

Shion chuckled at her own sick joke. She thought about her beloved St. Spica Girls' Institute, and the future of Amane and Hikari…

She was a bit glum.

At the furthest end of St. Lulim Girls' School's inner garden, where light-colored, delicately variegated box elder, maple, and ivy grew, there was an inconspicuous arbor, hidden under the shade of the trees.

Kizuna, Remon, and Kagome had been told to guard the area.

Today's theme was "Police." They wore sharp police uniforms, complete with patrol caps, and surveyed the area with watchful eyes.

"Inspector Remon, what is the situation?"

"Inspector Kizuna, no suspicious persons at this time!"

"Yes, Mr. Teddy Bear agrees!" Kagome chimed in gleefully, holding the bear with a necktie tied around its neck.

"Oh, that's great…" Kizuna patted Kagome's head, because she seemed so happy.

"What is this? Why did you call for me…?" Miyuki inquired. She sat on the arbor bench under the warm shade.

"Oh, I just wanted to invite you for some tea because the weather was so wonderful, President Miyuki. There's no need to be so paranoid." Chikaru smiled as she opened a can and offered it to Miyuki. "But unfortunately I only have *oshiruko*[7] instead of tea…"

Miyuki tried to hide her displeasure. "That's fine…thank you."

"Oh, wonderful! Miyuki-sama, do you like *oshiruko* too? A lot of Lulim students love sweets, so at their request we have *oshiruko* served in the cafeteria all year round. You're more than welcome to come and drink it at our cafeteria any time."

Miyuki didn't really like *oshiruko*, but she forced herself to drink it.

She grimaced. *It's so sweet…*

"Miyuki-sama, did you know that Makoto-chan has come back to Spica recently?" Chikaru beamed.

"Yes…I hear she's quite popular." Miyuki tried to get rid of the sweet taste in her mouth.

She looked around—the arbor blocked most of her view— and noticed four more cans of *oshiruko* sitting next to Chikaru on the bench, but no hot-water pots.

"Makoto-chan likes to be showy and exaggerated…tsk tsk." Chikaru laughed deliberately.

But Miyuki felt odd about it—Makoto-*chan*?

In contrast to Chikaru's laughter, Miyuki's face was serious as she looked straight at Chikaru.

"Did you…call her back…?" Miyuki asked.

"Yes. I'm the one that told her. I flew a white dove all the way to Russia…tsk. Miyuki-sama, isn't it fun to write letters by air mail? I like the very thin air-mail stationery—it's almost see-through and so pretty. I even acted like a noble lady and used quill and ink…" Chikaru tilted her head and smiled as she explained.

"Why did you do it?" Miyuki asked, dumbstruck.

Chikaru suddenly looked disheartened and hung her head. "Ohh…I'm so sorry… I wanted to apologize about that…which is why I called you here today."

She looked really apologetic as she explained her actions.

"I really didn't think it would blow all out of proportion like this… I always wrote letters to Makoto-chan…because I liked to use air-mail stationery. So in my letter this time, I just told her what was going on at school. Makoto-chan was a Spica student, and I thought she would like to hear about this year's *Étoile* competition, so…"

Chikaru smiled softly, almost nostalgically, as she recounted the events, but Miyuki seemed doubtful.

"Are you sure that's it?" she asked.

Chikaru's answer was just as Miyuki expected.

"Yes, of course. Would there be any other reason? This year's *Étoile* competition is mainly a fight between Spica and Miator. Lulim students, including myself, will just sit back and enjoy the show."

"But President Chikaru…don't you want Lulim to do well in the competition too…?"

Miyuki went straight to the heart of the matter, but Chikaru didn't bat an eye.

"Yes, of course. I have those hopes. But…"

She pointed to the arbor entrance. "Look at them. The future stars of Lulim are these adorable girls. They definitely have potential, so when they become fifth-year students, they'll have a good chance, but…at this point, they're still too young."

The three girls who were supposed to be guarding the area were now leaning against each other as they slept, with Kagome resting her head on Kizuna's lap.

"Lulim will probably have a golden age after I graduate. I might not be able to witness it, but…" Chikaru's face turned moody for the first time. "But it's okay…as long as these girls are happy. All I can do is teach them everything I know… prepare them for a glorious future. So Miyuki-sama, please don't worry about Lulim."

"I see," Miyuki said sympathetically.

Lulim was a relatively new school with only a few students who were well versed in school politics. In Miyuki's opinion, the only person who fit the bill was Chikaru, the reigning star of Lulim. Miyuki even felt pity for Chikaru, a lone star with no peers of her caliber.

"Chikaru-sama…if you were in Miator, you'd be more…" Miyuki started to say, but Chikaru smiled.

"No, don't say that. I dearly love Lulim…"

"I'm sorry," Miyuki said sincerely. *No wonder she's Lulim's Holy Mother. I don't even come close to Chikaru's immeasurable kindness.* But Miyuki's greatness was in the fact that she could admit to these things.

Chikaru continued, "Oh, I'm sorry…I got so gloomy. I'm the one who's supposed to apologize, Miyuki-sama. I'm very sorry Makoto-chan suddenly declared her intention to enter the *Étoile* competition and became the cause of all this turmoil…"

She grabbed another can of *oshiruko.*

"Would you like seconds?"

"N-No, thank you, I'm fine."

"Are you sure? Please don't hold back. Or…are you still angry…?"

Chikaru seemed so remorseful, and Miyuki hastily comforted her, then announced that she had to leave.

Before she left, Miyuki emphasized that Chikaru wasn't responsible for Kusanagi Makoto's behavior since she'd arrived, and Miator wasn't all that affected by it, so Chikaru didn't have to worry.

Miyuki scurried away, saying it was almost time for the afternoon classes.

Chikaru, watching Miyuki disappear, thought, *Are you relieved now, Miyuki-chan? I'm sorry for giving you sweet drinks you don't like…*

Fwoooo…

The winds whistled loudly. The dewy, stormy winds were still a bit chilly on the skin, but they carried a warm moistness.

Nagisa leaned on the roof railing and looked to the clouds in the sky. She held a small piece of paper.

This is real, right?

The person she was waiting for hadn't showed up yet, so she was a bit worried.

During lunch break, I will wait for you on the roof.
—Shizuma

It was a simple note, passed to her at the beginning of fourth period.

Who did she give it to in my absence?

It was such a spontaneous act, and was so very like Shizuma-oneesama, Nagisa had burst out in laughter when she'd read it.

Her heart thumped at the thought of meeting Shizuma, but these days instead of feeling nervous she actually felt refreshed— and her heart swelled with anticipation.

During lunch break, the announcements for the second round of the *Étoile* competition were to be posted, so the class had been filled with excitement. This was a great excuse to get away from it.

But…I was targeted immediately after the posting of the first-round announcements…

Groups of scary upperclassmen called me out and taunted me about not being worthy to be in the Étoile competition, especially as Shizuma-sama's partner…or they left me stuck with cleaning duties by myself…and that library incident culprit…

Looking back, I guess it was inevitable. I didn't know until I saw the Astraea School Directory…

Ah...

Nagisa realized. *The Étoile competition announcement... getting called out...and the fake letter...*

Don't tell me this is another...

Nagisa's face went white.

"Nagisa!"

A low, powerful, and lustrous voice came from behind her.

It's Shizuma-oneesama's voice. So it wasn't a mistake.

Nagisa didn't realize, as she sprang toward Shizuma, that she was more happy to see Shizuma than relieved about the note not being a trick.

Shizuma had just opened the door at the top of the stairs, but as soon as she saw Nagisa bounding toward her she opened her arms wide for her darling girl.

Nagisa's smile broadened some more.

Jump...Nagisa scampered up the three steps to the stairway entrance where Shizuma stood and bear-hugged her.

Shizuma-oneesama—Nagisa felt sort of nostalgic.

She burrowed her face into Shizuma's chest and felt happy, her worries melting away.

"Nagisa..."

Nagisa heard Shizuma's voice—which sounded lower, because it was traveling through Shizuma's body and echoing in Nagisa's ears.

Ah... Nagisa tried to hear what Shizuma wanted to say next, but...

Thump thump thump thump... All she could hear was the faint sound of Shizuma's heartbeats.

A very soft, warm sound. Nagisa felt excited to be so close to her, but also felt a strange sense of familiarity, a very blissful, soothing feeling…

She was enveloped in happiness, about to float away…

"Goodness, Nagisa…what's wrong? Were you feeling lonely? My darling little girl…" Shizuma softly laughed as she rubbed Nagisa's shoulder with her large hands.

Nagisa was coaxed into comfort, but… *Hah! I wonder if Shizuma-oneesama thinks I'm strange, since I bear-hugged her so suddenly…*

But when she looked up, she saw…the gentlest, kindest expression on Shizuma's face…

She tried to pull away, but Shizuma's arms locked her in, preventing her from moving.

Shizuma looked at Nagisa for a brief moment before saying, "Goodness, so Nagisa does like me, at least a little. I'm so glad." Her face moved even closer to Nagisa's.

Nagisa was pulled into Shizuma's beautiful eyes, full of strong will and determination, as the realization zoomed up on her…

Ah…she's gonna kiss me…

Nagisa closed her eyes to prepare for it, but…Shizuma sweetly nibbled her ear instead.

Nagisa's ear turned red, and a little wet. A brisk wind went by, and the dampness on her ear was chilled by the strong winds blowing across the roof.

Shizuma drew her face back and spoke. "Soon I won't be able to see you…so we need to hold back a bit."

O-Oh…so that's what it's about.

"A-Ahahahaha…"

Nagisa felt her body go limp and dropped to her knees.

Shizuma led Nagisa over next to the railing, the best vantage point to see the whole expanse of Maiden Park.

Shizuma's beautiful silver-gray locks waved in the wind. Nagisa felt as if something had been drained out of her as she stood next to Shizuma and looked at the sky.

The same sky that she'd been looking at as she had thought about Shizuma.

Shizuma-oneesama…Shizuma-oneesama, as you look at the sky, what are you thinking about?

Nagisa tilted her head as she pondered that question.

Maybe…maybe Shizuma-oneesama is thinking about… Sakuragi Kaori… The pure-hearted soul… Her most beloved girl who left the skies…

Shizuma-oneesama seems so sad…

Nagisa's anxiety poured out.

"Umm…are you feeling lonely, Shizuma-oneesama?"

Shizuma quickly turned to her. With a dumbfounded look, she said, "Oh, of course."

Oh, I thought so… Nagisa was disheartened.

"I'll be really lonely, knowing I can't see you for two weeks…"

Shizuma looked to the sky. "I'll be so lonely, I might want to die."

Huh…?! No, that's not what I meant…

It wasn't clear if Shizuma sensed Nagisa's concern or not. Shizuma licked her lips…

"Hey, Nagisa. For two weeks, don't cheat on me, okay? Truthfully, the Faceless Devil is such a drag, and I really didn't want to do it. Maybe I shouldn't have entered the *Étoile* competition after all."

Shizuma raised her arms up in an exaggerated way, as if to say *Ohh, God...*

"But I suppose I'll have to stick with it for Miator's sake... and as Miyuki said, I'm a bit curious to see how Prince Amane and her partner handle this event..." Her eyes had a mysterious twinkle.

"Well, my love is definite and strong, so I won't falter, but those two...seem like they won't be able to handle a long-distance relationship, don't you think? I'd love to see that tightly contained Prince Amane—who claimed to have no interest in girls—go stir-crazy with jealousy, you know...?"

Shizuma cracked up, but Nagisa was appalled.

"Gosh, Shizuma-oneesama...how could you say that! How mean... I feel sorry for Hikari-chan! She was almost thrown off the tower during the first round... I'm glad everything turned out all right, but if that sort of thing happened again, Hikari-chan would be so hurt..."

"Oh, Nagisa, what are you saying? You were the one who ended up hanging off the tower! You were lucky that I caught you right when you fell, but if I'd been late..."

"Aaah, well, that's true, but..."

Nagisa pouted as she recalled the incident. It had been right after Nagisa had found out about Sakuragi Kaori and Shizuma's past, which had made her want to withdraw from the *Étoile* competition—but then she had been saved by Shizuma's strong arms...

Shizuma continued, "Goodness, Nagisa, you're too nice... but I suppose that's one of your endearing qualities. Still..."

She wrapped her arms around Nagisa from behind and squeezed her tightly. Nagisa felt so much she couldn't say a word. She heard Shizuma's voice behind her.

"If you keep thinking about other people, your precious Shizuma-oneesama will be soooo worried about you...and won't be able to handle being away. Do you understand? So for two weeks...don't cheat on me, okay? I've already warned Tamao, too..."

What kind of warning?—Nagisa's heart jumped at the thought.

"I agree that you need a bodyguard while I'm away. But remember this...if you run into any kind of danger, or if I find out you've become too friendly with someone...I will surely run to your side. At that point, the Faceless Devil will disqualify us, and it will be game over. So...if you don't want to drop out and disappoint Miyuki, Chiyo-chan, Tamao-chan, and the other Miator students—behave for two weeks, okay? I...really don't care about the *Étoile* competition. My only wish is to be with you..."

Shizuma brought her face to Nagisa's neck. She carefully swept aside the stray hairs that covered the young girl's neck.

Nagisa's exposed neck felt cool as the breeze blew past.

The next moment.

Ah...

A warm, moist sensation as Shizuma kissed the nape of her neck.

Nagisa blushed, and her heart tightened…and she still couldn't say a word.

If something happened to Nagisa, Shizuma-sama would probably give up the *Étoile* competition just to be with her.

Oh, she's so hopeless—Nagisa thought happily.

"Will you two be able to handle staying apart…for two whole weeks?" Yaya asked as she put away tubes of paint. This was after school, in Spica's Third Year Class *Un* classroom.

Hikari answered Yaya's question with a bashful smile as she changed the water in the flower vase. "Gosh, Yaya-chan… I'll be okay. Since Amane-oneesama is such a lofty star…I can't see her much anyway. So unlike the other couples, who might have a hard time staying apart, I'm used to not seeing Amane-sama for more than two weeks at a time—so I'm actually glad they chose an event this easy."

Yaya narrowed her eyes and teased Hikari. "Yeah, but haven't you seen Amane-sama every day recently, Hikari?"

"Ah, well…it's just coincidence. It's not like Amane-oneesama and I make promises to meet, and we're not in the same clubs or anything…it's really a coincidence. We bump into each other in the lounge or in the hallway, that's all. Oh gosh, you should know that, Yaya-chan," Hikari giggled.

"That's why…geez, Hikari, you're so dense! Or are you

telling me this to convince yourself? So you don't get in over your head…?" Yaya stood next to Hikari, working at the sink.

"I'm not telling myself anything…" Hikari looked troubled, lowering her eyes, her cheeks coloring themselves pink.

Hikari is so adorable—Yaya shut her inner feelings off and continued.

"It can't be a coincidence! Amane-oneesama normally doesn't go out of her way to do things, and in fact she doesn't really leave her own classroom…in order to avoid her fans all over school. That Amane-sama has been acting strange since the *Étoile* competition began—no, long before that…though no one else knows about it, I'm sure…since the day you got homesick. Do you seriously think Amane-sama would mill around in the Third Year Class *Un* hallways for no reason…heck no!"

Yaya threw her hands up in disbelief.

"Oh golly…" Hikari's voice trailed off.

"That's why I'm telling you. I seriously doubt you two can stay apart for two weeks. You'll be okay, Hikari, but I don't know about Amane-oneesama. Truthfully, I don't want you to stick to Amane-sama, but since you two are now representing Spica, I don't want you to ruin the school's reputation with a dishonorable blunder, and…"

Yaya gnashed her teeth. "That Kusanagi Makoto!! I don't really care about some long-forgotten star with a permanent seat or whatever…isn't it really dirty to lure us with gifts?! I really hate people like that! She jumped into the situation without getting the whole picture, saying all kinds of crap and promising to rebuild Spica by being the next *Étoile*… I wish she'd stop blowing all that hot air. I'm pretty sure she'll jump into the Faceless Devil as one of the devils, but that's so obvious. Nobody will fall for that one!!"

Yaya, waving her fists in the air, finally stopped, panting for breath.

"Yaya-chan..." Hikari-chan was taken aback as she looked at Yaya. "Makoto is so pretty...I just assumed she was your type, Yaya-chan..."

Yaya smiled, embarrassed. "Well, I do admit she is pretty... really pretty. But Hikari, don't forget..."

She placed her hand on Hikari's neck and brought Hikari's face close to hers. She stared intently into Hikari's face.

"I really like you, Hikari. It's not like the pure, beautiful, sisterly love that Kusanagi Makoto touts, either."

The image of Hikari glancing down, veiling her eyes with her long eyelashes, burned itself into Yaya's mind. Yaya's heart jumped.

"What I'm talking about is a hot, burning desire. I want to...free you."

Oh gosh, I said it...!

Hikari, who was looking down in embarrassment with slightly reddened cheeks, lifted her face... She wore a puzzled look.

I want to free you...means...

Yaya tried to find a way out. Somehow.

"Well..." Yaya fished for words. "Well, umm, err..."

It was unusual for her to panic. Her inner voice told her to kiss Hikari and get it over with...but something stopped her from doing so.

"I mean…" She let go of Hikari and turned around. "I mean, I don't want Kusanagi Makoto to take over this place! That pure…equal sisterly love doesn't exist, at least for me…"

Her voice shook at the end of her statement.

"So… So you and Amane-sama need to win, for me…"

"Yaya-chan…" Hikari was nearly crying.

"Wh-What's…wrong?" Yaya turned around. *Did I say something to make her cry…?*

Hikari was full of emotions as tears welled up in her eyes.

"Yaya-chan… Yaya-chan, thank you… I… I…"

Tears rolled down Hikari's cheeks, and—she jumped into Yaya's arms.

Hikari buried her face in Yaya's chest and let tears stream down her face.

"I was actually really scared…at the thought of not seeing Amane-oneesama for two whole weeks. I was terrified to think that…maybe Amane-sama would find someone cuter than me…and leave me…"

She sobbed and tried to hold back her tears. "And I couldn't bear the thought of not seeing Amane-oneesama for more than a day, because I get so scared and worried…and I want to see her so much…two weeks will just drive me crazy. But Kusanagi-sama's arrived, insulting and denouncing Amane-sama—it's all my fault—so I decided to stay strong and win the *Étoile* competition to regain Spica's and Amana-sama's honor…"

"Stupid…Hikari…" Yaya stroked Hikari's hair. Her heart tightened, because Hikari was so endearing.

"But Yaya-chan, I'm glad you're supporting me… Thank

you, Yaya-chan. I'll do my best for Amane-oneesama. I'm going to do my best to win the second round…yes…"

Hikari was absorbed in her convictions…

While Yaya…had mixed emotions…

CHAPTER 5

A Black Wedge is Driven into the Towering Pile of Stones

It was the Month of St. John the Baptist, and the Day of St. Meriadoc…or June 7.

It was also the start of the rainy season.

It had been ten days since the students had switched over to their summer uniforms—it was the first time Nagisa had worn this version. The short-sleeved white blouse had intricate lace patterns in several places, and the jumper skirt was bright green. The summer uniform was boldly different in design from the winter uniform, but was nonetheless very classy and cute, like Miator, and was as popular as the winter uniform.

Nagisa came to school in the depressing rain and absent-mindedly stared out the window, watching the rainwater stream down the panes. She didn't have the luxury to enjoy her new uniform.

"Hey, are you daydreaming? You don't have time to do that,

Nagisa-chan! Let's get ready to go!!" Tamao snapped.

Nagisa sluggishly turned around. "Awwww, are we doing it again todaaaay...?" she asked groggily.

"Of course! We were authorized time to practice on our own, so we can't waste even a minute!" Tamao placed her hands on her hips. She was in a rare lecture mode.

"We're gonna practice again after school, so can't we take a break this morning?" Nagisa pleaded.

"No, no, no! Are you kidding! We only have ten days until the main event! You don't have time to lose, Nagisa-chan!"

"Aww, but my whole body is so sore..."

"That's because you don't exercise regularly! You seemed pretty athletic, Nagisa-chan, but I never expected you to *suck* this badly at dancing!!"

"I-I'm soooorry..."

Nagisa sounded really pathetic, but Tamao dragged her out of the room.

Their classmates chuckled at the sight; Nagisa's efforts were finally being accepted at Miator.

"One, two, three...one, two, three..."

Tamao clapped her hands in rhythm. *Clap clap clap...* The sound echoed through the vast Koubu Hall. It was the only ballroom or dance hall in Astraea, and was part of Miator's school complex. The ceiling above the wooden floor was at least five meters high and was made of stained glass. It depicted birds and flowers, drawn in a beautiful Japanese style. It had the feel of a retro-modern *Taisho* Era[8] building.

The main event of the second round of the *Étoile*

competition—Return from Temptation—would be held in this room. Those couples who had resisted and triumphed over the devils' temptations would reunite with each other, dance with each other despite not having met for two weeks, and display the strength of their love.

"One, two, three…one, two, three…come on, don't be so timid! Go more smoothly…yes, like that…aah, you're out of step!"

Tamao sounded irritated. "I taught you the back step on the first day, right? You keep taking an extra beat when you do that, Nagisa-chan. You're probably trying to do it in four beats, but the event dance will be a waltz, so it's a three-beat dance. This is actually the easiest step for a novice, so you need to master it really quickly…"

Tamao realized her words had been too harsh, because Nagisa shrank down in shame.

Tamao tried to make up for her tone. "Well, you know, Nagisa-chan, you're pretty athletic. I know your P.E. test scores. You run 50 meters in 7 seconds, and jump at least 50 centimeters high, and your bust is 79 centimeters, and you can reach down 30 centimeters past your toes…"

"H-h-how do you know that!?" Nagisa gurgled.

"Tsk, because I was interested in you."

"Even so, good heavens…" Nagisa was open-mouthed.

"Great, you're back to normal. Besides, you have potential, Nagisa-chan, so you could excel! But why are you so messed up? You've been out of step and clumsy…"

"Am I that messed up?" Nagisa asked, full of shame.

"You're usually so cheerful and give your all in everything you do, but…you don't seem to be with it, you know?"

"I'm sorry," Nagisa apologized weakly.

"Don't apologize…just keep trying. If you don't get better, who knows what Shizuma-oneesama will do to me…"

The image of Shizuma glaring at them as if she'd just beheaded an ogre crossed both of their minds. *"Hmph! You two pretended to practice dancing, but you fooled around instead, huh? Ohh, goodness! I need to inspect Nagisa-chan for any hickeys on her body…come here, Nagisa…"*

The two girls looked at each other, sighed…and nodded.

"So…why are you having problems? Do you absolutely despise dancing or something, Nagisa-chan?" Tamao asked seriously.

Nagisa gulped and finally decided to make a major confession.

"Tamao-chan, look…"

With the most pathetic look ever, Nagisa pointed below her waist—at the white organdy petticoat, with several semi-transparent layers. She wore a black, short-sleeved, full-body leotard, but the long petticoat over it almost reached to the ground.

"I…can't concentrate in this totally embarrassing outfit…" she whined.

Tamao burst out into laughter.

The Return from Temptation was different from Astraea's normal dance parties, because it was a competition, meaning there were judges and scoring.

It was customary in Astraea to be creative—because that was

one of the scoring categories. The creativeness was achieved by dressing up in costumes, of course.

During the *cadette* events, veils were worn, and for *aînée* events, costumes. For this dance, exquisite outfits were required. But because the three prestigious all-girl schools discouraged skimpy outfits, the dance outfits were all elegant, wide-skirted gowns, the type worn by noble ladies in the Renaissance.

"But you'll be wearing a heavy, layered dress, so your steps will be restricted...it'll be useless if you don't practice with this on..." Tamao couldn't believe she had to explain this.

But Nagisa persisted. "But...this outfit is soooo embarrassing... I probably won't look good in it...and look at my hair... Ohh, Tamao-chan, do I really have to wear it...?" Her voice trailed off.

"Of course you do! You might not know this, Nagisa-chan, but during the actual event, spotlights will be shining on you, and a chandelier will be hung from the ceiling, like in the Crystal Palace...and it will all look really glamorous! And all the spectators look forward to the *cadette* dressing like a real princess. If you don't wear that outfit, then you won't be a match for the other couples!"

"R-Really...?"

"Yes! Absolutely!! Oh jeez...I can't believe that was the reason you couldn't concentrate...no more slacking, Nagisa-san, because I am going to whip you in shape." Tamao laughed. "Otherwise...you will be thrown into the Repentance Room!"

Nagisa's replying laugh was weak. "Ohhh...please don't imitate Sister Fujii..."

"One, two, three…one, two, three…"

The cold voice echoed in the gymnasium. Another group was practicing dancing.

Konohana Hikari wore a practice dress as she danced in the St. Spica Girls' Institute gymnasium.

"Hey! There! Your arm is dropping, and you need to stand up straight!! You've got to turn more rapidly! As you turn, you need to keep your face like this…turn right here!"

With both hands, Kenjo Kaname grabbed Hikari's face, covered with sweat from the intense dance practice, and yanked it toward her.

They seemed to be practicing a very difficult dance, levels above what Nagisa and Tamao were doing.

"I can't believe you were allowed to come to Spica without mastering these simple basics! Okay, again from the top! Concentrate with your whole body…"

Kaname was one of the top five dancers in Spica. Her expertise was the male leading role.

Because she had been asked by the Student Council, she had reluctantly agreed to coach Hikari. At first, Kaname had rejected the idea out of spite, but Momomi had begged and cried, and said it was "for Amane-sama's honor." They couldn't afford to have Amane be a laughing stock at this event…

Kaname got fired up. *Perfect… I can torture this girl— whom Amane-sama is infatuated with—all I want.*

Kaname threw another scathing comment. "Hey! There! Your hips are off! Don't think you're hot stuff just because Amane-sama likes you!"

"Yes!"

Amazingly—Hikari somehow survived Kaname's torture.

Kaname was surprised. *You know...she has...potential... But this is the minimum standard, so she'd better not screw up.*

Hikari maintained her composure and continued to dance, not even wiping the sweat from her face. Kaname paused and actually examined her.

You know, she's actually really cute... She looks like the angel portrayed on the chapel's stained glass window...

Oh, I can sort of understand why Amane-sama would fall for her...

The jubilant "Kitten Waltz"[9] played in the gym.

Whump... Hikari slipped on her own sweat.

Kaname acted instinctively. "Are you all right...?"

She was about to run out to Hikari...but stopped in her tracks, frozen.

She looked at her outstretched hands. She had been about to...embrace Hikari.

Cold sweat covered Kaname's palms.

Meanwhile, Amane was quite worried.

She sat in the classroom and stared at the grain of her wooden desk in agony.

It had been four days since she'd last seen Hikari. During breaks between classes, she had used to wander around the campus, but these days she holed up in the classroom, with nowhere to go, and sat at her desk.

This is boring, Amane thought.

Until then, she hadn't realized that she always left the classroom during breaks.

But it finally dawned on her. *I was...looking for Hikari every chance I had.*

She'd used to think she left because she wanted to avoid her persistent fans—because they were so annoying. But that wasn't it.

Hey, Hikari...Even now, I want to see you so much... I wish I had said that to you before we separated...

As she stared at her desk, Amane recalled their final meeting, four days ago.

"I'm...really scared." Hikari's voice cracked; she sounded like she was about to cry.

The evening's gentle breeze drifted across the patio. It was the night before the second round of the *Étoile* competition— when they would have to separate for two weeks. Amane had asked Hikari to meet her at midnight.

Right outside the Spica Dorm lounge was a large patio that faced the forest of Maiden Park. Amane usually avoided public places, but that night she boldly chose a romantic rendezvous.

She found Hikari, who was wearing a slightly babyish nightgown, and thought she looked awfully cute.

"To tell you the truth…" Hikari admitted shyly. "I think I'm really selfish, and I didn't want to say this to you, Amane-sama. But…once the *Étoile* competition begins, people who don't like me will probably say things to you…and by chance, if something happens…like what happened at the Maiden Horse Race…I wouldn't know how to handle it alone…so I'm terrified. And if you meet a wonderful person in my absence…and like her more than me…then I don't know…"

Looking at Hikari, not listening to her nervous ramblings, Amane was captivated by her innocence…and chuckled.

"Tsk… You're so cute, Hikari."

Amane caressed her hair. Hikari flinched…and looked at Amane.

Illuminated by the patio light, Hikari's tears sparkled as they rolled a thin path down her cheeks, which were smooth as porcelain.

"Amane-sama…you're not afraid…?" Hikari's voice grew small. To hide her face, she walked toward the fence and gazed out at Maiden Park.

Amane chased after her. "Ah… I'm sorry, Hikari…that's not what I mean…"

Hikari continued her silent objection, but Amane enveloped Hikari from behind…placed her hand on Hikari's hand, and gently squeezed.

Amane tried not to peer into Hikari's face, but looked at the Maiden Park forest with her.

"Hey, Hikari. Two weeks will go by fast. Of course I'll be really worried about not seeing you, too."

Hikari's heart pounded faster as she listened to Amane's voice.

Thump thump…

Amane went on, "But…if you're worried…I'm sorry. I must be causing you to worry, Hikari…"

"No…it's me…and I just…" Hikari felt her face get hot.

"But I want you to believe me… I'm so horrible…and I don't think I can say this right, but…I just love you very much, Hikari."

Amane let the word "love" slip smoothly out of her mouth.

"You might find this weird, Hikari…but this is the first time I've felt like this…ha ha…so I don't know how to describe it…" Amane, embarrassed, mumbled her last words.

Hikari's heart jumped with joy and surprise, almost painfully…then…suddenly she was so embarrassed.

I don't know why, but somehow I knew Amane-sama's feelings all along…

Oddly enough, I don't feel presumptuous for thinking like that.

Maybe Amane-sama's feelings reached my heart…before her words…

Hikari had been waiting for her special feelings to be given a name.

The name that described the feelings that bloomed in both of them…

Amane's words—I love you, Hikari…

Hikari's heart took in those words…naturally… They gave her strength.

"It's all right. It's my fault for doubting you, Amane-sama…"

"I want you to know…you don't need to worry about me. Please believe in me. I promise not to do anything you don't wish for, Hikari."

Amane hugged Hikari. *Squeeeeze*…

Hikari's heart was squeezed along with her body…

"I'm really worried about you, Hikari. I'm also afraid you might find someone that doesn't cause you as much trouble as I do…a more dependable person…and you might be happier without me…"

"No! I can't think of doing this with anyone else but Amane-sama, even if I go to Heaven, I swear…"

Amane laughed at Hikari's forceful, exaggerated response.

"Even if you go to Heaven…are you sure? But…I'd be sad if you died so soon, Hikari…"

Locked in each other's arms, Amane's laughter vibrated through Hikari, causing her to giggle too.

"I've attended Spica for eleven years, since elementary school. In all those years, I've never fallen in love with anyone. I have lots of friends, sure. And I respect a lot of people, too. Back then, I thought it was strange for a girl to fall in love with another girl—I just assumed it was nothing but a very close friendship…and probably just another way the students broke the monotony here…by over-exaggerating the little things… That's why I tried to understand the reason they were raving about me, but at the same time I wanted them to leave me alone. Besides, I'm not the type that should be regarded as one of the Five Great Stars."

Hikari sympathized with Amane—*but you're definitely the brightest star on campus, so it's no wonder all the girls love you.* That was the thought in her heart…but she only nodded in silence.

Amane looked off into the distance as she continued.

"I wish I could tell you exactly how I feel, Hikari. But… even I don't understand my feelings. It's not a friendship. And it's not a simple adoration of a cute underclassman… But… love and having a relationship…well, since we're not man and woman…you know…"

Since we're not man and woman… Amane painfully repeated that phrase in her mind…and looked down.

Amane and Hikari were not man and woman… So if she said she loved Hikari as a woman…she was afraid of what would happen to them next…

Amane's bashful nature still prevented her feelings from pouring out.

"…It's okay." Hikari pulled away from Amane and softly placed her hand on Amane's cheek.

"…I'm sorry, Amane-sama. I…I just… Just being with you, like this, is enough for me to be happy."

She faced Amane…and looked into her eyes, her own eyes misty.

After a long pause, Amane gave a short reply. "…Yes, me too."

She gently…really gently…embraced Hikari, tenderly, as if she was the most fragile object in the world.

Their feelings for each other were all that was between

them. But they didn't know where to go from there…

What direction to take…

They just didn't know. The naïve couple didn't know how to express their overflowing affections toward one another…

They stayed together for a while longer, just listening to the angels sing from the heavens.

They were like two little birds, standing at the edge of a cliff, afraid to fly.

Amane lifted Hikari's face.

Seeing the taller Amane smiling so tenderly, Hikari lifted herself up on her toes…

Amane widened her eyes, startled.

The tiny bird pecked a kiss.

The little kiss lasted merely five seconds.

Hikari's heels eventually landed on the floor.

Neither of them really knew…how to feel. As they eventually broke their embrace, they smiled at each other.

"I'll take you back to your room," Amane said, and they left the patio.

On the way back, Amane thought about their happy future.

"I don't care about the *Étoile* competition any more. If Kusanagi Makoto wants to take my place and defend Spica's honor…" She smiled. "I'm ready to throw it all away…"

The rainy skies cleared. Strong sunshine poured between the trees.

In the inner garden of the Strawberry Dorms, on the first Friday afternoon after the second round had begun…

"Umm…is it okay to keep my glasses on…?" Remon asked with a shy duck of her head.

"Tsk…well, it's a bit strange, but since you look so cute with them, you can keep them on, Remon-chan!" Chikaru responded in a satisfied way, and she slipped a pair of bunny ears onto Remon's head.

"Okay, that leaves us with…" Two more girls.

"Wow, the bunny tail is so fluffy!"

"Why are there stockings attached to a swimsuit?"

Kizuna and Kagome hadn't changed into their outfits yet.

My, my… I have to pamper them, don't I…? Chikaru's heart fluttered.

The inner garden of the Strawberry Dorms was usually carpeted with grass, with a small fountain off to the side. But a large pool, fifteen meters in diameter, had appeared out of nowhere.

From the second week of June to the end of summer vacation, the triangular inner garden became host to a one-meter-deep, octagonal, temporary pool.

To liven up the Strawberry Dorms, every year at this season the pool was set up. Wooden decks were laid around it, with resort deck chairs and a drink bar that served free drinks on non-school days—a gorgeous setup that matched the style of the luxurious all-girl schools.

Today was the first day, Pool Opening Day.

Chikaru, the party-loving Costume Club President, who

never missed a chance to wear costumes, had volunteered her club to serve as pool attendants.

Today's theme was "Bunny Girl."

"Here, you need to stick out your butt…because I can't see."

Mmmm…! Kizuna, red-faced with embarrassment, scrunched her face and poked her butt out to Chikaru.

Chikaru, kneeling behind Kizuna…stared intently at Kizuna's butt.

What a cute butt, Chikaru thought as she repressed her urge to spank it…and slid her fingers along the French-cut edges of the suit.

Uhyayaha! Kizuna squirmed.

"Come on, stay still…"

Chikaru grasped Kizuna's hands to calm her. Kizuna endured the tickling sensations as Chikaru slowly and deliberately continued her movements.

She randomly rubbed Kizuna's butt, fondled it…and sometimes pinched her softly…which surprised Kizuna each time.

And finally…treating it like a precious treasure, she gently placed her lips on Kizuna's butt…and kissed it.

"All right, that should do it. Don't worry…it'll stay in place, no matter what."

Chikaru had been making sure that the French cut of Kizuna's swimsuit wouldn't shift.

"Okay, that should be everyone," she called to Remon and Kagome, who were already changed into their outfits and setting up a deck chair.

Looking at Kagome, still clutching her teddy bear, and

Remon, still wearing her glasses, Chikaru pondered... *Oh well. They look so cute anyway.*

Chikaru decided to let them be, satisfied with their outfits. She laughed to herself. *I hope more students will join my club when they see these girls...*

"Well, Costume Club members...let's have fun and do our best! We're here to serve as bunny-girl pool attendants. Don't let anyone touch you or get mixed up in any funny business. Be cheerful and cute! Let the party begin!"

"Yeaaah!"

As she saw the three girls yell out together, Chikaru shuddered with excitement.

"I wonder if Shizuma-oneesama is coming to the pool?"

"She probably excused herself today."

"Excused herself...?"

Tamao and Nagisa, wearing their dark blue Miator school swimsuits, arrived.

Nagisa loved baths, so she naturally enjoyed pools too, but—she seemed bashful. She probably wasn't used to her new swimsuit.

"You know the Faceless Devil has already begun, right? Even if it is Pool Opening Day, it would be horrible if you accidentally met each other here...and Shizuma-sama probably predicted you would want to come to the pool, since you're new here...so she excused herself today. See...you don't see any other stars here, do you?" Tamao asked.

Nagisa looked around and understood her point.

That's true…Amane-sama and Hikari and the other Étoile candidates aren't here.

"They're probably in their rooms right now. They need to avoid all kinds of dangers, you know."

"I see…"

Nagisa was pretty sure Shizuma-oneesama would have wanted to see her wearing the new swimsuit, so she was a bit let down.

"Oh…that's too bad, Nagisa-chan."

The voice came from in front of them. Nagisa raised her head and saw…Chikaru at the poolside bar, smiling. She offered Nagisa a sweating glass, filled with an icy-cold drink.

"It's too bad you can't show your wonderful swimsuit to Shizuma-sama…" Chikaru said as she approached Nagisa. She looked at Nagisa from all sides and tilted her head.

Nagisa was shocked at Chikaru's bunny-girl outfit. "Wow, your Costume Club wears these daring outfits too…?"

She couldn't hold back her curiosity. She reached out and… *pat*…Chikaru's breast was softer than she had imagined and bounced back delightfully. The material was…slippery.

"Oooh…" Chikaru, touched by Nagisa, exaggerated her swoon.

Nagisa hastily pulled back her hand. "I'm sorry, I…I…just wondered what the suit felt like. But…wow, it's so slick… "

Nagisa smiled bashfully at Tamao.

Both Tamao and Chikaru's eyes twinkled.

"Oh, Nagisa-chan…are you curious about this bunny-girl outfit?"

Their voices came out simultaneously. Tamao and Chikaru stared at each other in amazement. The next moment, they nodded as if they had made a silent agreement.

What? What are they doing? Nagisa didn't have time to think about it, though.

"If you like it so much…you can change into a bunny girl! We'll help you put it on."

The two girls dragged Nagisa out of the pool area.

"Umm…does this look all right? Isn't it…weird…?" Nagisa hesitated, but Chikaru reassured her.

"Oh no, it's fine. You look good in it, but…"

But…? Nagisa was suddenly scared.

In the locker room next to the inner garden, several wooden lockers were lined up. There was a sense of mysteriousness about it. Nagisa stood in an unfrequented area of the locker room as her heart thumped at the bold outfit she had on.

"But…we should fix it a bit…" Tamao commented.

"Oh, you think so too?" Chikaru added.

Fix what…? Nagisa was still confused.

"Excuse me…" Tamao's hand slipped into Nagisa's breast.

She pushed her hand into the tight space between the suit and Nagisa's breast.

Tamao and Nagisa felt a squishy sensation.

Squish squish… Squiggle squiggle…

Ohhh, nooo… Heedless of how uncomfortable Nagisa felt, Tamao slid her hand to Nagisa's underarm area and pushed

Nagisa's maturing breasts into the bunny-girl outfit's bra cup.

Only Nagisa's right breast filled the bra cup, and pointed up.

"Now that's sexy," Tamao grinned. "You're…so big, Nagisa-chan."

Nagisa's face blazed at Tamao's comment.

"Let's do the other side…"

"N-No, I'll do it myself…"

Nagisa tried to decline, but Chikaru cut in.

"Are you kidding, Nagisa-chan? If you fix it yourself, it won't settle in properly. Oh my, please don't tell me you've been doing it yourself all this time? Poor soul… Don't worry, you're in Astraea now! Tamao-chan and I will do it today…but I'm sure Shizuma-sama will do it for you from now on."

Shizuma-sama touching Nagisa's breast… Nagisa almost fainted at the thought.

Nagisa waved her arms. "Th-That will not happen…!"

Tamao hugged her. "Oh, of course, I know. It would be too insulting to have Shizuma-sama bow down just to fix your breasts, huh? But you're fine with me doing it, right? Tsk… I'll do anything for Nagisa-chan! You're better off with me, Nagisa-chan, since you aren't nervous around me. Ohh…let's fix your other side, too."

Tamao winked, turned Nagisa around, and dug her hands into her breasts.

This time…she slithered around deliberately.

Ahh…aaaaahhh… Nagisa writhed as little explosions went off in her head…and silently she screamed for help.

Shizuma-oneesama…am I supposed to be doing this…?

"Kyaaaah, so Makoto-sama, you lived in Russia since junior high?"

"Yes. I went there in order to become a professional violinist by sixteen…"

"By yourself?! Without a maid?"

"Yes. Of course, my parents wanted to send one, but I thought I might end up spending time making friends with the maid instead of studying, so…"

Makoto's smile caused the girls sitting around her to blush.

"Oh wow…if that's the case, you should have taken me, Makoto-sama! It must be pretty lonely, living in a foreign country, so if I'd been there I could have comforted you…"

The girl said it on purpose, so she could bring her chair right next to Makoto…and lean against her.

Makoto and her fans sat in Spica's pool dome. It had been a week since the Faceless Devil event had begun. Makoto hadn't done anything yet, but two couples were disqualified already.

Out of the three schools, Spica was known for its sports programs, so it had many specialized facilities, such as the horseback riding grounds, tennis courts, giant gymnasiums, and this pool dome.

This impressive pool facility had a 50-meter pool with depths ranging from 1.2 to 1.8 meters, a diving pool with a platform as high as 5 meters, and a glass-paned scuba tank.

Next to the pool, on a raised platform, was a small café

for the students. The café had ivory-colored parasols over each table, and Makoto, the center of attention, was surrounded by a slew of fans. She sat and relaxed.

The swim classes seemed to have ended. Makoto's black and silver swimsuit—she hadn't had time to order Spica's white one-piece school swimsuit—and matching shorts of the same pattern hung off her slender hips. She stood out in the crowd of white.

Students sitting at other tables began to notice her...

One of her fans spoke in a high-pitched voice.

"I'm looking forward to your mini-concert! It's so great for you to do a special performance for the Strawberry Dorms residents and show off your violin skills, fresh from Russia... I'm thrilled. You've defeated two couples already, so I wonder how many more fans you'll make... I just can't imagine. By the time the third round comes around in July, you'll surely be the world's best *Étoile*!"

"Ahahaha..." Makoto laughed out loud. "I hope so. I look forward to it, too. A star is supposed to garner attention, be praised by everyone, and shine. I believe Spica's white star should shine not only on Spica students, but on everyone in Astraea. I refuse to accept a star who doesn't like the attention. I think she must say that because she isn't confident of herself...she needs to have an escape route in case things don't work out."

Makoto's words became harsh. "Besides, a star shouldn't ever be monopolized by one person! A star is revered by everyone...so she should never...ever be monopolized by one person!"

Makoto's lips quivered, and the student next to her flinched. Makoto, noticing it, waved her forefinger in front of her face— *Tch tch tch tch!*

The girls focused on Makoto's expression.

"She...fell in love with a humble transfer student...and ruined Spica's chances of winning the *Étoile* competition... what a cheap story. That's why I came, to save Spica from the fake star and pull it out of the ruins. I want to shine Spica's white star on all of you," said the Emperor.

With that, Makoto stood up. "Otori Amane...is not the true star of Spica!"

The conversations around the café disappeared, and the students focused their attention on Makoto.

Meanwhile, Amane wanted to take a quick swim to gather her thoughts. The athletic prince wanted to work off her loneliness and worries about missing Hikari—with exercise.

She finished changing, grabbed a towel...and pushed the glass door to enter the pool dome.

She noticed the strange atmosphere as soon as she stepped inside. She didn't know the reason at first. She walked down the side of the pool and stood at the end of the lane.

Then...she realized.

She had no audience.

Every time Amane came to the pool, rumors would spread as soon as she entered the locker room, and by the time she reached the pool, a small gathering of fans would be watching from afar.

But today, when she looked around...no one.

There was a large crowd at the café.

Wondering if there was an event there, she glanced at it briefly, then looked down and tried to pass through...but...

"Hey, wait!"

A sharp voice, coming from the far side of the café, interjected.

Amane stopped. *Is she talking to me?*

When Amane looked up, not only was she surprised, but the crowd looking back at her was too. In the middle of the crowd, as if she was basking under a spotlight...stood Kusanagi Makoto.

Makoto...

Amane finally had the opportunity to look at Makoto up close. Amane was in the same class as Makoto, but by the time the students entered their fifth year, they had more elective classes. Amane took more science classes, while Makoto took more arts classes, so they only saw each other during brief homeroom periods in the morning and afternoon.

And ever since Makoto's arrival at the Strawberry Dorms, their fans—well, Amane considered them her "friends"—stuck closely to them and ensured that they didn't bump into each other.

And Amane...honestly...didn't have any negative thoughts about Makoto. In fact, she completely agreed with Makoto's opinion that girls loving each other romantically was totally wrong, and she would be relieved if Makoto would replace her as the star.

Amane seriously thought the *Étoile* should be a star who wasn't bashful.

That's what Amane wanted to say to Makoto—who hated Amane's guts. She wanted to say, *If you want to do so, I have absolutely no objections, so please do your best and claim the Étoile crown for Spica in my place. I quit.*

But…Makoto, standing on the other side of the pool, was surrounded by fans…so Amane couldn't even have a heart-to-heart conversation with her.

Amane forgot that she had been stopped…she shrugged her shoulders and tried to leave the pool.

"I told you to stop!"

Makoto, with her thin wispy bangs fluttering, walked toward Amane slowly and triumphantly.

Amane stopped once again and turned around to see Makoto, poised for action…

"Prince Amane, great timing! I challenge you to a duel!"

Makoto pointed her forefinger at Amane's nose.

The air tensed.

Pointing at someone's nose was Astraea's sign of challenge. This was the second time.

Even the gentle Amane felt something rustling inside of her, but she just swallowed hard and acted dumb. "Duel?"

"Yes, a duel to determine who will represent Spica in the *Étoile* competition. Let's settle this once and for all."

Makoto seemed a bit more excited than usual…probably because she'd just let off some steam.

"We can settle this in the actual *Étoile* competition. Why

here? You'll just disturb the people here," Amane said.

Makoto's fans had followed her, and soon enough a large audience surrounded the pair.

"Oh, running away, eh? Are you afraid? Since we're here and both have swimsuits on, let's have a swim race. Oh, don't tell me you can't swim…?"

The gallery murmured.

"Amane-sama is good at swimming. In fact she's good at…horseback riding, kendo, cross-country, dance, and so on… everyone at Spica knows she's a gifted athlete."

"Why did Makoto challenge her to a swim match?"

"Either she really doesn't know Amane-sama, or maybe she's confident of her skills…"

Amane was not interested in competing. "I don't want to cause trouble with other students using the pool during lunch break."

Makoto egged her on, undeterred. "Ahah…what a pathetic excuse. That just won't do. Look…"

The pool was empty. The students who, moments ago, had been swimming, had seen the confrontation and gotten out of the pool to witness the event.

Amane remained silent as Makoto continued, on a roll.

"Well, if you're not confident, you can run away from this challenge. But if you do, I'd feel sorry for the Spica students who thought you should be the leader of the Five Great Stars…" Makoto's voice grew louder.

The crowd became unsettled.

"Is Amane-sama going to run away…?" The concerned voices were angry at Makoto's insulting comments… "Amane-sama didn't do anything, and surely doesn't deserve those comments…"

Suddenly Amane turned her back on Makoto.

I have no time for this… Without a word, Amane tried to walk away.

Makoto immediately grabbed Amane's arm to stop her.

The tension sparked in the air, then dissipated.

Facing away, Amane stood still. In the next instant, she turned around and glared at Makoto.

Their eyes locked. There was at least a twenty-centimeter difference in height. Makoto looking up…and Amane looking down.

Makoto gulped, suddenly feeling oppressed.

Amane had a determined look. Had the sleeping lion finally awakened?

She looked straight into Makoto's eyes. "I have no reason to fight you."

Amane's stare was neither coy, adverse, nor disrespectful… she just stared right into Makoto's eyes. She almost felt sorry for Makoto, trying to find a reason to fight her…

And Makoto thought Amane's eyes looked almost like her dearly beloved's…

Makoto snapped out of it. *There's no way she resembles my dearly beloved… She doesn't look like her but… You shouldn't be worried about what others think of you—just do what you really want to do…*

For a moment…Makoto thought she heard her dearly beloved's voice.

It's true, Prince Amane... There is absolutely no reason for you to fight me.

Instantly, her fighting spirit rekindled.

But...I have a reason...yes, a big reason. If you are the Lion King, then I am the Black Dragon. I will breathe scorching fire, hot enough to melt metal, in order to get rid of you—and erase the record of a Spica star that fell to Earth.

For my dearly beloved...I vow to protect St. Spica Girls' Institute and its maiden holy grounds...and make Spica the number-one school in Astraea...for her...

But Amane freed her arm from Makoto's grasp...and left.

"Wait up!" Makoto called.

"I was given a difficult challenge...but it isn't to fight you..." Amane muttered to herself as she stared at the undulating surface of the water.

Noon...at the St. Lulim Girls' School...in the nurse's office.

Chikaru was organizing her outfits.

This cute pink nurse's uniform...is for my adorable Kizuna-chan. And this unusual light blue nurse's outfit will be for Kizuna-chan's classmate and best friend, Remon-chan...because her glasses will probably match it nicely...tsk...

And this amazing white jacket...is for the unsuspecting Kagome-chan. She'll make a really tiny but adorable doctor... hmm, she's actually really smart, so she might really become a doctor one day...

As Chikaru let her thoughts wander, she laid out the outfits, fully enjoying her fantasies.

Where was the school nurse? Chikaru had tricked her into vacating the office for a while, so she could use it freely.

Chikaru neatly folded the outfits and checked all the accessories that came with them. A small folder was on the table next to her. On the cover was "Today's Costume Club Plan"... and Chikaru's sketch of a nurse...

Knock knock knock... Someone knocked on the door.

A handsome voice spoke. "Excuse me..."

"Come in...my, you've come quite early. I thought you'd come a little later. I'm sorry for the mess..." Chikaru apologized loudly.

"Eh? I thought I came on time..." Kusanagi Makoto looked at the wall clock. The next moment, the one o'clock chime went off.

The St. Lulim Girls' School buildings consisted of beautiful, colonial-style wooden architecture. The annex-like building in the far corner, closest to Maiden Park—like a summer home— was the nurse's office.

A slowly turning fan with an attached chandelier hung from the high ceiling. Four large beds were placed in the middle. Chikaru arranged outfits on two of the beds as she enjoyed herself.

The wall clock played a beautiful music...

"Handel's oratorio...the *Messiah*," Makoto noted.

Chikaru smiled. "Mako-chan, you're probably the only one in Astraea who would comment like that about a simple Westminster chime."

"Well…" Makoto didn't have her usual sarcasm and seemed to be at ease when she was alone with Chikaru.

"But it's so ironic. The *Messiah*…a perfect song for me." Makoto grinned.

"So you really believe you're Spica's messiah…?" Chikaru asked with a smile.

Makoto hesitated a bit. "Yes…I refuse to accept Otori Amane as Spica's number-one star! Honestly, I probably can't fill those shoes either. But I'm way, way, way better than her! You understand it, right, Chika? The real star of Spica should be like my dearly beloved…"

Makoto looked up at the twirling ceiling fan, which rattled occasionally. She calmed herself.

"You'll root for me, won't you, Chika?" She approached Chikaru.

With a devilish grin Makoto continued, "Oh, you're finally speaking to me, my gentle Chika? You sent me that letter, but when I came back you totally ignored me, Chika-chan. I was shocked, you know? In the Spica Student Council room…"

Makoto recalled the incident as she hopped onto the other side of the bed, opposite to Chikaru.

"But…I knew you had your reasons…so I acted like I didn't know you. Hey, Chika…you know my feelings, right?"

She reached over and grabbed Chikaru's shoulders.

Unfazed, Chikaru smiled tenderly at Makoto. "Oh…what feelings?"

"Well, my feelings for my dearly beloved…and about wanting to become Spica's star and eventually the *Étoile* for her…and…" Makoto placed her hand on Chikaru's chin…

"And that I love Chika…just like my onee-san…"

Makoto used her thumb to rub Chikaru's lip. Without a word, she brought her face closer…and closed her eyes… As if she were a puppy, waiting for its master to pet its head…

Chikaru giggled, and gently caressed Makoto's small, soft head, over and over…ever so gently…ever so peacefully…

She might have a bigger scar than I expected…

The motherly instincts of St. Lulim's Madonna poured out…

After some time, Makoto opened her eyes and licked her lips with her red tongue. "Please root for me, okay? You can pretend you don't know me, but…you're my oneesan…"

She stopped. "Chika…do you already know…the secret behind me and my dearly beloved…?"

As if to cut off Makoto's question, Chikaru stood up and gave Makoto a serious look.

She smiled. "I'm so glad you regard me as an oneesan… Hey, Mako-chan, will you do me a little favor?"

Rustle rustle rustle… A gentle wind rolled through, bringing the light, sweet scent of flowers. The soft sunshine and the pleasant early summer air…

A small leaf hit Shizuma's face, but she blew it off.

In the center of Maiden Park, near the lake in front of the large chapel, Shizuma was alone, lying in the grass, trying to take a nap. She wondered if the afternoon classes had begun already. She didn't feel like going back to class...

With a sigh, she sank back down. She raised her hand to block the bright sunshine and slowly closed her eyes.

It felt good as she drifted off to sleep... Her eyelids seemed white...and she sweetly dreamed...

The early-blooming lavender that covered the area waved in the wind. It had also been blooming when a group of St. Miator Girls' Academy Strawberry Dorms residents went to summer school at one of the many second homes owned by the Hanazono family—at the edge of their Hokkaido ranch.

Shizuma, then a fourth-year student, split off from the group and went for a long horseback ride. As she sat amidst the blooming lavender at the top of the hill, her favorite black horse by her side...she looked at the full expanse of the Hanazono estate.

Under the warm, almost blinding early summer light, small beads of sweat formed on her forehead.

Someone called her. She turned around to see the short-haired Togi Hitomi. She had been Shizuma's classmate since elementary school, and the students considered her to be Shizuma's right-hand girl—and for a Miator student, she was unusually energetic and strong-natured.

Beside Hitomi was a girl with light pink cheeks, dragging her feet, looking down...

It was...Shizuma and Sakuragi Kaori's first fateful encounter.

Hitomi grinned. "So, what do you think, Shizuma-sama... this is the girl."

"Why?"

"Well, she's a big fan of yours, and has been dying to meet you… I told you about her yesterday, didn't I?"

"Yeah…so?"

"So…umm…well, that's why I brought her here! She was so excited to meet you, like she was going to Heaven or something…"

"Is she really that excited…because she's awfully *quiet*."

"Oh, she's probably really nervous to finally meet her favorite Shizuma-oneesama! But look! She's absolutely adorable. She's probably the cutest out of the whole Third Year class. I always thought she'd be a perfect match for you…" Hitomi smiled proudly, taking credit for her accomplishment. "I explained to you earlier, you should look for a partner for the upcoming *Étoile* competition. I think she'll shine just as much as you, Shizuma-sama…right, Kaori-chan?"

Hitomi peered into Kaori's face as she asked, but Kaori was even more embarrassed and silently tucked her face down.

"Ahahaha…gee, don't freeze up like that, Kaori-chan. Shizuma-sama is the big star on campus, but she's quite an approachable person, you know!"

As Hitomi rambled on, Shizuma decided that she didn't really like the girl, who just stood there, looking down. For some reason, she seemed to let Hitomi do all the talking, but wasn't willing to dirty her own hands…a cruel, unfair girl…Shizuma thought.

"Is she really that cute? If she's not willing to talk to me, I have no time for her!"

Shizuma turned around on purpose, acting as though she

was ignoring the quiet girl. "Come, Hitomi! Let's have some tea in the clubhouse. Mother is here too, so…"

"Eh, ah, but…what about…her…?" Hitomi said, flabbergasted.

Suddenly… *Hug*. Something grabbed Shizuma's leg.

"P-Please don't go… Shizuma…oneesama…"

The quiet girl, Sakuragi Kaori, threw herself at Shizuma, hugged her leg, and stopped Shizuma's movement.

"You…" Shizuma stopped, and something electrical ran from her legs through her whole body.

The girl, still looking at the ground, gathered all her courage, and said in a small voice, "I've…looked up to you since elementary school… I'm so honored to meet you, oneesama…"

It was a phrase she had practiced over and over in her heart.

Goodness… What a naïve and awkward girl…

She's begging me not to hate her… I can hear her inner voice, loud and clear.

Shizuma was moved by Kaori's clumsy, honest feelings. Shizuma's voice became gentle and sweet. "Please stand…"

The early summer breeze rolled past, carrying the sweet scent of flowers.

The dream skipped ahead…

A large cumulus cloud floated in the big blue sky.

It was summer vacation at the Strawberry Dorms. Students enjoyed the mid-afternoon summer beside the garden pool in the inner garden.

Shizuma had a pareo wrapped around her red and gold

patterned bikini as she relaxed at the poolside with Hitomi and Mizuho. Kaori sat quietly at the edge of their table.

Kaori had eventually become part of Shizuma's group, becoming less nervous around Shizuma, and she relished her happiness.

"Kaori, don't sit so far away...come here," Shizuma said.

Kaori shyly changed chairs. Shizuma held up a large glass, which held a light raspberry frozen drink. "This is too much for me. Will you help me out?"

Kaori nodded bashfully.

"Say 'ahhh...'"

Shizuma fed a spoonful to Kaori, like a baby. The crowd cheered, and the cicadas cried out noisily.

The dream changed again...the day had come.
The fateful news.

In the Maiden Park forest, trees full of leaves in shades of burning red...

It was that rare occasion on which Kaori had sent an invitation to Shizuma. Thinking that this was probably the first time she'd been called out by Kaori, Shizuma headed toward a particular section of Maiden Park.

Kaori was waiting for her.

"Shizuma-oneesama! I...I..." Her tears prevented further words.

As Shizuma comforted the sobbing Kaori, she asked what was wrong. Kaori told her.

"Is that true?" Shizuma asked.

Kaori could only sob.

"An incurable disease...dear God...no..."

It seemed as if the peaceful happiness she was embracing slowly crumbled. The whole world shook and felt like an ominous nightmare...

It was Shizuma's first shock.

"That's why I...can't stay by Shizuma-oneesama's side anymore..." Kaori madly sobbed.

Shizuma wrapped her arms around Kaori's trembling back...

I must protect my darling girl like a younger sister... she thought.

"I won't allow that to happen to you..." She hugged Kaori strongly. "I can't let you leave me like this..."

The pure white dream tormented Shizuma.

The first snows of winter fell outside one of the Strawberry Dorms rooms.

Inside, the stricken Kaori was lying in bed, with Shizuma sitting by her side. The room was silent.

The final hours approached quietly.

The white dream morphed into a horrible, black darkness...

Shizuma wandered in the darkness. She couldn't see a thing...a suffocating darkness.

How long had she been there...?

She finally saw a thin beam of light shining down.

A peach-colored flower petal…one, two, fell from the sky.

She reached out to catch it. It landed on her palm…softly, tenderly, seemingly almost familiar…

She was on a white cloud now.

"I…finally understand Shizuma-oneesama's true feelings…"

She hadn't realized an angel was sitting next to her. It was…Kaori.

Was this…Heaven?

"But I pretended that I didn't know. You made me so happy, Shizuma-oneesama, so I didn't want to lose it all."

Kaori's smile was so gentle and seemed to enfold her.

"Kaori…"

"Shizuma-oneesama, you were nice to me until the end. And I…am so happy to have met you. So please, Shizuma-oneesama…please find your real happiness…"

Shizuma thought… *Great. Kaori is finally free from the painful illness, free to feel so happy.*

Shizuma felt a wave of relief. Her body relaxed…and her face naturally formed a smile.

But the moment Shizuma tried to peer into Kaori's smiling face, Kaori's smile split in half.

The whole scene froze over…and a high-pitched voice pierced through it.

Shizuma was ripped back to reality.

Over and over… Every day, since that one lovely star—among a countless number of stars—had lost its luster, never to shine again, for eternity…

At the Astraea Chapel.

The entrance displayed a large white flower wreath.

Next to it was a small sign. It said…Funeral Mass.

The double doors were fully opened, and Miator students, veiled in black, came in and out of the chapel, lined up to offer flowers.

Unable to enter, Shizuma stood on the steps of the entrance and looked at the altar, deep inside.

Surrounded by white chrysanthemums was a picture of Kaori, smiling in June, surrounded by the scent of lavender. It was her most favorite picture.

As the solemn music of Mozart's Requiem played… Shizuma's mouth slightly opened under her black veil.

Suffering in this world
The dark night shall come
The hurt and fallen souls return to Heaven…

Shizuma awakened.

In front of her wasn't Heaven…but early summer on Astraea Hill.

The afternoon sun was still high in the air.

It was a dream…

She was in a cold sweat… *It's been a while since I dreamed of her…not for two months, since I met Nagisa.*

Today was the first time I saw her as an angel and spoke to her in the dream…

She was smiling…and told me she knew my true feelings.

She seemed so blissful…even if it was a dream.

I was so happy, but...Shizuma placed a hand on her heart and recalled the white funeral procession.

That day, deeply buried in tears and painful grief...

The sadness of losing her...I was probably in more sorrow than I imagined.

A gentle wind floated across and slowly rippled the pool's surface...

The light of the stars reflected on the water.

The cool breeze swept toward two girls.

In the inner garden, at nearly midnight...sat Hikari and Yaya.

Yaya had invited Hikari to come outside. *I can't sleep...* she had said.

Compared to the clamor of the day, the poolside at night seemed small, quiet, and somewhat lonely...

Only the night lamps softly illuminated the inner garden...and barely shone upon the two girls, sitting at the edge of the pool.

Squiggle squiggle...

It barely shone on the backs of their heels...wavering...as Yaya struggled to find words.

"Hikari...are you sad?"

Hikari weakly smiled at Yaya's question. "Eh...well..."

Yaya grimaced. *She's doing that smile...again. I know Hikari is sleepless. I know because, on the other side of the room, while I hold my breath...I can hear Hikari tossing around in her bed...*

Yaya was depressed. *Am I no longer able to suppress my feelings...?*

"You haven't seemed too happy these days, Hikari... On the surface, I know you've been giving it your all at dance practice... but...you don't seem to be here...as if your mind has left your body...leaving an empty shell behind or something..."

I can't bear to see you like this...

Yaya couldn't find the right words... Because she knew why Hikari was sad.

Because she hadn't seen Amane-sama.

Even during classes at school, and the dance lessons during breaks...and at the lounge during free time in the Strawberry Dorms, and the meal prayers at the large dining hall...Hikari was always looking for someone.

Subconsciously.

With her eyes.

All the time...

Looking for her white prince...

It had been a week since Hikari had last seen Amane. She had been trying so hard to keep her spirits up. She kept telling herself she needed to be a strong, cheerful girl, for Amane-sama.

Hikari-chan, you're so diligent, and much stronger... her classmates said. Some made insensitive jokes, that Amane might really turn into one of the Five Great Stars...

But to Yaya...it only caused her pain.

Ever since she's been separated from Amane...Hikari has been forcing her smiles. Somewhere in her body, she must have a small scar, so she forced a smile to hold down that pain...

It shows on her face. I don't want to see that kind of smile.

Something beyond frustration—a pressurized form of anger—welled up inside of Yaya.

In a small voice, her true thoughts spilled out.

"Come on, 'fess up...don't hold it in..."

In the dead silence of the night, even Yaya's soft whispers reached Hikari's ears. "Confess...?" Hikari, sitting next to Yaya, only turned her face. "I...don't have any confessions..."

Even as she denied it, tears welled in her eyes. Large drops rolled down her cheeks.

"I...don't have any confessions...nothing. I'm not sad. I know...you think I'm acting strange, Yaya-chan. But I'm not holding anything back...so don't be mad, Yaya-chan. There are times when I want to see Amane-sama...but...that's..." Hikari choked on her tears. And made that smile again. She scrunched her crying face to force the painful smile.

"Please...Yaya-chan...don't be so mean... If you left me, Yaya-chan...I'd be so sad...and wouldn't know what to do..."

Hikari's words sparked Yaya's jealousy.

Stupid, stupid, stupid...stupid Hikari... Why are you holding back so much...? Why do you force a smile...even though you're so sad and crying...?

Is it all for Amane-oneesama...? Why do you have to endure all this for Amane-oneesama, when she's the one making you this sad...?

Yaya couldn't help it anymore. She hugged Hikari violently. Hikari's hot, wet tears soaked Yaya's neck.

I…can't stand it. I want Hikari to be…really happy. My cute Hikari, who loves all things pretty and beautiful…You look a lot better with peach-colored tears of joy…not blue tears of sadness… You should have chosen someone who could make you happier…

Yaya heard a devil whisper in her heart.

Oh…here goes nothing…!

She pushed Hikari down onto the poolside deck.

"Ah… Ya-Yaya-chan, what are you…?"

Yaya hovered over Hikari, her searing eyes looking right into Hikari's.

Hikari couldn't say a word.

Tumble…

The two bodies fell into the pool.

Splash… The large splash echoed through the empty inner garden. Water sprayed in all directions.

Regardless of whether it was because Yaya moved, or Hikari moved, the pair, still in their pajamas, fell into the pool.

Hikari didn't understand what just had happened to her, and she struggled.

It's cold…

I can't breathe…

The wet clothes are restricting me…

I'm scared…

She panicked.

Yaya hugged the squirming Hikari.

Hikari almost heard Yaya's soft whispers in her ear…

"Don't worry. I'll always protect you."

Hikari realized she was standing in the center of the octagonal pool. The shallow part of the pool.

As if Yaya were a prince, holding the Mermaid Princess… she smiled gently. The pool water must have washed away her anxieties.

Hikari's dewy eyes sparkled as they reflected the dazzling surface of the water.

Yaya released Hikari from her embrace, had her stand there…and without a word began to undress her.

"Yaya-chan, why…?"

Yaya placed a finger on Hikari's lips and silenced her.

Hikari felt overpowered by Yaya's intensity…and lost her will to resist.

Yaya's gentle hands peeled Hikari's wet clothes off…and the night wind…stole Hikari's body heat.

It feels…so good…

The clouds eventually cleared…and the moon and a small star appeared.

Hikari's mind went blank as Yaya fondled her body.

Yaya felt Hikari's exposed body. Her white, wet skin was illuminated by the moonlight…and sparkled.

She was so alluring. Yaya wanted to have Hikari's whole body…

Yaya continued her caresses. "You're so beautiful, Hikari…" she whispered…

Hikari felt her soul jump to the skies as her mind went white…and only felt Yaya's kindness…

CHAPTER 6

Romeo and Juliet Always
Broke the Rules

"**H**urry…or we'll be late!"

"Aaahh, wait up! I'm late because today's dessert was the delicious fruit au gratin, and I went for seconds… I thought it was weird for all that dessert to be untouched…"

"Forget that…let's hurry!"

After dinner. The news had spread even to the Miator dining hall area.

Nagisa listened to the chatter as she passed along the line of couches in front of the dining hall.

"What's wrong?" Tamao asked. "Nagisa-chan, you look so scary… Ah, are you getting bored with me, because we've been together for so long?"

Tamao pretended to cry, but Nagisa snapped back coldly, "Gosh, enough of that already."

Oh my, Nagisa-chan is quite irritated… Tamao was

surprised. *She usually doesn't take it out on people...*

"Ah, Nagisa-chan, you're sooo scary. I'll be afraid to be with you if you're like that," Tamao pointed out lightly.

"I- I'm sorry, I didn't mean it... But I'd wanted to go too, so I'm a little frustrated..."

Tamao was even more surprised. "Did you really want to go...to Spica's violin mini-concert? I heard it was going to be a lovely setup, with a candlelit service inside the dark chapel... but I thought we talked through this already. Two couples have already dropped out of the *Étoile* competition, and though it's not likely...Kusanagi Makoto might be targeting you as the next victim of the Faceless Devil, so we decided not to go..."

"I know...but at this rate, the Miator dorm might empty out...and leave us behind..."

Sighing, Nagisa tried to shrug it off...and ended with a kicker. "I wonder if Shizuma-oneesama went too..."

Ohhh...so that's it, Tamao thought.

It had been ten days since Nagisa and Shizuma had separated. Nagisa acted like nothing was wrong, but her cheerfulness had been fading slowly, like a photo losing its color...

Ahahaha... Nagisa-chan acted like she wanted to go there, but all she really wanted was to see Shizuma-oneesama...

Tamao tried to blurt it out, but something stopped her from doing so.

The tears that welled up in Nagisa's eyes.

Tamao tried to cheer her up. "You're almost there, Nagisa-chan. It's only four more days...! The next time you see Shizuma-oneesama will be at the dance contest. If you don't dance well, you'll be picked on for life! Do you still want to see her, despite that?"

Nagisa shyly smiled and regained some of her cheerfulness. "Ahh…well, that wouldn't be good…" She blushed at the thought of reuniting with Shizuma…

Tamao felt something trying to come out of her throat, but held it back with a smile.

"Here, I brought back some leftover fruit au gratin. Let's eat this…and talk about the dance choreography in the small hall."

Nagisa grinned bashfully as if to say…*Okay, thank you!*… and nodded.

7:00 p.m. at the chapel.

Underneath the towering stained-glass windows, in front of the altar, a small stage had been set up.

It was extremely rare to hold an event in that holy place.

There were over a hundred Strawberry Dorms residents gathered there. The main lights had been turned off, but countless candles glowed along the wall.

It began quietly…with a violin rendition of a Tchaikovsky concerto. In the soft, warm glow of silence, at center stage, wearing an unadorned white tuxedo, Kusanagi Makoto played the violin.

In the soft glow of the candles…she was the center of attention.

A single red rose protruded from her white jacket's lapel,

and as her violin's music swelled to a crescendo…Makoto became more passionate.

Beautiful and lustrous, the violin vibrated violently yet sweetly…and it was utterly breathtaking… There was no accompanying orchestra or piano, but Makoto's presence filled the large room…

Everyone felt her incredible talent. Sighs poured out of the audience at the awe-inspiring performance.

Oh gee…there'll be another wave of Makoto-sama craziness stirring up tomorrow, thought Yaya, who sat at the back of the chapel.

She thought of Hikari, and it depressed her.

Hikari practiced hard with Kaname every day and tried so hard to keep her spirits up…"I'm going to do my best for Amane-sama…"

Hikari constantly repeated those words. And the smile that came with them was really forced…and worried Yaya to no end.

Hikari always does that…she says everything's okay, but the next moment she bursts into tears…

Yaya's heart ached at the thought. She didn't want to admit it, but Hikari had changed since she'd met Amane.

Hikari had used to let it all out…she'd cried when she was sad, she'd trembled and run away when she was scared, but… she had learned to endure some pain and to confront the things that she once had run away from.

Yaya didn't know whether the change was good or bad. Generally it was probably a good thing, but Yaya didn't want Hikari to feel so much pain, so…she recalled that night…

It was nice that Hikari was growing stronger, but Yaya just wanted Hikari to be happy.

She wanted Hikari to be the shy, bubbly angel who stayed innocent and pure.

Yaya didn't know where to keep her feelings, though. She couldn't hold it in anymore, and she reached over to hold Hikari's hand.

"Hikari, it's all right…just because she came back from Russia, it doesn't mean she's good at dancing. And honestly…it doesn't matter if you and Amane-sama become the *Étoile*…in fact, I'd rather you guys didn't…"

She finally noticed.

"Hikari? Where did you go…?"

Hikari was no longer sitting beside her.

Ten minutes earlier.

Hikari moved to the darkest corner of the hall.

She had come with Yaya discreetly, avoiding all the Makoto fans that might pick on her. They had arrived right before the concert started and had slipped into the center back row, which was only partially filled.

The performance began, and as the romantic feeling spread…Hikari was able to forget her worries for a while…and as a lover of beautiful things, she took in the soothing music and the beauty of the atmosphere created by Makoto.

Yaya was also absorbed in the performance.

Suddenly someone poked Hikari.

Who...?

Surprised, Hikari tried to turn around.

"Shh...quiet. Keep your face forward..."

She heard a familiar voice. Tears welled up.

"Please come to the back without being noticed..." the voice said, and that person slipped away.

Hikari checked on Yaya. She was completely focused on the concert. She had been pulled into Tchaikovsky's world...

Quietly Hikari left her seat.

Standing with her back to the dark wall was...Amane.

But Hikari couldn't make out her face. Hikari wanted to confirm it was really her, and she reached out.

Amane gently deflected her hand. "We shouldn't be seen together, so I'll keep it short. I just wanted to see your face..." Amane said in a low tone.

Hikari shuddered; Amane's tone was almost angry. Hikari wanted to see her so much...and was so happy to see her...but she couldn't move her legs.

From the darkness, Amane burned the image of Hikari's whole body, illuminated softly by the candles, into her mind.

But Hikari couldn't see Amane's face in the dark...

"Just four more days...hang in there."

Amane's words seemed so lonely. It almost sounded like she was bidding farewell for good...

Hikari...cried...

Trickle trickle trickle...the tears flowed uncontrollably. No matter how hard Hikari tried, she couldn't hold them back.

"Hikari…" Amane panicked.

She came out of the darkness and tried to hold Hikari.

"Hikari…Hikari…where are you…?"

Yaya's voice approached.

Amane stopped in her tracks. "Tonight at midnight…I'll be here."

Amane slipped away, her tight Spica uniform squeaking… and disappeared.

"Hey, why are you here, Hikari? Don't go off like that… Makoto's fans might ambush you, you know?"

It had been a close call.

Hikari wiped her tears as she listened to Yaya's lecture and smiled. "I'm sorry…I was so moved by the violin performance, it made me cry…so I thought I'd wash up in the bathroom…"

Yaya wryly smiled. "You sure love beautiful things, huh? But how could you be moved by Makoto, that little thing…? Stupid girl…"

Yaya loved Hikari's purity.

A set of eyes watched them…

The person on stage—the Emperor in the white tuxedo— had seen the whole thing.

Hikari wore a simple nightgown as she slipped away to Maiden Park.

She ran and ran, losing her breath…through the midnight forest.

The chapel's midnight bell was about to toll. A low, subdued midnight bell.

There was a legend that said misfortune would strike those who heard the midnight bell of the chapel…so most of the Strawberry Dorms residents stayed away from the chapel at night.

It was exactly why Amane had chosen that place, instead of a place in the Strawberry Dorms. There were too many eyes at the dorms.

Though she didn't care much for the *Étoile* competition, Amane still wanted to avoid the dishonor of getting caught for breaking the two-week separation rule. It would be a dishonor not only for Amane, but for Spica also.

Hikari was scared of the ominous jinx of the chapel bell, but…if she could see Amane-sama…she didn't care. She kept running. Into the dark night forest, toward the chapel…

She hadn't even told Yaya that she was going, and she had slipped out unnoticed…just to go and see Amane…

That's why Hikari didn't notice a figure, following her cautiously from behind…

B-tam…

Hikari had meant to close the chapel door quietly, but it slammed back and echoed through the hall, surprising her.

Inside, the chapel was a dark and empty void. It felt slightly moist and chilly. In the darkness, only a small, glowing red lamp was visible. It indicated the location of the holy water.

Hikari squinted toward the lamp. *That must be the altar.*

The next moment…*flick*…a match was struck.

A small candle, beside the red lamp, was lit.

The glow softly illuminated Amane's thin, white face.

Amane-sama… Hikari's heart filled with joy, rendering her speechless.

They had been separated for only ten days, but she felt such yearning. Her eyes filled, with tears of joy this time, which rolled down her cheeks without clouding her sight as she ran toward…

"Amane-sama!"

"Hikari!"

Hikari jumped straight into Amane's arms.

Amane clutched Hikari tightly.

Tightly…tightly…they hugged each other in silence. No words were needed. Words couldn't describe their feelings. They just hugged.

There were no words that could accurately capture how they felt.

After some time, Amane relaxed her arms and spoke to Hikari, who flinched.

"Please…show me your face. These ten days of separation have been so painful… I know we shouldn't be breaking the rules, but…I couldn't bear it anymore…" Amane confessed in a strained voice, and she placed a finger under Hikari's chin.

Amane-sama… As Hikari looked up, her heart throbbed painfully.

"Me too… I tried so hard to do my best for you, Amane-oneesama, so I practiced dancing with Kaname-sama…but I wanted to see you so much…"

"Yes…I know. I heard about you doing dance practice with Kaname, and I was so worried… I thought Kaname might have been torturing you…no, I couldn't bear it…if Kaname tried to touch you…"

"Oh no, Amane-sama…" Hikari was astonished. "That never happened…"

Amane lightly touched Hikari's lips with her forefinger.

"No, don't deny it…and…" Amane choked.

"And…?" *Is there something wrong with Amane-sama…?* Hikari suddenly felt anxious.

"And…" Amane deliberately played coy…as if she knew Hikari's anxious feelings…and turned away.

"Amane-sama? Amane—"

Hikari's lips…were suddenly sealed. With a warm…moist sensation.

Ah…

It was so…sudden and powerful. Like a storm.

Amane devoured Hikari's lips.

I can't…breathe… Hikari's heart tightened, and her whole body went stiff…

But Amane hugged Hikari really hard and wouldn't let go.

Something large and burning invaded Hikari's body. Hikari closed her eyes and felt a shivering ecstasy run through her head…

Oh golly… I can't…think…

Hikari's knees buckled…and she crumpled to the floor.

"Hikari…" Amane tried to hold her up.

"Ah, there they are, Sister Fujii!"

A flashlight beam slid across the walls.

Ah…

Amane and Hikari raised their hands to block the brightness as that large voice boomed.

Several light switches were clicked on. The darkness, guarded by the small candle's light, was gone in a flash, and the chapel turned into a blinding, unmerciful room of judgment.

Makoto's triumphant shouts echoed. "Feast your eyes on this, Student Council Presidents! Just as I reported. They're definitely here!" Makoto waved her arms dramatically.

"I'm really disappointed in you, Otori Amane! I can't believe you lost in such a pathetic way. You're a bigger fool than I imagined. You're no longer worthy of being called a prince… Are you seeing this, everyone? St. Spica Student Council President, Tomori Shion? Now you know Amane is not worthy to be an *Étoile*. She broke so many school and dorm regulations, just to have a midnight rendezvous at the chapel! Hey, Shion-kun, aren't you lucky I came back? Especially now?"

Inside the main entrance, next to the light switches, were the three schools' Student Council Presidents—Shion, Chikaru, and Miyuki—called out as witnesses.

Chikaru looked on with pity, while Miyuki bitterly smiled…

Shion…was horror-struck. *How could this happen…?*

But Amane protected Hikari.

Hikari trembled like a flightless little bird, still in the nest.

So Amane continued to protect Hikari with all her might.

The next morning, news of the incident spread through the Strawberry Dorms dining halls like wildfire.

In the brilliant white Spica dining hall…

"Hey, did you hear?"

"Eh…what?"

"Last night, at the chapel…"

Whispers throughout the hall.

"Eeeeh!? No, really?!"

"Yeah, it's…true."

"No way…mild-mannered Amane-sama…no…I can't believe it…"

The rumors wouldn't stop.

Tomori Shion watched the painful scene unfold. She couldn't even finish her breakfast muffin. After eating only two small slices of grapefruit, she left the room.

This rumor will surely saturate Spica by the end of the day. I need to figure out…a counter-plan…

She hurried down the hallway.

Amane and Hikari weren't in the dining hall. Last night, Sister Fujii had thrown them into the Repentance Room. In separate spaces, of course.

"Hey, did you hear? Amane-sama fell ill with a serious disease…"

"Eeehh, really?! I heard the new transfer student was disqualified, so Amane-sama and Kaname-sama were going to pair up…"

"Eeeeeehh, I heard that last night at midnight, Amane-sama and Makoto-sama had a duel at the chapel…"

The rumors raced.

An emergency meeting was held in the Spica Student Council room.

Because of its urgent nature, only a few members who were aware of the situation—the Strawberry Dorms residents—attended.

The room was heavy with silence.

"And so, last night it was confirmed that the Otori Amane–Konohana Hikari couple broke the rules of the Faceless Devil event by seeing each other before the two-week separation period was over. The two students are currently being detained in the Strawberry Dorms Repentance Room. They are under strict surveillance, which restricts them from school and outside contact, and only visitors authorized by the sisters will be allowed. We will announce this fact at a later date, but I believe the sisters will focus not on the situation surrounding the couple, but rather on the school and dorm rules that they've broken. They may receive severe punishment, including the possibility of being suspended from school." Shion made her announcement in a business-like tone.

"Thus…?"

"Thus what?!" Kaname exploded. She was always the first to interject at these meetings.

Shion sighed—*Here she goes again*—but felt relieved at the same time. She was glad Kaname had interjected, because she didn't want to finish what she had to say. She had known exactly when Kaname would explode…

"So…what's gonna happen? Don't talk like it's not personal! Isn't Amane-sama Spica's number-one star? How did we lose her…and fall into Makoto's trap! What are you gonna do about it, Student Council President!! Did you just stand there and watch Amane-sama being treated like a criminal as she was being taken away? There must have been something you could've done! Amane-sama didn't really want to enter the *Étoile* competition, but she made a painful decision to represent us at Spica…but look at this mess… It's no wonder the Student Council gets accused of being totally arrogant! And now Amane-sama is suffering stiff penalties…and that little Hikari, who endured my torturous dance lessons…oh man… they probably feared for their lives when Sister Fujii caught them…" Kaname's voice trembled slightly.

Tsubomi was utterly astonished at the whole turn of events…and felt the pressure of grief welling up inside her as she heard Kaname's unexpected comments about Hikari.

Ahh…even Kaname-sama is worried about Hikari-oneesama…yes, Hikari-oneesama practiced so hard…but…we at the Student Council couldn't protect her…

Shion wasn't fazed.

"Trap…? Criminal…? That had nothing to do with it. While it's true that Kusanagi Makoto has acted quite suspiciously on certain occasions…this incident was probably the result of Amane-sama's spontaneous actions, and took place of her own free will. Even if there were people trying to take her down, it's highly unlikely that Amane-sama would be lured out of the Strawberry Dorms and to the chapel at midnight. And as proof…"

Shion looked off in the distance. "Last night…when Amane-sama saw my face…she seemed so remorseful…like she was apologizing to me…"

Kaname screamed silently and clenched her fist.

"Yeah, Kaname-chan…don't blame everything on poor little Shion-chan," Momomi, who sat next to Kaname, said quietly. "Kaname-chan, you must have sensed it, too? Amane-sama hates to be showy…but she seriously intended to break the rules this time…"

Another heavy silence fell upon the room.

Tsubomi tried to say something, but seeing the tense reactions of the usually gentle upperclassmen made it difficult for her to find the right words.

Pheeew… Shion sighed. "It's highly regrettable, but there's nothing we can do at this point…"

In a strained voice she went on, "On behalf of the *Étoile* Executive Committee, we hereby disqualify the couple, Otori Amane and Konohana Hikari, from the *Étoile* competition…"

Knock knock knock…

A series of small, suppressed, but sharp raps echoed across the room.

Is someone late for this meeting...? Tsubomi, sitting at the last seat, jumped up to open the door.

"Good morning, St. Spica Student Council members...oh, and Shion-chan, sorry to bother you so early in the morning. I thought that maybe I could catch you here. Um, would you be interested in an idea I have?"

There stood the St. Lulim Student Council President, Minamoto Chikaru. She smiled pleasantly. As if she had predicted this strange turn of events...the gentle girl had a paper box full of freshly baked blueberry scones for everyone.

Meanwhile, Nagisa...plodded.

She walked around Maiden Park, on her way to school.

That path from the Strawberry Dorms to Miator ran along the outer perimeter of Maiden Park—it was the long way to school, so most of the students never used it. Even Nagisa rarely used this path, but...this morning was special.

It had been a week and three days since she'd last seen Shizuma.

Up until that day, Tamao had pretty much occupied each and every minute of her life, including showers and meals, but...maybe she had felt comfortable enough to leave Nagisa alone...or had just relaxed her grip on Nagisa...or she'd really had an urgent errand...

Either way, Tamao had had to stay back and do something

at the Strawberry Dorms, so she had asked Nagisa to go to school by herself.

And walking alone...Nagisa started to accept a normal life without Shizuma.

Shizuma-oneesama no longer barged into her classroom, and she hadn't bumped into Shizuma-oneesama in the hallways for all these days...

Her body no longer wondered if Shizuma would appear at the next corner...

And of course, she no longer experienced a rush of excitement flinging her up to Heaven, because she didn't have any more chance encounters.

And no more shocking news that dropped her down to Hell...

Nagisa was unaware of the mayhem at Spica. She noticed a yellow rose bush, ready to bloom, in Maiden Park.

It's so pretty...

Somehow she had walked past Maiden Park and ended up on the back side of Miator. She saw the steeples of Miator's auditorium down at the far end.

Oops...did I make a wrong turn? Oh well...I did make it to Miator...

The yellow roses were much too cute, so she reached out to pluck one.

I like red, white, and pink roses because they're so cool... and they might match Shizuma-sama or Tamao-chan...but they're too mature for Nagisa...

That's why I like cute yellow roses the most...

Right when she touched the rose… "O-Oww!"

"Hey, stop…who's trying to disturb the garden grave…?" a voice called out the moment she nicked her finger on a thorn.

It was a sharp voice.

Who…?

Nagisa spun around, and standing there, a look of total shock on her face was…Togi Hitomi.

Ah, I've seen this person before… Nagisa thought. *I recognize her short hair and handsome eyebrows…she's in the same class as Shizuma-oneesama…and usually sits with her in the cafeteria… Great…*

Nagisa smiled in relief. "U-Umm, excuse me. I just transferred here so I'm not sure…this rose…is called the garden grave? I didn't know I wasn't supposed to pick these flowers. It was so pretty, so I tried to take one… I'm sorry."

Nagisa bowed to apologize.

Hitomi was speechless.

Nagisa hastily filled the awkward silence. "Ah, but I haven't plucked it. When I touched the rose, I nicked my finger on the thorn… Ahaha…I guess I got punished for doing something wrong…ah…ahahaha…"

Nagisa's laughter echoed eerily.

Hitomi said, with a grim expression, "No excuses."

"Ah, I-I'm so sorry…"

Hitomi's face was so scary, it made Nagisa nervous.

"I'm very sorry. I promise not to touch these roses. I really didn't know…"

She bowed at the waist in a ninety-degree angle. As nervous

beads of sweat formed on her forehead, Nagisa looked at her feet.

But Hitomi didn't respond.

Nagisa held her bow for the longest time. *Huh? Did she go away or something…? Oh no…blood is rushing to my head… I'm getting dizzy…*

She didn't know what to do, so she lifted her head just a little to peek at the girl in front of her…

Hitomi covered her mouth with her hand and…sobbed.

Eh…eeeeehhh?! Wh-Why is she crying…?!

Nagisa was confused even more. "U-Umm, I'm sorry for doing such a horrible thing…" Her voice shook.

Hitomi replied in a surprisingly tender voice, "N-No…that's not it…" Her tears streamed down her face…and she couldn't finish her sentence.

Nagisa, worried about Hitomi, approached her.

"Umm…are you okay?"

Hitomi wiped her tears. Nagisa…stuck her hands in her dress pockets to fish for something. She handed Hitomi a freshly laundered polka-dot handkerchief.

"Thank you…you're so kind."

Hitomi hesitated a little before she took the handkerchief. She closed her eyes and looked up to Heaven…in a moment of silence.

"For some reason…the memories came back…you're so straightforward, simple, and cheerful…and totally the opposite of her. But maybe Shizuma-sama yearned for a girl like you, and never…"

She opened her eyes. She had no more tears.

"Maybe I was the one who was so hung up on…my idealized version of Shizuma-oneesama…only her beauty on the outside… I completely ignored her true desires and…"

And she looked at a small, cross-shaped stone monument… a grave-like structure planted with flowers that bloomed through the four seasons…

"I…want you to hear the story…since probably nobody else will tell you. But I think you've been curious about it. I want you to listen, for Shizuma-sama's sake. About the girl who passed away…"

The Spica Student Council room was stunned into silence…

Chikaru smiled. "Well then, everyone…may I take that as a yes?"

"But…what good will *that* do for Spica?" Kaname snapped.

Tsubomi nodded at Kaname's objection.

"Good? Oh, there will be a lot of benefits, Kaname-chan. Because…even if you forced Amane-chan and her partner to stay in the competition…well, that's probably impossible. I think Amane-chan will definitely receive some flack this time, and it will cut down on her chances to win the *Étoile* crown. But…if she gracefully withdraws now…Amane-chan will still be able to participate in next year's competition…"

Words flowed smoothly out of Chikaru's mouth, like a song.

"But Amane-sama will be a sixth-year student then…" Tsubomi pointed out.

"The second-place contestant, Shizuma-sama, is a sixth-year student. And…that's the main problem. Spica students, you don't want Miator to take the *Étoile* crown again this year, do you? To have Miator take the *Étoile* crown two years in a row, the year that Amane-sama was an eligible fifth-year student… and especially to have it taken by Shizuma-sama, who decided to participate on a *whim*…?"

"Well…" Kaname choked on Chikaru's words.

"Besides, Miator has been able to maintain their advantage during the *Étoile* tournaments all these years. The excitement stirring at Spica was based on breaking this cycle, right? And… the same goes for St. Lulim Girls' School."

"But Chikaru-sama, you've never indicated such a desire…" Even Momomi was taken aback by this comment.

"Well…I find it embarrassing to share it openly. 'I want the *Étoile* crown!'—I can't say that openly without sounding *rebellious*…so I didn't have the heart to say it. It's like a bride longing to wear her wedding gown without caring for the actual marriage itself…"

Kyaaah… Chikaru squirmed in embarrassment, much to the dismay of the students in the room.

"Umm…Chikaru-sama, are you insulting us…?" Shion's temple twitched in anger as she asked on behalf of the other students.

Chikaru apologized with a smile. "Ah, I apologize…I didn't mean it that way. It's a bad habit…"

"Well, it's understandable…" Shion grumbled.

Chikaru was known as the Holy Mother of St. Lulim Girls' School, but she was also the eccentric girl who had planned and established the Costume Club, nicknamed "the Madonna's Dress-up Club."

Everyone in the room agreed. Every girl dreamed of wearing a wedding dress someday…so being embarrassed at the thought of wearing one…was indeed a strange concept.

Shion struggled to continue. "But even if we do create a Spica-Lulim couple to go against Miator, do you have a strong candidate in Lulim, President Chikaru? At Spica, we have…"

She glanced at Kaname, but Kaname looked disgruntled. She had no interest in entering the *Étoile* competition with anyone other than her beloved Amane-sama.

Chuckling at the silent interaction, Chikaru answered.

"Oh, I sure do! I wouldn't come all the way out here empty-handed. Consider this to be my greatest form of generosity. Take a look…"

Chikaru pulled out a photo, folded into four sections, and slowly opened it.

"Th-This…" Kaname raised her voice.

In the picture was Kagome, looking like a French doll. She sat on a chair and had a childish smile, so cute and refined. Behind her stood Kizuna and Remon, wearing similar dresses…

At Kagome's feet, a teddy bear was dressed up in a tuxedo.

"This is a just a picture of your hobby!" Kaname bellowed.

Chikaru grinned. "Tsk… Don't they look like the Kusanagi

sisters? This is one of my recent projects. I chose dresses in honor of the second round of the *Étoile* competition. And…the girl sitting in the middle is Byakudan Kagome-chan. Kagome-chan is a first-year student who is a rare, enchanting girl from a very affluent family. She lived in England for a long time, so…she's a very good dancer."

The room stirred.

"If we paired this girl with…Spica's very popular violinist… won't we have a perfect victory in the second-round dance contest? I heard she defeated two other couples, also. They'll make a great pair. Please take a closer look at her picture."

Chikaru brought the other students in.

"And…Kagome-chan is very small…which makes her absolutely adorable, but look…she'll fit perfectly with Spica's little Emperor. And the new concept of a Spica-Lulim alliance will surely win the support of both schools…"

Chikaru placed Makoto's picture next to Kagome's. The two doll-like beauties…seemed to fit so well.

But Kaname retorted, "President Chikaru! We shouldn't be talking about fantasies! Excuse us, but we have a crisis at hand in Spica. If it was a plan to save Amane-sama, we'd listen, but we don't have time for your lighthearted daydreams! If that's all you've got for us, please leave…"

Had Kaname's jealousy over Amane-sama…caught fire?

Chikaru responded to Kaname's outrage calmly. She chuckled, "My, so short-tempered…"

But she stopped. Out of the corner of her eye, she had caught sight of a serious face.

Shion pressed her lips together tightly, silently ordering Kaname—who was about to continue—to shut up.

Momomi opened her folding fan with its panda logo and waved it at the sweat on her cheeks. Tsubomi swallowed hard, wondering what would happen next…

"I understand," Chikaru said. "You're not willing to cooperate without getting something else…so I'm prepared to share some information…only with this group."

Folding her arms across her stomach, she added with a wide smile, "But this hasn't been announced at Lulim yet. Please keep this between us…"

Turning around, she looked at the Spica Student Council members, and spoke in a hard, serious manner…

"Currently at Lulim, there's a movement to create a new department, which will collect unique, talented students… or specialists. Until now, Lulim has stood in the shadow of the two other schools, the historical and traditional Miator and the independent and athletic Spica. Lulim has been at a disadvantage…and hasn't been able to draw out its full potential yet. Its relaxed and broad-minded educational policy, which aims to create great housewives and mothers of the future, has been followed faithfully, but many former graduates have raised concerns about our many years of misfortune and an unclear future. At the same time, in recent years Lulim's free-spirited environment has attracted many unique individuals. The three girls here are prime examples of the success that we've had so far. And…"

Chikaru's smile returned.

"This year, these three girls came to our school in hopes of transferring into our new department…our first candidates."

New department…unique, talented student candidates…

The Spica students were rendered speechless, listening to Chikaru's mind-boggling new concept.

"Lulim hopes this new department will create bright young hopefuls that will contribute greatly to society. At the same time…Lulim will emerge from beneath the overbearing shadows of long-standing Miator and Spica to gain glory for a successful future…"

Facing the large glass wall, Chikaru looked out into the distance.

"And the name of the new department is…"

Everyone in the room gulped.

"St. Lulim Girls' School Z Class. It will commonly be known as…the Public Entertainment Department."

A shock of silence filled the room.

Chikaru waited, with a gorgeous smile, for that name to sink in.

"To tell you the truth, I wanted to make Lulim my little harem, full of cute girls. I wanted to gather adorable girls that could become TV idols… So I need Lulim to win the *Étoile* soon. If a student in the Public Entertainment Department becomes an *Étoile*, more students will want to attend Lulim…and in turn, they'll bring in *more* cute girls…"

Chikaru's cheeks turned pink. "So…I want to take advantage of the *Étoile* entry privilege that Makoto-chan, your little Emperor, has acquired. And for Spica, you'll gain the Lulim votes, so it'll be a big plus for your school, too. If we don't create an alliance now…the number-one candidate, Prince Amane, will be disqualified…and the new transfer student, Makoto-chan, will become a star but won't be on good terms with the Student Council…and she won't be able to find a good partner, and Miator's Shizuma-sama will monopolize the competition…"

The room went cold with silence.

Huff huff huff…

Nagisa raced to school as she ran out of breath.

She just ran…she didn't know how to feel. She hadn't heard Hitomi trying to stop her, as she ran off in the middle of the story.

Her heart and head were so full she was about to explode.

Shizuma-oneesama and…Sakuragi Kaori…

Hitomi had explained how Kaori had been beautiful, pure, and withdrawn…but she had secured a place next to Shizuma-sama and had been very happy.

Shizuma might not have loved her as much as she'd loved Shizuma, but nonetheless Shizuma had enjoyed taking care of her beautiful young girl.

Hitomi had probably explained it to Nagisa in such a careful way, but Nagisa didn't care about that anymore. Hearing about Kaori's incurable illness—and the way Shizuma had battled the illness with Kaori—was shocking to Nagisa, as if she had been struck by lightning.

Hitomi's recollection of the two girls' past was too beautiful…and too tender…

And much too fragile and sad.

Nagisa didn't know how to feel.

"After Kaori passed away, Shizuma-sama…was empty, like a shell. That bright, powerful person, who was like a sun, couldn't smile or laugh. Whenever she looked to the sky or looked at a flower…she would only sigh. I honestly didn't think Shizuma-sama had loved Kaori that much…it surprised me, but really…"

Hitomi had looked at Nagisa.

"It was so painful to see Shizuma-sama back then. If she saw a cute girl, she didn't even respond…she stopped her playful teasing. I didn't recognize Shizuma-sama anymore. I almost became jealous of Kaori…and I prayed that Kaori wouldn't take Shizuma-sama away from me. But Shizuma-sama slowly recovered…regaining her usual cheerfulness…and when she decided to enter the *Étoile* competition, she became so joyful and energetic. There were rumors that Shizuma-sama wouldn't compete. But we—me, Mizuho, and Shizuma-sama's close friends—convinced her that she had to mark her time in history as an *Étoile*.

"Kaori had looked forward to Shizuma-sama becoming the *Étoile*…so Shizuma-sama needed to show it to her up in Heaven. Shizuma-sama agreed reluctantly, with dark eyes, but from the next day on…she was the powerful Shizuma-sama again. We were happy she was back to normal, but…during the coronation ceremony, when we heard Shizuma-sama cry out, 'All my love to you'…we finally understood Shizuma-sama's true feelings…"

That had been Nagisa's limit.

She'd just had to… She had felt that she had to ask Shizuma something…

And before she'd realized it, she had run off. Maybe she'd just wanted to run away from that place…

"Ah, wait…" Hitomi had yelled to Nagisa to stop, but it was no use. Hitomi's last words never reached Nagisa's ears.

"Shizuma-sama…was probably crushed by guilt. Shizuma-sama's feelings toward Kaori were…not love…"

Nagisa ran.

She just ran.

Toward the Sixth Year Snow Class classroom.

She's not here.

Nagisa went to the teachers' office.

She's not here either.

Nagisa ran all over the school to find Shizuma. She couldn't find Shizuma anywhere.

She ran along the path to Maiden Park again. The path where she had first met Shizuma…

But Shizuma wasn't there. *Not here, either…*

As memories of being with Shizuma flashed through her mind…Nagisa ran all around Astraea.

The Mouth of Truth event of the *Étoile* competition…the chapel where they had retrieved holy water…and…

She looked up at the large stone castle.

She remembered Shizuma's sweet voice. *The Secret Garden…*

It was the library.

She was drawn to the entrance…and opened the door.

Tmp tmp tmp tmp…

Nagisa's feet tapped the stone floor of the library as she trotted through it.

She walked around…and finally reached the vacant second-floor hallway.

Nagisa saw her.

"Ohh…here you are…" Nagisa said out loud, relieved.

Shizuma looked at her, puzzled…and really surprised.

"Nagisa…"

Shizuma looked around. Nagisa was panting and almost dropped to her knees. Shizuma wrapped her arms around Nagisa's waist, picked her whole body up, and carried her to a hidden area behind the bookshelves.

"You shouldn't be here…people will see you. You know about this morning's commotion, right? But…I'm glad you couldn't hold back and came to see me…"

Still holding Nagisa, Shizuma tried to kiss her forehead, but…

Nagisa deflected it instinctively. "No…"

"Nagisa…?" Shizuma was surprised…then lookcd sad.

Nagisa thought—*oh no*—as she slowly turned to face Shizuma.

"I…have a question I've wanted to ask you for a long, long time. That's why I came here…"

Nagisa's hands trembled.

Shizuma, seeing Nagisa's troubled state, stood up straight. She spoke in a low tone.

"I see…so what's your question, Nagisa?"

It felt like a large lump was stuck in Nagisa's throat… because her voice wouldn't come out…

She swallowed the lump, and tried hard to keep her voice from cracking, but it only made her voice loud.

"Wh-what did you think of Sakuragi Kaori-san…Shizuma-oneesama?"

She almost yelled it. She regretted asking the question almost instantly. But…she couldn't take back it now.

Shizuma…remained still, as if she had expected this question. But…to Nagisa's eyes, Shizuma's face tightened… and seemed a bit sad.

"Nagisa…you don't believe in me…?"

"N-No, that's not what I mean…I just…" Nagisa was serious.

Shizuma continued as if she hadn't heard Nagisa. "Well…I can't hide it from you anymore."

Shizuma looked as if she were laughing softly. Yet she seemed so sad…as if she had some very deep sorrow…

Nagisa became fearful. *Maybe I shouldn't have asked… But it's too late.*

As Shizuma began to speak, she grabbed Nagisa's hand and led her to a bench in a secluded area.

"She was very cute…a girl you'd have loved to have as your younger sister."

Shizuma's words were so sweet and gentle. They pricked Nagisa's heart. She wanted to run away, but Shizuma held Nagisa's hands, wrapping them tenderly in her own.

Nagisa was able to hold back her urge to bolt and listened.

"Hitomi introduced her to me... Back then, I was really tough...tsk...and truthfully, I didn't think she was cute. No, she looked cute, but... Hitomi complimented her looks so much... I thought...she was a quiet girl who was spoiled by everyone. She seemed so boring. She was so introverted that someone had to bring her to me... I hated girls like that. But when I tried to walk away...she threw herself at my feet to stop me. I was really surprised by her clumsy, honest feelings..."

Tsk tsk...Shizuma occasionally chuckled or smiled sadly as she told the story. She looked through Nagisa, as if she were looking at something beyond the horizon...

Kaori had been a very beautiful girl, and had looked perfect with Shizuma. But she had been physically weak, so she'd sat under the parasols while everyone frolicked at the pool.

She had always been by Shizuma's side, a reigning presence amidst her friends, and had always smiled happily. She hadn't been flashy by any means, but she had always been mild and peaceful and seemingly so fragile...a serene beauty that Shizuma had loved.

Shizuma...had loved...her...

Shizuma explained softly, to keep Nagisa calm.

Nagisa understood her intent.But Nagisa wanted Shizuma to tell her...straight to her face...*I love you now.*

Once...just once...

Nagisa knew Shizuma had cared about Kaori so much that she'd claimed the *Étoile* crown for her. But she wanted Shizuma to tell her…*I love you more*…

Even if it was a lie.

Nagisa's eyes glazed as she stood. She was so scared…she couldn't hear the whole explanation.

Shizuma usually would have sensed Nagisa's hidden emotions and held her back…but she was probably distracted by the memories of Kaori.

"I'm sorry…I need to go…since it's almost homeroom time…"

"Okay… Nagisa, are you okay? You don't seem too well…"

"I-I'm fine! Thank you…very much. Shizuma-oneesama… I'm sorry for asking you so suddenly… I'm okay… I'll leave before someone finds us here…"

Shizuma is such a nice person. She probably wouldn't compare people, or rank who she loved the most and stuff…

Nagisa tried to convince herself.

But…knowing Shizuma-oneesama…if she really loved me, she'd surely say it straight to my face…

"I love you more than Kaori, so don't worry…I really love you…"

I…can't do it. I can't win against…a deceased person.

No matter how much I try…I'm surprised I want to "win" someone's love…but it's much harder to give up at this stage.

Oh gosh… I…I really love Shizuma-oneesama…and want to be her number one…

But that's an impossible dream…

Tsubomi, with sweat on her forehead, reached as high as she could to post the new announcement on the bulletin board.

As soon as the paper was secured to the board, she scampered away before the crowds could gather.

The announcement was written simply…

ANNOUNCEMENT
The candidates listed below have been disqualified from the second round of the *Étoile* Competition due to violations of specified competition rules.

NAMES
St. Spica Girls' Institute

Fifth Year, Class Trois   *Third Year,* Class *Un*
Otori Amane   Konohana Hikari

—*Étoile* Competition Executive Committee

Screams and cheers and angry yells swirled at Spica.

Meanwhile, in the Miator Fourth Year Moon Class classroom…

Nagisa was gloomy as she entered the room, so Tamao

raised her voice on purpose to welcome her.

"Ohh, Nagisa-chan, where were you? I looked all over for you…"

Tamao sensed the severity of Nagisa's depression and peered into her face, concerned.

"What…happened? Did the library culprit appear? Ah, was it Spica's Emperor Makoto…?"

"No…it was nothing… I'm fine! Really…"

Tamao watched Nagisa slump in her chair. She bit her finger, looked at Nagisa suspiciously…and was dying to ask…

"Heeeeey, did you hear about it already? About Prince Amane…?"

"What…? Prince Amane…as in the *Étoile* candidate…?"

Nagisa recalled Prince Amane on a white horse, gallantly saving Hikari in the first round of the *Étoile* competition, during the Maiden Horse Race.

Nagisa's heart ached. *Ahhh…those two must really love each other… I feel a little wistful and envious… Oh gosh…I hate this feeling…*

Tamao, oblivious to Nagisa's feelings, said enthusiastically, "Yes, that mild-mannered Prince Amane and her partner, Konohana Hikari, were caught last night during a rendezvous at the chapel. They were disqualified from the competition and sent to separate Repentance Rooms, on restriction…"

"Eeeeeehhh?!"

Gadunk… Nagisa knocked her chair down as she stood in astonishment. *What in the world…?*

She remembered Amane, cradling the sobbing Princess

Hikari in her arms, comforting Hikari with gentle whispers. It was so obvious and almost blinding how much Amane cared for Hikari.

And at the same time, Hikari had believed and depended on Amane…with all her heart.

In contrast, Shizuma-oneesama and I are…

She recalled Shizuma's distant gaze, going right through her, smiling at past memories…

We aren't worthy of competing in the Étoile competition.

The moment she thought of it.

Ah…

It dawned on Nagisa.

I…broke the rules, too…

Nagisa hadn't recalled until then that seeing Shizuma was a major no-no…

"Well…then I'm disqualified, too! I just met Shizuma-oneesama…" she cried out in a daze.

Her classmates wondered what had just happened. But in the next moment, Tamao, although taken by surprise at Nagisa's volatile confession, immediately covered Nagisa's mouth.

"O-Oh goodness…what are you saying? Nagisa-chan, don't say such nonsense just because you're stressed out from the competition… You were with me all morning! You shouldn't lie like that, and because you've gotten this far, you can't quit. Miator's honor is on the line…!"

Tamao's laughing face had gone white…she fervently looked around the classroom as she covered Nagisa's mouth.

Oh, Nagisa's just whining again… A few classmates who

understood Nagisa and Tamao's relationship wryly smiled or sympathized…and returned to their conversations.

Ding dong…

The starting bell rang.

Tamao whispered to Nagisa, who sat limply in her chair, "Don't worry—from the looks of it, nobody saw you, right? No one will know. Let's go report it to Miyuki-oneesama… okay?"

CHAPTER 7

On the Morning of the Escape,
a Promise is Broken, Then Fulfilled

$\mathbf{F}$our days later…

Nagisa and Shizuma managed to stay apart for four more days.

Nagisa was dragged off by Tamao to talk to Miyuki, and was told that, in order to avoid embarrassing Shizuma, Nagisa shouldn't tell anyone what had happened, so the only thing she could do was keep it quiet.

At Spica, the rumors about Amane and Hikari were scandalous…

Couldn't they wait for just two short weeks, those impatient fools…?

Angry rumors might have come from the hard-core fans whose hopes had been betrayed, but it was disenchanting to know that these fans, who used to cherish their stars, could turn around so easily and spread such insidious rumors…

Miyuki explained to Nagisa the recklessness of her mindless actions, and the only thought that crossed Nagisa's mind was…*I have to protect Shizuma-oneesama's reputation…*

But in keeping this incident under wraps, Nagisa couldn't overlook her own dishonesty and unfairness…and she wanted to run away from it all.

Spica's Amane and Hikari stayed in the Repentance Room for only two days, but they were sent to their rooms, under restriction, after that.

Thinking about that couple drove Nagisa insane.

As Nagisa practiced dancing with Tamao…one question stuck in her mind.

What should I do…? When I'm not even worthy of being in the Étoile competition?

And then…it was the day of the main event.

Shion came to school very early in the morning and sat in the Student Council room.

She liked this privilege—to come to school first, alone, as the Student Council President.

The empty school building seemed cold and quiet. She rode the elevator up to the eighth floor, where the Student Council room was, and by the time she reached it, the sun was up. Now the glass-walled room would slowly become warm and humid.

As she checked the agenda one last time, Shion went back over the events that had led up to this day.

The day she had entered the Repentance Room to tell Amane she had been disqualified from the *Étoile* competition…

Amane had been in a cheap, cramped room with only a small, simple white bed and an old Bible on the desk. Amane had sprung up at the sight of Shion…and when Shion had explained the official decision in a serious tone… *"I'm so sorry…"* Amane had apologized, and had bowed her head to Shion.

Amane had understood Shion's strong desire for Amane to claim the *Étoile* crown for Spica that year, no matter what…

Considering Amane's bashful nature, there were many things Amane had had to compromise and endure to take part in the *Étoile* competition. But one thing was certain…Amane was a Spica student who truly loved her school.

The thought pained Shion's heart.

Shion ultimately felt responsible for putting Amane into this position…and she had inadvertently blurted, *"Oh no, it's not your fault, Prince Amane,"* which had made both of them burst out in laughter.

It might have been Shion's mistake—based on Makoto and Miyuki's requests—to choose the Faceless Devil event. But—two weeks—it had been Amane and Hikari's fault for not being able to wait for only two weeks.

Shion and Amane had felt a little better after they'd laughed about it. Shion was finally able to give up her long-standing dream, and Amane didn't care about being locked up. She had worried more about Hikari, who had just transferred, and had gotten mixed up into this whole mess. She was probably scared to death.

Shion had nodded in agreement, and Amane had asked her to please check on Hikari. Shion felt partially responsible for pulling Hikari into this mess too, so she had pounded on her chest and said, "*Sure thing!*" and then had gone to Hikari's room.

Hikari had been trembling with overbearing guilt.

Shion understood her feelings. That's why she had tried to explain everything to Hikari in the most logical fashion.

She had said she'd just met with Amane, who didn't care much about this incident. Sure, a lot of rumors would spread, but those would eventually go away, so she had said not to worry about it. In fact, they were lucky to have Makoto back, because she had eliminated three couples...which meant she could officially enter the *Étoile* competition, starting with the dance contest...and she would protect Spica's reputation, so Hikari had nothing to worry about.

Shion had also told her that Amane was really worried about her. Amane had asked Shion to please pass on to Hikari how much she wanted to see her.

According to Shion, it was the first time she had seen Amane agonizing over something so much.

Hikari had said, in a thin voice and with tears streaming down her face, that she wanted to see Amane-sama, too.

Ohh, just thinking about those two really pains me. Unable to take the pain, Shion changed the subject of her thoughts.

Then there had been the tense scene in the Student Council room with Chikaru.

Oh yes, Chikaru... I wondered what that strange proposal was about.

Now that Amane had been eliminated, Chikaru had suggested that Makoto and Kagome—a Spica-Lulim alliance—should pair up and enter the *Étoile* competition...an idea Shion had never expected.

After the meeting...Shion had grabbed Chikaru and asked her what she was up to.

Chikaru had just smiled.

"Oh, I just...want to gather a lot of cute girls in my little harem at Lulim, that's all... If Lulim has an Étoile, it'll attract a lot of students here, and more cute girls will come..."

Lulim's Public Entertainment Department, Class Z...what a far-fetched idea. But after checking with everyone, they had agreed to the Makoto-Kagome coupling and entry, just as Chikaru had planned. Even Miyuki hadn't objected.

For some reason the *Étoile* competition had turned into an effort to avenge Amane's defeat. Chikaru's bold plan to create a couple from students of different schools—an unprecedented coupling in Astraea's *Étoile* competition history—had riled up a festival-like excitement at Spica and Lulim. The alliance was creating a friendly atmosphere, for sure.

But will this ultimately be a good move for Spica...?

Shion wasn't sure. Amane and Hikari stuck in her mind.

Hikari's painful, teary smile tore at her heart.

Tap tap...she tapped the pile of papers on the table.

Today was the main event...

Hikari felt the heaviness of the situation sink in.

When she had first transferred here, she had been impressed with her beautiful dorm room, the chic art décor style.

Hikari was still restricted to her room. Her roommate, Yaya, had left for school already.

Hikari sat on her bed and turned to her thoughts. About the rule she had broken…and the trouble she had caused Spica, and how she had ruined Amane's reputation…

She tried to hold back her tears, but couldn't.

I did such a horrible thing…

Knock knock knock… Small knocks at the door.

The door opened.

It was Amane. She wore her nicest smile.

Hikari was so surprised she couldn't speak or cry…

Amane carried a small bag. She opened her arms and hugged Hikari.

"Hey, let's go…we don't belong here any-more…"

The Koubu Hall was filled with excitement…and people.

The students had been jittery during morning classes, anxious about the main event in the afternoon.

They finally gathered after lunch.

The main event received a lot of attention, especially this

year because it followed a number of disturbing incidents. As the students tried to guess who would win…the enthusiasm grew.

Miator's dark green uniforms, Spica's pure-white uniforms, and Lulim's pink uniforms…

The Koubu Hall, inside the Miator School grounds, was the location of the *Étoile* competition's second-round dance contest.

This was Astraea's only dance hall, owned by Miator, and was only used for that purpose. Dance class was a required course for all three Astraea schools, so all the students had set foot into this hall at least once during their academic career.

Most of the gathered students were in their uniforms, but a few were dressed as noble ladies and gentlemen. They were the *Étoile* candidates.

Eight judges presided over this point-based dance contest. Nine *Étoile* candidate couples would dance at the same time…and be scored. The judges would find the average of all the scores, and those who were below the average would be disqualified.

The highest scoring couple would be the second-round winner, and receive the second *Petite couronne*.

"Hey…which couple do you think will win?"

"Hmmm…I think the Kusanagi Makoto pair will. Since she just returned from Russia…and her partner is Kagome-chan…"

"D-Do you know anything about her? I heard she's a first-year student. She just came out of nowhere…but this is her first year here, so can she really dance?"

"Oh…Kagome-chan, following her family's traditions, was

home-schooled. And her house is in England, so she's rumored to be a super-talented dancer."

"Woow, really? Lulim is so lucky to get a talented girl like her…"

"Yeah, she's Lulim's super heavyweight star!"

"Uh-huh."

Meanwhile…

In Maiden Park, under the shade of the trees, was a tall girl carrying a small bag…and a small girl, beside her.

In the clear summer morning, they cut across the green Maiden Park.

The tall girl unlocked the small gate, which was right next to the larger gate, with a hidden key…and slowly opened it.

The two girls slipped away, unnoticed.

"Are you sure?"

"Yes…"

B-tam—only the sound of the closing gate was left behind.

Nagisa stood alone in front of the Miator Student Council room.

She couldn't look the Student Council President in the face.

But she was able to open her mouth. At first, it trembled, but she pulled it off better than she imagined…

"I…wish to withdraw from the *Étoile* competition."

Nagisa chose…to leave Shizuma.

Shizuma-oneesama…Shizuma-oneesama will surely be mad at my decision.

That's all Nagisa knew.

I can't do this anymore. I want to stay by your side. But I didn't know how painful it was to be with you…

I…finally realized.

Nagisa turned around and walked away.

The Student Council President, Rokujo Miyuki, was speechless…and just watched her leave.

For one month…the girls' fates had intertwined…

Countless intersecting feelings at Astraea Hill had turned into infinite raindrops that fell to chill and soak the earth.

What would come at the end of the rainy season…? A violent, black, raging storm? Or perhaps a brilliant mid-summer sky, blue as can be?

At this point, no one knows…

Strawberry Panic!

Girls' School in Full Bloom

Eheheh... I'm a little embarrassed...

Summer has arrived on Astrea Hill, and with it, the change into seasonal summer uniforms. Nagisa's summer uniform was delivered to her room, so she invited her friends to see her try it on. Everyone complimented Nagisa, making her blush.

Today, we fight
the final battle!

November School Festival

The most popular event in the Tri-School Festival is the play performed by Strawberry Dorm residents. In addition to Shizuma and Amane, the three school presidents also appear, bringing the play to its climax. What will be the outcome of the "final battle" between the Five Stars…?!

Holy Mother, please
bless my little angels...

December Christmas Eve

A holy night. After the party, Santa Chikaru and her little helper appear. Chikaru seems to be leaving gifts in the rooms of the underclassmen. Kizuna and the girls sleep as Oneesama lovingly watches over them.

PROLOGUE

The Midsummer Winds Attract Worrisome Dreams

*T*hump, *thump, thump, thump…*

Nagisa's heart fluttered anxiously. The fingers of her tightly clenched fists pressed together as a light breeze slid across her stomach. It felt as if something precious was slipping through her pale, dry fingertips like sand, and she gripped her hand even tighter.

Oh gosh…Am I…Am I doing something completely outrageous…?

Nagisa grew nervous, picking up her pace as she cut through Maiden Park toward the Strawberry Dorms.

I never left class early, or the school, for that matter. I also never felt this anxious until today. It's so nerve-wracking…

No, it's different.

It wasn't nervousness that tormented Nagisa, but pain, sorrow, and uncertainty. Frustration.

No, I've made up my mind...I made my decision the moment I declared my withdrawal from the competition. And I don't want to admit that I regret it already. There was nothing else I could do. It couldn't be helped.

Nagisa shuffled faster. Her confusion was so great that she couldn't think of anything else to do but stare blankly at a small point of empty air ahead of her while she continued her steps along the slightly overgrown path. She pushed through the wind, defying its resistance, and forged ahead. The dark green cuffs of her Miator uniform fluttered violently.

This turbulence describes my feelings perfectly, Nagisa thought with a wry smile, but when she looked at the sky, like a daydream, she was called back into that memory.

It had been a windy day, like today, and the wind scattered the cherry blossoms across Astream Hill. Nagisa was lost, and suddenly a goddess appeared, standing proud—she was so beautiful and divine. The goddess seemed fearless and untouchable.

Back then, I didn't know who she was—it was our first encounter. I asked her for directions. The first time I laid eyes on her, from that moment on... I couldn't take my eyes off of her. Yes, ever since then a part of my heart has belonged to her.

I wonder: why was I so obsessed with Shizuma-oneesama? It wasn't a matter of whether I liked her or not, I was just captivated by her beauty. The first time I saw her, I was in awe. I gasped because I never imagined that a girl could be so beautiful.

And on top of that, I couldn't believe such a beautiful girl paid attention to me. Hard to believe now, but it's true.

Nagisa shook her head, pushing the memories away. *I was being toyed with, but I couldn't resist. I was at her mercy. And before I knew it, I did something I shouldn't have done.*

I got so scared that I let go.

Nagisa stopped and looked at her hands. Her palms were coated in sweat. She had been lost in her thoughts and walking at such a heavy pace that she had run out of breath and was sweating profusely.

Finally she saw the front gate of the Strawberry Dorms. It was unusually quiet and vacant. Nagisa had it all to herself. She was half-relieved Shizuma wasn't there, especially since Nagisa had withdrawn from the competition, but also half-disappointed as well. That was the story of their relationship. She always wanted to be with Shizuma, yet at the same time didn't want to be with her. Because she liked Shizuma, and at the same time was afraid of her. No, that wasn't it. Nagisa liked Shizuma so much that she was *afraid* to be with her—a feeling she had never felt before.

She didn't even recognize the feeling…it was love.

With mixed emotions, she clutched her traditional Miator leather school bag—a little heavy for a young girl—and entered the gate. For a brief moment, the memory of Shizuma guiding her to this dorm on her first day of school flashed through her mind. The memory was enchanting, like a magic spell.

And like a curse, it would not let her go.

CHAPTER 1

The Escapees Walk Down a White Path at High Noon

Growing excitement and anticipation stirred in one of the buildings on campus—Miator's Koubu Hall. The second round of the *Étoile* competition—which determined the best couple to represent the three prestigious all—girl schools-had been held here.

And the winners were about to be announced.

The students, usually so prim and proper, chattered with excitement, but the announcement broke through the clamor.

"Everyone, we ask for your attention. We would like to make an announcement. The winning couple of the second round of this year's *Étoile* competition is…"

The crowd fell silent.

"…Kusanagi Makoto, from St. Spica Girls' Institute, and Byakudan Kagome, from St. Lulim Girls' School!"

The crowd broke into wild cheers.

"Woooow!"

"Those two?"

"I knew they would win."

"That's great"

"What a wonderful surprise."

Praises filled the hall as students showed their approval. But beneath the compliments, voices of criticism could also be heard.

"I can't believe this... What a scam." In the back row of the bleachers, Kenjo Kaname leaned against the wall, staring at Makoto as she raised her hand in victory.

Beside Kaname stood Kiyashiki Momomi, who covered her mouth with a folding fan and snickered, "You're ticked off... yet again." She turned to Kaname and smiled. "You're such a sourpuss, Kaname. Just think, with Prince Amane eliminated from this round, this outcome was predictable, wasn't it? Of course, even I'm surprised that Shizuma-oneesama dropped out, but she never should have participated in the first place."

With no response from Kaname, Momomi sighed and continued to share her thoughts with the little panda on her folding fan. "I'm really sad that Amane-sama was disqualified, but all things considered, even if the partner is from Lulim, I hope Makoto wins for Spica's sake."

"Did you say 'Makoto'?! Since when did you get so intimate with her to call her by her first name!" Kaname jerked her head around to look at Momomi, flames burning in her eyes.

"Oooh, you're soo scary. Gee, you almost make me sound like a traitor or something." Momomi patted Kaname's shoulder.

"Of course I wanted to see Amane-sama have a glorious victory. She would have shone as the stunning white prince. But, you know, we can't wish for that anymore."

Because the damage has been done.

Momomi shrugged, as if giving up, and pointed to the group on stage. She bit her lip, as if she was trying to hold herself back, and continued. "Besides, I don't think Makoto is a bad girl at heart. Sure, she comes off as stubborn and rebellious, but she seems to be upfront, with no evil intentions. I mean, even though she sounds really rebellious and all, she didn't trick Amane-sama or anything. She says a lot of things bluntly, but she doesn't seem to be tricky or anything. I think she's upfront and honest. I mean, think about it. If Princess Rokujo and the Miator Student Council were behind this, they would have planned a lot of underhanded scheming to take down Amane-sama, you know—"

Kaname interrupted. "But Miator forced their way into the competition at the last minute. You know the Miator Student Council was behind Shizuma-sama's sudden jump into the competition. But I don't think they had any secret plans—"

Momomi interjected, "Oh my gosh! Hey, Kaname, do you remember? Who was the first person who recommended Makoto's transfer to Spica? And who gained the most from Makoto's victory in this round? I also heard that Shizuma-sama's participation was a complete surprise to the Miator Student Council. Everyone knows that Shizuma-sama entered the competition on a whim, as a tool to get closer to the new transfer student, Aoi Nagisa. Other than Rokujo Miyuki, Miator didn't have any strong candidates in the Fifth Year classes. They were all overshadowed, virtually unnoticed, because of Shizuma-sama's powerful presence. Also, the Miator Student Council couldn't stand the way President Shion cockily hyped up Amane-sama's impending victory. So they backed up Shizuma-sama's participation, just to beat our school." Momomi voiced her opinion with her usual machine gun rapidity, overwhelming Kaname.

"Well, that might all be true…but if Miator wasn't serious at first…" Kaname muttered. She was surprised that Momomi, who was usually light-hearted, was taking things so seriously.

Kaname continued, "It was Lulim President Chikaru-sama who introduced Makoto to the *Étoile* Executive Committee… and the person who benefits most from Makoto's victory is…"

Subconsciously, Kaname began to say "Makoto" without the honorifics, without hesitation. "Makoto herself, right?"

Momomi quickly replied to Kaname's lazy analysis. "What will she gain from winning the *Étoile* crown?"

"Gain?" Kaname pondered.

"Jeez. Instead of going to Junior High here at Spica, Makoto went overseas to study music. There is absolutely no value in her coming back to study at Astraea. And I know this might sound really disrespectful, but… I'm pretty sure she thinks this whole *Étoile* thing is a big joke."

Kaname's expression hardened. "A big joke?!"

Momomi tried to calm her down. "Ohh… sorry, it's not how *I* feel about it. I was just explaining how she might be feeling, okay? But… the *Étoile*… the *Étoile* is the true star of campus, the most revered couple. Outsiders probably don't understand our point of view about it, so…"

"I guess I see your point…" Kaname agreed; even she was aware that the excitement over the *Étoile* probably sounded absurd to most people. But Astraea Hill, isolated from the rest of the world, had nothing besides the three prestigious all-girl schools. The *Étoile* competition was the only big event for the students, and it was especially important to long-time Astraea residents like Kaname and Momomi.

The *Étoile*—the biggest star, shining over Astraea. Every year as the time of the competition drew near, the maidens of Astraea became obsessed with the contest, wondering which couple would become the next *Étoile*, and rule over the school for the coming year.

The girls all knew there was no decisive factor for choosing an *Étoile*. There weren't any any specific qualities one had to have in order to become an *Étoile*.

Beauty didn't matter.

Leadership didn't matter.

Good grades or being active in club activities didn't matter.

Fashion sense and volunteer activities didn't matter.

In fact, there were no clear-cut selection standards that qualified a couple to become an *Étoile*. The *Accord d'Étoile*—Rules of the *Étoile*—which were supposedly held in the Miator archives, stated, "Once a year, one senior and one junior *Étoile* shall be chosen to represent the student body. The pair shall serve as role models for the all of the maidens that live on Astraea Hill."

Étoile... the one star that illuminated the entire hill. Roughly two thousand girls from affluent families were gathered in the three schools. Astrea brought together all the young flowers of the world, like lilies, cherry blossoms, peonies, and roses, producing a powerful yet sweet fragrance. The beautiful and powerful star must have an attractive force strong enough to become the center of this rich universe. The type of star no one could keep her eyes off of.

The star must be able to shine in the beautiful sky, dazzling all the girls below, a couple that all the girls admire and long for, ever-perfect role models that energized the hill to its core.

That was the world of Astrea Hill.

"If that's all true, and Mokoto thinks this is some kind of joke, I don't want her to win at all." Kaname stared at the stage, her expression handsome instead of harsh. It was a look Momomi hasn't seen before. She became lost in her admiration of Kaname's face. *I never noticed how pretty she is.* Momomi's cheeks turned rosy pink and she hoped her thoughts were not apparent on her face.

Kaname loved Spica. It was a place where she could be her true self. She always felt that she should have been born a male, but here she could express herself freely, without worrying about how others thought of her.

Many girls in this beloved flower garden loved her dearly. And it was here that she met Amane, the prince of her dreams. In the Prince she finally found a person to emulate. Even after Amane was eliminated, Kaname's feelings for Amane were the same. She wished for happiness at this very place, where she found true love.

"A mere transfer student cannot possibly become our *Étoile*," Kaname muttered. Her throat was suddenly dry, and she wondered if she would be able to share her thoughts without biting her own tongue. "I won't allow a childish shorty like her to trample on our feelings." Her fingers dug into her palms as she clenched her fists hard.

Momomi looked shocked. *Does she really think Makoto is such a threat?*

"Yes, Makoto is still like a child in many ways. She's simple and honest, and in my opinion, I don't think she's *Étoile* material, but instead is longing for a reliable, older oneesama. That's why I don't believe Makoto is capable of tricking people. But there is someone who is known to scheme, and unlike Makoto, can benefit from this victory."

Kaname knew exactly who Momomi was talking about. *Yes, that person appears from time to time, softly urging things to go her way...* Just as she finished the thought, she glared at Momomi. "I told you not to say 'Makoto'!"

Momomi rolled her eyes. "Jeez, don't take it wrong. It's not like I talked to her directly or anything, okay? But it sounds weird to call her 'Kusanagi-san', and 'Makoto-chan' sounds so..."

"Humph! She's not cute enough to be called 'Makoto-chan'!! She looks like some sort of overhyped, snotty teen idol," Kaname grumbled.

Momomi was amused at how seriously Kaname reacted.

"Oh, on second thought, 'Makoto-chan' is very fitting. She's more of an actress than an *Étoile.*"

Momomi chuckled, hiding her mouth with her folding fan.

"Oh my gosh! You won't believe it! Amane-sama and Hikari-oneesama!" The shout came from Okuwaka Tsubomi. She burst into the hall, a royal blue student council insignia embroidered on her uniform sleeve. On her face was a look of total shock, her jaws opening and closing like a fish. She took center stage in the fully packed dance hall, huffing and puffing with reddened cheeks, breathing so hard she could barely finish her announcement.

Kaname stepped up to help her. "What's wrong, Tsubomi? What happened to Amane-sama and Hikari-oneesama?"

At the same time, a different voice overlapped Kaname's. It was Spica's President, Tomori Shion. Though she was supposed to be presenting the awards on stage, she left the stage and approached Tsubomi, distress in her voice

"What happened to those two...?" Both she and Kaname grabbed Tsubomi from each side. No one had seen Shion this frantic before.

"The both of them..." Tsubomi stammered nervously, her upper lip beaded with sweat. "Aaahh, umm... I overheard the nuns speaking... and..."

Everyone else in the hall began to quiet down. The girls directed their attention to Tsubomi. Murmurs swept through the crowd.

What's wrong?

What happened to Spica's star, the prince who lost her glory?

When the crowd fell silent, Tsubomi continued in a feeble voice. "Amane-sama and Hikari-oneesama… escaped from school…"

Shion froze in shock, and her face went pale. She staggered backward, falling on the floor.

The next instant the crowd erupted, voices of anger and excitement thundering around the ballroom. Spica's proud white prince, disqualified from the *Étoile* competition and stripped of her glory, had escaped from the school with her partner.

There weren't any clear details of what their disappearance meant, or even if it was true, but excitement brewed as the faces of the girls in the hall turned either blue from shock or red in anger.

After a while, Shion stood up again. "Everyone, please simmer down. The award ceremony is now over. Everyone please exit the hall immediately."

Makoto stood on the empty stage, witnessing the commotion, her mind a blank except for one thought. *What happened?! They left school…?*

Her perplexed partner, Kagome, gazed up at Makoto. Her face was ghastly white as she stared off to a distance, like Kagome wasn't there at all. Kagome, afraid, closed her eyes and tightly hugged her teddy bear. Makoto lost her balance and crumbled to the floor.

While most of the people had left the stage to ask Tsubomi for details, Chikaru went to Makoto's side. Right before Makoto hit the floor, Chikaru reached out and caught her. "Phew…that was close," Chikaru said.

Chikaru and Kagome were the only witnesses to the silent tears that rolled down Makoto's cheeks.

Shizuma ran through the campus like a vicious god. *I must find Nagisa immediately.* She respected Miator's rules and loved the uniform, so she rarely ran while wearing it. She felt the classical uniform skirt wasn't made for running, and besides, it wasn't proper for a lady to run.

Miator's queen, Hanazono Shizuma, usually made it a point to walk calmly, gracefully, and elegantly. But when she heard the news from Miyuki and left the student council room, Shizuma's steps became heavier and heavier, and soon she was running.

I can't accept this situation. It must be a misunderstanding. It happened so long ago, so why? Frustration and doubt circled Shizuma's mind. *I must hear it from her mouth to believe it.*

Miyuki's words echoed in Shizuma's head. *Nagisa has probably reached her limit. I tried to have her reconsider, but when I saw her eyes…I couldn't say anything.*

"Her limit? What do you mean?" Shizuma questioned in anger.

"I believe the pressure of being by your side, Shizuma-sama, was too much for her. Being a new transfer student must have multiplied it a hundred times," Miyuki had replied.

"But why now?"

"As I stated, she probably reached her limit today and…"

"I cannot believe this!"

"Shizuma-sama, a strong person like you does not understand such pressure. But those who are weak must always fight the temptation to flee. She had barely arrived when she was pressured to participate in the *Étoile* competition, the biggest event of Astraea. And as you know, there was more anticipation and excitement for this year's competition than ever before." Miyuki hesitated. "Nagisa *did* state that the main reason she chose to withdraw was because she broke the rule and saw you during the "Faceless Devil" trials, but…"

"But?"

"While I told her she was honest and conscientious, and those are both good qualities, Suzumi-san and I both tried to explain to her that she need not resign over it. So I don't believe that the infraction was the only reason behind her withdrawal. If she really cared at all about Miator and Shizuma-sama, then…"

Shizuma was extremely irked by Miyuki's comment. She kicked the chair as she stood. "Well, maybe you guys weren't convincing enough? Face it, I don't think she'd listen to you or Tamao. That's why I should go talk to her," Shizuma blurted.

Miyuki tried to stop Shizuma. "Please wait, it's…" With a troubled look, she stopped short, clapped a hand over her mouth, and looked away.

Shizuma narrowed her eyes. "I haven't seen you make a face like that in a while. You must know the other reason for Nagisa's withdrawal… right?" She sat back down. "Miyuki…?"

What are you afraid to say? Shizuma's voice was cold and fearful.

"Tell me now."

Miyuki froze. She looked at the table and said in a trembling voice, "Y-Yes… it's…" After a brief pause… "She probably felt threatened by the enormous amount of pressure created around the *Étoile* competition…" Miyuki shook in her chair, her whole body trembling.

Shizuma kicked the chair. "Enough already." She stormed out of the room, creating a lot of noise, but Miyuki was too scared to look up.

Shizuma ran faster, as if she was trying to suppress her growing anger. *Don't make a foolish mistake, Nagisa…*

I must find her and set things straight. I cannot allow her to quit the Étoile competition without my consent. It's not like her to quit like this. My Nagisa is always bright and cheerful, never gives up, and is so very sweet. Her love and care for others is as deep as the ocean. I want to kiss her for being so beautiful and pure.

Her thoughts were interrupted by a shout.

"Shizuma-sama!"

The sound stopped Shizuma cold. She was about to leave the school building, instinctively headed for the place she and Nagisa last spoke—a section of the large Miator library called the Secret Garden. The voice came from the same direction.

Nagisa? Is she waiting for me?

Shizuma ran towards down the dim hall and up three small flights of stairs. When she reached the door that led to the garden, the bright early summer light burst through a window, momentarily blinding her. When her eyes adjusted, she saw a girl's silhouette underneath the door's arch.

"Hitomi?"

Togi Hitomi was in the same grade as Shizuma, and also one of her closest friends. Shizuma thought it was strange for her friend to be waiting for her like this.

"You seem to be in a hurry, eh?" Hitomi slyly smiled.

It's no use explaining things to her, Shizuma thought as she tried to slip past Hitomi. "Yes, I'm searching for something," Shizuma said as she tried to squeeze past Hitomi.

Hitomi grabbed her arm. She didn't look at Shizuma, but kept her eyes forward, gazing into the distance.

"Are you looking for that girl? Even if you find her, she won't be convinced." Hitomi's confrontational tone took Shizuma by surprise.

Hitomi slowly turned her head, a very serious look on her face. "Shizuma-sama…how do you…really…how did you really feel about…Kaori?"

Hitomi was usually very brash and aggressive, but she deeply admired and respected Shizuma. This was the first time she had directly confronted her friend.

"I don't need to explain myself to you," Shizuma snapped. She didn't want to waste her time here, not when she needed to find Nagisa before she got too far away.

Shizuma didn't look at Hitomi's face either, and an air of uneasiness dropped over the two childhood friends. Suddenly, Hitomi began to cry.

"Kaori…," Hitomi said between sobs, "…really loved you,

Shizuma-sama…which is why I brought her to you…" She gripped Shizuma's wrist and looked her straight in the eye. Teardrops rolled from the corners of Hitomi's red eyes. "If she was happy to be with you, then I was fine with that…"

Hitomi, overcome, looked down. Shizuma, standing at an awkward angle, couldn't hide her shock.

"Hitomi, don't tell me you had feelings for her?"

*It all makes sense now…*Shizuma embraced Hitomi before she crumbled to the ground. Hitomi leaned into Shizuma and cried in her arms. Hitomi's tears, spurred by her feelings for Kaori, covered Shizuma's bosom and stained her uniform.

She held her feelings in all this time…

Shizuma recalled the darkest day of her life. At Kaori's funeral ceremony, Shizuma remembered Hitomi standing in the shadows next to the chapel. Mizuho, who was always by her side, wasn't with her. Instead of sharing her grief with others inside the chapel, Hitomi stood alone, crying in silence, trying to hide her tears. She had looked hopelessly sad.

Shizuma had found Hitomi's behavior at the funeral to be peculiar. *I didn't realize how terrible Kaori's death was for her…*

Shizuma pulled Hitomi away and looked at her face. With one finger, she lifted Hitomi's chin so she could see her properly.

Hitomi didn't want to show Shizuma her tear-soaked face, but she complied. She was compelled to stare into Shizuma's eyes. Shizuma planted a kiss on Hitomi's forehead.

I'm sorry…I'm so sorry for not knowing your feelings for her. When you introduced Kaori to me for the first time in

Hokkaido, in early summer, had I known about your feelings, I wouldn't have grown so close to Kaori...

"Panties, socks... pajamas, towel... and umm..." Nagisa turned to look at her uniform hanging in front of the closet. It was a dark green one-piece dress—the color dubbed "Miator green"—with an off-white short-sleeve blouse.

Though it was a lightweight summer uniform, the pannier added volume and the black lace trim added finesse, giving it a classical and elegant look. It fluttered with the breeze that blew through the window.

The summer uniform was similar to the charcoal-gray winter one, which had intricate lace trim on the cuffs and collars. Its style totally set it apart from the other all-girl schools.

Nagisa recalled the excitement and worries of when she first held this uniform. "I thought I was too childish for this mature uniform," she muttered to the empty room. She continued to pack.

I was right. This school is too mature for me. Nagisa held back her tears and stuffed her bag. *Yeah, I need to leave today. I don't belong here anymore...*

She had only been at Miator for three months, but every day had been exciting. Meeting Shizuma-oneesama, sharing a room with a good friend like Tamao-chan. And the way the younger Chiyo-chan looked up to her was kind of flattering.

This place is totally different than my old neighborhood

schools. Astraea Hill has a rich history, and long-standing traditions, and everyone here lives with such high standards and discipline.

Regardless of their year, everyone around Nagisa acted so mature and independent, and always looked into the future.

Maybe it's because they have a college in mind, something to strive for, but every student always thinks about their goals in life.

Upper-class life, and the expectations that surrounded these affluent girls, made their families cautious and prudent. The girls were expected to get good grades and, here at Astrea, they could be shut out from the rest of the world. But their lives were also troubled as they were pulled into their families' squabbles regarding heirs and the old tradition of political marriages.

Nagisa had never been exposed to such things until now. It surprised her to learn that some of the students were already engaged. What was even more surprising was that these girls, as a way to escape from the reality of their lives and to enjoy their brief youth, often had serious feelings for other girls. Such a revelation had shocked Nagisa, but, before she realized it, she had fallen right in the middle of their drama.

Nagisa had never been attracted to anyone before. All the girls around her, since elementary school—no, even kindergarten—always talked about their crushes.

Some girls had crushes on boys in their class, and some had crushes on their teacher. Others had crushes on their older cousins, and some even vowed to marry their favorite singers. But Nagisa had had no interest in such games.

"Nagisa-chan, who do you have a crush on?"

Every time someone asked me that question, I always just scratched my head and said that I didn't have anyone in mind. But nobody believed me, and they teased me for hiding my feelings. But, I really...

Nagisa had only been at Miator for three months, but she had accumulated a lot of things. She tried to stuff them into her bag.

I really didn't *have any crushes back then. I was just happy to be with my family and had lots of fun with all my friends. The thought of having a crush never occurred to me.*

Nagisa's happiness came from simple things: pretty meadowsweet blossoms, or eating a delicious apple pie with friends at a classy café. She had never experienced the excitement of seeing a person she liked at school, or being able to talk to the person she liked at the student council. She couldn't even imagine how she'd feel if she ever fell in love with someone.

But when Shizuma...oh, how my heart throbbed!

Nagisa blushed at her own thoughts. Her first kiss had been with another girl whom she just met, before she could experience first love with a boy.

Nagisa's hands, busy packing, stopped. She thought about what she had done at this school. Her hands flew to her mouth as her tears bubbled up in her eyes.

I never realized how much...I love Shizuma-oneesama...

Nagisa realized she had experienced her first love. *Oh jeez...*

She didn't even bother to wipe her tears, but just stood there, lost in her overwhelming emotions. Then another thought occurred to her, like a stab to the heart. She was leaving.

I can't go back now...

The Miator students would never forgive Nagisa for quitting the esteemed *Étoile* competition. Many students at Miator thought a new transfer student like Nagisa shouldn't have entered the competition, but had grudgingly accepted her because Miator didn't have any other viable candidates.

Of course, Nagisa wasn't the person everyone was rooting for—the Miator students had put all their hopes into Miator's Queen, Hanazomo Shizuma. She was the only person who had a chance to defeat Prince Amane, Spica's white prince, the most likely to win the *Étoile* crown.

Knowing how Shizuma was—confident and overindulgent—and no matter how spontaneous her decision, she chose Nagisa to be her partner. The students had no choice but to accept Nagisa to ensure Miator's chance at victory.

It was the only reason Nagisa was tolerated.

Well, we did win second place in the first round...for Miator...

The Miator students had supported them, for the sake of Miator's honor, as they watched the competition. *I was just a tag-along,* Nagisa thought. *They never said anything, but I knew they all wanted me to just stay silent and ride on the coattails of Shizuma-sama's glories.*

But I was okay with that, because, while being with Shizuma-sama brought me immeasurable amounts of anxiety and nervousness, I also felt an indescribable happiness. I didn't expect Shizuma-oneesama to care for me so much. It was a little overbearing.

The way Shizuma's whim had stirred up Nagisa's life she

couldn't enjoy normal campus life because of all the jealousy and whispers. She readily admitted that she wasn't the right person to be Shizuma-sama's partner.

"I know Shizuma-oneesama is a really wonderful person and all, but I'm not a good match for her. It's got to be some sort of mistake. I'm really honored that she wants to be with me, but I don't know what to do."

I must have been smiling when I said that, because everyone shrugged off my concerns. They must have thought that I enjoyed the attention. But I told them I didn't want to compete.

Knock, knock, knock, knock...
The startled Nagisa dropped the clothing in her hands. A pair of white panties landed on her knees.

"No! Please! Nagisa-chan, don't go...!"

Suzumi Tamao burst into the room and threw herself at Nagisa, sobbing.

Two girls walked under the bright sun, along a small wooded path that led to the coast. The sound of waves could be heard from a distance.

"Ah, the gymnaster flowers are blooming," Hikari said. She pranced to the side of the path and picked a tiny, light blue flower. She looked over her shoulder, excited. "This flower blooms at this time of year. It's really plain, but awfully cute, and it's one of my favorites."

Amane reached out to Hikari's hand holding the flower. "Yes, this flower is pretty. Like you, Hikari."

Instead of reaching for the flower, Amane reached for Hikari's hand. Hikari jumped and dropped the flower. Amane scooped up the flower before it reached the ground and brought it to Hikari's face.

Hikari's cheeks turned crimson. "Sorry, I'm so clumsy." She covered her reddened cheeks with her hand, a gesture that Amane thought was endearing. She chuckled and patted Hikari's head.

"You're so adorable, Hikari." Amane put the flower in Hikari's hand and kissed it. Hikari's cheeks turned an even deeper shade of red.

Hikari and Amane were enjoying their brief escape from reality. They didn't know where their spontaneous decision to leave Astrea would lead them, but they didn't care. They were just happy to bask under the bright summer sun, enjoying this blissful moment.

Hikari was thinking about the rumors she had heard before they left. *Maybe Amane-oneesama couldn't bear the Spica lifestyle anymore, and that's why she left with me.*

Even Hikari had noticed the enormous amount of pressure put upon Amane at school. *Of course it was all because she is a stunning prince.* Hikari watched Amane walking down to the beach with a handsome posture, and understood why Amane captivated everyone's hearts. Every morning, the Amane-wannabees met her at the gate. In the hallways, the lowerclassmen cheered and whispered as she walked by, and during lunch, the students lined up outside her classroom and made up excuses just to see her. There were crowds of fans around her all day long, even after school at the horse track, and in the Strawberry Dorms upon her return. It had gotten so stressful, Amane had told Hikari that she had stopped going to the large bath in the Strawberry Dorms three years ago, and that she avoided the midnight parties if she could.

Hikari had had an uncomfortable experience at a midnight party, but everyone else seemed to enjoy it, and if Kaname hadn't said those things, Hikari could have enjoyed the tea and sweets.

It was a shame that Amane-sama couldn't even enjoy such an event. *How much pain did Amane-sama have to endure when she declared that she wanted to be normal, like everyone else?*

Hikari understood the feelings of Amane's fans all too well, but she only knew a little about *Amane's* feelings. She knew that Amane loved Spica, which was why she had agreed to enter the *Étoile* competition, even if it was only half-heartedly. But despite their best efforts, Kusanagi Makoto appeared and ruined everything.

It was Hikari's fault for getting disqualified and sent to their rooms, under restriction.

At least that's what Amane's fans all said. Hikari thought it wouldn't be surprising if Amane hated Spica by now. Hikari was happy that Amane had chosen, and her heart was warmed by the golden rays of the sun.

How did we end up like this? Amane wondered. *Ever since I met Hikari, I've been acting really strange. I wanted to see*

Hikari so bad I broke the Étoile competition rules.

Amane would usually never do such a thing. *We only had to hold on for only four more days!* If Amane had been stronger, they wouldn't have been disqualified from the second round, and they wouldn't have had to run away from Astrea Hill.

Though Amane felt the *Étoile* competition was pretty outrageous at times, she was never angry about it. No matter how much she despised being treated like a prince she accepted it, as long as she was able to attend Spica. She had been at the school since she was four years old, and she loved Spica.

If she could bear it for two more years, she would finish her obligations. After all, there weren't many places like Spica, which allowed her to ride horses all she wanted. She enjoyed the simple regimen of going to school and coming back to the Strawberry Dorms each day.

To be able to enjoy life at Spica was worth giving up some freedom. At least, that's what Amane had always thought. But when Hikari appeared, it was as if a bright light had cut through the clouds, and an angelic voice had come down.

A turbulent storm riled Amane's heart. Even now Amane didn't understand why she had such an overwhelming desire to see Hikari that night. After all, she only had to wait only four more days to see her. That was it. She had been stupid enough to think she wouldn't be caught. It hadn't even crossed her mind that her secret meeting with Hikari might have been exposed. *Maybe, subconsciously, I was angry over a rule that prevented me from seeing Hikari.*

That evening, Amane went to the chapel just to see Hikari.

When Amane saw her little flower, she wanted to hold Hikari in her arms. She asked Hikari to meet her at the chapel again later.

She was surprised that Makoto had told the sisters about their meeting, but she wasn't angry. It wasn't Makoto's fault. It was Amane's. She had convinced Hikari, who wasn't familiar enough with Spica's rules to know any better, to come meet her, which caused Hikari to get locked up in her own room, under restriction.

And now, she had Hikari flee from the school with her. Amane felt bad for Hikari, but was overjoyed to be alone with her. Hikari, laughing under the bright sunlight, was simply dazzling.

No, Amane had no regrets about leaving Astrea.

This was the only thing we could do.

"Amane-sama! I can see the ocean!" Hikari yelled. The sparkling blue water peeked between the trees, winking at them in the sun, begging them to come and play.

The summer sun turned orange. It was near sunset.

"Your clothes are getting dirty," Amane said with a chuckle.

Hikari tried to pat off the sand that stuck to her skirt. "Goodness, it's really dirty. And I was being so careful not to get it wet."

Hikari, cheerful as ever, lifted her skirt, exposing her pale white thighs.

"Your panties will show if you raise it any higher," Amane said softly.

"Huh? Oh my gosh! Don't look, Amane-sama." Hikari blushed and tried to lower her skirt.

Amane grabbed Hikari's hand. "Stop! Your skirt will get wet." Amane's hands stopped on Hikari's thighs.

Hikari's heart jumped and something swelled in her throat.

"Ah, umm… but…" Hikari weakly pushed away Amane's hand.

"Don't worry. There's no one around but me. You shouldn't get your skirt wet." Amane pushed against Hikari's hands and slid her hands up Hikari's thighs.

Hikari gasped and froze, her eyes closed. Amane slowly dropped to her knees, her face almost scraping Hikari's body. She grasped the edges of Hikari's skirt, stuck between her thighs and pulled it out. The cool sunset breeze gently passed through the gap between her thighs.

Hikari felt a single drop of nectar trickle from inside her body.

Amane inhaled Hikari's sweet fragrance, an enchanting floral scent, and swooned. She swallowed deeply and shook her head to clear away the sweet temptation. "Let's go."

Amane led Hikari to her family's beachside mansion. The modern one-story house was made of bright gray concrete and glass windows and, compared to the dark rooms Hikari had been stuck in during restriction, the building looked brilliant.

Amane brought Hikari to the shower room, accessible

directly from the outside. Both girls removed their sandy clothes. There were three booths in the white-tiled shower room.

"Please use any of them. I'll go get some towels," Amane said.

Each shower booth was separated by beautiful frosted glass partitions. Hikari bashfully hid her body and ran inside the booth on the end. She turned the knob to let the hot water spurt out.

"Ahh…that feels so good."

Hikari's body, which had been chilled by the sea breezes, was warmed by the shower's hot water. She closed her eyes, lost in her thoughts. Images of Amane swam through her mind, smiling and laughing.

Amane-sama…

Hikari felt unexpectedly carefree and really happy, despite having run away from school with Amane.

I thought I would be really nervous with Amane today, because I adore her. Until now, every time I was with Amane-sama, I was both honored and somewhat nervous to be with her.

But today when Amane-sama touched me, my heart thumped wildly, but I also felt at ease… and looked Amane-sama in the eye without hesitation. My nervousness was lost in the happiness of being with Amane-sama. I'm just so happy.

Hikari's hearted swelled with emotion, and tears leapt to her eyes.

"What's wrong, Hikari?" Amane, wearing only a large white shirt, held a waffle patterned bath towel and robe.

"A-Amane-sama! It's nothing."

Hikari tried to rub the tears from her eyes, but Amane entered the booth before she got a chance. Amane wrapped her arms around Hikari and lifted her face. Hikari's face was wet from the shower, but small teardrops fell from her eyes and clung to her cheeks.

Amane looked concerned. "Are you crying?" *It's my fault… Is she thinking about school? Maybe she feels helpless, like I forced her to run away.*

On impulse, Amane placed her lips over Hikari's closed eye. She licked Hikari's tears.

"Ah…" Hikari moaned.

When Amane heard the sound her animal instincts took over. Only the sound of the shower was heard as Amane sealed Hikari's lips with hers. Hikari's body stiffened from surprise, but Amane pushed her against the wall and pressed her body against Hikari's.

I'm never letting go of you. I'm going to be with you forever…

Amane placed her lips on Hikari's neck. "You're mine, Hikari…" *Hikari's body is really hot. I wonder if the shower warmed her up.*

She touched Hikari's breast. Beneath the small, teacup-sized bud of flesh, Amane could feel Hikari's heart pounding.

"You're absolutely beautiful." Amane leaned down and tried to kiss Hikari's bosom.

"Ah… aahhh… no…" Hikari suddenly shoved Amane.

"Hikari?"

Amane was pushed out of the shower booth, confused about what had happened. She stood there, water falling from her short bangs. *Why?* Amane looked up—Hikari was beet red and trembling. She looked down at her hands as if they weren't her own.

"Do you not want me to touch you?" Amane asked.

Amane looked really sad, and Hikari suddenly realized what she had just done.

"N-No, that's not it... I really love you, Amane-sama!" Hikari replied quickly. "But I've never been touched like that before, so I was surprised." *Why did I push her away? This is so embarrassing! If Amane-sama wants me, I'd give myself to her... I really want to.* This was the first time Hikari had ever been in this situation, and she was so confused. *I mean, before coming to Spica, I never imagined being with a girl like this...*

"I just got so nervous, thinking about being with my beloved Amane-same, and..." Hikari as she looked down, embarrassed.

"You're so beautiful, Hikari," Amane said. "Don't worry. I'll protect you forever."

Hikari recalled the night her breasts had been kissed by another girl. That time she didn't feel uncomfortable being intimate. Instead of the fluttering excitement she had felt with Amane, she had been overcome by a sense of security and sensual pleasure, so she allowed herself to be caressed by the other girl. Amane's hands had brought those memories to the surface. The other girl's hands had slid all over Hikari's body so naturally, slowly building inside Hirkari a deep ecstasy. In the back of Hikari's mind she knew this wasn't a normal type of intimacy, but for some reason, she felt that what Yaya did to her was okay. Right up until this moment with Amane, Hikari had felt it was an expression of friendship.

"Yaya-chan…"

When she heard that girl's name, Amane couldn't maintain her cool. Her face twitched.

"Yaya? What did Yaya do?"

"Um, the other night, Yaya-chan…"Hikari stopped. She didn't know how to finish the sentence. She closed her eyes and thought about what to say to Amane. Hikari had believed that happened between her and Yaya was an act of friendship. Not with her head, but with her body. A normal friendship wouldn't lead to that sort of thing, but because it was Yaya… It was true that Yaya had taken off Hikari's clothes, caressed her body, and kissed her ears, fingers, and breasts. But at the same time, Yaya had also petted Hikari's head, hugged her, and whispered into her ear.

"Don't worry, I'll protect you. You should have more confidence in yourself, because a person like me loves you very much."

Hikari had been waiting for someone to tell her.

Have more confidence in yourself. Yaya whispered sweet words in her ear. The pool in the evening, with steam rising, under the moon, was like a dream. With those words and sensual hands, Hikari relaxed her body.

And Hikari knew that Yaya truly loved her, and that she wished for Hikari's happiness. What their classmates said about

Yaya wasn't true—she wasn't just full of lust. Hikari felt Yaya's deep friendship. She showed her love not only with her words, but with her whole body, because that was how she expressed herself.

Hikari had accepted Yaya's feelings with her body. But how could Hikari explain it to Amane? Even now Hikari didn't feel guilty about it. Yaya was her friend. The way she expressed herself was a bit peculiar, but it had actually helped Hikari to feel better about herself, and her situation at school. She didn't think it was an act of betrayal towards Amane.

But how would Amane react? Hikari was afraid to find out.

"Hikari? Amane called out to her again. "Hikari, did Yaya do something to you?" Amane's last words trembled. Amane knew about Yaya's love for women.

When Hikari opened her eyes, Amane was drenched from head to toe, and her face was ghostly white. She stared at Hikari, wearing a look of disbelief. The rain-drop sound of the shower was so distant. Hikari fidgeted. She didn't want Amane to misunderstand the situation.

"Oh, no! Yaya-chan just tried to cheer me up. I know people misunderstand her, but she's my best friend. She has always supported me for being with Amane-sama. I depended on Yaya-chan a lot. But, you know, she's that kind of person, and she did hug me quite often. But it's different from the way you hug me, Amane-sama. Because I… I… love you, Amane-sama…"

Hikari didn't know why, but her heart ached as she said it. "I love you so much, Amane-sama…so when you touch me, I get so…" Hikari started crying again.

Amane was taken aback by Hikari's explanations. She reached in and turned off the shower. Everything seemed to drop into sudden quiet.

"I see. I'm sorry for saying such a stupid thing." Amane covered Hikari's head with a towel. With her face hidden, she hugged Hikari.

"I don't doubt you, Hikari."

She put the bath robe around Hikari's shoulders. "Here. Get dressed before you catch a cold." She gave Hikari a gentle, reassuring smile.

Hikari borrowed clothes from Amane, but they were so big on her, it made her giggle. When she was dressed, she went into the large living room that faced the ocean. She sat on the sofa next to Amane. Amane had prepared some warm ginger tea. Hikari took a drink, and the warmth and sweetness went down her throat, soothing Hikari's dry mouth.

Hikari tried her best to explain again what had happened between her and Yaya. She spoke deliberately, and carefully tried to clear any misunderstanding. Hikari wanted Amane to understand Yaya's feelings. She explained everything, told Amane every last detail of that night. Yaya did take off Hikari's clothes and fondled her body. But that was Yaya's way of expressing her friendship. Hikari believed it was the only way Yaya knew how to express her feelings.

After Hikari finished speaking, she looked up at Amane, worry lining her face.

Amane paused before she responded. "If… it helped you,

Hikari, I guess I need to go thank her as well. If she hadn't been around to help you, you might've quit the *Étoile* competition and disappeared from my life forever."

"No way…" Hikari blurted out, making Amane laugh.

"But we ended up quitting anyway, and running away, so I guess it doesn't matter, huh? If we run into Yaya, I'm sure she'd be mad at us. How scary!" Amane joked.

Hikari laughed. "Oh, Amane-sama… I think…" She blushed. "I think Yaya-chan would be happy for us."

Amane patted Hikari's head, stood up, and told her she'd be back with more ginger tea. As she turned her back to Hikari and walked towards the kitchen door, Amane's expression darkened.

There's no mistake that Yaya really loves Hikari. She loves her so much that she accepts my relationship with Hikari. Hikari just doesn't realize it. What kind of person caresses a girl as an act of friendship? I find it hard to believe. I know my desire to touch Hikari's body is NOT from friendship.

Especially with Yaya…

Yaya claims to only love women, so it's hard to believe that Yaya was able to make Hikari feel at ease while she was being passionately fondled…

Would I have been able to hold back like Yaya, if I were in her shoes?

"What are you doing?" a surprised Nagisa asked Tamao.

"Well gee, that's what I came to talk to you about. I didn't see you at Koubu Hall, and then they made that shocking announcement about your withdrawal and… then, I rush back here and find you getting ready to run away from home!"

"Run away from home? Well, umm…" Nagisa stammered. "I-I'm not…"

"Oh, come on, I see your luggage! I knew you'd do this, Nagisa-chan. I assume that since you quit the *Étoile* competition, you convinced yourself that you couldn't stay here any longer, right?"

"Y-Yeah…"

"That's why I came back, to beg you to reconsider. Gosh, I don't know why you decided to quit, but… Wait, I know! You couldn't forgive yourself for hiding out in the bathroom, right? But that was unavoidable. You don't need to worry about that stuff, Nagisa-chan! Or, did you finally realize you wanted to dance with me instead of Shizuma-sama? Aww, gee, Nagisa-chan, you're so honest! Of course you'd love me over Shizuma-sama." She winked at Nagisa, laughing. "Come on, don't run away from home…" Tamao chattered so fast Nagisa could barely get in a reply. But Tamao's teasing made Nagisa's despair disappear.

"Run away from home? Gosh, I'm not running away *from* home. I'm trying to run *back* home!"

"Jeez, Nagisa-chan, are you still thinking like that? Don't you know that Strawberry Dorm is your home now? And since I'm your roommate, I'm your family. Actually, I don't really care about why you quit the *Étoile*. Oh, fine, I'll come clean. I was lying when I said I was rooting for you as a fellow Miator student!"

"Ehh?" Nagisa was taken by complete surprise at her comment.

"Ah, well, I *did* want you to do your best. But Nagisa-chan, you're actually mine, so I didn't want you to compete in the *Étoile* competition with Shizuma-sama. If you're with me, I guarantee that you'll have fun. I mean, my biggest pleasure in life is to provide you with great tasting desserts. I'll do homework with you, sleep in the same bed with you, and I'll even massage you whenever you want." Tamao sat beside Nagisa and hugged her, then slid down and placed her head in Nagisa's lap.

"Ahaha… that tickles!" Nagisa cried out.

"Oh, good. Do you want me to tickle you some more?" Tamao tickled Nagisa in various places.

"Kyaah! Stop! You know I'm very ticklish…" Nagisa tried to squirm away, but Tamao pinned her down.

After a while, both of them had red faces, sweating, gasping, and laughing. Before she knew it, all of Nagisa's negative thoughts were gone.

"Darnit, I was trying to leave before anyone noticed," she mumbled, staring at the bright sunshine that poured through the window.

"You know I wouldn't let you get away like that," Tamao said. "Would you like some tea? I have some of your favorite crescent cookies left over."

But Nagisa replied, "Thanks, but I really should leave."

"Nagisa-chan…" Tamao looked up. "You should just forget about Shizuma-oneesama," muttered Tamao. Nagisa became quiet.

I guess that wasn't convincing enough. Tamao thought…
and unlike her usual character, became adamant.

"Shizuma-oneesama probably won't be mad at you for
withdrawing from the *Étoile* competition, regardless of your
reasons. And now that you've withdrawn, you can't undo it. On
top of that, if you leave Shizuma-sama, I'm sure she'll recover
in no time. Shizuma-sama can choose anyone from her pool
of hopefuls. Her policy is to accept all and chase no one; in
fact, she changes partners almost monthly. She'll go out with
anyone as long as they're cute. You can bet she'll find a new girl
without missing a beat."

*I think my words were a bit harsh. It pains my heart to be so
blunt with her. I hope she's not hurt.*

Tamao cautiously checked Nagisa's expression. Nagisa had
a big smile on her face.

"Yeah, you're right. Shizuma-oneesama only thought of me
as a stupid, naïve transfer student, so she wouldn't miss me if I
left her."

I didn't mean to be so mean, Nagisa. Tamao tried to say
something, but Nagisa kind of knew what Tamao was trying to
say, so she pretended to be mature and looked at Tamao.

"I won't think about Shizuma-sama anymore."

A chill ran down Tamao's spine as Nagisa continued. "I
know that I don't match Shizuma-sama at all. That's why I've
given up. My withdrawal may mean nothing to Shizuma-sama,
or might she might even be relieved she doesn't have to deal
with me anymore. But everyone at Miator might feel differently,
right?" Nagisa's said, half-hoping.

Tamao gulped. *Ohh, she's given up completely. Where did my innocent little Nagisa learn to make such a face?* The idea of Nagisa's heart breaking made Tamao want to cry.

Nagisa went on. "Everyone is probably mad at me. I didn't mean to, but a transfer student like me, who participated in the *Étoile* competition half-heartedly, only to quit halfway and stuff... I can't blame them if they accuse me of not taking the *Étoile* competition seriously."

"Ohh, Nagisa-chan, don't think like that."

Tamao was jealous of Shizuma, because Nagisa cared for her so much. It made Tamao sad. And upset that Nagisa harbored such feelings about Shizuma and not her.

"Ohh, Nagisa-chan, you're just going crazy because everyone's bullied you so much!" Tamao finally chattered again. "But you don't need to worry about any of that!" She hugged Nagisa. "If you decide to leave Shizuma-sama, that's fine. And don't worry about the *Étoile* competition. Everyone assumed the Prince would take the crown this year, so no one at Miator expected to win. And you were bullied so much, because all the other students were jealous of you, having the campus queen pay you so much attention."

Tamao made a silent vow to Nagisa. *Everything will be okay from now on, because I won't let Shizuma-sama near you anymore. Rest assured, I'll protect you. I'll make you forget Shizuma-sama.*

"Hey, Nagisa-chan, how about this? Promise me that you won't see Shizuma-sama ever again. Just tell everyone that Shizuma-sama dumped you. That way, no one will say anything bad about you. They all know Shizuma-sama changes partners on a whim. And you can enter the *Étoile* competition with me next year! What do you think?"

Nagisa's laugh was weak. "Why would you want to do that?"

"Come on, we can win for sure next year! If we do, then everyone will have to accept you, right? Right? Don't you think it's a brilliant plan?" Tamao playfully pinched sad Nagisa's cheeks and pulled them up.

"Nagisa-chan, if you're with me, I think we can win the *Étoile* crown. Actually, President Rokujo has been asking me to enter, but I wasn't really interested. But if I pair up with you, Nagisa-chan, I'll have a lot of fun. And we can actually put all that dance practice to good use!"

Nagisa hung her head. "Yeah, I'm sorry about that. You taught me so much, Tamao-chan, but all that effort was wasted. I'm so sorry, Tamao-chan." She dropped her head lower.

Tamao hugged her happily. "Yeah, that's right! Now I remember. Nagisa-chan, you're absolutely right! You totally used me. I skipped all my club practices and council meetings just to coach you, Nagisa-chan!"

"I know." Nagisa shrank behind her shoulders, but Tamao grabbed her arms.

"If you want to make it up to me, you need to win the *Étoile* crown with me. It's a promise, okay? And don't ever see Shizuma-oneesama." Tamao grinned.

Nagisa wasn't sure how all of it connected, but Tamao was trying so hard to cheer her up. As she heard Tamao blather, her feelings of desperation went away, and she felt better.

"Gosh… Tamao-chan, you're so silly…" Nagisa chuckled. Her desire to leave the school grew smaller and smaller. *Oh well, whatever. I'll just stay here a little longer.* She didn't want to leave Tamao-chan and her kindness just yet. *I'll stay until I gather enough courage to leave again.*

Tamao didn't notice Nagisa's change in heart. "Promise? Great. Okay, it's time to celebrate with some delicious tea! I'll break out the vanilla tea, my special blend, and… Nagisa-chan's favorite crumble pie."

Nagisa jumped up. "What? We still had some left over?! You told me we ate it all."

"Tsk…I knew you liked it so much, Nagisa-chan, I ordered a new batch the next day! I was holding onto it for an emergency."

"Emergency?" Nagisa asked, perplexed.

"Yes, for celebrations like today, and other purposes…"

Tamao sat next to Nagisa again and hugged her. "And, for things like…" Tamao stared into Nagisa's eyes and brought her face closer.

Nagisa was confused …*Hmm? This is…weird…what is she trying to…*

Tamao was so close they were almost touching. "Okay? This is to promise that you won't meet Shizuma-oneesama anymore. And that you'll enter the *Étoile* competition with me."

Tamao leaned into a dazed Nagisa, and lightly placed her lips on Nagisa's.

Knock, knock, knock…

Someone knocked on the door. Before either Nagisa or Tamao could do anything, the door opened.

"Excuse me...Kyaaaah!" Chiyo's scream echoed through the hallway.

Tamao snapped her fingers. "Aww, I almost had her."

Nagisa snapped out of her trance. "Chiyo-chan, what's wrong...?"

Tsukidate Chiyo's face was beet red as she answered, "U-Umm, I was worried about Nagisa-oneesama. I thought Nagisa-oneesama was upset or something, so I thought I'd make some tea."

Tamao switched back to her usual self. "Aww, Chiyo-chan, you're so sweet for worrying about her. That's wonderful. We'd be glad to have some tea." Tamao added a wink.

As commotion stirred all over campus, in the Student Council room, Rokujo Miyuki sank in the president's chair. The enormous leather chair enveloped her whole body, including her head. It was her personal chair, one she brought into the room. She loved that chair; it was the chair of St. Miator Girls' Academy Student Council President. But in her current miserable state, she knew it was only a matter of time before she'd lose this special privilege.

Miyuki was alone in the silent council room. Anytime she wanted to think, she came here. She'd only come when she was sure no one was around, during classes or breaks. But today was different. She was ashamed of herself, but running here was the only way she could deal with this situation. Shameful as it was, she was using this place to hide.

She couldn't bring herself to go to Koubu Hall, where the second round of the *Étoile* competition was being held.

The winners of the round are probably being announced about now. I wonder which couple won? Did the Spica-Lulim pair of Kusanagi Makoto and Byakudan Kagome—the first couple in history that paired up students from two schools— sweep the competition? Oh well, all that means nothing to me now.

Even though Miator students had entered the contest, Miyuki no longer cared about the *Étoile* competition. Not now, since Shizuma and Nagisa had quit.

Though she had urged Shizuma's participation in the competition, Miyuki had kind of expected this outcome. *I miscalculated everything.*

Miyuki recalled Nagisa's face when she declared her withdrawal. *She looked so desperate. And though she never stated clearly why she wanted to quit, judging from her facial expression, I have some ideas. Someone either fooled Nagisa with false information, or she was hurt by jealousy, or maybe it had something to do with Sakuragi Kaori. Regardless, she probably felt she could no longer be with Shizuma. Nagisa probably couldn't bear it anymore. One way or another, I expected this to occur.*

Miyuki stopped her self-loathing for a moment, switching to repentance. *I feel bad for putting Nagisa through all this.*

Shizuma-sama's starry brilliance is much too strong. She burns out all the other little stars surrounding her. Shizuma is like a large, fixed star that continues to expand. The only way other stars can survive is either to be just as strong and passionate, or stay far out of her orbit to avoid being sucked in by her gravity.

Neither option is easy. It's hard to maintain your sense of self next to Shizuma's overpowering presence, and even if you try to keep your distance, before you know it you're pulled into Shizuma's aura.

Miyuki shook herself free from melancholy and stood up.

This is not the time to reflect on Shizuma. How will the Miator students react to this turn of events? Miator has lost all chances to attain the Étoile crown this year. Non-participation was one thing, but having candidates compete in the competition, only to quit mid-way is unacceptable. Considering this is Shizuma's second chance in the competition, and all the coordination that was involved, the student body will demand something from me for this horrible outcome. Should I expect to get fired? Or should I take responsibility and submit my resignation before that happens?

While Miyuki stood pondering, the door opened. The fragrant aroma of olives filled the room, and Marikoya Aiko, the Miator Secretary, entered the room, looking down. She gasped when she looked up and saw Miyuki.

"I apologize. I didn't expect anyone to be here."

Miyuki waved her hand languidly, as if to say, "Don't worry about me."

Aiko smirked at Miyuki's obviously depressed state.

Huh? Miyuki, thought, surprised. She didn't expect that reaction from Aiko. The girl was tall and quite beautiful, so she was really popular among the lowerclassmen. There were several reasons she was content to being just a secretary, though she could have aspired much higher. Her face was always a mask, emotionless, a result of her upbringing in a former noble family.

So when Aiko smiled happily, Miyuki knew something big was up.

"But I am glad you're here, Miyuki-sama." Aiko held out the folder in her hands. "I found a document that you may find interesting."

She silently walked over to Miyuki. "I hope you find this useful. For the person I admire…"

Aiko bowed to Miyuki and knelt beside her chair. She presented Miyuki with the file. It was an official document with the St. Miator Student Council watermark. The cover bore these words:

Emergency Report Regarding the Expulsion of Kusanagi Masaki, the first permanent *Étoile*

It was dated roughly nine years ago.

CHAPTER 2

The Hidden Road Sign Invites
Those Who Are Lost

Okuwaka Tsubomi ran around, cleaning the empty Koubu Hall. Several other First and Second year students, also wearing council member armbands, were also there, pushing mops and rags across the floor. All the decorations and bleachers had been put away. The Koubu Hall gradually returned to its usual quiet state.

Yaya sat at the edge of the stage, watching the workers run around like busy bees.

I wonder how Hikari is doing? What was I thinking, when I...?

She recalled that night. In the evening light, Hikari had been so strikingly beautiful. She put her complete trust in Yaya. It could be felt through her soft, white skin. In the silence, Yaya removed her clothes, fondled her beautiful budding breasts, and kissed her neck. And the whole time she completely trusted Yaya as her close friend. Which is why Yaya hadn't gone all the way.

She bit her lips in frustration.

I'm so stupid. I went so far, and I just couldn't go all the way. I normally wouldn't stop halfway, so why did I? Ahahah... She almost laughed out loud, as she stared up at the ceiling. Koubu Hall's ceiling was about five meters high. In the center hung an extravagant chandelier that sparkled in the sunlight that poured through the windows.

Now that I look back, it was probably for the best, I guess. Hikari was able to regain her confidence and her smile.

Yaya didn't know how her words and actions had been taken. The next morning, neither of them could talk about what happened the night before. When they had tea during breakfast, she noticed Hikari's rosy face, filled with happiness.

Yaya was afraid to break the silence. She wanted to tell Hikari to just forget what had happened the previous night, only she had been too scared. Maybe there was just a little hope in her heart that Hikari had accepted Yaya's feelings, that maybe she actually loved Yaya.

But, deep down inside, she knew the truth. *Hikari only sees me as her friend. Even while I was making out with her, she probably thought I was expressing my friendship in a strange way.*

It hurts that she only sees me that way. Hikari is clueless, but that cluelessness was probably the only thing that allowed me to maintain my close friendship to Hikari. If she had realized the true meaning behind my actions—which most people would have—it would have been the end of our friendship. Hikari probably would have run screaming. Luckily she didn't notice. And she still needs me.

Though Hikari had been forsaken by everyone, Yaya had given her love and brought back her confidence.

Oh, maybe Hikari didn't notice my true feelings. Or maybe she didn't want to acknowledge it. Ohh, this is ridiculous. Why am I wasting my time, thinking so negatively? Snap out of it, Nanto Yaya! If you had so much time to muddle around in your thoughts, then you should've just gone all the way. Have you forgotten what you always tell yourself? A love relationship without sex doesn't exist... Love is spawned from body heat and physical intimacy, so if you love the body, then love of the heart will follow suit. I don't believe in such a laughable thing as platonic love...do I?

Sigh... Yaya stretched her arms. It was torture, thinking about how Hikari was no longer hers, but a relief at the same time. At this point, she could only wish for Hikari to stick it through with Amane. If Hikari couldn't be Yaya's, then the girl needed to go far away, out of her reach.

Tsubomi ran through the Hall's entrance, on the other side of the room, and made straight for the stage.

"Yaya-oneesama!"

Another girl, wearing the white Spica uniform, was with Tsubomi. It was the school's Student Council President, Tomori Shion.

Tsubomi swirled her cleaning rag in large circles as she called out to Yaya. "President Shion would like to talk to you, Yaya-oneesama."

Yaya tried to jump down from the stage, but Shion waved to stop her, and slowly walked towards her, Tsubomi following behind like a puppy. Tomori Shion had an extremely slim figure, and her normally pale face looked even moreso today, probably from exhaustion.

I can understand why she would look beat.

Shion's plan for the *Étoile* competition had been thrown all out of whack, first with Shizuma's entry, then the nomination of Hikari, and then Makoto's sudden appearance. The final straw had come with Amane and Hikari's infractions and disqualification, and their escape from the detention rooms on the day of the second round. She had utterly lost face as the Student Council President.

Yaya felt kind of sorry for her, so her smile was sympathetic. "How can I help you?"

Shion nodded politely, as if to acknowledge Yaya's gesture. "Nanto-san, I understand that you share rooms with Konohana-san?"

Yaya nodded.

Shion's smile was small and fleeting. "By any chance, were you aware of what they were planning to do?"

Yaya hadn't expected the question, but she tried not to show her surprise. "Why would I know anything?"

Shion found Yaya's smile and quick response suspicious. "All right, then, do you know where they might have gone?"

"There's no way in hell I could know such a thing."

Yaya's protest was a bit overdramatic, which did nothing to asssuade Shion's suspicions. "But *I* heard that even though others despised Konohana-san, you were on her side. Konohana-san isn't the type of girl who would make a move as bold as running away without giving it some thought, isn't that right? Which is why I presumed she may have discussed her problems with you."

Yaya, suddenly infuriated, cut off Shion before she could say anything else. "What would make you think that, President Shion? Hikari and I don't have a special relationship. We're just roommates. The fact that Hikari 'ran off' with her partner should prove that. Don't ask me, ask Amane-sama. I really don't know anything."

"Oh, I see." Shion was surprised at Yaya's outburst.

From behind Shion, Tsubomi chuckled. "President Shion, if Yaya-oneesama knew something, she'd surely have stopped it from happening! Because Yaya-oneesama reeeaally likes Hikari-oneesama! I mean, she only gave her up because Hikari-oneesama likes Amane-sama, but really, she's…"

"Hey! Tsubomi! Why are you bringing that up?" Yaya waved her fist.

Tsubomi stuck out her tongue at Yaya. "But don't think you're alone. You're not the only one who likes Hikari-oneesama! I'm also really worried about Hikari-oneesama. I mean, as long as she's with Amane-sama, I'm sure she won't get into any accidents or anything, but I hope they're okay." Tsubomi looked as if she was about cry, so Shion jumped in.

"O-Okay, I get it! Enough of this subject. Let's move on."

Konohana-san's popularity is surprising, Shion thought. *If the Étoile competition had progressed as planned, we probably would have had a solid victory.*

Her thoughts were interrupted by the loud click of the public address being turned on. A voice boomed from the speakers, making an announcement: "Attention please. Would Tomori Shion-sama from St. Spica Girls' Institute, Fifth Year Class *Deux*, and Nanto Yaya-sama from St. Spica Girls' Institute, Third Year Class *Un*, please report to the faculty room immediately."

The three girls looked at each other, all wondering what had happened to Hikari, and then Yaya and Shion raced from the room.

Behind the Secret Garden—otherwise known as the library, a large, stone castle-like building—a figure walked over the shadowy grass. Shizuma was disgusted with everything that was going on with the *Étoile* competition and with school in general, so she decided to leave her classes early.

It was early summer, and the lawn behind the library was green and lush. But right now all Shizuma wanted to do was pluck every blade of grass in sight, one by one, until the lawn was bare.

I've been so foolish. And so selfish—about Kaori, then Hitomi, and now Nagisa. My selfishness has hurt the feelings of many girls. It frustrates me to no end.

She had done so much damage without meaning to. And an action without evil intent is the biggest sin of all, because it cannot be repented. Shizuma was strong-willed. She knew that and liked it. And she couldn't help but draw attention to herself; she was quite an alluring girl.

Shizuma thanked God for her attractive qualities, but she knew her strong personality wasn't envied by others. Despite that, many girls were attracted to her. Like Sakuragi Kaori. And Shizuma, fierce and strong as she was, protected all those who loved her. It was a new development for Shizuma, ever since her encounter with Kaori. Before that, Shizuma had had a very different attitude. She hadn't cared for people who couldn't take care of themselves. She had looked down upon girls who adored her, as if she had to fulfill some void in their lives that they couldn't fill themselves. She felt sorry for those who placed hope in others instead of themselves.

But when Shizuma met Kaori, she realized the existence of true love. For an independent girl like Shizuma, it was difficult to believe in selfless love. She had felt the girls who liked her must have had some kind of ulterior motive. Shizuma had beauty, power, intelligence, and was a fearless daredevil; maybe the girls wanted to attain those qualities through Shizuma, without making their own efforts, to ride on her coattails and stand in her spotlight.

That was what she had thought, but now she realized those were merely illusions spawned from Shizuma's suspicious mind. The girls instinctively sought someone to love and to develop an intimate relationship with. It wasn't because of any logical choice, but stemmed rather from a physical desire, and one of the predominant natural instincts of a human. To want someone, to love them and be loved. Shizuma felt in her soul it was the most happiness a human could have.

Kaori had lived her life like that, right until her death. It was the most important lesson she had taught Shizuma. And once she realized the truth, she appreciated her life with the maidens of Astraea, and even grew to respect them.

She vowed never to hurt anyone's feelings again. *According to Hitomi, Kaori was happy to be with me, but I wonder if she was really happy? Before she died, she may have seen right through my heart. Though I tried to protect her, I really...*

"Oww..."

Shizuma had walked through the bushes and accidentally snapped a stem off of a thorny brush. A little thorn was stuck in her pinky. The red blood swelled into a small droplet. Shizuma licked it, thinking it served her right, this little pain, after everything she had caused.

"What is the matter?" a voice asked. There was a rustling in the flowering trees and shrubs behind Shizuma.

"Who's there?" Shizuma turned around.

Rokujo Miyuki stepped through the bushes. A tall girl was right behind her—Marikoya Aiko.

"We were looking for you. I would like to share some confidential information," Miyuki said graciously.

"I don't feel like talking to anyone right now," Shizuma replied coldly. She tried to turn and walk away.

"It has something to do with Aoi Nagisa-san."

The sound of luxurious, rushing water echoed throughout the giant bathroom.

Clouds of steam saturated the room.

"So, how did we all end up here?" Shizuma asked Miyuki as she wiped the sweat from her face with a small towel. Brilliant sunshine flooded through the large window that looked out onto the inner garden. The white wisps of fog looked like gentle snow, and felt like heaven. The girls were sitting inside Miator's public bath.

"Well, I suppose it is a little hot at this time of year to take a midday bath," Miyuki replied nonchalantely. "But I assure you there is a good reason."

"Err, is there a reason why I was brought here, also?" Marikoya Aiko, blushing, sat next to Shizuma.

"You're definitely here to entertain me." Shizuma pointed at Aiko's breasts. "You're thin enough to be a model, but you sure have a great pair."

Aiko squirmed. "Please don't look at me like that." She didn't last long in hot baths, they made her dizzy.

Miyuki cut in. "Please don't tease my secretary too much. Actually, I thought this would be the best place to discuss a confidential matter with you, Shizuma-sama. We should finish before she passes out."

Oh, so you brought someone to distract me from toying with you, eh? Shizuma mentally cursed, but she was intrigued by Miyuki's secrecy. *What is going on in her mind?*

"Do tell." Shizuma leaned against Aiko to keep her from fainting. Aiko, nervous, cast a sidelong glance at Shizuma's deliberate movements.

Miyuki began to explain. "Today, in the St. Miator Girls'

Academy Student Council room, we found an interesting document. Something I've been looking for, regarding Spica's legendary *Étoile*, Kusanagi Masaki."

"Kusanagi…" Shizuma was surprised at the familiar name. Miyuki continued with the details.

"Makoto is the younger sister of the legendary *Étoile*, Kusanagi Masaki. Their ages are far apart, possibly because they have different mothers. There are no records of the legendary *Étoile* graduating, apparently because she dropped out of school after the competition.

"As if that isn't enough, immediately after her older sister's disappearance, Makoto graduated from Spica Elementary School and left the country. This might be just a rumor, but the first *Étoile* may have run off with her lover, never to come back to school."

Shizuma was taken aback by the details, but acknowledged them as if she was watching a play, the story detatched from herself. "So what does that have to do with me and Nagisa?" She glanced at Marikoya Aiko, waiting for a chance to tug away the towel that hid her body.

"What does it… have to do…" Miyuki sputtered. "Well, I was hoping you would consider re-entering the *Étoile* competition—"

Miyuki tried to finish her sentence, but Shizuma interrupted by successfully yanking the towel away from Aiko, who shrieked.

"Ahah, gotcha! You don't need a towel in the bathtub." Shizuma joked, happy to get another eyeful of Marikoya Aiko's gorgeous breasts.

Miyuki, exasperated, interjected. "Shizuma-sama! Please! Were you listening to me at all? You seemed to be infatuated

with Aoi Nagisa, yet you fool around like this? It was this kind of behavior that probably cost Nagisa's confidence in herself, Shizuma-sama."

Shizuma dropped her hand and pouted. "It's over. She probably hates me." She turned her back on the two girls. Suddenly she stood up and mumbled, "I'm going to wash off."

Miyuki expected Shizuma to snap back at her, but she was speechless at the tame response.

A small splashing sound made Miyuki turn around. Marikoya Aiko had fainted.

As sunset rapidly approached, Amane sat thinking. Though it was early summer, the sea breeze felt chilly. Amane leaned her head against the window, looking out to the shore. The sound of waves breaking on the shore could just be heard through the glass. Amane thought about Hikari, lying in the guest room. She had lain, cradled in Amane's arms, and quickly drifted off into sleep.

This must have been one hell of a day for her. First being put on restriction, then running away, and then frolicking on the beach. Ever since we were sent to our rooms, Hikari hasn't had any time to relax. She tends to be hard on herself, so she when she finally did relax, she fell fast asleep.

Amane sighed deeply. *I guess I'm tired, too.* She laughed to herself, but at the same time a bitter concern filled her heart. Hikari's words played in her memory.

I know Yaya had feelings for Hikari. Everyone knows about

her hatred of men, and that she's the only genuine lesbian on campus. But Hikari was so innocent and pure that I hadn't the faintest clue. I had assumed they never went past being good roommates. I was wrong. Amane laughed some more, not cheerfully. *Of course Yaya didn't. I should've noticed earlier. Yaya saw her the way I did.*

Amane couldn't believe her foolishness. When she acknowledged Yaya as her rival to win Hikari's heart, a flame lit within her. But Yaya had encouraged Hikari to be with Amane, who was clearly her love rival. Most people would burn with jealousy over what Yaya had done, but for some reason, Amane wasn't angry. She actually appreciated that Yaya cared so much about Hikari. If the rumors were true about Yaya, then she probably could have used every trick in the book to get have her way with Hikari, but she had restrained herself.

Amane was filled with competitive spirit. This burning desire to win was something Amane hadn't felt in a while.

Amane had almost lost herself when she first encountered love, but she had found herself again. *Hikari loves me. And I love her. I must provide for her happiness, more than Yaya.*

In order to that, I know what I must do.

Amane stood, reached to the top of the unused fireplace and picked up the phone.

"You two really have no idea what happened to them?" Sister Carina, the disciplinary head, drilled Shion and Yaya. The two girls stood at attention in St. Spica Girls' Institute Faculty Room. They were not permitted to sit.

Sister Carina was a brunette with well-defined European features and rimless glasses. Her appearance made her seem glamorous, but she was actually a very gentle and caring sister, even though she was in charge of discipline. It was well known that she was very lenient and understanding in most cases.

But today, Sister Carina was unbelievably furious. So furious that she forgot to let them sit. Shion and Yaya cringed in fear.

"If you girls are hiding something, then you will be charged with the same infractions as them. Understood?" The sister eyed the girls suspiciously.

Yaya couldn't keep from asking. "Umm, what are they charged with?"

Sister Carina's sharp glare almost physically hurt Yaya. "It is a major infraction for a Strawberry Dorm resident to leave the campus grounds, but to have them leave while they are under restriction—*dear God!*" The sister made the sign of the cross, holding onto the rosary around her neck. "I cannot imagine the number of punishments they will receive for that. We must find those two before they get into more trouble. If they are not found soon… Oh, Lord… At this point, they might receive the highest form of punishment anyway."

The sister raised her hands in the air and crossed herself three more times.

"Don't tell me the highest form of punishment is—?" Yaya whispered.

Upon seeing the sister's reaction and finally understanding the school's position on the matter, Shion's face went blue. *This is no longer just about the Étoile competition. If they're not found soon, their whole futures will be jeopardized.*

Sister Maria, the receptionist entered the room, interrupting the conversation. "Sister Carina, you have a phone call from St. Miator Girls' Academy."

Sister Carina did not even turn around. "Oh, please have them call back later. I'm in the middle of an important conversation—"

"But, oh…" Sister Maria, with a troubled look on her face, whispered something into Sister Carina's ear.

Sister Carina's face changed color. "The School Chancellor said that?" After a long pause, she waved Yaya and Shion away. "The two of you are dismissed. Please do not share this conversation with anyone."

She stood up and ran out the door, leaving Yaya and Shion looking at each other, wondering what had happened.

Chikaru accidentally dropped the the phone back onto the cradle with a loud clang. She spun around to check. Kusanagi Mako lay still on the bed. She moved her hand but didn't wake up.

Phew, that was close. She should sleep a little more.

Chikaru was in the Strawberry Dorm observation room, watching Makoto sleep.

The sun was in its final stages before disappearing from the horizon, the burning orange rays pouring through the windows slowing turned to darkness.

Makoto's face seemed pale and ill, stricken.

I'm so sorry, Chikaru thought sadly. *Mako-chan, I didn't expect things to turn out like this.*

Chikaru looked into Makoto's face. The girl had fainted when she heard the words, "run away" during the commotion in Koubu Hall. Chikaru hadn't realized how deep Makoto's emotional scars were. She just wanted Makoto to confront and overcome her past, by competing in the *Étoile* competition... no, by winning the *Étoile* crown.

In Chikaru's mind, maybe Makoto would understand her beloved sister's feelings if she experienced the same things she had. And if Makoto saw Amane with Hikari, maybe she'd understand what true love was.

But, I wonder if it was a little too early for the poor thing.

Chikaru lightly poked Makoto's nose. She thought, not about about Makoto, but two people who were in a much more desperate situation.

Amane and Hikari.

Chikaru never imagined Amane and Hikari would run off like that. Honestly, Chikaru hadn't thought their disqualification from the *Étoile* competition wasn't a big deal. Those two were serious, though, which was why everyone had focused all their jealousy on them. Chikaru thought Amane should capture the *Étoile* crown just once. Amane was *Étoile* material, but she didn't seem to have enough self-confidence. Chikaru just wanted her to shine and be the star she was meant to be. But

Hikari had appeared out of nowhere causing Amane to fall head over heels in love.

The reason why Amane entered the *Étoile* competition was not for the crown, but for Hikari. With such an ulterior motive there was no way Amane would achieve victory. As expected, rumors were rampant about the forsaken couple. If the awkward Amane and timid Hikari couldn't bear the stress then both *should* be released from the pressures of the *Étoile* competition, Chikaru thought.

I'll clean up the mess you two left behind... no problem.

She had tried to come up with a good plan. *Well, it really wasn't much of a plan, huh,* Chikaru thought. All she had done was write a letter to Makoto and tell her what was going on. Really it was just a good chance for Lulim to slip in and win an *Étoile* crown. Chikaru grinned. Her plan had made it easier for the other two girls to ease out. Chikaru knew Mikato couldn't resist coming back, a new candidate worthy of the *Étoile* crown appeared, and Amane's popularity waned. In the end, Amane and Hikari broke a cardinal rule and were disqualified.

Being disqualified was a major dishonor in itself, but really, how much damage did Amane sustain from this turn of events? After all was said and done, she only had to sit in her room under restriction. Surely it wasn't so bad they had to leave campus. Maybe Amane had put too much pressure upon herself because of her feelings towards Hikari?

Chikaru continued to ponder about the clumsy prince's struggles of dealing with her newfound emotions of love. *Cinderella only got her handsome prince with the help of a fairy godmother, right? I'm partially responsible for the way things turned out.*

She looked at the phone, thinking over the converstation she had just had. *I never wanted to have to rely on* her. *She'll hold the fact I asked her for help over my head forever. I wanted to be free of her, that's the reason I chose to go to Lulim in the first place. Sigh...but I bit the bullet and asked... I wonder if I should give up on the Class Z idea?*

She sighed again. The sun had set, and the room went dark. Chikaru moved to turn on the lights. The moment she stood...

"Hrmm..." Makoto woke up.

"Oh, you're up, Mako-chan." Chikaru greeted her with a smile. "Do you feel better?"

Makoto squinted and eyed her surroundings. "Where are we?

"You don't remember? We're in the Strawberry Dorms' observation room. Mako-chan, after the competition in the Koubu Hall, you felt sick and wanted to rest, so I brought you here. This used to be a temporary clinic for small ailments, but these days, most students go straight to the hospital for treatment."

"Oh..." Makoto nodded, still squinting. "I had a dream."

"What did you see? Was it a wonderful dream about the dance?"

"I saw Masaki-oneesan in my dream. My beloved Masaki-oneesan, my sister, whom I can never see again."

The name came out of Makoto's mouth rather naturally. Makoto and Chikaru were both surprised. They looked at each other and started laughing. When they got control of themselves,

Makoto wondered, "Why couldn't I say her name until now?"

"Well, because you probably loved her so much, that's why," Chikaru smiled.

"Yeah I really loved and respected her. I was really shocked at what happened. So when Prince Amane ran away like that, I guess all the bad memories came back to me."

Makoto looked up to the ceiling with distant eyes. Her expression cleared as if she was at peace.

Chikaru was startled. "So, what was your dream about?" she asked slowly, careful not to disturb the fragile moment. *Just let it out and confess your feelings...*

Makoto seemed to pick up Chikaru's wishes. She stumbled over her words at first, but explained everything while wearing a gentle, carefree smile.

"It was...the very first time I met her. I remember it so well. I always had short hair like a tomboy, but the "oneesan" who appeared before me was really beautiful, like a doll with long, straight black hair.

"I was nervous. We were going to my new father's house for the first time. It felt like walking into enemy territory. This was going to be my new house, and I was still a kid. I thought Masaki-oneesan and her mother, the Mistress of the house, were enemies to me and my mom."Makoto looked down bashfully. "Wasn't that a dumb thought? But I really didn't understand the reason behind things, you know? When I finally met my sister, I thought she was so nice and pretty. She told me that I looked like a boy, pure and gallant. No one had ever called me gallant before. It made my spine tingle. Then, she said that she was glad I was a tomboy, because she always wanted a younger sister who was active and not too girly, and looked forward to catching horned beetles with me.

"The Kusanagi estate had a large wooded area, with a lot of horned beetles. I don't know how she knew I liked to catch insects, and I didn't expect a pretty girl like Masaki-oneesan to ask me to hunt insects with her. But anyway, I felt welcomed, and accepted, so I was really happy. Looking back, I'm sure she said that about the insects to please me.

"Up until that day, I always wondered why my last name was different than my dad's and why he never came home at night." Makoto shrugged. "I just stared figuring things out. So I was just happy that I finally had a place to call home. Dad would come back to our big home every night, plus I gained a beautiful sister. I had never had a place to call home before that, so this was complete happiness. I went to the same school as Masaki-neesan, and wanted to grow up to be like her. Masaki-neesan was really sweet and feminine, and I wanted to protect her, since I was a tomboy… such silly thoughts.

"But then Neesan was gone one day. And I couldn't forgive myself, because I thought it was my fault. I didn't notice anything the whole time I was there. It was so obvious, too, thinking back on it. I mean, with me and my mom there, Masaki-oneesan must have been deeply hurt. But she held it in, never said a word. Of course, I was totally ignorant, and kept snuggling up to her, saying, 'Neesan, Neesan.'"

Makoto humphed. "Neesan probably couldn't wait to leave that house. Otherwise, she wouldn't have run off with a plain girl. Neesan was the campus superstar, adored by everyone, the legendary *Étoile* of Spica. But she threw all that away and left with her partner. I actually don't think she really wanted to run away like that. I think she couldn't stand to be in the house with my mom and me there. I should have been the one to leave the house. It wasn't until after Neesan was gone that I found out about her feelings and left the house also. But since I was too young to live on my own, I begged my parents to allow me to study abroad instead. Of course, it was kind of pointless because it was after the fact. Neesan had disappeared."

Makoto paused and looked up at Chikaru. "When I got the letter from you, my skin crawled. I couldn't forgive the person who ruined the reputation of my Neesan's beloved Spica and her venerable *Étoile* crown." She rolled her eyes. "I'm so stupid. I tried so hard to punish myself and vowed never to return to that house. But I came right back to defend Neesan's honor, even though Neesan wasn't there. When Amane and Hikari ran away together, I was overcome with fears of my past. I'm embarrassed I passed out, though. I don't think anyone should be forced to run like that."

Clang clang... Nagisa scraped her knife and fork together, making an annoying, grating sound.

Girls across the table coughed to warn her it was rude.

Nagisa blushed. "Ah... oh, sorry..." She was eating in the Miator Cafeteria inside the Strawberry Dorms. After Tamao had calmed her down, Nagisa had lost her will to leave. She was invited to eat dinner at the cafeteria. Today's menu had Nagisa's favorites, Saltimbocca[10] and Gâteau à l'ananas[11], so she decided to come, but now she was wondering if it was the right choice.

I won't die if I skip one dinner... Nagisa could feel the cold, piercing stares from the girls around her.

Yeah, I expected this much, since it's my fault that I quit the Étoile competition.

Although no one confronted her directly, the girls sitting around Nagisa were unusually quiet. Tamao, sitting next to her, was quiet as a rock, unwilling to disturb the artificial peace.

But I want to go back to my room, right away... Tears welled in Nagisa's eyes. Under the tablecloth, Tamao gently placed her hand on Nagisa's knee.

We're almost done. Hang in there...

Nagisa understood her silent but heartwarming encouragement.

She subtly wiped the tears from her eyes and brought her face up. *Okay... I'm gonna hang on.* She scanned the room. Her biggest fear was bumping into Shizuma, but there had been no sign of her when Nagisa first entered the room. Tamao had reassured her that upperclassmen were allowed to take meals in their room, and Shizuma would be considerate enough to do so at a time like this. Nagisa didn't understand what she meant by "a time like this," so she continued to scan the area for Shizuma. But she wasn't there. Nagisa was both relieved and disappointed.

Dinnertime was almost over. Nagisa tried to stand up, but was stopped by a soft voice behind her.

"May I join you?"

Who...? Don't tell me... Nagisa gulped and turned. Behind her was the library staffer and Shizuma's former *Cadette*, Kano Mizuho.

After dinner, the sky was already dark. Dusk surrounded the sunroom, where Nagisa and Mizuho faced each other. Not too many people used the sunroom at night, so they were the only ones present. Except for Tamao, who was about two steps behind Nagisa. Mizuho had requested to speak with Nagisa alone, but Tamao insisted on keeping her company.

The sunroom was quiet, with a damp warmth and sweet aroma of flowers surrounding them. In the glass window ceiling, the stars glittered above, their only witnesses.

Mizuho broke the awkward silence. "I want to talk about Shizuma-sama and Kaori."

Nagisa's shoulders quivered. "I... don't..." She took a step back, wanting to run.

"No! You misunderstand." Mizuho spoke gently, softly, but with certainty.

"Misunderstand? But I heard from Togi-sama..." Nagisa blurted.

It was just as Mizuho suspected. "Hitomi told me about that. I'm sorry. Hitomi tends to say things bluntly, but she's doesn't know everything."

Nagisa still seemed suspicious, so Mizuho continued. "I'm probably the only one Kaori ever told. Shizuma-sama and Hitomi weren't aware of Kaori's true feelings."

Nagisa leaned back, ready to take another step away, but she felt a warm presence behind her.

"You should let her finish, Nagisa-chan." Tamao's tone was serious as she placed her hands on Nagisa's shoulders.

The train roared as it thundered through the area. Outside the train windows, the sky was already pitch-black. Inside the small compartment, two girls faced each other in the old, green four-man booth.

Earlier, Hikari woke up to find Amane sitting beside her, wearing her Spica uniform. She seemed different than the day before, quieter. Amane didn't say a word, but her smile was radiant, as if she had been renewed and, as she wrapped her arms around Hikari, there was a fierceness Hikari hadn't felt before. Up until that moment, Hikari had felt that Amane was really wonderful and quite passionate, but at the same time, she she was subdued and vulnerable, which made Hikari feel relaxed and comfortable. She wasn't sure how to react to Amane's change.

When Hikari tried to ask a question, Amane reassured her

that she'd taken care of everything, but wouldn't go into details. Amane had asked Hikari to get up and put on her Spica uniform. They packed their things and left the Otori mansion. They retraced their journey, and after making several transfers on the local trains, they ended up at a large, unfamiliar station around midnight. Despite the time of night, the station was lively with throngs of people—something Hikari hadn't seen since she moved to Astraea Hill.

The lights inside the station shone in the dark night, revealing large crowds running to their platforms. Hikari could barely keep up with Amane, who protected her as they wove between people. They were on their train before Hikari knew it, the train pulling away from the platform before Hikari had a chance to check their destination. Unfortunately, the old-fashioned train didn't have a destination sign, either.

Once they boarded the train, Amane was soft and gentle as usual, but she gradually spoke less, and finally stopped talking and looked out the window.

I'll be fine if I stick with her, Hikari told herself, despite the anxious knot in her stomach.

In the low candlelight, the only sound was the gentle splash of tea being poured.

"Oh no… I spilled some."

"Ehh?"

"Kyaah! Oh gosh, the cake will get wet!"

The tea spilled onto the small table, which was cluttered with four tea sets and a plate of cake.

"Towel, get a towel!"

"Move the cake!"

"And the teddy bear, too!"

The tabletop candles wobbled, and the girls' faint cries overlapped one another. Minamoto Chikaru's Costume Club members were having a tea party in the Lulim dorm. Candles glowed inside the dark room, providing the only light. Kizuna, who was in charge of serving the tea, wore a white satin tuxedo and matching cape with the collar up. She usually wore her hair in pigtails, but tonight it was down which, with her costume, made her look like a pretty boy.

Natsume Remon, who swiftly wiped the table, saving the cake from the spilled tea, wore a black velvet tuxedo with little black bat wings on her back.

Kagome, the smallest of the bunch, had a tiny pair of paper fangs in her mouth like the rest of the girls. She wore a very feminine nineteenth-century one-piece dress with lots of frills and ribbons. She sat on a chair, holding her teddy bear, which she had dressed in tails and a top hat for the occasion.

"Gosh, if we keep these in, we can't eat our cakes," Kagome said to her bear. She pointed to the fangs in her mouth. Kagome chomped down and crushed the fangs.

Once the excitement over the tea spilling had abated, Kizuna and Remon gave a sigh of relief. They looked at each other's fangs, then cringed and hesitantly turned around to face their leader. Chikaru sat in a chair, facing Kizuna. She wore a mermaid-style dress of ivory and sat upright, playing out her role of a proper lady. She looked at the clumsy girls and heaved a sigh. "I didn't expect this to happen."

Kizuna tried to explain, "But they're made of paper, so we can make them again."

Before Kizuna finished her sentence, Remon jumped in and whispered, "No, the paper will get wet again in your mouths and we'll end up with the same result." Remon's paper fangs had stuck to her mouth.

Chikaru held her forehead in distress, but finally said, "Well, I suppose it cannot be helped. You can all remove your fangs, just for today."

Kizuna and Remon jumped for joy.

"Cool! Now I can eat my cake real fast!"

"Great! I was actually really careful not to crush my fangs."

Chikaru cringed when she realized the fangs were quite unpopular, but she shrugged it off. "Oh, well! This was our first attempt at playing *Poe's Clan*[13]." She looked at all the girls. "All of you look great in your outfits. The 'pretty boy' theme works for us! We just need to get rid of the fangs. Anyway, this is a celebration for Kagome-chan's victory in the *Étoile* competition, so let's eat!" She raised her teacup and toasted.

"*Yay…!*" The three girls cheered in unison, flicked their fangs off, toasted Kagome, and ate their cake in silence.

"Kagome-chan, you were really wonderful today! I thought you were just an adorable little girl, Kagome-chan. But you

were so confident that I was totally impressed. I didn't know you were so good at dancing!" Kizuna said as she finished her cake and licked her fingers.

Remon chimed in. "Yes, Spica's Kusanagi-sama was a good dancer, but you were just as good, Kagome-chan! You two looked like a prince and princess from a fairy tale."

"Yes, you made a great couple," Chikaru heartily agreed, smiling. She tried to pet Kagome's head as a compliment, but Kagome frowned and buried her face into her teddy bear. She squeezed her eyes shut, and her soft cheeks were pushed out of shape by the bear as she pouted. Cake crumbs sprinkled onto the bear's head.

"What's wrong, Kagome-chan?" Kizuna had never seen Kagome make such a face before.

Kagome petted her bear solemnly. "I don't want to be with Spica's little Emperor."

"Wh-Why? Did she do something to you?!" Remon asked.

Kagome kept her eyes on her bear as she replied. "She told me Mr. Teddy Bear was just a silly doll, and I couldn't hold him while we danced."

"B-But…" Remon wanted to agree with Makoto that it was just common sense, but she covered her mouth.

"Oh, that's no good." Kizuna deeply sympathized with Kagome. *That bear means everything to Kagome. Everyone knows she won't let go of the bear, even for a second. Of course, dancing with the bear would have been difficult.*

Kagome nodded at Kizuna's explanation, and tears welled up in her eyes. "And when Kagome shared Mr. Teddy Bear's thoughts with Makoto, she laughed. And she gets mad when Kagome falls asleep… and… and…"

Well, Makoto-sama is pretty blunt, so I can see why Kagome-chan wouldn't get along with her, Remon thought as she quickly moved over to comfort Kagome. *Yes, we understand what you're going through, Kagome-chan, but everyone is rooting for you in the Étoile competition, so is there any way you can just make it through? Please?*

Kizuna jumped in to help. "I see… I really feel sorry for you. How about I talk to Makoto-sama! I'll tell her that Kagome-chan and Mr. Teddy Bear are really close, and ask her to understand. I think if we explain it to Makoto-sama, she'll feel bad for treating you that way."

Kagome smiled from ear to ear and hugged Kizuna. "Kagome wants to be in the *Étoile* competition with Kizuna-oneesama."

"Eeeehhh?! Wh-What do you mean?" Kizuna exclaimed. She looked at Remon in surprise. How could Kizuna reply? She looked at Chikaru for guidance. She had been unusually silent through the whole conversation, wearing a grave look, absorbed in her own thoughts.

The small candle lights flickered in the darkness and dimly lit Chikaru's face.

CHAPTER 3

A Sunless Sky Illuminates
the Invisible Truth Below

The eastern skies had just begun to show hints of white. Shizuma wandered around the Maiden Park, alone. She climbed up the gentle slope and stood at the center of Astraea Hill, at the edge of the lake. The predawn sky was still wrapped in darkness, but fresh morning air wafted over everything.

Shizuma slowly sighed and stared at the surface of the lake. The lake's calm, still water showed a reflected Shizuma, wearing a white quilted gown over her off-white silk negligee.

I look like I'm sick. Maybe it was her face, pale from lack of sleep that made her look ill. She hadn't been able to sleep at all last night, and when she sat up and checked the clock, it was before dawn.

Oh yes, she *used to comment that my face looked pale, like a patient, didn't she...*

Shizuma tried to keep the past behind her... but the memories swept over her again.

She recalled the conversation she'd had with Miyuki in the bath. Because Amane had suddenly disappeared, Miyuki wanted to request a rematch of the *Étoile* second round. She had begged Shizuma to find Nagisa and return to the *Étoile* competition. If that wasn't possible, Miyuki would reveal Makoto's past.

It was a ploy, Shizuma knew. Miyuki would never do that, unless she had no other choice. Shizuma had replied, "What would that accomplish? You, of all people should know that a person's family situation is beyond one's control. Besides, it was you who originally asked me *not* to chase after Nagisa."

Shizuma thought Miyuki was going to be flustered, but she had been ready for Shizuma's argument.

"I do admit that I am among those whose family situation is constraining. Which is why I had second thoughts about you and Nagisa. I am able to shine like a bright star here on campus. I can enjoy my freedom until I leave school and lose my wings. You should be able to do the same."

Shizuma had never seen Mizuki so serious. She had all but flat-out admitted that she was obsessed with keeping her position as the Student Council President. If Shizuma and Nagisa withdrew from the *Étoile* competition, St. Miator Girls' Academy would be dishonored, and things might escalate to the point where the students might demand the Student Council members to take responsibility and resign. Miyuki really enjoyed her role as the president. When she left St. Miator's, Miyuki would be stripped of her freedom, so she wanted to cling to her only bright light of glory as long as possible. It was a frank revelation from a girl who was usually quite reserved.

Shizuma couldn't find the words to form an appropriate reply. She already knew about Miyuki's saga. It was an unchallenged truth of a rich girls' school, a sad, dark part of the life of a daughter from an affluent family. At the same time, it was the reason the girls at this hill strived to shine so brilliantly. To be desperate enough for Miyuki to spell it out so bluntly meant she had something in mind.

At this point, she'd use any method to win this year's *Étoile* competition, so she could finish out her duties as the St. Miator Student Council President in a glorious fashion. Miyuki had half-given up hopes for this year's *Étoile* competition at first, but through Nagisa, a lucky card, she was able to recruit the help of Shizuma; and once she had acquired a chance at victory, she would do anything to attain it. Miator still had a good chance of winning, Miyuki confidently stated. With Shizuma, victory was possible. So now, Miyuki wouldn't hesitate to use any option available. She had come up with a plan to take down Makoto.

With Amane and Shizuma out of the competition, and once Makoto was taken out as well, the main competitors would be missing. If Makoto finally dropped out, it would be obvious to everyone that all the viable candidates were effectively removed at that point, making it a three-way draw. A rematch would be necessary. Miyuki pictured a drastic event, like the "Faceless Devil."

Miyuki had explained all of this to Shziuma, her expression cold and calculating.

"So, I'm not sure what transpired between Shizuma-sama and Aoi-san, but, please, Shizuma-sama, please convince Aoi-san to compete again. It should be an easy task, requiring only one little phrase—'you're my one and only, Nagisa'—to get her back. Just like you did during the 'Mouth of Truth'. Unless you didn't really mean it then?"

Shizuma stared into the deep blue water of the lake and thought about the girls of this hill and their fates. *Oh, Miyuki… Acting as if you know nothing about the issues between me and Nagisa. You, of all people, know the circumstances all too well. Look at your harsh expression… I'm sure you don't mean it at all.*

Compared to the rest of the world, the girls of this hill were beautiful like flowers, angelic, innocent, and naïve. They could have anything they want, and were promised a safe, bountiful future, and they seemed to live a luxurious lifestyle.

But their reality was far from glamourous.

Miyuki had a fiancé, pre-selected before she was even born. After she graduated from high school she'd spend a year learning some home-making skills, then she must marry her fiancé. Wealthy girls had to marry at a young age, so they could give birth to an heir as soon as possible—a ridiculous logic, indeed,

Shizuma thought. No matter how intelligent Miyuki was, her family had told her that a lady does not require education.

In contrast, Makoto grew up away from her household. Shizuma had gotten the gist of her situation from Miyuki's explanation. Makoto was an unwanted child. The harsh truth was that she was an illegitimate child. It must have been shocking to finally realize that she had been born because her mother had an affair.

Of course, Makoto was not to blame. But Shizuma wondered how Makoto must have felt when she realized it. The thoughts that must have run through her head, Shizuma could only speculate—*Why was I born? Why did my mother give birth to me, knowing that it would destroy another family?*

And then realizing the turmoil her most adored, beloved sister must have gone through all along, Makoto must have thought she was the cause of all the unhappiness, and blamed herself for her sister's actions. Maybe Makoto was so brash because it was her only defense mechanism.

On the other hand, if you poke around Astraea, you will hear another story.

Shizuma had talked with St. Spica Girls' Institute's Nanto Yaya. Yaya openly despised men, and it was well-known she was a true lesbian. She was often compared to Shizuma in terms of the number of girls they fooled around with, so Shizuma was curious about her.

It was when Yaya had decided not to go home during summer vacation, and Shizuma had to stay back to complete a few tasks as the newly crowned *Étoile*. With fewer students residing in the Strawberry Dorms at that time, they had become "acquainted" with each other.

Yaya shared her thoughts with Shizuma about the father she hated. He never came home, going from one affair to another. A very foolish father, unable to hide it from her mother. Her mother had stopped loving her father, but asked for compensation for his affairs, receiving expensive jewelry and clothing, and partying around. Yaya's parents should have split long ago, but because her father had married into the Nanto family's wealth, it was hard for him to leave the cushy company president's seat.

Her mother was just as bad. She had given up on men, but as long as her father kept the business afloat, she was fine with all his philandering, because it maintained her high status.

Yaya's father had told her ever since she was a child, *If only you were a boy.*

At first, Yaya thought he just wanted an heir to his business. But nothing could be further from the truth, because by then, Yaya already had several half-brothers. The Nanto business was to be passed onto a male heir, but the oldest and only legitimate child was Yaya. Though she was the oldest, if any of the half-brothers wanted to stake a claim to the business, Yaya would have to defend her position. Once she realized that, she stopped talking to her father.

On the rare occasion when her father would come home, he'd ask her how she was doing with her studies, but it was doubtful that he even knew her age or anything else, for that matter.

Yaya had recounted her bitter situation to Shizuma. It was the reason Yaya hated men—she couldn't fathom touching such a filthy creature. Yaya vowed never to marry, and regardless of what others said, for the rest of her life, she was going to live with girls she loved.

Shizuma watched her face in the water and reflected on the situations that surrounded Miyuki, Makoto, Yaya, and many of the other girls of Astraea. She looked into the sky as it grew lighter and thought,

If there really is a heaven, are you there, Kaori? Are you looking over me?

What is going through your mind as you watch me and Nagisa? If only I could hear from you.

Shizuma raised her hands. A stiff morning breeze blew over the lake and rippled its surface, the cold, damp air fluttering the edges of Shizuma's nightgown.

Nagisa, I envy you. You are so honest and carefree, with nothing evil about you. I must seem so unreasonable to you. Not just me, but compared to you, Miyuki, Makoto, and everyone else must seem so strange.

Shizuma closed her eyes and thought about her impending fate. Shizuma shared the fate common to most girls in Astraea. She had enough inner strength to keep the pressure from fazing her, and she tried to ignore it, but her spirit was the polar opposite of Nagisa's, as carefree and bright as the blue sky.

Farewell, Nagisa. I don't want to draw you into any more trouble. I set you free. Because I love you.

Shizuma looked into the summer sky, a brilliant blue. *My dear Kaori, did you, perhaps, feel like this, too?*

Shizuma confronted Nagisa. "It's time to bid farewell."

Nagisa stood there, speechless.

"Thank you for entertaining me. You helped me pass some time."

Oh gosh, I was used to pass time? It felt like something was caught in Nagisa's throat, and she broke out in a cold sweat. *It hurts. Shizuma-oneesama, how could you?*

"…No…" she finally muttered. She had shaken off whatever was holding her voice captive.

"No… what?" Shizuma peered into Nagisa's face, her expression cold, and frightening. "You're trying to go against my wishes?"

Nagisa, terrified, covered her face. Her face reddened and her whole body shook violently.

"I didn't mean to. I'm sorry," Nagisa pleaded.

A voice called Shizuma from behind. "Shizuma-oneesama, we should go now." It was a sweet, childish voice.

Shizuma suddenly softened her expression as she turned around and answered, her voice gentle. "Oh, you've come for me already?"

Nagisa raised her face in astonishment, and looked in the direction of the voice. A little girl stood there, here face concealed by a light, peach-colored mist.

When did it turn so foggy? Nagisa scanned her surroundings. She had just been standing near the lake at the top of Astraea Hill. Suddenly, she was enveloped by white fog.

Oh gosh, I can't see where I'm going. Ah... she reached out, searching for Shizuma.

But Shizuma was no longer there.

Ahh... Nagisa's hand grasped thin air. She could just see Shizuma through the fog, far ahead of her.

How did she get so far away?

Shizuma held hands with the little girl. Though the two girls were far away, Nagisa could see Shizuma's soft, blissful smile. She whispered into the little girl's ear and chuckled.

Nagisa's chest tightened. *Why?* Her cry of agony was silent. The couple faded away into the distance.

No! I won't know what to do without Shizuma-oneesama...

Something painful pierced through Nagisa's heart. Her throat was dry, her head spun, and her eyes blurred until she couldn't see Shizuma anymore.

"Noooo!" Nagisa screamed. Nagisa closed her eyes, and felt something change. Shizuma, who was supposed to have disappeared, spoke directly into Nagisa's mind.

"Don't worry. I will protect you forever. I will be above the clouds looking after you. You must find happiness without me."

Nagisa opened her eyes, and a goddess stood before her. Large white wings grew from Shizuma's back. She floated just above Nagisa, looking down on her with the most divine smile as she gracefully flew away.

"No, don't do this to me!" Nagisa cried. "I cannot be happy without you!" Hot tears streamed from her eyes and ran down her cheeks.

The heat from her tears jarred Nagisa awake.

Oh, it was a dream.

She lay in her bed in her room at the Strawberry Dorms. After wiping the tears from her face, she looked at her wet hands, dazed.

What a horrible dream. I am such a fool. I was the one who ran away from her. After that dream, I feel so much pain and remorse. My heart still aches, even when I'm fully awake.

Nagisa looked over to the window. The sky outside was getting lighter. She checked the bedside clock; it was five-thirty in the morning. She turned over in her bed, pulled up the blanket, and forced her eyes shut.

It was just a dream. I need to move on.

"Good morning, my dear Oneesamas. I brought some breakfast tea for you." The voice on the other side of the door was cheerful.

"Come in," Tamao called. She looked at Nagisa to ask for approval. Nagisa nodded, and Chiyo entered the room. She wore the apron of a room assistant, and in her hands were a teapot and a small silver vase.

"I brought some herb tea and some *konpeito*[13] for the tired Nagisa-oneesama."

Chiyo smiled as she walked past them. Despite the fact that Nagisa and Tamao had just woken up and still wore their pajamas, she diligently opened the curtains and neatly tucked them at the sides, prepared some tea, and made their beds.

"Hey, don't worry about that, I'll do the beds myself." Nagisa wasn't used to the room assistant program—where the underclassmen of St. Miator were assigned to the room of an upperclassman in order to take take care of their personal needs—so she didn't feel comfortable having Chiyo do so much for her.

"Please, Nagisa-oneesama, I am obligated to perform these duties. And I would like to be of use. I am glad to serve Nagisa-oneesama." Chiyo brought her cleaning rag to her blushing cheeks.

"Oh jeez, Chiyo-chan, don't put a rag on your face," Nagisa said, but Tamao found it amusing.

"Yes, Nagisa-chan, St. Miator's program allows students to understand the intricacies of running a household, so you shouldn't interfere. You know that many of the students here have maids at home, right? Without the program, they might never have a chance to do household chores. It is important to teach the students about the enjoyment of service."

Chiyo smiled, looking proud.

Nagisa was surprised at the conversation between the two. *Oh, I wonder if Chiyo-chan comes from a large home? But, come to think of it, St. Miator probably has students from all kinds of influential families, like Shizuma-sama and Chiyo-chan.* She recalled the picture she had seen of the large Hanazono family ranch and compared it to her small, 4-bedroom house. Her humble background was embarrassing.

"So are you going to be the successor of your family, Chiyo-chan?" Tamao nonchalantly asked.

"I don't think so. I have an older brother who will probably succeed. When I reach *genpuku*[14] at age 15, the family will decide."

"Oh, don't you mean *mogi*[15]?" Tamao wondered.

"I am from a martial arts family," Chiyo answered self-consciously.

Tamao quickly grasped what Chiyo was talking about. "So until a successor is decided upon, you're treated like a boy, right, Chiyo-chan? But if you have an older brother, you may not have to succeed, eh? You won't have to be the oldest female master."

"Yes!" Chiyo happily replied.

Nagisa wiped her face with a towel, not having the faintest clue what they were talking about.

How weird. I thought it would be good to be the successor of a family. What a wasted opportunity. I mean, I'd probably succeed. Nagisa pondered as she stared at her puffy eyes in the mirror.

I hope this looks better. I guess it's best to ice it, but I'd have to go all the way to the cafeteria to get the ice. I'm so stupid. Why did I cry over a dream? I mean, I don't have any right to cry over Shizuma anymore.

She thought about her conversation last night with Mizuho in the sun room. She had said some unbelievable things. Shizuma hadn't cared for Kaori much, or something like that.

Nagisa shook her head. *No way...*

But Mizuho had spoken softly and clearly, and gradually Nagisa became convinced.

"After Kaori's tragic death, no one, especially Shizuma herself, would dare say this. But Shizuma didn't really love

Kaori. I know, because I was one of Shizuma's closest friends. She really needs someone like you, Nagisa."

But Nagisa just couldn't believe what Mizuho said...

"Thank you for your kind words," Nagisa had replied. "But I don't need to know about it anymore. Whatever happened is over."

Nagisa let the Mizuho's words echo in her mind again. *Even if it was true, Shizuma wouldn't forgive me for running away the way I did.*

It was morning, time for students to go to the schools on Astraea Hill. The maidens walked straight to the gates of the three schools, a sea of colorful green, white, and pink uniforms that decorated the summer hill like little blossoms.

Chikaru enjoyed the nervous tension that surrounded her as she walked to school with Shion.

"I'm so glad to bump into to you this morning, Shion-chan," Chikaru said with a smile. She had caught sight of Shion as she was leaving the Strawberry Dorms. Shion was trudging along, shoulders slumped.

"Good morning, Shion-chan, fancy meeting you here," Chikaru had said.

Shion had jumped, startled, and looked at Chikaru as if she were frightened of her. Chikaru tried not to be offended.

"You seem to be running a bit late today, aren't you, Shion-chan?"

"Well, there's no particular reason for that." Shion spoke less than normal today, obviously depressed.

Chikaru felt bad for yanking Shion around with all her little schemes, but she hadn't expected Shion to react like this. She thought Shion would come back at her with some wild reaction, like St. Miator President Rokujo. It would have made things exciting.

On the other hand, if she did overreact, maybe things will get worse. After all, it's my fault for causing all this. Although Shion-chan is the Student Council president and quite intelligent, she is unable to hide her emotions. It's adorable. She must be really depressed after Amane-chan's disappearance. Tsk... Shion-chan is so bad at hiding her feelings. I'm surprised no one noticed Shion-chan's depression. No, wait. Maybe Momomi-chan and Kaname-chan have seen it.

She glanced sideways at Shion. "Hey, Shion-chan, what is the third round event of the *Étoile* competition?"

Shion flinched as if she had been hit. Her brows furrowed. "I'm sorry, wc haven't finalized it yet." She hid her face momentarily as she played with her bangs and adjusted her posture.

"My apologies. Though we had tentatively decided on an event for the third round, unexpected circumstances have affected our plans. But thanks to your gracious offer, Chikaru-sama, our Spica candidate, Kusanagi Makoto, and your candidate, Miss Byakudan Kagome, will more than likely take the crown, so I am not too concerned about the final event."

Shion's expression changed to a cool and collected poker face. Even so, Shion was disgusted with the emptiness of her bluff.

Why should I be sorry? At this point, I don't care anymore about the results of the Étoile competition.

Shion was surprised at the revelation, and her indifference towards the *Étoile* crown. Almost immediately, her guilty conscience stabbed her heart.

No. As the Spica Student Council President, I am supposed to bring the Étoile crown to Spica. So why do I not care about the competition? What was I working so hard for all this time?

Shion stood there, dazed, her mind a total blank.

Chikaru, knowing exactly what was on Shion's mind, put on a sympathetic smile.

You're doing fine, Shion-chan. An intelligent girl like you needs to face your feelings and become stronger for it. You need to acknowledge your own feelings and make your desires come true. Life is short. I want you to enjoy this brief but relaxing life as a maiden of this hill. You may not realize this yet, but the reason you don't care about the Étoile is that Amane-chan is gone. You don't want the Étoile crown for Spica, but rather, for Amane-chan. You want your most adored Amane-chan to shine as the best Étoile of Astraea.

Suddenly, Chikaru waved her hands in an exaggerated manner, pushing away the melancholy that had dropped over them.

"Oh, I'm sorry, Shion-chan. Umm…I shouldn't be saying this because it was my idea in the first place, but…I've run into a problem."

"Eh…a problem?" Shion was surprised again, and snapped out of her daze.

Chikaru hugged her bag to her chest. "Well, Kagome-chan isn't really getting along with Makoto-chan."

"Not getting along?" Shion asked.

"For some reason Kagome-chan and Makoto-chan aren't compatible with each other. I know it's a surprise, but I found out yesterday. Kagome-chan told me that because Makoto-chan doesn't care about Mr. Teddy Bear, she no longer wants to be her partner."

"M…Mr. Teddy…Bear?" Shion repeated, dumbfounded.

"Yes. Kagome-chan is a really good girl, but she is a bit unique, and can be a little difficult sometimes!" Chikaru let her bag fall back onto her shoulder as she clasped her hands together and stretched her arms out in front of her.

"But don't worry. We only have one more round left in the competition, so I think she can hold on until then. After all, the reputations of Spica and Lulim are at stake. It'll be fine if Makoto-chan can give her lots of candy and be more careful of Mr. Teddy Bear. That's why I was curious as to what the third round event was going to be. I hope it's not difficult." Chikaru laughed nervously, as if she were anxious.

"Excuse me. Umm…may I see Yaya-oneesama?"

It was lunch break at the St. Spica Girls' Institute, Third Year, Class *Un*. Tsubomi stood at the entrance to Yaya's classroom.

The student sitting nearest the door frowned and pointed to a desk near the window.

Sitting at the desk was a girl with long, jet black hair. She didn't move. Her beautiful black hair hung down like a silk curtain, covering her face. It was hard to tell if she was awake or asleep.

"Is that her?" Tsubomi asked.

The upperclassmen chuckled at Tsubomi's confused look. "Yes, that's her. She's been like that since morning. What a nuisance, she was like that during classes, too. The teachers eventually just ignored her. You know, we understand her loneliness after Konohana-san's disappearance, but it's really surprising for Yaya, usually full of pride, to be so openly depressed."

Tsubomi's eyebrows lifted in surprise. "Oh, I see."

To completely collapse the way Yaya had was quite shameful in Astraea, and it was the first time Tsubomi had ever seen someone do it. No matter how upset a person could get, Yaya was probably the only person on the hill who would express her sadness so openly.

Yaya was pouting.

She's being so blatant about it, too, Tsubomi thought. *Come to think of it, it is pretty amusing.*

She giggled in delight. "It is very much like Yaya-oneesama to act like that."

The girl smiled, "Yes, absolutely. It is so Yaya."

The two girls laughed. A Third Year student appeared beside Tsubomi. "It is rather funny, but please, cheer her up any way you can." She patted Tsubomi's shoulder.

"Leave it to me!" Tsubomi clenched her fists, committed to her task, and bounced into the classroom.

"Yaya-oneesama!" Tsubomi waved her hand and stomped towards Yaya.

The black curtain of hair slowly rustled. It moved, the light reflecting off of her beautiful locks. White skin peeked between the strands of hair.

Yaya-oneesama is beautiful as ever, Tsubomi thought. "Gosh, please get up already, Yaya-oneesama! You shouldn't be taking a nap at a time like this."

Yaya's head snapped up. It didn't seem like she was sleeping at all when she spoke. "Hey, why are you here? I didn't ask for you, Tsubomi."

Tsubomi flinched in the face of Yaya's anger, but she wouldn't give up.

"Yaya-oneesama, I know what's bugging you. You want to know about Hikari-oneesama and Amane-sama, don't you?"

Yaya's gaze shifted away. "No, why should I…" *Care about them…* Yaya started to say, but she stopped herself before the words escaped. She grabbed Tsubomi's shoulders.

"Don't tell me you know where they are?" Yaya's face went pale.

Tsubomi was overwhelmed by her sudden change, but managed to reply. "Sorry, no! I'm good at picking up news, but not that fast!" She stuck her tongue out. "Actually, you probably know more than I, since you were called into the sister's office."

"Hmph. Don't get ahead of yourself. The sister didn't tell

me anything. She drilled *us* with questions instead. If I knew anything about those two, I wouldn't be so jealous right now," Yaya folded her arms. She was about 15 centimeters taller than Tsubomi though Yaya was only two years older. Tsubomi looked up, envious of the difference in height.

Tsubomi persevered. "Oh gosh, Yaya-oneesama, you totally missed your chance to get information from the teachers."

Then Yaya understood Tsubmomi's sudden appearance. *Oh, so Tsubomi is here to find out what happened to me yesterday.* Disappointed, she slumped back into her chair.

"President Shion was completely rattled, so I was counting on Yaya-oneesama to fill me in or something," Tsubomi mumbled.

Yaya collapsed onto her desk again. *I'm so tired of everything.*

"Umm, Yaya-oneesama, didn't you ask the sister *anything* back in the faculty room? This morning, President Shion looked so depressed. Well, it's only natural for her to feel depressed, because she worked so hard to put Amane-sama into the *Étoile* competition. So I totally understand President Shion to be shocked over Amane-sama and Hikari-oneesama's disappearance. But she acted so strange in this morning's staff meeting. I mean, she let Kiyashiki-san run the meeting, and Shion didn't say a word. The other council members said they've never seen her like this before. But since it's Spica's turn to manage the *Étoile* competition, we have to run the third round without fail. We don't know what to do with a president who has turned into a lifeless shell, so I'm so worried."

Yaya didn't respond, but repeated Tsubomi's words in her mind. *Lifeless shell, huh? I'm probably the same. Now that my beloved Hikari is no longer here, my soul is like an empty shell.*

She loathed herself for thinking that way. *I should have taken her, body and soul.* She coiled her hair around her finger.

Tsubomi hesitated before she spoke again. "Yaya-oneesama, are you sure you don't know their whereabouts? I mean, you were so close to Hikari-oneesama, so a lot of council members assumed you had to know something."

If I knew something, I'd tell everyone in a heartbeat, Yaya thought. She ran her tongue over her teeth.

"Tsubomi, just shut up. I'm going to sleep." Yaya buried her face in the desk and stopped moving.

"Oh for pity's sake, Yaya-oneesama!" Tsubomi's face turned red with anger and she stomped her feet as she left Yaya's classroom, even though she understood Yaya's feelings.

Hikari-oneesama and Amane-sama, please come back to Spica soon. Everyone is waiting for your return.

"Oh, Princess Nagisa…are you on cleanup duty again? Must be hard being Cinderella," said Iohata Momiji, Nagisa's classmate, as she opened the classroom door, smiled, then waved her hand and left.

With a triangular bandanna covering her head, Nagisa grinned dryly as she watched her classmate leave. Because

Nagisa selfishly withdrew from the *Étoile* competition, she was assigned classroom cleanup duties alone, for a week, as punishment.

St. Miator Girls' Academy, Fourth Year Moon Class's classroom was cheery, with girls scurrying to leave, anticipating a fun time after school. Nagisa hesitantly moved her broom back and forth, trying to avoid the girls' eyes as they left the room.

Tamao noticed Nagisa's misery and deliberately took her time packing up. When the classroom was half-empty, Tamao looked Nagisa in the eye.

Nagisa laughed in embarrassment.

Tamao was miffed at her classmates. *Nagisa-chan, you had your reasons for withdrawing from the Étoile competition. Everyone isn't aware of your true motives, so they just accused you of leaving a black mark on the honorable history of St. Miator Girls' Academy, or whatever.*

If that was the case, Shizuma was just as guilty, but only Nagisa had been punished for dropping out of the *Étoile* competition.

Nagia always shook off such comments, protecting Shizuma. "It's all my fault this happened," she said over and over. "Not Shizuma-oneesama's."

Tamao did not care much for warped feelings of love. *Nagisa-chan, you're such a fool. If you loved Shizuma, why did you withdraw? If you had enough courage to take the blows for the person you love, then why didn't you use that courage to confront Shizuma-oneesama about Kaori?*

Tamao couldn't help but think like that. *Nagisa hadn't been herself since the morning after Prince Amane's disqualification. Then she tried to leave school without telling anyone.*

If she loves Shizuma-sama so much, she should just tell her.

That's so unlike you, Nagisa-chan, to keep things inside. Sigh. But I suppose if you did that, you'd probably cause trouble for her.

A wicked thought crossed Tamao's mind. *I'm so mean. I told Nagisa-chan to forget Shizuma-sama, even though I knew Nagisa's true feelings. I guess I'm the one who's holding Nagisa back from talking to Shizuma.*

Tamao's shoulders heaved with her sigh. *But if Nagisa-chan mustered some courage and expressed her feelings to Shizuma-sama, I'd have no chance at winning Nagisa's heart.*

Tamao bit her lip. *It's been a while since I felt so hopeless. When did I start to feel so seriously about her?* Tamao used to run from things that required too much effort or that had the potential to hurt her heart. Suddenly she was angry with Nagisa.

What had started out as a little desire to play with the new transfer student had changed, after seeing Nagisa jump into the *Étoile* competition shortly upon her arrival. Despite Shizuma's overbearing presence, Nagisa's pure heart prevented her from feeling bitter towards anyone, and she was so simple and honest that tea and cakes made her forget her worries in an instant.

Tamao's anger ebbed when she realized she truly loved Nagisa's strength.

Please don't change, Nagisa, Tamao thought. She wanted to protect Nagisa from the overbearing Shizuma. Tamao was sure her love would be noticed by Nagisa one day. Instead of burning out from Shizuma's wavering feelings, it was better for Nagisa to be with her.

Watching Nagisa cleaning, seeing her suffering, Tamao's desire mounted, and she wanted Nagisa. She remembered Nagisa's sad face yesterday when she announced that she wouldn't think about Shizuma-sama anymore.

I want Nagisa-chan to love me. Tamao realized. *But I don't want her to resent me for keeping her from Shizuma-sama. It's too early for her to see Shizuma-sama just yet.*

Tamao imagined Shizuma, like a grim reaper, sweeping Nagisa away before her eyes. She shook her head in denial. *I refuse to give up my precious Persephone to Hades.*

A voice broke through Tamao's thoughts. "You shouldn't go easy on her, okay? You and Shizuma-sama were too lenient on her and look what happened." Tamao turned her head toward the voice. Another student had approached Tamao, a stern look on her face.

"I know I shouldn't," replied Tamao. "But now that Nagisa-chan has withdrawn from the *Étoile* competition, she won't be meeting Shizuma-sama anymore, so there's no reason to be mad at her, I think." She smiled.

The student, taken aback at the reply, responded, "Well… I guess you're right," She looked at Nagisa sympathetically. Nagisa noticed Tamao and the other student looking at her, and started to fidget uncomfortably.

"I suppose if she gets through this week, everyone will warm up to her again. Nagisa-san, try to tough it out, okay?" The student smiled.

Nagisa cautiously returned the smile and nodded. Tamao sneaked a quick wink, and moved her mouth silently, so that only Nagisa could see.

I-will-help-with-clean-up.

Nagisa's shoulders relaxed in relief. *Great! Tamao-chan, you're so nice.* She had noticed Tamao's angry face a few moments before, but now her heart jumped. *When we return to the Strawberry Dorms, I need to thank Tamao-chan! Cakes and tea are okay, but it's always on her tab. Oh, maybe I can give her a massage? Tamao-chan probably likes massages, since she always massages me. Okay, today, I'll...*

Her thoughts were interrupted by the sound of the classroom doorknob rattling behind her. She turned her head to see who was entering, and a tingle ran down her spine. She knew in her heart that something special was about to happen.

Tamao's body froze, and there was a feeling like a large wave crashing against her. A black, ominous presence. She caught sight of the person entering the room and her expression turned dark. She stood and rushed to jump in front of Nagisa, trying to protect her from the presence in the doorway. Tamao spread her arms out to block Nagisa's view.

Nagisa tried to look around Tamao, but couldn't get a clear view of the newcomer.

Tamao confronted the intruder. "Why are you here?"

It was the first time Nagisa heard Tamao speak so coldly. The air in the room turned so tense it pressed against them.

Nagisa, suddenly afraid, had no idea what was going on. She didn't want to know.

"Goodness, such pleasant greetings, Tamao-chan."

Nagisa heard the voice, a voice she didn't want to hear. Her heart tugged painfully, and the back of her throat burned. She was suddenly dizzy.

"Shizuma-oneesama…" Tamao said in a low voice, trying not to let Nagisa hear the name. She glanced over her shoulder to check on Nagisa, then declared, "You have no reason to come to this class anymore!"

Shizuma was taken aback by Tamao's bravado, but she recovered quickly with a brilliant smile.

"Oh, that's not true." She took one step towards Tamao, then another.

Nagisa's body began to shake violently. *Shizuma's going to yell at me.* She couldn't face Shizuma; she was terrified.

What should I do? Shizuma-oneesama must be really mad that I withdrew without telling her first. My mind was made up then, but how could I tell Shizuma-sama?

Oh gosh, I'm so stupid. I should have left Astraea when I had the chance.

The classroom fell silent. Shizuma stopped in her tracks.

Ohh… she's almost here… Nagisa, red-faced, hid behind Tamao and closed her eyes. *She will probably just pull me out of here…*

The next moment…

"Tamao, thank you. I am relieved that you're here to protect her," Shizuma stated cheerfully.

Nagisa felt Tamao's body relax for a moment and brush up against her. The next moment, Tamao's body moved away as

Shizuma's arms wrapped around Tamao's hips and pulled her close, leaving Nagisa completely exposed.

Surprised, Nagisa looked up at Tamao, as if she was asking for Tamao's help. She inadvertently caught Shizuma out of the corner of her eye.

What in the world? Tamao was confused by Shizuma's sudden action.

Shizuma suddenly kissed Tamao on the mouth. To keep Tamao confused, she kissed her for three whole seconds.

What the? Shizuma-sama, no…

Tamao pushed Shizuma away with full force. Shizuma's lips were wet, like peach-colored coral.

"Wh-What are you doing?" Tamao yelled.

Shizuma grinned slyly. "Oh, it was for old time's sake. After all, this isn't the first time we've done this, remember?" she said playfully.

"But! That was a really long time ago!" Tamao blurted out before she remembered Nagisa was still standing there.

If she knew about what had happened between us in the past, she'd never speak to me again.

But Nagisa had witnessed everything. Shizuma had taken Tamao and showered her with love.

Tamao tried to explain. "Nagisa-chan, it's not like that! This is Shizuma-sama'a sick joke! She's trying to get back at me because I'm trying to protect you from her." She tried her best to convince Nagisa, but Nagisa just stood there with a blank look on her face.

Shizuma added the final blow. Standing sideways, without looking at Nagisa, she said in a low, cold, extremely serious voice.

"Nagisa…"

Tears welled in Nagisa's eyes.

"I understand your decision, so I will no longer be a nuisance to you."

A teardrop rolled down Nagisa's face.

"Goodbye. It's time to bid farewell."

Shizuma said the words, though they were like a knife to her heart. She turned on her heel.

"Sorry for bothering you. Please excuse me. Take care, Nagisa."

With her back towards them, Shizuma left the room like the wind.

Shizuma's words echoed in Nagisa's ears.

It's time to bid farewell…

Take care, Nagisa…

Her last words were completely generic, something that an upperclassmen—no, the campus queen—would say to a random underclassmen.

Shizuma-sama… Nagisa didn't even bother to wipe the tears from her cheeks as she fell to her knees.

Ding dong…

The bells of Astraea tolled in the distance. It was time to leave school.

Ding dong…

The warning for the first dismissal bell rang. At St. Lulim

Girls' School, the closest school to the Strawberry Dorms, a white-uniformed Spica student, Kusanagi Makoto, stood at its gate.

She leaned against one of the gate's large brick columns, looking bored as she waited for someone. A large crowd of Lulim students admired her from a distance.

"Look…that's Spica's little Emperor…"

"Up close, she has such a beautiful face…"

"She looks great in Spica's miniskirt, almost like a handsome boy…"

The little whispers and gasps Makoto heard half-annoyed, half-pleased her. They felt a bit strange, if she was honest about it. Unlike Spica students, who passionately adored her, the students at St. Lulim's calmly enjoyed their chance to see Astraea's new idol.

Makoto had suddenly felt the urge to look at Lulim's campus this morning. *Because Chika attends this place, I needed to see it for myself. This school has quite a unique atmosphere…oh, there she is!*

She took a little step and ran towards a little girl with curly hair. Makoto's steps were light, almost a prance. When she finally reached the curly-haired girl, she stopped in front of her and kneeled before her.

"Good day, my princess. I have a little gift for you today."

Makoto presented the little girl with a bouquet. The semi-transparent flowers were made of beautifully-colored candy, with shiny, colorful wrapping paper filled with chocolate clusters in between. Makoto had carefully researched all of Kagome's favorites.

Kagome smelled the sweet aroma wafting towards her. "Wow, what pretty candy flowers!"

Without acknowledging Makoto at all, Kagome plucked one candy flower and gave it to a surprised Kizuna, who stood beside her.

"Here. This one is for Kizuna-oneesama."

Kizuna was doubly surprised, but not as surprised as Makoto. Then Kagome plucked another flower and gave it to Remon, who stood next to Kizuna.

"Here. This one is for Remon-oneesama."

Makoto finally lost her cool. "Hey, what is the little princess thinking? This is my present to you—" She poked her head out from underneath the bouquet.

"Kyaaaaaaah!"

Kagome, finally noticing Makoto, gave out a blood-curdling yell.

No, no... She shook her head, and dove behind Kizuna. She hid her face in fear and shook, her teddy bear clutched to her chest.

Kizuna hastily picked up the bouquet Kagome had dropped and thanked Makoto.

"Kagome-chan was just taken by surprise, but I'm sure she'll thank you later, Makoto-sama."

Makoto clicked her tongue, irritated. *She's so difficult, and becoming really annoying. What doesn't she like about me? Chika chose her to be my partner, but why do I have to stoop down and cater to this girl?*

Chikaru stood in the distance, watching Makoto and the girls, witnessing Kagome's display. She sighed deeply.

I guess I have no choice.

"I think it's good you said that," Hitomi said. She turned and looked out of a glass window so clear it seemed a breath might pass right through it. The night sky outside was already dark with a quiet Maiden Park below.

In one of the upperclassmen's rooms, on the Miator side of the Strawberry Dorms, Togi Hitomi and Kano Mizuho—publicly and privately known as Hanazono Shizuma's closest friends—were deep in discussion after dinner.

Mizuho, the main resident of the room, responded. "But Nagisa might still be misunderstanding some things." The soft, orange light illuminated Mizuho's gentle face, which looked worried.

Hitomi's turned away from the window, her expression serious. "True…she didn't listen to my story to the end. I'll admit she may have prematurely withdrawn because of my partial explanation."

"But after you explained, didn't she have a talk with Shizuma-sama? I recall Shizuma-sama mentioning that she tried to explain things to Nagisa, without lying. So I think Nagisa's decision to withdraw from the *Étoile* competition was completely her own. In her mind, if she couldn't believe in herself, there was no possible way she could continue to be with Shizuma-sama. Those who aren't sure of themselves have no right to be with Shizuma-sama," Hitomi's last speech came out more passionately than she had intended.

Mizuho dropped her head and sat in the chair that leaned against the wall, staring at the white lace of her uniform. "Nagisa-chan is a sweet, honest girl. But as a transfer student, she should have been given more time to adjust to the environment of St. Miator Girls' Academy. I would say that confident people, like you and Shizuma-sama, are rare indeed. To think, the first person Nagisa encountered was Shizuma-sama! It must have been a huge shock. I believe she tried her best to adjust to her new situation."

"Tried her best? What do you mean?" Hitomi took a sip of dark, bitter coffee, and scrunched her face.

Mizuho smiled at Hitomi's reaction. "Of course, she tried her best for Shizuma-sama. I only spoke to Nagisa-chan briefly, but she seemed really honest and caring. I could tell just by looking at her. She's the type of girl who would wish for Shizuma-sama's happiness over her own."

"Well, I wish for the same myself," Hitomi shot back.

"Tsk. Gosh, Hitomi, of course I feel the same as you, too. After being with Shizuma-sama for such a long time, I know all about Kaori and the first *Étoile* competition, and how Shizuma-sama hasn't been herself recently. We both know it all too well."

Hitomi nodded. "That's true…"

"But Nagisa's life has been in turmoil since she arrived. She met Shizuma-sama the same day she came here, then not long after she was thrown into the fire because of Shizuma-sama," said Mizuho.

"Are you saying that the *Étoile* competition is a fire?" Hitomi tried to protest, but Mizuho calmed her down.

"She had just come to Astraea in April, you know? I really

think she didn't want to enter the *Étoile* competition in the first place, especially if her partner was Shizuma-sama. And I heard that she was bullied quite a bit as a result. Hitomi, don't you know what happened during the first round, 'Mouth of Truth'?"

Hitomi flinched, but said nothing. Mizuho waited for a moment, and then continued.

"Just before that event, Nagisa-chan was called to the library, where she discovered the facts about Kaori. It was a cruel trick. I was there when she found out, so I know how hurt she was. Shizuma-sama is a wonderful person, and she smothered Nagisa-chan with love. She must have felt like she was flying, and finding out about Kaori like that must have been like cold water being dumped on her. It was really sad to see. Nobody can blame her for loving and being loved by Shizuma-sama. Think about Kaori. Kaori was oblivious to her surroundings, because she could only see Shizuma-sama. She didn't pay attention to all the jealous people around her, and continued to profess her love to Shizuma-sama openly and honestly. That was one of her good points, but I believe Shizuma-sama was a bit troubled by it. She tried to protect Kaori from all the negativity, but…"

Mizuho's cheeks relaxed, and she smiled.

"Nagisa-chan is so reserved, and though she had become the center of Shizuma-sama's—the campus queen's—attention, she was so apologetic to everyone over it. Which turned her into a perfect target for bullying. I think she really wanted to withdraw as soon as possible. But she couldn't give up Shizuma-sama so easily. Because…"

Hitomi couldn't resist cutting in on Mizuho's explanation.

"Of course! No one would want to let go of Shizuma-sama if she smothered them with love. She's got some sort of magic charm!" Hitomi admitted.

Mizuho chuckled. "I agree, she does have a spell-binding quality. You and I are great examples."

Hitomi blushed.

"But Nagisa-chan is different. Hitomi, haven't you noticed it, too? I know you have; you just haven't admitted it yet."

Hitomi looked off to the side. She gulped down the rest of the coffee and almost cried from its bitterness.

"After hearing Kaori's story, Nagisa-chan probably wanted to heal Shizuma-sama's wounds. So she chose to stay by Shizuma-sama's side, even though it upset her to do so."

"Yeah, I knew that already," Hitomi huffed.

"We feel we can help Shizuma-sama because she doesn't consider us to be her lovers, but good friends. With all due respect, of course."

"Yeah…" Hitomi's voice grew smaller.

"But Nagisa-chan could have been even more jealous of Kaori if she wanted to. And she should have confronted Shizuma-sama, told her to choose between her and Kaori. I'm sure Shizuma-sama would have easily chosen Nagisa over Kaori, but it would have been torture for Shizuma-sama, and Nagisa would never want that. After Kaori's death, Shizuma-sama pondered whether her feelings for Kaori were true or not. She might have even felt guilty or lost some confidence in herself."

The two girls fell silent.

Hitomi swallowed deeply and looked at Mizuho. Mizuho,

who was as calm and gentle as a *Bosatsu*[16].

"So you had the same thought as me, Mizuho?"

"Yes."

"I have my regrets."

"Yes, I know."

"I shouldn't have introduced Kaori to Shizuma-sama."

Mizuho didn't respond.

"What I did was to cause grief for both of them, and troubled Shizuma-sama in the end. And this time, I pulled another girl into this mess."

Mizuho tried to comfort Hitomi. "That's not true. Nobody knew Kaori had such a short life ahead of her. "

Hitomi, on the verge of tears, nodded.

"Hitomi, you must have had a hard time, also." Mizuho patted Hitomi's shoulder.

Hitomi could barely speak, her voice trembled so badly. "…I…I didn't go through…anything…"

Mizuho sat on the bed next to Hitomi.

"At least Kaori found happiness."

"Are you sure?" Hitomi looked down and sniffled.

Mizuho brought Hitomi's head into her chest. "Deep down Kaori knew Shizuma-sama's heart was not hers."

Hitomi was speechless.

"But I believe Kaori was happy enough. Just being with Shizuma-sama dispelled all her fears about dying so young."

Hitomi finally chuckled. "Gee, what a great way to look at things."

"She had such a pure, innocent soul, and was sent to heaven

at such an early age. She was so different from Nagisa-chan. Kaori was a young girl with an angel's attitude."

"Absolutely."Hitomi rested her head on Mizuho's shoulder and thought about Kaori.

Mizuho was gentle, but continued to explain things bluntly. "Shizuma-sama probably needs someone like Nagisa-chan."

"You may be right." Hitomi nodded. "There aren't many underclassmen who would want to save Shizuma-sama." She laughed and sniffled.

Mizuho did not join Hitomi in laughter. "She never asked— not even once—to have Shizuma-sama all to herself. Any girl with Shizuma-sama would feel insecure. They would doubt that they are worthy of being with Shizuma-sama. And they would naturally express their insecurities to Shizuma-sama. Several times, at least, which would annoy Shizuma-sama. But Nagisa-chan was different. She chose to part with Shizuma-sama. She must have misunderstood something. Or maybe she refrained from asking, thinking that Shizuma-sama really didn't need her."

Suddenly, Hitomi burst into laughter.

"Gee, Mizuho, you like Nagisa, don't you?"

Mizuho blushed in embarrassment. "Well, I didn't mean it like that."

"Don't worry, I know. I like her, too. She's a very sweet and bright." Hitomi continued, "We are both wrapped around Shizuma-sama's finger, aren't we? She owes us a lot."

Hitomi patted Mizuho's head once, and stood. She faced Mizuho, and raised her hand. "I put in one vote for supporting Nagisa-chan. I still think those two want to be together, after all."

CHAPTER 4

How the King of Truth Became Known

It was way past bedtime, a quiet midnight in the Strawberry Dorms. In her Spica dorm room, Yaya fell asleep, alone again.

*Gracious, how many days has it been...one, two...*she counted in her head. How many days since Hikari went missing? *About six days already. Almost a whole week. I never expected this to happen.*

She glanced across the room at Hikari's empty bed. The wrinkle-free, light peach satin cover seemed dull and solemn.

Until now, I never felt so lonely being in a room by myself.

Yaya pulled her futon cover over her head. *I should stop thinking about anything, or I'll never get to sleep. I'm so tired.*

The little emergency light was turned off, making the room completely dark. The only sound was Yaya's breathing. She tried to fight back the tears that welled inside her. Eventually, she drifted off to sleep.

Yaya dreamed of Hikari. She wore a short, white, robe like an angel, smiling shyly at Yaya. She stretched her hand out to Yaya, inviting Yaya to take Hikari in her arms. Tempted, Yaya took her hand, and brought Hikari close.

Hikari gasped as she sank against Yaya's chest. Yaya stamped out all her fears and hugged Hikari as tightly as she could, nearly crushing her bones.

"Hikari," she whispered.

Hikari, wearing a glowing smile, buried her face into Yaya's bosom. Yaya couldn't hold herself back anymore. She ran her hands all over Hikari's body, reaching for every part of her, over and over, as if she wanted to confirm that Hikari was really in her arms. She kissed Hikari's lips relentlessly, as if trying to make up for all the time she couldn't kiss her. Yaya kissed her so hard she ran out of breath. After a brief release she kissed her again.

The moment their lips parted, Yaya felt insecure, as if Hikari would disappear, and so she began her kissing again. She kissed Hikari's lips, cheeks, neck. Her breasts. Then explored every part of Hikari's body with kisses.

Hikari, lost in ecstasy, let Yaya take control.

Yaya peeled off Hikari's clothing. Hikari shivered in anticipation.

"Hikari, you're so beautiful." Yaya was captivated by Hikari's white, alluring skin. It drew Yaya to her lover, like a spell.

Yaya made love to Hikari.

Hikari, lost in ecstasy, whispered into Yaya's ear. *Ohh… Yaya-chan…Yaya-chan…* She writhed in Yaya's arms, burning with passion so hot she nearly melted Yaya in the process.

"Oh, Hikari. My Hikari. Please tell me that you only love me."

Yaya rubbed her body against Hikari, breathing heavily and asking the question again and again. Hikari arched her back and moaned with pleasure. *Ahh, Yaya-chan...*

But she never answered Yaya's question.

Hikari reached her climax. She clutched Yaya's body, and her moan was like honey to Yaya's ears.

Yes, that's it, come with me, Hikari...

Yaya poured all her love into Hikari, and the two girls reached the end of the earth together. Yaya was intoxicated on the feeling that she and Hikari were the only people on earth.

Hikari relaxed and closed her eyes, her body glowing with the pleasure of what Yaya had given her.

Suddenly, a halo rolled down from the top of Hikari's head.

Yaya hadn't noticed the golden circlet above Hikari before. It was the halo of an angel who had appeared on Earth. The halo glowed white for an instant, then melted into nothing.

Ahhhh, no, Hikari! Yaya cried. She had been filled with happiness just moments before, but she was now completely empty. Hot tears rolled down her cheeks.

With a gasp, Yaya opened her eyes and saw the darkness. She wiped her cheeks, surprised by the tears she found there. She looked down at her hands. The sensation of Hikari's body lingered in her trembling hands, but Yaya sighed with relief. *I'm glad it was just a dream. Thank goodness I didn't go all the way with Hikari like that. I really don't want to do that to her. I mean, I'd probably be happy if I did make love to her, but...*

A smiled slowly crept onto Yaya's face. With tear-soaked cheeks, she felt indescribable happiness. She laughed, carefree.

Yes, what I want the most is not to make love to her.

I want to be Hikari's best friend.

Again the sun rose on Astraea Hill.

One week had passed since the second round of the *Étoile* competition, and each school was different than it had been just seven days before.

At the St. Miator Girls' Academy, the rumor that Shizuma had dumped Nagisa faded into the background. Nagisa's life had settled into an almost comfortable lull. She no longer felt like she wanted to leave school.

Shizuma withdrew from the *Étoile* competition, and like many other Sixth Year students, didn't appear in public too often anymore.

Nagisa just went with the flow of everyday life. What Shizuma did to Tamao on that last day was a little shocking, but what she had said to Tamao was even more shocking. Shizuma's final word to Nagisa was the biggest shock of all.

Goodbye...

Nagisa refused to think about it. Whenever she tried to think of the reason for it, her heart tightened and her mind went blank.

I should just forget everything. I won't think about Shizuma-sama ever again.

Tamao didn't bring up the subject either, so between the two of them, it was like that final meeting had never happened. Since then, Nagisa spent her unbelievably pleasant days with Tamao always by her side.

At St. Spica Girls' Institute, Makoto was still the flamboyant Emperor. She had won the second round of the *Étoile* competition. Things were slowly approaching their conclusion. Amane and Hikari had not been seen since their disappearance, but the teachers and Sisters acted like nothing had happened. Students, possibly feeling guilty that they had excessively pressured the two girls, found it hard to bring up the subject.

Originally, Amane's hard-core fans, the Amane-wannabees, had caused a ruckus—thinking that Amane and Hikari would eventually be expelled from school—but once they realized that their commotion might prevent their prince's return, they changed their minds and waited patiently in silence. Everyone believed the two girls would eventually come back.

Finally, at the St. Lulim Girls' School, Student Council President Minamoto Chikaru smiled like the Madonna and enjoyed the day at her Costume Club. Chikaru's smile was for Kagome, who wore an overly frilly nurse's outfit.

"Hey, do you really refuse to enter the third round with Makoto-chan?"

"Yes,"Kagome replied immediately, smiling, while she snuggled her teddy bear.

Chikaru sighed.

In this brief time of peace, only the Spica Student Council worried about the final round of the *Étoile* competition.

Lunch break. On the Spica campus, in the Spica Student Council Room, at the highest floor of the tower far beyond the throngs of girls clamoring in the cafeteria, the Student Council members waited nervously for something to arrive. President Shion, still completely depressed, sat with Kaname and Momomi, who were both nervous. All three waited patiently. The rest of the council members became nervous as well, and there was not a sound to be heard. If someone looked up from the green expanse of the Maiden Park, the only things they would see through the large glass windows were the back sides of white uniforms quietly sitting at the table.

Knock, knock, knock...

Shion clenched her fist. *Here we go. It's time for me to take responsibility and get impeached.*

"Excuse me..."

The St. Lulim Student Council President, Minamoto Chikaru, and the St. Miator Student Council President, Rokujo Miyuki, entered the room. Their three key staff members followed behind. The two presidents wore business-like smiles, which was not unexpected. Today was a day for business. Today was the periodic Tri-School Joint Student Council meeting.

"Welcome, and thank you for coming." Shion stood, spreading her arms to welcome the guests inside, but her trembling hands were clamped shut. *Hang in there...*

The agenda for today's joint council meeting was to cover the results of the second round of the *Étoile* competition, and to discuss what event to conduct in the third round.

"Regarding the second round," Shion began once everyone was seated. "Spica's first round winners, the Amane pair, were disqualified. They broke cardinal school rules, and left school without authorization."

It was a major embarrassment for Shion to announce such shameful results. But, since she was in the highest position of power, she had to endure this shame. Once it was over, she needed to figure out the best way to decide on the third round.

Somehow I must bear this trial and restore Spica's glory.

The overwhelming pressure made her dizzy. Shion couldn't bear to look Chikaru and Miyuki in the eyes.

"Well, so, let's begin. First, I would like to report on the execution and results of the second round of the *Étoile* competition. Please review the handout." Shion tried to control her shaking voice as the handouts were passed around the room, and the Tri-School Joint Student Council meeting began.

Shion reported the *Petite couronne* winners of the second round: St. Spica Girls' Institute, Fifth Year, Class *Trois*, Kusanagi Makoto, and St. Lulim Girls' School, First Year, Class C, Byakudan Kagome.

"We've tentatively scheduled a coronation ceremony for after the commotion at the schools has simmered down. Unfortunately, the second round had resulted in several disqualifications and withdrawals, but it did end smoothly so regarding the third and final round…"

Shion flew through the report rather quickly, thankful the job was nearly over.

"I object." Miyuki interjected and raised her hand.

"Huh?" Shion stopped. *Well...here it comes.* "Yes, what is it, St. Miator Girls' Academy President Rokujo?"

Miyuki kept her gaze on the table top as she stood, then snapped her face up to stare at Shion. "President Tomori, you state it all so simply, but how are we going to deal with the disappearance of the winners of the first round, St. Spica Girls' Institute's Otori Amane – Konohana Hikari pair?"

Urk... Shion nearly choked, but tried to regain her composure. *It's okay...calm down. This line of questioning was expected,* Shion reminded herself.

"Regarding that case, I express my deepest apologies. Our school is to blame. I acknowledge that this act was incredibly dishonorable and unprecedented, but since the couple has already received due punishment for being disqualified from the first half of the second round, "The Faceless Devil," I do not believe further corrective actions are required." Shion said it all with her eyes closed.

Yes, there's no other way to explain this situation. How much more should Spica suffer from this tragedy? There is no other penalty that could hurt Spica more than losing Amane.

Miyuki countered, "That is not what I meant. I understand that the two students were duly punished. It would have been understandable if they had only broken the rules with the framework of "The Faceless Devil," but they also went missing from school, causing a major uproar, on the day they were supposed to participate in the latter event of the second round. Do you not think their actions were both unforgivable and dishonorable for Astraea?"

Urk... This time Shion was really stuck for a reply. Miyuki continued to pile it on.

"In fact, the couple in question won the first round, and was in the running for the final crown. They had the potential to be Astraea's best and hold a very honorable position."

Yes, that's true... Shion thought. *Why did Amane make such a foolish decision to leave school?*

"So why did the two students make such a selfish decision to leave school?" Miyuki's continued as if she could read Shion's mind. "Shouldn't the Spica Student Council have made sure that a strong couple, who dominated the first round in such an impressive manner, be monitored to prevent such an incident in the first place?"

Oh...so that's where she's going...

Shion spoke carefully, hiding her anger. "Are you suggesting, President Rokujo, that punitive measures be taken against the Spica Student Council itself?"

What in the world will that accomplish? Is she suggesting that I resign from my presidency?

When Miyuki did not answer, Shion snickered. "If my resignation would undo this mess, I would have done so instantly. But even if I stepped down, there's no guarantee that the two girls would return, so I believe I should stay on until this whole situation is resolved."

She thought about Shizuma. *If that's your argument, St. Miator Girls' Academy had a couple drop out as well.* "And how about the situation at the St. Miator Girls' Academy? The previous *Étoile* jumped into the competition at the last minute, only to drop out prematurely. Isn't your school just as guilty of stirring up the *Étoile* competition?"

Miyuki continued her argument without changing her expression. "Yes, of course. I am ready to take responsibility for the trouble my fellow students have caused. That is why I am proposing a course of action."

Shion narrowed her eyes. *Eh...what do you mean...?*

Miyuki spread her arms and shrugged her shoulders. "In other words, I just wanted to say there's no point in continuing the *Étoile* competition." She gave Shion an evil grin.

"Look, I will somehow convince the previous *Étoile* to re-enter the competition. So it would be great if everyone at Spica can find Amane-sama and Konohana-san to have them re-enter the competition, also. With the first and second place winners of the first round dropping out the way they did, all of the students who had high hopes for those two couples were utterly disappointed. They turned the competition turn into a big joke. Besides, there aren't any couples who have charisma like those two couples, so I'm suggesting we redo the second round once they all return." Miyuki spoke rather frankly.

Shion sat back in her chair, astonished. "B-But even if we both agree to that, President Miyuki, what about Lulim?" She looked at Chikaru.

Chikaru was laughing in amusement.

"Yes, Lulim probably won't agree to redo the second round, especially since one of their students won the *Petite couronne*."

But despite the way the conversation had gone, Miyuki pulled out the final ace up her sleeve.

"Yes, regarding that…unfortunately, I came across a 'rumor' that I feel I must report here." Miyuki gave a sidelong glance to Chikaru, who was still chuckling.

"The subject in question is Kusanagi Makoto, who entered from the second round and came out as winner. It is a fact that she is the younger sister of Kusanagi Masaki, the legendary *Étoile* from nine years ago, correct?"

Everyone in the room was shocked into silence. Shion looked like she had tasted something bitter. Chikaru maintained her smile, which only convinced Miyuki that she was getting close to the heart of the matter.

"When I researched Kusanagi Masaki I came across an interesting fact." Miyuki waved the file in question. "What I have here is a report about Kusanagi Masaki, compiled by the former Miator Student Council. According to this report, there are no graduation records for the legendary *Étoile*, Kusanagi Masaki. And in addition, there are hints of her dropping out of school."

Commotion spread throughout the room.

Dropping out of school? An Astraea student, dropping out?

Miyuki sensed the confusion in the room and lifted the report a little higher. "The main reason for her dropping out was probably due to her sudden disappearance."

Shion jolted in her seat. *This is unexpected.*

Miyuki continued, "The reason for her disappearance appears to be related to the secret behind the birth of her sister, Kusanagi Makoto—"

Chikaru stood suddenly, causing a lot of noise. She spoke loud enough to drown out Miyuki's last words.

"Umm… President Miyuki? I truly apologize for interrupting you during your explanation, but…"

What now? Miyuki looked upset.

Chikaru didn't seem to notice and rattled on. "It seems like the Spica and Miator councils are really concerned about their students dropping out or withdrawing, so I'm quite hesitant to say this, but…"

She put on a coquettish smile. "Actually, I have an important announcement to make to everyone here."

Chikaru blushed playing her part to the fullest extent. "Err… the student paired with Makoto-chan, Lulim's First Year student, Byakudan Kagome…well, Kagome-chan…doesn't seem to get along with Makoto-chan, and has insisted on withdrawing from the *Étoile* competition."

The room was now in utter chaos.

At the time Chikaru was making her announcement, in the St. Miator Faculty Tower, the campus queen, Hanazono Shizuma, stood before a large, heavy oak door. There was a white envelope in her hand.

She was deciding whether or not to go inside.

If I just say the words…it'll be all over.

Shizuma straightened her posture and grabbed the doorknob.

"St. Miator Girls' Academy, Sixth Year, Snow Class, Hanazono Shizuma, entering!"

Her voice was gallant, yet lustrous.

"Come in," a calm, female voice acknowledged Shizuma.

Shizuma's feet sank into the dark green carpet. She placed the white envelope onto the large desk. The lady who occupied the office remained in her chair as she spoke.

"Are you sure?" the woman asked, her eyes narrowing. The faint scent of her Wild Orchid perfume lingered in the air.

"Yes, Chancellor."

Shizuma closed her eyes and searched deep into her soul. She used to have some thoughts of wanting to stay back. But she thought it was best for her to do this, and she had convinced herself. Now she was fully determined to see it through.

"I had assumed you'd stay at this school until graduation." The young, beautiful chancellor smiled as she opened one of the shiny drawers of the mahogany desk. She put Shizuma's white envelope away. The outside of the envelope bore the words "Request for Withdrawal" inked in black calligraphy. It was Shizuma's request to drop out of school.

"I really enjoyed attending the St. Miator Girls' Academy, and hoped to graduate from here, but…" Shizuma wryly grinned. "I suppose I need to end my naïve life at this paradise."

"Oh, you're silly. You need not hasten becoming an adult. It's quite boring, you know."

The Chancellor tapped her forefinger on Shizuma's nose. "But I suppose it can't be helped, especially when it's due to family reasons."

She tried to hug Shizuma's shoulder, but the phone on her desk rang like a little bird.

"Oh, my line is ringing." She grabbed the phone and waved Shizuma away, silently motioning…*that's all, you're dismissed.*

Shizuma took a deep bow and headed out. Just as she touched the door, she overheard the chancellor say, "Yes…Now?!"

Shizuma turned to see what had made the chancellor so surprised. Instead, she saw a strange object outside the window behind the chancellor's desk.

What is that thing?

The Chancellor hung up the phone, and motioned to the object that hovered in the distance. It came closer, and when Shizuma saw the green star on its side, she knew what it was.

It's the Miator helicopter.

Shion was so angry she was sure steam was rising from her head. She had taken blow after blow in her weakened, depressed state.

Miyuki's accusations, Makoto's hidden secret of some sort, and now Chikaru's explosive revelation. Just what in the world is Chikaru up to? Wasn't it she who wanted Kagome to enter the Étoile competition in the first place? And wasn't it her idea to bring Makoto back to Spica? Now her girl wants to drop out and totally kill any chance of Spica's getting the Étoile crown?

Shion had the strange feeling that all of this was part of Chikaru's plan.

"Are you out of your mind?" Kaname pounded the table and stood up.

Shion lost her train of thought.

"What the heck? How come Spica takes the blame for everything! Such audacity! You all have no right to pin this on us!" Kaname fiercely growled.

"No, Kaname-chan...don't talk to President Miyuki like that..." Momomi, sitting beside Kaname, tried to softly warn her.

"Hell no... You want me to sit here and allow everyone to blame Spica? We had already decided on the second round event, but it was you who insisted on changing it to the "Faceless Devil," President Miyuki!"

Kaname forgot to speak politely. She pointed her finger at Miyuki.

Ah... Excitement ran through the room. Pointing was Astraea's sign of a challenge. Now that Kaname had started, she could not stop.

"And you, President Chikaru!"

Kaname pointed her finger at Chikaru's nose as well. "Because of you, we had to bring that shorty, Kusanagi Makoto, into the competition! Because of her, Spica was thrown into dire confusion, and caused Amane-sama to..."

Kaname realized that she just referred to her own upperclassman as "shorty". She stopped and hung her shoulders in shame.

"Amane-sama and Hikari lost their places in Spica." Kaname's voice trembled.

"Kaname." Momomi looked at the saddened Kaname and sniffed. "We shouldn't think about those two anymore, because it's beyond our control. They are probably living happily together. It was fairly obvious how attracted they were to each other."

Momomi thought back to the first round of the *Étoile* competition, "The Mouth of Truth". How Amane had carried Hikari in her arms and vowed to love her, and Amane's intense emotion as she chased after Hikari during the pajama party. She knew how hard Hikari trained to improve her mediocre dancing skills, all with a smile. And how Kaname's feelings for Hikari eventually softened.

"Every student who attends Spica probably shares the same feelings. We all wish for Amane-sama's happiness with her first love, even though it's a little frustrating to see a girl monopolize the prince...so some students may become jealous...but..."

Momomi rubbed Kaname's back, speaking softly.

"I think everyone knows our devotion to Amane-sama. This may sound rude, but I don't think Makoto could be considered Amane-sama's rival. Amane-sama has been Spica's number one prince, overwhelmingly popular, which is why you don't hear anyone at Spica lay blame on Amane-sama and Hikari-chan, right? We were much too demanding and pushed them over the edge. But in the end, though they may not say it out loud, I think everyone wishes for their happiness—regardless of whether they stayed at Spica or not."

Shion choked up watching Kaname and Momomi's inner struggle. Miyuki's words echoed in her heart. They resonated differently now, though.

—"There's no point in continuing the *Étoile* competition."

—"Find Amane-sama and Konohana-san to have them re-enter the competition…"

—"With the first and second place winners of the first round dropping out the way they did, all of the students who had high hopes for those two couples were utterly disappointed. They turned the competition turn into a big joke."

One way or another, we're being asked to locate Amane-sama, aren't we?

Shion's thoughts over the past week, which were hazy at first, finally began to take form.

I should go back to square one. First, I strived to win the Étoile crown once Amane-sama, our biggest, unchallenged star, agreed to enter the contest. I wanted nothing but to have her win the crown that she truly deserved. That was my original intent. As the student council president, I wanted our rarely-found Spica star to become the Étoile.

I knew she didn't need any help from me to win it, but Amane-sama was really very shy and didn't enjoy exposing herself to the public. So I wanted to assist her in any way I could, that's all.

Amane-sama, ohh, where in the world have you gone?

Shion looked out of the thick glass window pane staring into the distance. Outside the window lay Maiden Park forest, quiet as usual, under the big blue sky.

Those two girls are somewhere on the other end of this sky. Ohh, but I have no idea where exactly they are.

A small flash in the distance, like the sun reflecting off of something shiny, shook Shion from her thoughts.

"Huh, what is that?" Tsubomi, looking in the same direction as Shion, cried out.

In the sky there was a small, black dot. It grew bigger as it came closer and soon the machine's roar shook the room.

Everyone in the room stood up in amazement. The deafening roar got even louder, turning into an unbearable, ear-splitting noise. The black, shiny object grew larger and gradually, the imprinted small, green star became visible. The helicopter rose straight up until...

It's right above us...Kaname bolted out of the room first.

The other council members were right behind her.

Kaname ran up the emergency staircase, stomping on the bare metal steps. Shion, who had lost her patience with the slow-moving elevator, followed on Kaname's heels.

When the student council members arrived on the roof, they found several other students had already gathered.

The St. Spica Girls' Institute Tower Building was the tallest structure on Astraea Hill. On its roof a large, vicious black bird equipped with giant rotary blades had landed—the Miator school helicopter.

Strong gusts of wind blew across the high roof. Shion struggled to keep her hair out of her face, as she squinted to get a better look.

The twirling rotor blades slowly came to a halt. The center helicopter hatch opened, and two girls sat in the black leather seats. They hopped out of the helicopter, and everyone gasped at once.

It was Spica's Prince and Princess.

*Ahh...*Tears flowed out of Shion's eyes before she could stop them. She covered her mouth to hold back her cries of joy.

Is this a dream? If this is a dream, then it's a wonderful dream!

The astonished crowd began to whisper among themselves.

One student after another began to cry. Amane shaded her eyes with her hand and scanned the faces until she found who she was looking for. Amane corrected her posture and made a deep bow to Shion. She stood back up, with her shoulders square.

*I'm sorry...*Amane did not have to say the words for Shion to know how she felt.

Something was different about Amane.

What's different? I don't know exactly, but she just seems different. Spica's ivory Prince looks so clean, so white, and cleansed of impurities. She looks so peaceful.

Amane was illuminated by the early summer sun on the roof, surrounded by a golden halo of light. To Shion, Amane seemed magnificent.

Amane was taken aback by the large crowd that welcomed them. She guarded Hikari while she searched for a place to retreat, but almost immediately, an army of nuns, their faces flushed in surprise, began to pour out from the elevator room on the roof.

Shion thought, *As expected, the chaperons have arrived. I'm not sure why Amane arrived in a Miator helicopter, and at least it brought them safely to Spica. But there is no way Amane and her partner would go unpunished.*

What if they get expelled?

A shiver ran down Shion's spine. It had been a while since she felt such excitement.

She felt a surge of energy from within, and couldn't help but smile.

As the Student Council President of Spica, I cannot allow that to happen. Now that Amane-sama has returned, I can surely bring the school back together.

The students of Spica were filled with sorrow without our Prince Amane. No one wishes for her expulsion. I will submit petitions, conduct boycotts, and do anything and everything to convince the faculty to keep her in school. One way or another, I must prove the innocence of Amane-sama and Konohana-san, and even if it doesn't work out this year, I will somehow find a way to enter them into the Étoile competition next year.

Shion burned with her motivation. She hadn't felt like this in a long time—not since she became the Student Council President and won the executive power to conduct the *Étoile* competition at the beginning of the year, all for Amane.

I will protect them, no matter what, Shion vowed with a clenched fist. The sisters, who were leading Amane and her partner to the elevator, suddenly stopped in their tracks.

Ding.

The elevator chime rang and the doors opened. Standing

inside was an attractive woman in her forties. She wore a pin-striped charcoal gray suit, with a tight knee-length skirt, and a hunter green silk blouse. A power suit. Her soft, wavy black hair flowed down the side of her face, accentuating her prominent eyes and nose. Her smile was noble and gentle, and her stiletto heels, three inches high, clacked as she exited the elevator.

The sisters looked absolutely stunned, and instinctively stepped back to let her through. The woman ignored the sisters and instead walked straight towards Amane. The smell of her perfume—wild orchids—wafted on the air as she passed.

Amane stood her ground, wearing a determined but slightly unsure look. But she was not intimidated by the woman who stood in her way. Hikari hid partially behind Amane, worried.

A different female voice came from behind the woman.

"Goodness, where are we going, Chancellor?"

Shizuma appeared behind the woman. She wore a puzzled look, and was unusually out of breath.

Chancellor? Is she the Chancellor of Miator?

Shion was flabbergasted. *If I understand correctly, the most powerful person in Astraea is the Chancellor of Miator. Astraea is owned and operated by one family, and the Chancellor of Miator is always a female heir of that family. Daughters of the family must attend Miator by tradition, but it's never publicly disclosed who they are, in order to keep their identities a secret. I never expected the Chancellor to be so young and beautiful, though. Why is she involved in Spica's problems?*

Shion couldn't figure it out just yet.

"Welcome back! The Prince of Spica is really handsome, isn't she?" The Chancellor gleefully said. "It's the first time I've seen her!" She turned her head to get a response from Shizuma, who was behind her.

"Yes, I suppose," replied Shizuma. She pressed her hand to her temple, trying in vain to contain her irritation and discomfort.

The Chancellor, though she'd asked the question, ignored Shizuma's response, and like a sniper taking aim at a target, pointed a finger at Amane's nose.

Gulp...the crowd fell silent. Finger-pointing meant a challenge to a duel.

But the Chancellor humphed; she obviously didn't mean nor care about the implications of her actions. The elegance she had displayed when she got off the elevator all but disappeared, to be replaced with a mature, lustful smile.

"I want her." The Chancellor, almost licking her lips, looked at Amane as if she were some kind of prey. She drew closer to Amane. Standing close to Amane, she caressed Amane's cheek with her hand. Her hand moved slowly and deliberately.

Hikari, who was hiding behind Amane, trembled. *Amane-sama doesn't like this at all.*

Shion, observing the situation, desperately hoped that Amane wouldn't lose her temper and swat the Chancellor's hand away. *The Amane I know wouldn't tolerate this. She would have gotten angry or red-faced and pushed that hand away already.*

But Amane didn't budge, only gazed at the Chancellor, seeming neither angry nor embarrassed. She simply stood there, hiding nothing, showing her true self. She planted her feet firmly on the ground, confident. From her straightforward stance, she asked a straightforward question.

"And who in the world are you?"

The Chancellor and Amane looked each other in the eye. Amane, finally returned to Spica, stood tall in the face of her biggest challenge yet. She projected a majestic aura, her presence sparkling in the eyes of the observers that surrounded her.

*Amane-sama has changed…*Shion swallowed.

The Chancellor stared at the unmoving Amane and let out a breath.

"Excuse me."

She lowered her hand from Amane's cheek. Though she retained a sense of elegance and glamour, her expression turned soft and caring, into the face of a gentle educator.

You are quite lovely. A pure white star shimmering in gold.

"Your predicament is rather…unfortunate. I'm aware of your situation, Ms. Otori Amane, Spica, Fifth Year, Trois Class. You lost your patience, dropped out of the *Étoile* competition, and out of desperation fled from school, right? I never expected a student who ran away from school to have this much courage. A person like you, with the strength of a king, is best fit for our St. Miator Girls' Academy, don't you think?"

The Chancellor turned and winked at Shizuma. Shizuma didn't think Miator was the best school for Amane, but knew it was impolite to contradict the Chancellor.

"I suppose…"

The Chancellor went on. "You know after causing all this trouble, she'll eventually get expelled from Spica, right? Once that happens, there shouldn't be any problems transferring her to Miator. Spica's reputation will be maintained, Prince Amane's records will be wiped clean, and Miator will gain yet another outstanding student. A brilliant plan, right? Oh, I'm sorry, I haven't introduced myself, have I? I am the Chancellor of St. Miator Girls' Academy."

As the Chancellor introduced herself, she fished for a business card in the breast pocket of her suit.

"Stop it!!"

Shion's voice pierced the air.

"Please stop!! Amane-sama is Spica's one and only bright star. We cannot stand idly by and watch our most revered star be swept away to Miator."

Shion's pleas hung over the crowd. The helicopter's sudden appearance had attracted the attention of many Spica students, and in fact a significant portion of them had gathered on the rooftop. The several dozen students, naturally grouped by class, formed a large ring around the helicopter.

Shion shook in anger as she approached the center of the ring and cut in between Amane and the Chancellor.

The Chancellor lifted an eyebrow, surprised at this sudden outburst. "Oh, you say that, but didn't the students of Spica persecute Prince Amane for breaking the rules? I heard about the arrival of Kusanagi Makoto—the younger sister of the legendary *Étoile*—who split the Spica supporters in half. It seems a waste to keep a magnificent student like her in a school full of disloyal students."

Shion spread her arms out, protecting Amane. "Despite the differing opinions, the fact of the matter is that Amane-sama is the person who best represents Spica! The small fraction of Spica students who prematurely ceased their support for Amane-sama lost their focus a bit. A temporary delusion, that's all. Every Spica student knows the truth deep down. Amane-sama is our only hope.

"No matter how dark the skies are, and no matter how much rain pours down, the strongest star of Spica is Amane-sama. When she disappeared from school, none of the students made a fuss about her whereabouts. On the surface, it may have seemed like nobody cared, or that nobody loved her, but we were only keeping silent in order to prevent further troubles. We didn't want anything to block Amane-sama's return, because the students of Spica believed that Amana-sama would come back to us someday.

"That is why none of the students took action. They just couldn't. We will not allow Amane-sama to be taken from us ever! I will never allow that to happen!"

Shion bellowed her last words as tears welled in her eyes.

Amane was struck by Shion's words. She closed her eyes.

Shion's words… The students of Spica need me… I can't just leave the Spica students behind…

Amane's shoulders relaxed. She even smiled.

So, that's it…

She looked at Hikari, anxiously standing by her side.

It actually feels good to be needed by someone.

Amane gently patted Hikari's head and stepped in front of Shion.

"Chancellor, I appreciate your generosity of transporting us back here. But I don't have the strength of a king. I just hope that I have enough strength to protect the ones I love. The little bit of strength I have now didn't come from me, though."

Amane took a deep breath and looked up to the sky.

"I received this strength from the skies of Spica."

She looked at Hikari and everyone around her. She looked into each student's face. Every one of them watched Amane, supporting her with their hearts.

Amane smiled triumphantly, her white teeth gleaming.

"And from all the Spica students who love and support me."

Oh, Amane-sama, the students whispered between tears of joy.

"I am humbled by your offer, but I will not transfer to Miator. I love Spica. When I realized I might not be able to return to Spica, it made me realize how much I loved this school. Hikari probably feels the same way, too."

Amane firmly gripped Hikari's hand.

"I want to make Hikari happy at Spica. No, I want to be happy with Hikari. I now know that we couldn't be truly happy if we kept on running. And it made me discover that I wanted to enrich the happiness of everyone who supports me. I am happy when Hikari is happy. I want Hikari to be the happiest person alive. I shouldn't be fearful of all this happiness. I wish for all the students of Spica to be happy as they can be."

Amane raised Hikari's hand high in the air for everyone to see, then she lowered Hikari's hand and kissed it. Then she kneeled on the ground, as if she was praying or repenting.

"As punishment for my ignorance, I will accept expulsion from Spica."

Amane closed her eyes. The crowd fell silent. The girls around her could not speak.

Clap, clap, clap clap…

Someone clapped their hands, slowly and deliberately. The sound traveled through the crowd until everyone applauded Amane.

"Well, it looks like your total defeat, Chancellor. Or should I address you as 'Mother'?"

The speaker broke through the center of the crowd, and approached Shion from behind.

"Currently at Miator, you have the Four Saints, with Shizuma-sama, Miyuki-sama, and Marikoya-sama leading the pack. There is a potential star candidate in the Fourth Year, Suzumi-san, plus a new type of heroine, Aoi-san, as well. How many more stars do you want, Mother?"

The person repeatedly addressed the Chancellor as "Mother."

The Chancellor seemed distraught. "Chikaru…" But the next moment she straightened her posture and smirked.

"Oh, but it was you who requested their readmission, wasn't it? That's why I went to all the trouble of bringing them back."

"No, what I asked was to re-admit them to Spica. How could you overlook such an obvious detail? But then again, I suppose

you always end up manipulating things to your advantage."
Chikaru shrugged.

"Of course I do. You know me too well, my daughter."

The growing crowd was taken aback by the insidious
conversation.

Is Chikaru-sama…perhaps…?

The Chancellor walked towards Chikaru.

"You know the reason I continue to search for new stars is
because you left me. Remember? Fine, since you finally came
and addressed me as your mother in public, why don't you just
leave Lulim and come back to me and Miator? Yes, that's a
great idea." The Chancellor's eyes twinkled mischeviously.
"Chikaru-chan, if you transfer to Miator, I promise to have these
two safely readmitted to Spica."

Amane held up her hand to stop the conversation. "Hold it!
I'm not asking for a deal! The reason I called President Chikaru
is because I just wanted to come back to Astraea Hill. I never
expected to be re-admitted."

Chikaru let out a loud sigh, as if to blow off the Chancellor's
offer.

"This is exactly why I chose to enter Lulim, Mother!" she
snapped, glaring at the Chancellor.

"You know that the only time I call you 'Mother' is…?"

"When you're mad at me, right?" the Chancellor snickered.

"Correct. Ever since I was a child, you have openly followed
your own desires, and failed to consider the feelings of others.
So I made sure my actions and feelings were understood clearly
by you."

By this time Remon and Kizuna had joined the growing crowd. The two girls were shocked at Chikaru's conversation.

We never imagined Chikaru-oneesama to have such a thorny upbringing.

The appearance of the Miator Chancellor, Minamoto Chihiro, had taken everyone by surprise. The news had spread like wildfire that the Miator helicopter had brought back the Prince. The crowd was twice the size it had been when the Chancellor had arrived.

"You're so blunt, Chikaru-chan. You should be more lenient with your own daughter," the Chancellor joked.

"Gee, I'm the daughter, not you. I never wanted to attend Miator anyway. I didn't want to glide down the Miator path automatically. The same path that my mother, grandmother, and great-grandmother followed. Especially since my mother is the Chancellor and has such a self-centered attitude"

Chikaru skirted away from her mother until she stood behind Amane. She lightly pushed Amane's shoulders.

"Like your selfish plan for her transfer," Chikaru said. "It's quite obvious that my school life would have been negatively affected by your antics. That's why I wanted to create my own path. I chose Lulim. Yes, I know you think it's the bridal preparation school for commoners, the newest and most relaxed school of Astraea. But the freedom, warmth, and beauty of Lulim best fits me."

What a foolish child. The Chancellor threw her hands into the air, disappointed. "Indeed. You made such a rash decision because you're too inexperienced. Watch, you'll regret not choosing Miator when you become an adult and want to advance your career."

Chikaru's tone was serious. "I will not regret it at all. I love Lulim. Lulim gave me freedom, youth, love." She scanned the crowd, and eventually found Kizuna and Remon, far in the back. The little girls were jumping up and down, trying to catch a glimpse of Chikaru above the tall crowd.

When Chikaru saw the girls she was overjoyed.

Their faces are so red. They're worrying about me, I'm sure. Oh, my cute little angels. Those girls are my true family.

Chikaru, moved, closed her eyes.

"I found my true family at Lulim. I believe Otori-san feels the same way about her school."

She patted Amane's shoulders, lending her support to Amane and Hikari.

"I completely understand her desire to start over at Spica, the school where she found her love. Due to her God-given talents, she had to bear mounting pressure. Over the years I am certain that there were moments when she wanted to escape from it all, but she returned to become Spica's star again of her own volition. It would be pointless for her to be admitted to a school other than Spica."

Chikaru focused back on Chancellor Chihiro.

"As an educator, can you please give consideration to her plight?"

There was a brief pause. Everyone gathered held their breath as they waited for the Chancellor's decision.

Amane broke the silence, speaking clearly in a low, sultry voice.

"I would like another chance to become Spica's star."

She put on a big, bashful grin for the crowd. "If everyone can forgive me, that is."

Half a heartbeat went by before the cheers broke out, like a wave of sound. The girls in white uniforms, which made up the majority of the crowd, were elated. Some clapped, and some cried, but all cheered.

"Amane-sama…"

"Our White Prince…"

"We will gladly welcome you back…"

Amane tried to hold back her tears as she scanned the group.

I will never forget this day for the rest of my life…

Chikaru patted Amane's shoulder again, as tears welled up in Hikari's eyes.

"Amane-sama, I'm so glad," said Hikari.

Hikari's frail voice was so irresistible that Amane hugged her. The cheers grew louder.

"Amane-sama…"

"We support you, and wish you happiness…"

"We're envious of Hikari-chan…"

"Thank you, everyone. I vow to all who support me that I will make Hikari happy, and for all the students of Spica, I will win the *Étoile* crown!"

She spread her arms out as the crowd roared.

Amane hugged Hikari's shoulder and kissed her on the cheek.

"I promise to make you happy," Amane whispered into Hikari's ear, making her blush.

Thunderous applause, and tears of joy.

Cutting through the storm of applause, another student came running onto the roof.

"So, Amane, you've come back!"

Kusanagi Makoto emerged from the elevator and waded through the tightly packed throng. She had been on her way to Lulim to check on Kagome, but changed her course when she saw the Miator helicopter land on the roof.

The air grew tense. Up until this moment, Amane and Hikari had won over the crowd. But their biggest opponent had just arrived. Kusanagi Makoto, the little Emperor, who had protested Amane's competing in the *Étoile*, and had acted openly hostile towards Amane, berating her.

The group wondered what Makoto was going to say to Amane…

Will she say…how irresponsible…selfish…unfair…and pathetic to come back?

The tension was almost unbearable, and the crowd froze. The only person moving was pale-faced Makoto, silent as she brazenly pushed her way through the crowd, heading straight for Amane.

By the time she stood in front of Amane, she was out of breath.

"Why are you the only ones returning?"

No one else could hear her whisper.

The next moment, Makoto straightened her back and fixed her eyes on Amane. She raised a fist.

She's going to punch me..., thought Amane as she clenched her teeth.

But Makoto's cold, nervous fingers only touched Amane's cheek. Gently, she stroked Amane's face. Her expression relaxed, and a thin stream of tears glided down her cheeks.

Makoto saw Amane through her tears, a blurry image that resembled the person she loved most.

She's back. The person I love most. She didn't abandon me.

"Oh, I'm so glad that you're back, Oneesan."

Makoto, unaware of her mistake, gently hugged Amane.

"Mako-chan," Chikaru said, surprised. "That's not your oneesan. I'm sorry."

Makoto looked up at Amane, her eyes clear, and then dropped to her knees.

Kagome, who had followed Makoto to the roof and stood next to Chikaru with her teddy bear, went to Makoto and patted her head.

CHAPTER 5

The Maidens Drew Water from the Fountain of Courage

*D*ing dong...

Astraea Hill's second dismissal bell rang.

The shocking scene on the rooftop had been prolonged by the Chancellor's sudden appearance and Makoto's teary one. But at the sound of the bell, the Spica nuns came to their senses.

"Please excuse us," the sisters said politely to the Chancellor as they escorted Amane and Hikari off the roof.

The two girls, tired from their adventure, were actually relieved to leave the scene and followed the sisters willingly. The elevator was already at the roof, thanks to the most recent visitor, so the group entered it and descended, headed for the Spica Chancellor's office on the first floor of the tower.

The crowd gradually dissipated. Students who weren't participating in clubs and after-school activities were not allowed to stay on campus past the second bell. That night at the Strawberry Dorms there was a boatload of students on additional duties as punishment for violating that rule.

Tomori Shion was worried about Amane and Hikari, so she followed the sisters, and asked the remaining student council members of each school to quickly usher the rest of the students out of school.

The students continued to share their excitement with fellow classmates, hesitant to leave, but the student council members slowly but surely managed to get them back to the Strawberry Dorms.

The only people left on the roof were Chikaru, Miyuki, Shizuma, and the Chancellor.

Chikaru remarked, "I didn't expect Makoto-chan to cry like that."

After Makoto's breakdown, Kizuna and Remon had comforted her. Makoto had sobbed as she left, Kagome pulling her by the hand.

Miyuki, her gaze distant, commented, "Though she fiercely competed against Amane-sama, deep inside, she had projected the image of her older sister onto Amane-sama."

She felt terrible for trying to manipulate Makoto and orchestrate a large scandal. She glanced at Shizuma, who stood there in silence, smiling peacefully.

The Chancellor threw a quizzical look at Shizuma, then faced Chikaru.

"So, Chikaru…" The Chancellor smiled, but Chikaru only looked disgusted.

"Will you consider my proposition?"

"Proposition?" asked Chikaru.

"Aww, did you forget already? About your transfer. I'll convince the Spica Chancellor to readmit Prince Amane and her partner, so won't you come to Miator?"

"Oh, did you expect me to fall for that? After I had a big argument with you and left the house?" Chikaru's smile was spiteful.

Like mother, like daughter, Miyuki thought. *Chikaru is absolutely unbelievable.*

Miyuki was unnerved. She smiled wryly at the Chancellor.

"Chikaru-sama is highly regarded as Lulim's Holy Mother and is therefore an indispensable person at Lulim. Even if she transfers, she will have less than two years before she graduates. I recommend Chikaru-sama stay where she is."

Chikaru was encouraged by Miyuki's words.

"That's right, my long-awaited dream of establishing Class Z is about to happen. I'm never giving up my dream of creating my own harem!" Chikaru declared, playfully punching her fist into the sky.

During the conversation, Shizuma stood at a distance, observing. Chikaru looked back at Shizuma, who instinctively averted her eyes to avoid her gaze.

Acting as if she was looking at her watch, she said quietly, "Chikaru-sama should come to Miator, Miyuki, because I will be leaving soon."

Miyuki's and Chikaru's jaws dropped.

Yaya stood in front of the chancellor's office, waiting for the two girls. She wasn't motivated to sing today, so she skipped choir practice and read a book on the grassy knolls of Maiden Garden. She never went up to the roof.

She heard the excited voices of students on their way home, walking past her as she lay on the grass.

The girls squealed and gossiped, and Yaya overheard bits of what had happened.

They came back? Yaya's heart leapt and she became restless. She ran straight to the Chancellor's office, where the girls had supposedly been escorted.

Yaya eagerly stood by in front of the Chancellor's office, waiting for them to come out. She stared at one spot on the wall, not moving an inch, and waited patiently.

One question whirled through Yaya's mind: *Is this a dream? Maybe I'll wake up in my room, and see Hikari's empty bed again. That would be too sad.*

Yaya shut her eyes at the fearful thought. There was a faint noise as the door opened.

Creak...

Yaya opened her eyes, and there stood her golden angel.

Wow... Yaya thought of all the things she had wanted to say when she reunited with Hikari. *Are you tired from the long trip? You were stupid for leaving? Maybe if I winked at her and said never to leave me, she'll be relieved.*

But instead, Yaya just hugged Hikari without saying a word. First softly, then tighter. She did it right in front of Amane without a care in the world. The best way for Yaya and Hikari to communicate their feelings was to embrace. They were both crying.

"I'm sorry for making you worry, Yaya-chan."

"It's all right. As long as you're happy, Hikari-chan."

Yaya was simply happy to see Hikari again, to touch her. It was a lot simpler and better than her dreams about Hikari. Hugging fulfilled and empowered her.

Based on the Miator Chancellor's endorsement, Spica granted Amane's and Hikari's request for readmittance. Regarding the prohibited entry into the chapel, the school staff concluded that "both students were chasing after an unknown intruder at midnight,"and dropped the charges.

One week later, at St. Miator Girls' Academy, stories of Amane and Hikari's dramatic return had spread throughout the Miator campus from first-hand witnesses. The two girls' bold escape from the Strawberry Dorms—the biggest elopement ever—the ostentatious return on a helicopter chartered by Chikaru, plus Amane's public proposal of love to Hikari, and finally, the vow to capture the *Étoile* crown had captured the hearts of the rivaling Miator students. It quickly became a fad for Miator couples to make promises to "elope," and the campus was permeated by the legendary story of Amane and Hikari.

Meanwhile, Nagisa and Tamao were eating lunch in the

inner garden. Tamao pulled out an egg salad sandwich, Nagisa's favorite, and shared it with her. Nagisa politely took the sandwich, but was lost in her thoughts. She was recalling the stories of Amane and Hikari that gossip-loving Iohata Momiji shared.

Momiji had pounded on the desk repeatedly, she was so moved by the two girls' deep love for each other. Nagisa listened to the story and agreed with Momiji—those two were made for each other. Prince Amane came back to Spica and begged for forgiveness, all for Hikari, and was somehow forgiven.

According to Momiji, the sheer beauty of the two lovers moved the crowd, and prompted everyone to support them.

Nagisa tried to recreate the scene in her mind.

I can actually imagine that.

She recalled the Maiden horse race in the first round of the *Étoile* competition.

I remember Hikari-chan, desperately trying to pull me up, because I fell off the tower in place of her. Amane-sama made a heroic effort to rescue us.

As she munched on the egg salad sandwich, Nagisa thought, *Those two are probably empowered by each other. In the end, Shizuma-sama saved me, but unfortunately I'm not with her anymore. I let go of that strong, beautiful hand...*

Her hand stopped. There was a lump in her throat as her heart squeezed tight.

"Hey, Nagisa-chan... you're dropping crumbs everywhere," Tamao said.

"Oh, I'm sorry, I was daydreaming," Nagisa replied.

"I see. Listen, Nagisa-chan. It was really brief, but

Shizuma-sama came on to me once."

"Eh?"

The topic changed so suddenly that Nagisa barely heard what Tamao had said.

"It happened when Shizuma-sama was in junior high. I was a new First Year student, so I was really surprised. Shizuma-sama was a big deal at this school and she was as wonderful then as she is now. But I was afraid and ran from her."

Nagisa was utterly confused.

Tamao-chan had prior relations with Shizuma-sama? Neither of them shared that with me until now. So, in the classroom, is that why she kissed Tamao-chan?

Nagisa's mind was filled with questions. Tamao ignored Nagisa's bewilderment and continued.

"So that kiss was just Shizuma-oneesama's petty joke," Tamao commented, as if she had read Nagisa's mind. "If you get in a serious relationship with Shizuma-sama, it'll definitely wear you out."

Nagisa didn't know how to respond. There was a long silence, with Tamao avoiding Nagisa's gaze. Finally she asked the dreaded question.

"Are you in love with Shizuma-sama?"

Nagisa began to cry. "I don't know."

That day, as if it had waited for Amane and Hikari to return, the announcement of the third and final round of the *Étoile* competition was posted. At the end of lunch hour under the clear, blue skies, the student council members of each school posted the announcement on their bulletin boards.

ANNOUNCEMENT

Notice of this year's *Étoile* Competition Third Round

The final round of the *Étoile* Competition, entitled *"Le Dernier Miracle,"* will be conducted on the date specified below.
All students must purify their bodies and souls to prepare for and await the birth of the new *Étoile.*
There will be no further changes to the third round event from this day forward.

THIRD ROUND
Le Dernier Miracle (The Last Miracle)
Seventh Month on the Day of Saint Thomas
Event: Fencing Duel

Amane and Hikari's names were included in the list of participating couples. Also posted on the board, near the edge, was another announcement so small that most Spica students failed to notice it.

<u>NOTICE</u>

The student noted below will leave Astraea Hill at the end of July.

St. Miator Girls' Academy
Sixth Year, Snow Class
Hanazono Shizuma

Action: Dismissal from school
Reason: Foreign study in Europe

At Miator, news of Shizuma's impending travel abroad spread through the campus like wildfire. The sudden news caused students to be surprised, angered by the irrational decision, and deeply saddened by the seriousness of the situation.

All regarded Shizuma as Miator's undisputed queen, so this earth-shattering news threw the Miator students into a state of confusion. During every break for the next few days, the students would gather and chatter about what would happen once they lost Shizuma.

"*Shizuma-sama is probably going to Europe because Aoi-san dumped her, right?*"

"*No, you've got it backwards... Shizuma-sama is studying*

abroad, so she decided to withdraw from the Étoile competition!"

"I heard that Shizuma-sama got over Aoi-san and moved on to Suzumi-san. Someone saw them kissing in the classroom after school!"

"Really? Maybe Suzumi-san will join her and they'll study abroad together? Oh my gosh! If that happens, then once the Fifth Year class graduates, Miator will lose viable candidates for the Étoile competition."

"Have you heard the rumor about Minamoto Chikaru-sama transferring from Lulim to Miator to replace Shizuma-sama?"

"Dummy, that was a joke made by the Chancellor during Prince Amane's return."

Rumors begat more rumors, leaving Miator in a storm of chaos. But Shizuma never opened her mouth on the subject, and in fact, refused to talk with anyone. She was aware that Hitomi and Mizuho were quietly watching her in the classroom, worried looks on their faces, but she even refused to explain things to her closest friends.

Hitomi and Mizuho were obviously worried. They knew exactly why Shizuma withdrew from the *Étoile* competition—because Hitomi had dredged up the past and told Nagisa about Kaori.

But watching Shizuma, Hitomi and Mizuho had the same thoughts.

Is she serious about leaving? If she really wanted Nagisa, nothing would have stopped her. What happened to Shizuma-sama?

Hitomi wondered if it was Nagisa herself that had something

to do with Shizuma's change in personality. Shizuma's tranquil silence only increased Hitomi and Mizuho's concerns.

Maybe Shizuma is trying to change.

The pair could not figure out Shizuma's intentions. As longtime friends of Shizuma, this was the first time they felt this way. For some reason, they wanted Shizuma to talk to Nagisa.

If Shizuma-sama talked to the girl one more time, maybe she would go back to being her normal self—bright, strong, and true to herself like before. Or did Shizuma-sama change because she broke up with Nagisa?

Hitomi shuddered at the thought of what she might have caused.

I wasn't able to sort out my feelings, and I took it out on Shizuma. I was in love with Kaori, but Kaori was in love with Shizuma. And Shizuma eventually let Kaori go and pursued Nagisa and loved her. I felt sorry for Kaori, like Shizuma was dishonoring her memory, but I turned a blind eye to Shizuma's new feelings. In my mind, I kept attacking Shizuma for pursuing Nagisa. And when Shizuma tried to chase after Nagisa I interfered.

Of course, I knew that didn't cause her to give up Nagisa. It was something else. Something inside Shizuma caused her to change. Darnit, I'm so ashamed of myself. I'm supposed to be Shizuma-sama's best friend. But I wonder if Shizuma saw that love was more important than friendship?

Soon, Hitomi began to accept Shizuma's decision to study abroad. *Am I just looking for an excuse to avoid responsibility? No, that's not it.*

Shizuma's foreign study was actually something the female members of the famous Hanazono clan were scheduled to do. The Miator students should have already been aware of that fact. Shizuma was the only daughter of the Hanazono syndicate. The Hanazono clan had grown into a large conglomerate, owning several businesses. It was so large it was often regarded as a kingdom.

Shizuma was the sole heiress to this kingdom. She was a young, beautiful daughter who had been a queen from birth.

This young queen had other news, which she had been keeping secret, but which was soon being covered on TV and in magazines across the globe for days. Even the isolated maidens of Astraea became aware of it, but nobody had the courage to bring up the subject.

The other news was a potential engagement.

Engagement was a common happening in Miator, and especially with Shizuma, who received many proposals of marriage throughout the year. No one expected the proud Shizuma to give in to her parents' wishes and accept a marriage proposal, though. After a few times, nobody paid attention to her potential engagements.

Even Hitomi and Mizuho couldn't hide their surprise at the recent news article. And with Shizuma remaining silent, they couldn't possibly confirm it.

The subject was too touchy and scary.

The headline of the paper read: "Hanazono Syndicate's only daughter is the best candidate for our next Empress."

Shizuma had received a marriage proposal from royalty.

"I apologize for calling you out here."

Makoto, looking refreshed, turned around and looked at Chikaru.

She's starting to look like her sister, thought Chikaru. *Tsk... Mako-chan would probably make a fuss if I said that.*

"Oh, no problem." Chikaru's voice echoed in the empty chapel.

It was third period. The only ones skipping class were Makoto, who had lost the motivation to study, and Chikaru, who, as student council president, had the special privilege of being able to leave class at any time.

It was the beginning of July. The inside of the chapel was usually cool from the high ceilings, but it seemed a bit hot and muggy now. Makoto stared at the large, stained glass window above the altar. It depicted the Savior going to Heaven, the moment a human child became a child of God.

She looked over to the pictures on the walls. The standard pictures of the Savior's struggles circled the walls of the chapel. Makoto stared at each picture in succession.

At the end, after all the struggles, was a miraculous resurrection.

"I thought...my Neesan was unhappy because of me." Makoto shyly smiled.

"I kept telling you it wasn't your fault," responded Chikaru.

"Yeah, you were right, Chika. But I didn't want to believe it."

Makoto was straightforward and mature. She had a sharp, boyish face, like it was polished.

"But I was so jealous. I can't believe my Neesan chose that person over us!"

She no longer harbored any extra emotional baggage, and spoke from the heart. "I kept telling myself it was my fault, just so I would have a reason. So I would feel better about forcing myself into her life."

Makoto didn't face Chikaru. Instead, her words were directed at the sky. She closed her eyes, trusting the heavens, and imagined the blue summer sky of Russia.

"That's how it feels to be in love." Chikaru laughed.

Makoto opened her eyes. She wore a soft, beautiful expression that Chikaru had never seen on Makoto's face.

Makoto laughed.

"Have you ever been in love, Chika?"

Chikaru thought about it. "Hmm...who knows? But when I look at Amane-sama and Hikari-chan..."

Makoto finished her sentence, "Yeah, looking at the two of them... I knew that those two were really happy to be with each other. They were destined to be together, you know? Just like my sister and her love."

Chikaru smiled silently. Makoto closed her eyes again, remembering her sister's face, Amane's face, and Chikaru's face.

"I think I'm already in love with someone. And I'm glad that those two returned to school."

Makoto bid farewell to the stained glass picture of the

resurrection, and turned to face Chikaru. She seemed somehow cleansed.

"Neesan never came back, but they did. I hope they become a wonderful *Étoile*. Chika… I'm sorry, but I want to withdraw from the *Étoile* competition."

Chikaru, pleased to hear that, smiled. Makoto was relieved to see her smile, but at the same time, she felt a little lonely.

Chika is aware of my feelings for her. Despite that, she's smiling.

She remembered the picture she had found hidden behind the altar and snuck into her suitcase, hidden behind the altar.

I'm glad to have come back, even for a short period of time. Glad to obtain a picture of the legendary Étoile, Kusanagi Masaki, being crowned, and that I was able to take a picture with my gentle Chika. That's good enough for me…

"I'm going back to Russia, since I no longer have a reason to stay."

She jumped onto the altar, with her back to Chikaru, like she was praying. Warm sunlight filtered through the stained glass and showered Makoto with color as she loudly declared, "I love you just as much as my Oneesan, Chika!"

*Yes, thank you…*Chikaru replied in her heart. She placed something in Makoto's hand.

"What's this?" Makoto asked, regaining her innocent smile.

She'll be fine.

Chikaru's heart bloomed in her chest. "Mako-chan, I couldn't give this to you while you had a chip on your shoulder. Because you despised your brother-in-law, and men in general, in order to hold yourself together, I feared that you might be ruined by this. But I think you can handle it now. After seeing Amane-chan and her love, you finally understand, don't you? It doesn't matter if your love is a male or female, it only matters that you are happy."

When Makoto opened her hand, there was a paper, folded in half. It was a one-way plane ticket to Vienna.

"Please send my regards to Masaki-sama," smiled Chikaru.

My happiness is to be with you, Makoto thought, but did not say it out loud. She waved behind her as she departed with a smile.

Nagisa was at the lowest point of her life ever. Even a casual observer could tell, it was so obvious. The Miator campus without Shizuma looked bare to Nagisa's eyes.

Ever since the day Shizuma came to say goodbye to Nagisa, she knew she'd never see Shizuma again.

In her heart, she longed for Shizuma. Each time Nagisa heard rumors about Shizuma at school, she was reminded of how much she didn't know about Shizuma. Like, that studying abroad was a normal part of the Hanazono clan's curriculum.

Shizuma had insisted on staying until Sixth Year, but her family had insisted she complete her obligation abroad. Nagisa knew Shizuma came from a wealthy family, but didn't know how famous they were. A marriage proposal from royalty! To Nagisa, that was mind-shattering news. Shizuma had probably chosen to study abroad in order to decline the engagement offer, another concept beyond Nagisa's comprehension.

To anyone else it would be the ultimate Cinderella dream, but to Shizuma it was a cue to run. Of course, Shizuma wasn't a rags-to-riches princess, but still, it was far beyond Nagisa's wildest imagination.

Shizuma-sama decided to go away...oh...gosh...and she even turned down the offer...

Even Nagisa knew that refusing an engagement proposal from royalty came with a price. Shizuma had chosen to hide in Europe for a while, to lessen the dire consequences. According to the rumors, for the Hanazono clan marrying into royalty was not only unattractive, but an unnecessary burden.

Oh gosh, what kind of world does Shizuma-sama live in?

Every story Nagisa heard was unbelievably shocking and scary. It dawned on her that she was just an ignorant newbie. *No wonder other people hate me, and laugh at me. I definitely didn't know a lot of things.*

She surely didn't know much about Shizuma's precarious situation, either.

Shizuma had stopped attending classes so that she could prepare for her study abroad. Nagisa couldn't share her thoughts with Tamao, who seemed to be treating her coldly for some reason. Ever since Tamao asked her if she was in love with Shizuma, Tamao had seemed to be lost in her thoughts.

My heart aches so much without Shizuma-oneesama.

Nagisa couldn't dare share that with Tamao. She didn't know what to do, but she would go crazy if she stayed put. So she decided to wander around the Miator school buildings. She felt hollow and lonely. Her legs instinctively walked towards the Sixth Year classrooms in Tower Five. She stood in front, but couldn't bring herself to enter the building full of upperclassmen, especially since she knew Shizuma wasn't there anymore. Nagisa did an awkward about-face in front of the Tower Five entrance and wandered away.

Somehow she ended up in Maiden Garden. She looked up to the hot, blue sky, sweat rolling down her neck. The white summer roses that used to bloom all throughout Maiden Garden were no longer there, and in their place, lush greenery filled the area. The smell of fresh grass was overwhelming.

Wow. Nagisa shielded her eyes with her hand as she looked up. It was summer already.

Where should I go? she wondered.

In front of her was a small path that led to the library. Trotting down the path towards her was Chiyo.

Ah, Chiyo-chan.

Nagisa stared at her blankly, forgetting to greet Chiyo-chan.

"Nagisa-oneesama! Good day! Are you going to the library?" Chiyo smiled.

She was probably on her way back from library duty. Nagisa forgot to respond, and looked at Chiyo-chan like she was far away.

Chiyo-chan's smile is cute as a little meadowsweet flower, Nagisa thought.

And she remembered that day. The first day she arrived at

Miator—a pleasant, sunny day, like today. It was spring, and the white meadowsweets were in full bloom. Nagisa recalled that she had been looking forward to the start of her new adventure that day.

That was the day she first met Shizuma. It seemed like it had happened so long ago.

"Nagisa-oneesama."

Teary-eyed, Chiyo called out to Nagisa, staring off into the distance.

"I'm sorry, what are you saying, Chiyo-sama?"

"Umm... maybe you should...go see Shizuma-sama one more time?"

Nagisa's heart swelled at the suggestion.

Yes, I want to see her.

Nagisa woke up the next morning, her mind made up. It was the morning of the third round of *Étoile* competition. Upon Amane's return to school, the rainy season cleared up and left dry, sunny weather.

When Nagisa sat up in her bed, Tamao was already in the shower room, getting ready for school. The *Étoile* competition Sequence of Events guide lay on the table next to Tamao's bed.

There were no other events in Astraea that day. To celebrate the birth of a new holy *Étoile*...all classes, clubs, and after-school activities were cancelled, while the students anticipated, then cheered for, and crowned the new *Étoile*.

The third round was a fencing duel—a one-on-one fencing competition. On the cover of the Sequence of Events guide were illustrations of the *Aînée* contestants, dressed up as medieval knights, and the *Cadettes,* wearing medieval princess outfits, as costume-loving Astraea traditions called for.

This year's *Étoile* Executive Committee was run by the Spica Student Council, so among illustrations was a short-haired knight wearing a feathered hat, and a delicate princess with curly, golden locks wearing a high-waist dress—similar to Juliet's dress in Romeo and Juliet—which somewhat resembled Amane and Hikari.

Nagisa stared at the cover for a while.

We were supposed to be in this competition, too. Shizuma-oneesama was supposed to fight for me like this.

A small tear drop fell.

I'm so stupid. I love her so much, but I ran away. There's nothing I can do about it now. Shizuma-sama probably decided to go abroad because she grew tired of a whiny girl like me. I should have never let her go. I'll never meet someone like her, ever again.

Her heart burned with regret.

Will I never see her again? Once Shizuma-sama goes to England, will I ever get a chance to see her face again?

Memories of being with Shizuma flashed through her mind. Shizuma, suddenly bursting into Nagisa's classroom without warning. Shizuma, who normally had no reason to visit underclassmen towers, regularly visiting her. Shizuma, inviting Nagisa to take a bath with her at the Strawberry Dorms.

And Shizuma, always hugging her. Shizuma, forcibly kissing her.

Shizuma, whispering that she loved Nagisa.

My Shizuma-oneesama…

She couldn't hold it back anymore. Her feelings for Shizuma were so great, hot tears flowed down her cheeks.

I need to see her. I don't care if she's mean to me, or picks on me. I don't care if she says goodbye to me again. I need to see Shizuma-oneesama one more time. I can't let her leave me like that, and I can't deny my feelings anymore.

Nagisa put aside all her hesitation, and was filled with strong love for Shizuma.

I feel so stupid for holding back, trying not to upset Kaori. It shouldn't have mattered in the first place. I like Shizuma-sama. That's all. Even if Shizuma-sama doesn't like me anymore, as long as I have feelings for her, I'll be happy just being by her side.

I was being selfish, Nagisa thought. *But why did I feel that way? I should have believed in Shizuma-sama.*

The door closed with a small sound. She left quietly so that Tamao wouldn't notice.

Nagisa fought excitement and hesitation all the way to Shizuma's room. The upperclassman's single person rooms lined the hallway on the top floor. It was a place underclassmen had to be most careful. Nagisa could bump into anyone at any moment, and she would have to explain herself.

Nagisa, hunched over, nervously walked down the hall. But because of the *Étoile* competition, there was not a soul in sight.

She tiptoed across the deep green carpets that lined the hallway floor.

She finally made it to Shizuma's room.

Room No. 6001   S. Hanazono

Her name was in gold font on a green nameplate. Nagisa used her trembling hand to knock on the door. She rapped on it so softly that it barely made a sound. But there was no answer.

Oh no. Should I knock harder?

Nagisa shuddered with nervousness, but mustered enough courage to knock once more.

This time, it was too loud, and Nagisa became even more flustered.

Oh jeez…I knocked too hard…

Nagisa, scared, tried to flee. She took a few steps back, but the creak of another door opening in the hallway stopped her cold.

Room No. 6002   H. Togi

Hitomi and Mizuho peeked out from the doorway.

"Well, who is it? We're not attending the *Étoile* competition so I thought we told the room assistants not to visit our room today," Hitomi grumbled as she stepped out of the room. Her eyes widened when she saw Nagisa.

"Y-You're here! Why?"

Mizuho knew why Nagisa was here.

"Oh, I'm sorry… Shizuma-sama is already…"

Nagisa sensed the sadness is Mizuho's voice, and knew she was too late.

She's gone already.

Nagisa was in a daze, drained of energy. *I won't be able to see her again...ever. The person I love most, the strong, beautiful and glamorous queen who was so nice to me and loved me back. Hanazono Shizuma-sama is gone.*

"I can't believe this," Hitomi snorted." Why do two people who love each other have to be so stupid and split up?"

Mizuho was taken aback. "Hitomi?"

Hitomi shook her head. "I hate this situation. There are so many people in this world who love their partner so much, but can't express it or have to leave them."

Hitomi stood in front of Nagisa, who was about to crumble to her knees.

"Hey, you. Do you really love Shizuma-sama?" Hitomi asked, her voice cold.

"Yes," Nagisa answered meekly.

"Really? Can you promise to make her happy?"

Nagisa gulped at the question.

Can I do that? Can I...make a person being sought after by royalty...happy? Am I allowed to give her happiness?

"Yes, I can." Nagisa responded. "I love Shizuma-oneesama, so even if if seems I'm not capable of doing it, I will find a way. But only if Shizuma-oneesama forgives me."

Nagisa clenched her hand so hard it shook.

Hitomi was satisfied with Nagisa's honest answer and grinned.

"Good. If that's what you think then I'll help you! Right, Mizuho? We still have a chance to chase after Shizuma-sama!"

Hitomi turned to Mizuho, but Mizuho sadly shook her head.

"No, we won't make it in time. Shizuma-sama is departing at 9 o'clock in a private jet." She pointed to her watch. It was already 7:30 AM.

Ah... Nagisa froze.

"It'll take at least two hours to get to the airport. I'm sorry," Mizuho lamented.

Hitomi persisted. "It's a private jet, right? Then we can ask to delay its departure."

"Just because it's a privately owned aircraft doesn't mean it can do as it pleases. The runway scheduling is packed tight, so it will be difficult to adjust. And Shizuma-sama made the hard decision to study abroad, so it might be difficult to convince her."

"Silly, we have the ultimate weapon! We can overturn her 'hard decision!'"

"But…"

Hitomi lost patience with Mizuho's whimpers. "Okay already! Mizuho, don't you want Shizuma-sama to come back?! Didn't you say you'd be lonely if Shizuma-sama left?!"

"Well…"

"We've been friends with Shizuma-sama for thirteen years, and we only have nine months left until we graduate. This is our last chance to get Shizuma-sama back. We might not get another chance," Hitomi said in a serious tone.

Mizuho bit her lip. "So you're trying to manipulate Nagisa-chan to achieve your goals?"

Another voice, familiar to Nagisa, chimed in. A voice Nagisa instantly recognized.

Uh-oh.

Tamao-chan, who had always supported Nagisa no matter what…

"Tamao-chan…" *How did you know I was here?*

"Nagisa-chan, you shouldn't be fooled by these oneesama, you know? All they're trying to do is use you just to get Shizuma-oneesama back."

"What are you saying?"

Ignoring Hitomi's protests, Tamao, all dressed and ready to go, walked to Nagisa. She touched Nagisa's hair.

"Oh my, you ran out while I was taking a shower. Your hair's a mess. You can't go to Shizuma-oneesama looking like this." She stroked Nagisa's ponytail.

"Tamao-chan…"

Nagisa could barely speak, but she repeated Tamao's name.

"Tamao-chan… Tamao-chan… Tamao-chan, Tamao-chan, Tamao-chan…"

She cried and hugged Tamao.

"There, there…you shouldn't cry so much, especially before you go see your love, okay?"

Nagisa sniffed and silently nodded.

"Can I go?" Nagisa asked. She looked up from Tamao's embrace, with tears streaming down her face.

"You love Shizuma-oneesama, right?" Tamao asked softly.

Nagisa answered without hesitation. "Yes."

Tamao looked up as she continued to hug Nagisa. "You should have told me earlier, Nagisa-chan. What a fool you are."

"I know, but…Tamao-chan… I…"Nagisa sobbed.

Tamao laughed. "I know what you're trying to say. 'But I like you as much as her,' right?"

Hitomi burst out in laughter.

"Tamao-chan…" Nagisa looked like a sad, wet puppy.

"I have two more years until I reach Shizuma-oneesama's age. If I'm even with her now, look out. I'm confident that you'll like me more by then, Nagisa-chan." Tamao giggled.

"Silly girl, Shizuma-sama will be an even more attractive university student by then," joked Hitomi.

"Oh, you have it all wrong, Hitomi-oneesama. A high school student has more appeal than a college student because she can be in the same class and spend all her time with her love," Tamao coolly shot back.

Nagisa's tears dried up as she heard the two girls joking back and forth.

Thank you, Tamao-chan… And Togi-san and Kano-san, too.

"Tamao-oneesama! I put…the request through! It will land…on the school…grounds…in ten…minutes," Chiyo yelled between gasps as she ran down the long hallway towards them.

"Oh, don't yell like that. The neighbors will hear you." Tamao covered her eyes.

"Land on the school grounds? Did you…?" Mizuho asked.

"Yes. I figured we didn't have much time left, so I requested a helicopter. Just like Amane-sama did, of course."

Tamao grinned.

Helicopter? Nagisa was dumbfounded.

"We're… just in time…"

Chiyo, out of breath, stopped in front of Nagisa.

"Good thing Tamao-oneesama's home is nearby! The Suzumi Resort Group's company helicopter happened to be parked at home this morning."

"Resort? Company helicopter?" Nagisa mumbled as Chiyo reported the outrageous details.

"Will I be able to see Shizuma-sama in time?"

Tamao grabbed the confused Nagisa and pushed her down the hall.

"Stop mumbling and start running!"

The other girls followed suit.

Shizuma sat near the window of the departure lobby of the large airport and stared outside. In the special lobby specifically reserved for the Hanazono clan, no visitors were admitted to bid farewell, so there were only a few staffers in black suits. She completed her check-in, and her luggage was loaded onto the small, silver plane parked in the distance. Shizuma could see it through the window.

It's almost time. She placed her empty coffee cup on the window sill. *Ever since I entered junior high, I knew that I'd have to study abroad sooner or later.*

Studying in another country was part of a required education for a Hanazono, but for Shizuma, the timing of this trip served another purpose—to avoid a particular marriage proposal. In actuality, she was past due to complete her studies abroad. Shizuma looked at cargo and ladder vehicles running back and forth.

School life was enjoyable. I really wanted to stay there until I graduated.

Memories of Kaori flashed through her mind. *She was a good girl and left me with great memories. Yes, Kaori probably knew my true feelings. I loved Kaori. Not as a lover, but like a sister. When Kaori died, I was so sad and sorry for her. When I found out about Kaori's fatal condition, I didn't want to regret anything. I just wanted to cherish every moment that I spent with her, no matter how brief. The other students glorified our relationship as a tragic love story. But what Kaori and I experienced wasn't tragic; we made great memories. No matter how much I search in my heart, I don't regret a thing about Kaori.*

The one thing that remains is guilt. I felt helpless when Kaori passed, and guilty about not being able to love her as a lover. I really don't know what Kaori truly wanted from me. But now that I've left Nagisa, I realize that no matter how much time I spent with Kaori, I would have never fallen in love with her.

And when Kaori passed away, she left me behind and wished for my happiness…

Nagisa's face came to mind, and her heart ached. She shouldn't have given up on Nagisa, and properly expressed her feelings. But she couldn't do that, because she was afraid of hurting Nagisa again.

Nagisa had endured ·a tough life at Astrea, all because Shizuma had pursued her. Even though it wasn't Nagisa's fault, they had been relentless.

It was the first time Shizuma had experienced such agony. Up until now, Shizuma had taken whatever she wanted without hesitation. But that was no longer the case.

Now that I'm far away from her, Nagisa seems like a most precious, sparkling treasure to me. She has special qualities I don't have. She's pure, honest, energetic, and carefree. She would show her warm, soft, gentle glow only to me. And when I took Nagisa in my arms, I felt at peace, enveloped by her warmth.

Why? Shizuma asked herself. *Why is she the only one I want?*

Tears rolled from Shizuma's eyes, and she batted them away. *She probably wouldn't like me to be this weak.*

Strong gusts blew across the runway. Shizuma got out of the car that had transported her from the lobby to the runway, and walked toward the boarding ramp. She climbed to the top of the ramp and lowered her head to board the plane. The cabin attendant standing next to the door smiled.

"*Bon voyage.* Have a nice trip."

Shizuma repeated in her mind.

Bon voyage...Have a nice trip...The time has finally come...

With her heart broken and full of pain, Shizuma stepped into the plane.

"Shizuma-oneesama."

She heard an unbelievable voice in the distance.

A very familiar voice. Her heart burned and swelled at the irresistible sound. It was the voice of Shizuma's most adorable girl.

Her eyes opened wide, but she was afraid to turn around.

"Shizuma-oneesama…wait! Shizuma-oneesama!"

Is this real?

Shizuma froze in place, listening as the voice got closer. She turned around slowly. There was Nagisa, red-faced and full of tears, running toward her. Behind her were Tamao, Hitomi, Mizuho, and Chiyo, closing in.

The girls screamed, "Shizuma-oneesama… Shizuma-sama"

"All of you." Shizuma had a lump in her throat.

Nagisa stopped at the bottom of the ramp.

"Shizuma-oneesama! I… I…"

Nagisa also had a lump in her throat. Her tears blurred her vision. "I…came for you!" she blurted.

Shizuma covered her mouth, trying to hold in her surprise. Without a word, she spread her trembling arms. *Come to me*…

Nagisa understood the silent message and darted up the ramp. *Oh*…

Nagisa's tears—burning tears of joy—soaked Shizuma's chest.

"Shizuma-oneesama, it's not fair. You left me behind without

even telling me. I…I…love you so much, Shizuma-oneesama."

Nagisa buried her face in Shizuma's chest.

Shizuma embraced Nagisa's warm tears and held her tight. *Oh, Nagisa. What a girl. You chased me all the way here. You make me so happy. I can be myself when you're with me. You're the only one in this world that I love.*

They hugged for a while, then Shizuma raised Nagisa's face. Nagisa tried to hide her teary face and runny nose, but Shizuma would not allow it.

"I'm not unfair. I will take responsibility, so don't move."

Nagisa's face turned beet red. Shizuma gently stroked Nagisa's cheek. Unlike her usual surprise attack, she pulled close to Nagisa's face like any lover would and kissed her on the lips. After a long, deep kiss…

"You're the first girl to scold me like that," Shizuma remarked as she walked down the ramp.

EPILOGUE

The Sacred *Étoile*

Ding dong...
   Ding dong...
   Ding dong...
   The celebratory bells rang, and the girls' cheers resonated in the air. Astraea Hill was filled with happiness. At the edge of the lake was a large tent and numerous parasols with tables underneath them covering the area. There were bright hunter green one-piece dresses, white two-pieces suits with skirts, and soft, light pink plaid sailor outfits all about. The students of the three prim and proper schools of Astraea Hill—St. Miator Girls' Academy, St. Spica Girls' Institute, and St. Lulim Girls' School—mingled with each other enjoying tea and sweets.
   Today was the annual Astraea Tea Party. The bells tolled to celebrate the crowning of the new *Étoile*. It echoed in the background, under the clear summer sky.

"Come to think of it… I should have taken you with me to Europe, huh?" Shizuma whispered into Nagisa's ear, which made her choke on a piece of chicken.

"Grrk…ack. Wh-What are you saying, Shizuma-sama! If you did that, then everyone would hate you." Nagisa remembered how she ran faster than Tamao, Chiyo, Hitomi, and Mizuho the day they had chased Shizuma to the airport.

"Goodness, you needn't get so mad. Think about it… maybe everyone would have congratulated us. This year's *Étoile* coronation is boring! I'd rather take you on a trip to Europe and have plenty of fun."

Rokujo Miyuki, a glass in one hand, interjected.

"Please engage in those activities after you graduate. Yes, why don't you just marry Aoi-san then? A honeymoon in Europe sounds quite lovely, wouldn't you say?"

Tomori Shion sat next to Miyuki and chuckled. "Please let us enjoy ourselves this year. You'll have another shot at the *Étoile* crown next year, Shizuma-sama."

"Next year?! I can't possibly do that!" Shizuma blurted.

"Oh? Shizuma-sama, I thought for sure you'd be able to pull off a stunt like that for Aoi-san," Yaya snickered.

Tamao, who sat next to Yaya, shook her finger. "Don't worry. I, Suzumi Tamao, will not allow such a thing! Next year Nagisa-chan and I will win back the *Étoile* crown for Miator."

Chiyo clasped her hands. "Wow, that's wonderful, Tamao-oneesama."

"Wait. Isn't the *Étoile* couple supposed to be a pairing of an upperclassman and an underclassman?" Tsubomi questioned.

Chikaru chimed in.

"Good point. Maybe Nagisa-chan should transfer to Lulim instead? You're one of the best stars around. Kizuna-chan, Remon-chan, and Kagome-chan are younger than you, so it'll be perfect! Come on, everyone line up! Yes, you all look quite lovely!"

Kizuna, Remon, and Kagome scampered toward Nagisa and surrounded her.

"Yay, Chikaru-oneesama, we have one more student to join us in Class Z! ♥"

"Eh, ah, wait…hold on…" Nagisa stuttered.

"Oh, what a great idea! Maybe I should transfer to Lulim as well?" Shizuma commented.

Everyone laughed at her joke.

If we're not careful, Shizuma-sama might just do that.

"By the way, where are they?" Momomi asked. "The winners of the competition?"

"Oh…they're probably having their pictures taken right now, in their *Étoile* outfits," Kaname answered bluntly.

One last bell.

Ding dong…

A celebratory bell rang its last note. The doors of the chapel were opened wide and the Prince and Princess came out. The blue summer sky was boundless, and the winds smelled sweet as flowers as it swept through the hills. The girls' cheers grew louder as a flurry of white flower petals swirled in the air.

Flower petals slowly showered on all the young maidens, as though the heavens were cherishing this special moment. Time stopped briefly, while the girls' dreams and loves were locked in eternity.

FIN

TRANSLATION NOTES

[1] Double bridal wreath: Also known as Reeves' spirea (*Spiraea cantoniensis*). The Japanese name, *kodemari*, means "little hand ball." It has clusters of small white flowers. It is in the rose family.

[2] The good seed: Shizuma's speech about the "good seed" is a play off the Parable of the Seeds from the Bible, found in Matthew 13. In the original parable, the "seed" is someone who hears the gospel of the Lord, and falling on "the side of the road," on "rocks" or on "good ground" is a metaphor describing that person's reaction to hearing the gospel.

[3] Mouth of Truth: In Italian, *La Bocca della Verità*. The sculpted image of a face (perhaps of the sea god Neptune) found in Rome. The mouth of the face is a hole. Legend has it that if one places one's hand in the mouth and tells a lie, one's hand will get bitten off.

[4] *Financier:* A French almond cake.

[5] *Dokudami cha:* A tea made with *Houttuynia cordata* herbs and other tea leaves. It is also known as "heartleaf" and "lizardtail" in English, and *dokudami, gyoseisou,* or *juuyaku* in Japanese. Used for medicinal purposes and as a health beverage.

[6] *Teki ni katsu:* "Defeat the opponent"—a pun derived from *steeki katsuretsu* (steak cutlets). Japanese people tend to use puns involving food items as lucky charms for certain events, such as college entrance exams, sports competitions, and work projects. In this case, Nagisa's old elementary school served lucky steak cutlets so each class would have a good chance to win on Field Day.

[7] *Oshiruko: azuki,* or sweet red bean, soup. Normally served in a bowl as hot *azuki* soup with *mochi* (rice cake) for dessert, but in this case Chikaru hands Miyuki the canned beverage version.

[8] *Taisho* Era: The reign of Emperor Yoshihito (1912–1926). The Japanese often use years of the Emperor as eras for official documents. (For example, the year AD 2007 is *Heisei* 19.) The era is named not after the Emperor himself, but to describe or predict the era.

[9] "Kitten Waltz": Chopin's Waltz No. 4 in F Major, Opus 34, No. 3. In Japanese, it is known as "The Kitten Waltz" or "*koneko no warutsu*."

[10] *Saltimbocca*: Marinated veal, chicken, or pork dish, topped with prosciutto and sage, popular in Switzerland, Italy, Spain and Greece (Italian).

[11] *Gâteau à l'ananas:* French pineapple cake (French).

[12] *Poe's Clan ("Poe no Ichizoku")* was a historical shoujo manga published in 1972 to 1976 by renowned manga artist Moto Hagio about a family of vampires.

[13] *Konpeito*: Japanese hard candy originally made in Portugal. Comes from the Portuguese word *confeito*, which means "sugar candy."

[14] *Genpuku* is a coming-of-age ceremony for boys between the ages of 11-17.

[15] *Mogi*: A female equivalent coming-of-age ceremony for girls between the ages of 12-14 for traditional samurai families. *Seijin shiki* is the modern day version of the coming-of-age ceremony for girls and boys who reach the age of 20.

[16] Bosatsu: Bodhisattva, or "enlightened being" in the Buddhist religion. In this case, the most likely Bosatsu Mizuho resembled was the Japanese "Kannon Bosatsu" or "Goddess of Mercy."

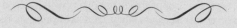

ABOUT THE AUTHOR
Sakurako Kimino
Place of Origin: Tokyo
Blood type: O

Familiar to many as the creator of *Sister Princess*, a sister moe title that became a sensation in the bishoujo realm. In this series, she writes a pure, traditional yuri story freely drawn from her own experiences in an all-girls school.

ABOUT THE ARTIST
Takuminamuchi

Illustrator of the comic version of *Strawberry Panic!* (published in *Dengeki G's Magazine*).